# Crafting the Culture and History of French Chocolate

Frontispiece. The October 1997 marché aux chocolats featured costumed elders of the French Confrérie des Chocolatiers gathered around a chocolate replica of the Aztec god Quetzalcoatl and a 4.5 meter "Grand Totem" dedicated to his glory. Through such symbolically rich events, artisans craft not only chocolates but the culture and history of the foodstuff itself.

# Crafting the Culture and History of French Chocolate

Susan J. Terrio

UNIVERSITY OF CALIFORNIA PRESS

*Berkeley / Los Angeles / London*

University of California Press
Berkeley and Los Angeles, California

University of California Press, Ltd.
London, England

© 2000 by the Regents of the University of California


Library of Congress Cataloging-in-Publication Data

Terrio, Susan, J. (Susan Jane), 1950–.
Crafting the culture and history of French chocolate / Susan J. Terrio.
   p.   cm.
Includes bibliographical references and index.
ISBN 0-520-22125-7 (cloth: alk. paper). —
ISBN 0-520-22126-5 (pbk. : alk paper)
1. Chocolate—History.  2. Chocolate—France—History.
3. Chocolate industry—History.  I. Title.
TX817.C4 T47 2000
641.3'374'0944—dc21                               99–046119
                                                 CIP

Manufactured in the United States of America

09  08  07  06  05  04  03  02  01  00

10  9  8  7  6  5  4  3  2  1

A section of chapter 3 was published as "Crafting *grand cru* chocolates in contemporary France," in *American Anthropologist* 98 (1): 67–
79; portions of chapters 4 and 5 appeared in "Performing Craft for
Heritage Tourists in Southwest France," *City and Society*, 1999, and
are reprinted with permission of the American Anthropological Association; part of chapter 7 was published as "Des maîtres chocolatiers
aujourd'hui. Bayonne et la Côte basque," in *Ethnologie française* 27
(2): 205–213; and the epilogue and a section of the introduction
appeared as "Deconstructing Fieldwork in Contemporary Urban
France," in *Anthropological Quarterly* 71 (1): 18–31.

*For*
*Owen M. Lynch*
*In Memory of*
*Carolyn Jean Hamm*

# Contents

# Illustrations

# Acknowledgments

It is with bittersweet feelings that I acknowledge my numerous debts now that this book is complete. I begin by expressing my profound appreciation to the craft families, workers, and apprentices whose stories form the core of this book. Their enthusiastic cooperation helped me to know their craft, lives, and histories. I am particularly grateful to Francis Boucher and his wife Christiane in Paris and to all the craft families in the southwest who were extraordinarily patient and diligent in ensuring that my own apprenticeship stayed on course. My most heartfelt thanks go to two Bayonnais families who appear under the pseudonyms "Harcaut" and "Sarlate." They drew me into their lives, and the friendships we formed made my stay more memorable and less solitary. I want to thank the craft activist from Pau, who appears in these pages as "Jean Mourier," for his tireless assistance in opening doors that might otherwise have remained closed.

I conducted archival research at the Bayonne Chamber of Commerce and Industry as well as the Chamber of Trades. My special thanks go to the staff at both organizations, in particular, to Monsieur Arnaudin, then president of the Bayonne Chamber of Trades, who graciously permitted me to observe practicum classes; to Françoise Caillaba for her help with my apprenticeship research; and to the craft instructors who welcomed me into their classes. At the Chamber of Commerce and Industry, archivist Laurent Bossavie provided critical assistance in accessing local business records. I was particularly blessed in finding wonderful landlords in Bayonne, Maïté, and Pierre Bousquet, who became like surrogate parents to me.

I owe an enormous debt to national craft leaders. Within the Centre féminin d'études de la pâtisserie, I am particularly grateful to past presidents Bourguignon and Bassignana. At the professional organization of *chocolatiers* in Paris, three people were critical to my research: Alain Grangé, Francis Boucher, and Guy Urbain. They not only provided unrestricted access to archives but were enormously generous with their own time. Other members of the executive board also granted interviews: Jacqueline Lombard, Jacques Daumoinx, René Chaleix and his wife, Benoît Digeon, Christophe Chambeau, Suzanne Lioret, Florence Boucher, and Alain Urbain. I would like to thank the staff at the Paris headquarters of the *chocolatiers,* in particular, Maïté Guérin. At the Paris School for the Food Trades, the principal Henriette Sauvage and her assistant, Isabelle Kaminsky, were extremely helpful. Interviews with celebrated masters were indispensable, and I thank the following *chocolatiers* for their kind indulgence of my many questions: Robert Linxe, Michel Chaudun, Jean-Pierre Richard, Pascal Brunstein, and Fabrice Gillotte.

This book began as a doctoral dissertation in the Department of Anthropology and the Institute for French Studies at New York University. As an anthropologist I have been fortunate in having fine teachers. I want to thank Susan Rogers for her help in defining my project in its earliest stages and for initiating me into the mysteries of grantsmanship. For their helpful critiques and steadfast support during the write-up phase, I am grateful to Fred Myers, Karen Blu, the late Annette Weiner, the late Nicholas Wahl, and historian Herrick Chapman. My deepest debt goes to Owen Lynch, whose insightful commentary and unflagging faith in my abilities were crucial to my success. Academic, like craft, masters come in many varieties, some demanding and harsh, others encouraging and generous. Owen Lynch is a master in the best sense, guiding his apprentice scholars through the rituals of initiation while providing the creative space necessary for them to realize their full and unique potential.

My fieldwork was funded by a Social Science Research Council/ American Council of Learned Societies/German Marshall Fund grant, a National Science Foundation Dissertation Improvement Award, and the Bourse Chateaubriand from the French government. New York University provided a year of write-up support with the Yves-André Istel Fellowship. I wish to thank Georgetown University for generously supporting two return trips to France with three summer research grants and for providing a semester's research leave.

Many colleagues on both sides of the Atlantic have offered intellectual guidance and emotional encouragement. In France I want to thank

Jacques Revel, Martine Segalen, Françoise Zonabend, Jean-Louis Flandrin, Brune Biebuyck, and Nikita Harwich. I am particularly indebted to Colette Pétonnet for sharing her wise counsel and unerring instincts as an ethnographer during my fieldwork. For his indispensable suggestions on how to transcend my dissertation, I acknowledge and thank Charles Leslie. For their thorough readings and critical insights on the entire manuscript I am deeply grateful to Daniel Bradburd and Patti Sunderland and to colleagues who read portions of the evolving book: Gwendolyn Mikell, Joanne Rappaport, David Gow, Jean-Paul Dumont, Denise Brennan, Mark Ingram, Colleen Cotter, Eusebio Mujal-Leon, Michèle Sarde, Sylvie Durmelat, Alexandra Jaffe, Debbie Lesko Baker, Stephanie Millington Terrio, and Kristin Terrio De Leonardis. My deepest appreciation goes to the reviewers of the manuscript, Michael Herzfeld and Carole Crumley, for their thorough and judicious commentary, and to Stan Holwitz for his generous editorial support.

To the dear friends and close family members whose support and good humor have sustained me on this long journey I acknowledge myriad debts of the heart: Patti Sunderland, Irène Tobaly, Hazel Cramer, Cozette Griffin, Rebecca Kline, Nancy Sullivan, Martha Flannery, Jean Hamm, Joan McCloskey, Jill Santoro, Linda Long, my oldest and great friend Karen Moody, my brother Mark, who has graciously shouldered the primary responsibility of caregiver for our mother, the newest member of my family, John De Leonardis, just for being himself, and Debbie Lesko Baker, whose friendship has immeasurably enriched my life and enlarged the circle of family since my arrival at Georgetown. Finally, my greatest debts are to my husband Steve for his unceasing patience, generosity of spirit, and unswerving support of me and this project through many difficult times; to my mother Helen Millington Hoy, and all the Millington women, who have provided daunting models as mothers, wives, and professionals; to my daughters, Kristin and Stephanie, who, during the time I conceived and wrote this book, have grown up, becoming two accomplished and beautiful young women of whom I am immensely proud.

# CHAPTER 1

# Introduction

The idea for this book began naturally enough from a stop at a Parisian *chocolaterie*. It was a beautiful September day in 1988, and I was touring part of the Faubourg St. Antoine with Colette Pétonnet, an anthropologist whose work on (im)migrants is a cornerstone of French urban anthropology. I was in Paris for a year to complete doctoral coursework and to define a thesis topic, at that point only vaguely articulated around the notion of the adaptation and reproduction of artisanship in contemporary France. Pétonnet, along with the other anthropologists and historians whom I saw in the first months of my stay, urged me to narrow my focus and to choose a specific craft.

Given that she lived near the Faubourg St. Antoine, the Paris center of furniture-making trades since the Middle Ages, Pétonnet began by showing me the workshops of furniture sculptors, carpenters, leather workers, gilders, varnishers, locksmiths, and bronze, mirror, and marble makers. This first contact with the crafting world that I had previously only encountered in books—historical, ethnographic, and fictional— provoked feelings of excitement but also disorientation. Except for the ubiquitous craft fair or the living heritage museum, consumers in the late twentieth century have little if any direct experience with production, artisanal or industrial. By late afternoon I was reeling from fatigue. Sensing my overload, she suggested that we end our work for that day with a visit to her local *chocolatier*. "We'll get some *éclairs au chocolat* and eat them in the street like children. How does that sound?"

A few minutes later we arrived at the *chocolaterie* close to her apartment on the rue Main d'Or. We inspected the chocolates invitingly displayed in the boutique window and then went in. Looking back now, what I recall most vividly are not visual images, although they were striking enough, but the olfactory ones—the intense aroma of chocolate. The saleslady was on the phone so we took a few minutes to study the chocolates in the display case. There were rows upon rows of candies arranged like jewels under glass. Most were tiny and dark with a smooth, lustrous sheen. Some were dusted with gold leaf, others crowned with walnut halves, slivers of almond, whole coffee beans, or sugared fruit peel. For contrast, these dark beauties alternated with the occasional row of brilliant foil-covered candies or warm brown milk chocolate bonbons.

I distinctly remember my surprise. Their size, aesthetic display, and evocative names suggested radically different symbolic meanings and social uses than the—dare I admit it—chocolate bars I purchased at home. Even after twenty-five years of speaking French and long experience with French cuisine, the specialized candy terms—*praliné, ganache, gianduja, pâte d'amande, mendiants, truffes*—were new to me. As Pétonnet paid for our *éclairs* and explained my interest in artisanship to the saleslady, we got fleeting glimpses of male artisans producing goods in an adjacent workshop. The "saleslady" turned out to be married to the artisan who periodically handed her trays through the workshop door. They owned the business and employed a full-time worker and an apprentice. Business was slow so she described the seasonal rhythms of chocolate production, the gifting relations associated with confectionery consumption (the *éclairs* were after all a gift from a professor to her student), and her husband's skill hard won through long years of apprenticeship and, later, work experience in other businesses before he became self-employed. She also alluded to the difficulties facing small producers on the eve of proposed European Community (EC) reforms. Another customer arrived so we said our good-byes and left. Outside in the street we looked at one another and Pétonnet said what we were both thinking, "What about *chocolatiers?*"

Stimulated by my questions and observations over the course of that year, Pétonnet turned her ethnographic gaze on this most familiar of neighborhood crafts, making it strange, achieving the double vision that results from fieldwork inquiry at home (compare Okely 1996, 22–26). This distancing made the familiar strange for her, and it was the beginning of a long process that made the initially strange familiar for me. For six months during that academic year I combined coursework with fieldwork involving weekly visits to a *chocolaterie*, interviews with craft leaders of the *chocolatiers'* professional organization, and archival research at libraries, museums, and the organization's headquarters. By the time I left Paris in 1989, an anthropological problem and fieldwork sites had come into focus.

In 1989, French *chocolatiers* were attempting to affirm and authenticate a unique culture and history of artisanal chocolate production. Because craft leaders spoke for and elaborated numerous strategies on behalf of a national membership, I wanted to investigate how these strategies were perceived and managed by *chocolatiers* outside of Paris. On the suggestion of both French academics and Parisian *chocolatiers,* I made an exploratory trip to the city of Bayonne, where local artisans were themselves actively promoting both the historic and contemporary importance of southwest France as a regional center of chocolate production (see map 1). I returned to conduct primary fieldwork among French *chocolatiers* in the southwest and in Paris from September 1990 through May 1991, and for shorter stays in October 1991, 1995, 1996, and 1998.

## Evolving Chocolate Landscapes

It has been ten years since my visit to that Parisian *chocolaterie.* In 1988 it would have been difficult to predict that French *chocolatiers* and their products would become, in the words of one well-informed Parisian observer, *"un phénomène de société,"* a societal phenomenon. Every year since then, new events have been organized and new narratives recounted in which French chocolate is celebrated as both living artisanal tradition and enduring gastronomic patrimony. Chocolate has been ever more exuberantly displayed as an object of ludic spectacle, artistic prowess, and culinary refinement. In 1998, for example, the New Year began with the birth of the Académie Française du Chocolat et de la Confiserie. The Académie was explicitly modeled on the classicist institution inaugurated in 1634 to purify, standardize, and defend French language usage. Like their literary colleagues, the chocolate *immortels* pursued the same elitist enterprise and had undertaken the weighty task of writing the first official confectionery dictionary.

Soon afterward, the thirty-third chapter of the Confrérie des Chocolatiers de France (Brotherhood of French Chocolatiers) was created at Intersuc, the annual Paris show for small-scale chocolate producers.

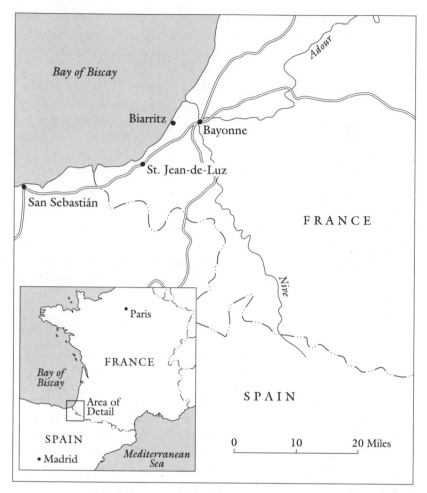

Map 1. Basque coast cities in southwest France.

Founded in 1986 by small business owners to increase demand for vintage chocolate, the Confrérie stages colorful costumed processions and public induction ceremonies (see fig. 1). In the fall of 1996, France's Prime Minister Alain Juppé happily agreed to receive the Confrérie's symbolic attribution of membership—an imitation cacao bean pod—and to swear his loyalty to the "spirit of French chocolate" in Bordeaux, where he was also mayor.[1]

Intersuc 1998 also featured the newest addition to the Parisian chocolate scene—the first Festival de l'Art Gourmand (Festival of Gourmet Art). Artisans at that event crafted chocolate necklaces, earrings

Figure 1. Induction ceremony, Confrérie des Chocolatiers de France, 1999.

and rings, *dragée* (sugar-coated almonds) bouquets, sugar corsets and gowns, as well as paintings, both originals and reproductions, in white, dark, and colored chocolate and marzipan.

Near the end of 1998 the fourth annual Salon du Chocolat opened. The latest of the ubiquitous Parisian exhibits of consumer goods, the Salon du Chocolat is mounted on a grand scale by Sylvie Douce, heir to the founder of the Havas communication empire. When it first opened in 1995, the Salon drew an astounding 40,000 visitors. Government ministers, the mayor of Paris, scholars, physicians, artists, writers, gastronomes, pastry chefs, restaurateurs, members of exclusive Parisian chocolate clubs, and *chocolatiers*—from small family-owned businesses to large industrial enterprises—all gathered to promote the French art of chocolate making. The Salon featured scholarly conferences and connoisseur tastings rating the body, bouquet, and palate quality of chocolate. Visitors witnessed the spectacle of chocolate being melted, tempered, hand-dipped, sculpted, molded, even modeled in a haute couture fashion review (fig. 2). Salon invitations invoked a "chocolate dress code—dark, white, or milk." Entertainment included gastronomic theatrical sketches, an "exotic" mime, and a parade of master craftsmen—all to the strains of a steel band. Financed by Ms. Douce's own public relations firm, Event International, along with industrial partners including

Figure 2. Chocolate corset designed by Chantal Thomas and Christian Constant, Chocolate Show, New York, November 1998.

the French firm Valrhona and the foreign multinationals Jacobs Suchard and Nestlé, the Salon grew steadily in popularity, attracting 80,000 visitors in 1998. Just a few weeks later, the Event International group organized the inaugural New York Chocolate Show, which drew over 10,000 visitors.[2]

Paris had by no means a monopoly on ludic extravagance. Bayonne officially proclaimed 1996 the Year of Chocolate, and to commemorate the city as the historic cradle of French chocolate, municipal authorities, local craftsmen, and the officers of the newly founded Académie du Chocolat de Bayonne planned a year-long round of events, including lectures, public tastings, the hand-dipping of candies, and the crafting of chocolate sculptures in the medieval downtown quarter. In the same year a *chocolatier* from the neighboring seaside resort of Biarritz opened a chocolate museum featuring his original chocolate sculptures, a titillating collection of nudes, nymphs, and lovers.

## Texts and Contexts

It is clear that I initially envisioned the craft in somewhat romanticized terms, naively assuming the ideology of craft to be a description of reality. I later came to understand that this ideology is integral to the practice of craft in late capitalism. In response to the challenges posed by shifting national and international circumstances, French *chocolatiers* write craft culture and make their own history through texts  written, visual, and performative. These texts are commemorative and take myriad forms: published memoirs, oral histories, public lectures, gastronomic essays, recorded interviews; window displays, photographic documentation, and videotapes; and the craft events and the narrative discourses that accompany them, such as induction rituals, connoisseur tastings, and craft contests.

These commemorative texts and the discursive narratives *chocolatiers* used to describe their work seduced me from the very beginning. They were so convincing because of their remarkable consistency. When asked about their reproductive practices, craftspeople gave virtually identical answers, answers that corresponded to received popular notions concerning the seamless familial continuity in the practice of artisanship. However, the ethnographic nature of my research revealed a sharp divergence between *chocolatiers'* discursive assertions and their lived practices. Had I limited my study to discourse analysis or text deconstruction, I would have had a very different understanding of their work and lives. It was only by living among *chocolatiers* over time that I began to grasp the complexities of craft identities within family businesses as strategic assertions that inevitably suppress differences and contradictions.

In this book, craft work, identities, commodities, and communities are not treated as fixed, ahistorical constructs, the ideal types of Weberian sociology, the living vestiges of Tönnie's gemeinschaft or the doomed remnants of Marx's historical materialism. Rather, this book is situated within a practice or processual anthropology that asks how a particular craft—chocolate making—is constituted, maintained, contested, represented, and reproduced through the practices and discourses of the people who perform it (Kondo 1990; Ortner 1984). It focuses on the social and historical construction of this craft within the everyday contexts of work and family as well as the extraordinary realms of performance and ritual. It is a chronicle of French *chocolatiers'* attempts to manage their work successfully in the present and to ensure its continuity in the future.

This is a tale that privileges events over structures because it eschews the study of culture as a stable, durable process reproducing constitutive patterns through time. Rather, this story emphasizes both continuity and innovation, fixity and rupture, and the processes whose outcomes may be unforeseen. Contrary to the depiction of craft producers in much of the social science literature (see below), *chocolatiers* emerge here as knowledgeable social actors with a keen understanding of their own culture as well as an astute appreciation of history's importance in the construction of knowledge about France and in the shaping of French identity. At the same time, they are situated within complex, shifting fields of power associated with a particular historical and cultural moment, postwar France and, more specifically, the 1980s and early 1990s. Located within and beyond the workplace, these fields of power shape and limit their practices in particular ways. *Chocolatiers* operate within the constraints of culturally salient French notions of family, gender, education, class, nationhood, and historically resonant notions surrounding artisanship. Their agency is also mediated and shaped in unintended ways by developments in local, national, and transnational arenas.

This is a chronicle of the tenacious efforts of French *chocolatiers*—members of a tiny craft in a postindustrial society—to reinscribe themselves into the history and the sociology of the nation-state. Their efforts engaged and continue to engage them directly with the representatives and structures of power from socially prominent tastemakers and the CEOs of industrial chocolate manufacturers to politically powerful technocrats in Paris and Brussels, members of their own craft and a changing clientele.[3] The story of this engagement and the unforeseen consequences it entailed provides an important corrective to historical and anthropological scholarship. This scholarship has neglected both the existence of craft work and the adaptive agency of craft producers within first world centers. Despite a plethora of works on the logic of consumption in late capitalism, relatively little is known about the economic and sociocultural dimensions of craft commodity production in advanced capitalism.[4] I explore the largely unexamined ways in which craft modes of production, training practices, and work identities interact *dialectically* with macro processes (compare Comaroff and Comaroff 1997). These processes include the policies of centralized bureaucratic institutions, both French and European, rapid taste shifts tied to transnational cultural trends, identity struggles among competing national cultures within the EC, and the continuing expansion of advanced capitalism itself. At the same time, I focus centrally on questions of identity, community, and historical consciousness among contemporary artisans.

## The People without History

Since the 1970s, French *chocolatiers* have faced diverse challenges in the form of intrusive EC regulation, intensified international competition, and changing confectionery consumption habits. These challenges have involved them in ongoing negotiations with technocrats in Paris and Brussels on critical issues ranging from training and certification to new norms of production and taste. At the outset, these negotiations were complicated by the fact that French *chocolatiers* were a people without history (Wolf 1982). France has long enjoyed global recognition, if not hegemony, in the culinary arts and, in particular, dessert cuisine. Yet few French people understood chocolate making to have had a distinctive place in French history, in Bayonne or elsewhere, in the same way as fine porcelain, tapestries, sculpted furniture, fashion, wine, or bread making. Fewer still had any knowledge of *chocolatiers* as constituting a craft distinct from confectioners or pastry makers. Worse still, in the 1980s foreign franchise outlets began to make a swift incursion into the French artisanal market because few consumers were able to differentiate between authentic artisanally produced chocolates and foreign mass-produced candies.

*Chocolatiers* were the people without history for several reasons. First, they were not documented in historians' history of preindustrial French guilds (Coornaert 1968; Hauser 1927; Sewell 1980), in folklorists' writings on traditional French crafts (Sébillot 1895; Van Gennep 1946), or in life histories produced by craftsmen themselves. *Chocolatiers* had no distinct corporate identity because the practice of the premodern craft was strictly regulated and restricted by the French Crown to particular individuals, often apothecaries and pharmacists.

Chocolate was initially considered to be a powerful drug with little-understood medicinal properties. Consumed initially as a sweetened hot beverage, chocolate became such a popular repast at the seventeenth-century French court and in noble salons that in 1705 the Crown finally allowed the guild of Paris coffeehouse owners *(limonadiers)* to produce and sell it by the cup *(Larousse gastronomique* 1988). Since chocolate was introduced to France in the late sixteenth century, chocolate making has largely been practiced within or alongside a number of companion crafts, including apothecaries, pharmacists, grocers, café owners, liquor distillers, and, in the modern era, pastry makers and confectioners. Moreover, in the wake of legislation permitting the formation of trade unions (1864) and professional associations (1901), artisanal *chocolatiers* were consistently subsumed within the organizations of grocers, confectioners, pastry makers, and industrial manufacturers of chocolate.

French *chocolatiers* were a people without history in part because France itself is not a country historically famous for its luxury chocolates. Only recently has France been acknowledged to be in the international vanguard of chocolate production. The candies best known in France are typically regional specialties, many made of sugar or from a sugar-nut base—as anyone knows who has sampled *calissons* in Aix-en-Provence, *nougat* in Montélimar, *berlingots* in Nancy, *bêtises* in Cambrai, *sucre d'orge* in Vichy, or *tourons* in Bayonne. The nations that have earned renown in chocolate manufacture are those associated with strategic advances in *industrial* processing phases. A prime example are the Swiss, who, in the nineteenth century, invented both milk chocolate and the blending process known as conching, or the Dutch, who discovered the processing phase required to create solid chocolate bars. In Belgium, too, chocolate manufacture has a long and distinguished history (Mercier 1989).

Even the history of the introduction of chocolate to French society is uncertain due to the existence of several competing theories. Cacao beans arrived from Mexico first in Spain, not France, and spread gradually from there to the rest of Europe, although the exact path and timing of this diffusion are unclear. The most popular theories feature the arrival of chocolate at the seventeenth-century French court on the occasion of royal nuptials uniting Spanish princesses with French kings: either the Infanta's marriage to Louis XIII in 1615, or Maria Teresa's marriage to Louis XIV in 1659. Another theory posits the diffusion of chocolate among clerics and monastic orders and still another the royal grant of refuge in southwest France to Iberian Jewish *chocolatiers* escaping religious persecution in the late sixteenth or early seventeenth centuries.[5]

As chocolate production became industrialized in the nineteenth century, it appeared in new forms—a powdered drink and solid bars—with reduced cocoa solids and added sugar. This lowered the cost of chocolate, thus ensuring that its consumption would democratize and expand. These chocolate products became and to this day remain items of popular consumption. Yet as a sweetened stimulant, hot chocolate never played the transformative role in French industrialization, colonialism, or work and social patterns that hot sugared tea played in England (Mintz 1985). In contrast to the free market created for sugar in England, French state intervention in chocolate manufacture was and remains substantial. The French state defines and regulates chocolate production, and its consumption in most forms is taxed at the same rate as luxury products (Union of Industrial Chocolate Makers 1990).

Although overall consumption of chocolate in all forms rose steadily throughout the nineteenth century, and sharply during the 1980s, in contrast to other European countries, French annual per capita consumption of chocolate remains low and is still linked to seasonal and ceremonial occasions (Casella 1989). Moreover, recent evidence suggests that French consumers know well their local confections but demonstrate little knowledge of the national chocolate cuisine lately promoted as part of their gastronomic patrimony (Mathieu 1990).

Most significantly, *chocolatiers* were a people without history because of their ambiguous role in a postwar history whose master narrative was constructed around the themes of modernization and professionalization. It was assumed that petty bourgeois craftspeople did not make history but, rather, impeded its forward march. My fieldwork among *chocolatiers* occurred at a time when French sociologists, many writing from a Marxist viewpoint, had turned away from the so-called declining petite bourgeoisie associated with traditional craftsmen (Baudelot and Establet 1974; Bourdieu 1984) and focused instead on the rising middle classes employed in new categories of salaried work (Boltanski 1988). Sociologists overwhelmingly dismissed artisans as volatile and archaic leftovers unequal to the demands of modernity and, therefore, destined to disappear or survive marginally.[6] One well-known sociological study of artisanal bakers (Bertaux and Bertaux-Wiame 1978) was the exception that proved the rule. French sociology increasingly centered on the aftershocks associated with decolonization and the end of the thirty-year period of rapid growth and state-led modernization known as *les trente glorieuses* (1945–1975).

At the same time, historians of modern France wrote artisanship out of contemporary history by documenting the definitive separation of household and workplace and the progressive decline of artisanal workshops in the twentieth century. This decline was considered emblematic of changes that had arrived later in France than elsewhere but effected an equally fundamental reorganization and differentiation of production and space (Prost and Vincent 1991, 9–49). Artisans were deemed to be synonymous with an older categorization of work marked by independent occupation, undivided labor, informal validation of skill, and personal ownership of the means of production. This history assumed that the work of both rural and urban artisans was inherently incompatible with modernization.

Similarly, many of the French anthropologists with whom I had contact favored a study of contemporary *chocolatiers* in part because it was consistent with objects of long-standing interest to French ethnology, with its deep roots in folklore and museum studies, namely, the "traditional" social groups associated with rural, preindustrial France. They were primarily interested in how the documentation of a chocolate craft *habitus* rooted in workshop culture and internalized predispositions such as gestures, tools, linguistic phrases, and technical prowess could contribute to the huge body of data assembled by folklorists. French anthropologists' interest in my study focused less on the dynamics of change that are often at the heart of Anglo-American ethnographies of France (see Badone 1991, Brettell 1995; McDonald 1989; Raissiguier 1994; Reed-Danahay 1996b; Rogers 1991; Rosenberg 1988; and Ulin 1996) than on the imperatives of loss engendered by the inevitable disappearance of now scarce work and social forms such as artisanship (see Blasquez 1976; Chalvon-Demersay 1984).

When one considers artisanship as a cultural category, it is clear that *chocolatiers* possess an intermediate, highly ambivalent class position and social status.[7] This is so because they embody a set of contradictions and tensions based on their dual functions as artisans and entrepreneurs. As craftsmen they evoke small-scale, skill-based, family-centered modes of production. The use of the label *fabrication artisanale* still connotes honest work and high-quality goods produced on the premises, whether the label corresponds to reality or not. Artisans represent what the French like to tell themselves about themselves in terms of a traditional work ethic, family values, community cohesion, and the noncompetitive practices of small business. However, artisans are manual workers, albeit highly skilled in some cases, in a society where intellectual work has the highest cultural value. In this society, economic rewards are thought to be properly contingent upon the educational credentials that lead logically to intellectual work. Indeed, the value of intellectual work has intensified in the postwar period through the burgeoning of a service sector and a concomitant ideology of professionalization. Most craftsmen complete an abbreviated vocational track in school and hold diplomas that have little cultural capital.

Artisans also embody a set of contradictions as business owners. Self-employment and freedom from bosses are attractive because they afford the possibility of social mobility for business owners and/or their children. Yet artisans are entrepreneurs in a context where business proprietorship offers considerable economic rewards but less social status than liberal professions, high civil service, or executive management positions. Artisans are not only business owners with little educational capital (Bourdieu 1984, 333) but also manual workers whose businesses require considerable self-exploitation. This intermediate status—neither workers nor capitalists—marginalizes them with regard to class and economics. As petty bourgeois capitalists, they tend to be dismissed as anachronisms at best. At worst they represent a cautionary tale that the French must tell themselves regarding class conflict, economic exploitation, and political extremism. In many scholarly and fictional accounts, petty bourgeois entrepreneurs are depicted as vulnerable to economic greed (hoarding products, overcharging customers, exploiting salaried help) and receptive to extremist ideas.[8]

## Craft and Capitalism

France is only one ethnographic case in point of general anthropological inattention to the existence of craft producers and communities in advanced capitalism. Despite the tenacious persistence of traditional crafts and the continuous emergence of new ones, artisanship has been neglected as a subject of serious ethnographic inquiry in first world centers. One reason for the dearth of work on craft has to do with the set of well-known dichotomies and evolutionary schema with which the social sciences conceptualized the shift from precapitalist to capitalist society as well as the reorganization of time, space, and production said to accompany this shift. In the industrializing context of the nineteenth century, this shift was theorized as a unilinear evolution from status to contract, gemeinschaft to gesellschaft, gift to commodity, simple to complex division of labor, and mechanical to organic solidarity. Changes in nineteenth-century Europe convinced Western social scientists that a craft mode of production would be definitively eradicated.

Evolutionist assumptions still strongly inform an essentialist master narrative that looks back to a golden age of craft tradition and contrasts it to the alienation of modern work. This narrative denies the vitality of craft in the present by linking it inextricably to the premodern and the precapitalist. It is informed by the basic tenet of evolutionary thinking which says that change inevitably proceeds to greater complexity, leveling or marginalizing the simpler forms that preceded. This narrative continues to assimilate craft work to only one set of the oppositions noted above: undivided labor, the essentially similar activities of mechanical solidarity, the undifferentiated social formations of gemeinschaft, and a collective ethos grounded in kinship and mutuality. It assumes the incapacity of craft workers to adapt to modernity because it denies them the same temporal existence as modern workers. Just as anthropological paradigms postulated a different time for the Other (Fabian 1983), contemporary craft is constructed not as an object of study for the present but one properly measured against the standard of the past. It is judged by how well it conforms to or deviates from its preindustrial ideal type. If it deviates it cannot be "true" craft, if it conforms it cannot survive. The received wisdom concerning the nature and direction of change says that craft is anachronistic.[9]

This image of craft exemplifies a prevalent theme in the depiction of Western modernity itself—the notion of cultural anachronism (Chakrabarty 1992). This concept of craft as anachronism relies strongly on the assumption that artisans are dominated by and subject to myriad forces beyond their control—tradition, the market, and the nation-state, or supranational entities such as the European Community (compare Kearney 1995b, 64–65). At the same time, this image allows craftspeople to emerge as a set of symbols that authenticate but simultaneously embody the evolutionary roots of the West (Nadel-Klein 1995). Whether as objects of romantic fascination or modernizing zeal, French craftspeople are, like artisans in Greece (Herzfeld 1995, 1997) or Greeks within Europe (Herzfeld 1987), the imagined primitives at home. They are disturbing because they remind us of what the modern West has lost and blur the boundary between the anthropological Self and the ethnographic Other.

## The Politics of Authenticity

In the 1980s, as proposed EC reforms threatened to undermine French norms of chocolate production and foreign franchise outlets steadily gained market share, *chocolatiers* began to engage in a complex politics of cultural authenticity. They were outraged that franchise outlets sold mass-produced candies in storefronts that not only consciously replicated a French craft model of production and sales but were purposely positioned close to traditional confectionery boutiques. French *chocolatiers* denounced foreign candies as fakes and formulated their own counterclaims of authenticity. The politics of authenticity continues to be vigorously played out in various venues, including the mass media, government ministry offices, public schools, individual boutiques, and craft events organized prominently in the public spaces of French cities.

In 1989, Parisian craft leaders, local southwest *chocolatiers,* and the state officials to whom they appealed all agreed on the imperative to develop an appropriate model by which to authenticate French craftsmen and their chocolates. All three groups had specific agendas that alternately converged or diverged in pursuit of the politics of cultural authenticity.

State officials were receptive to *chocolatier* appeals for a number of reasons. First, in the post-1975 period, state policies and public attitudes regarding artisanship shifted. A number of legislative reforms and policy initiatives aimed to preserve and even to promote artisanal training models, certification procedures, and cultural forms. In 1980 the creation of the Year of *Le Patrimoine* (Patrimony) ushered in a period of frenetic heritage festivals commemorating various manifestations of French national identity (Nora 1992). That same year, the Office of Ethnological Patrimony under the aegis of the National Ministry of Culture began to fund ethnographic research on traditional artisanal skills in danger of disappearing or in need of reviving. This program intended "to document cultural remnants of traditional France" and "to resuscitate" endangered production models by promoting them as authentic living cultural forms (Programme savoir-faire et techniques, dossier 1, 1988). In 1989, the Ministry of Culture also created the National Council of Culinary Arts and charged it with protecting French gastronomy through initiatives ranging from the documentation of major sites of French culinary production to the creation of a French gastronomy museum (Fantasia 1995, 203). It is no accident that my fieldwork among contemporary artisanal *chocolatiers* in the southwest cradle of chocolate production was funded in part by the French state (albeit a different funding source, the Chateaubriand Fellowship).

Second, EC representatives had proposed a set of European norms for chocolate production that threatened to undercut existing French legislation. The French state and its legions of bureaucrats take very seriously the protection of their language and cultural forms from intrusive foreign influences—such as attempts in Brussels to harmonize and eradicate unique national cultural forms in favor of a common European culture. Thus, even as France asserted its diplomatic, political, and economic presence in preparation for membership within the "new" Europe, the arena of culture remained highly charged and contested.

For their part, *chocolatiers*—both craft leaders and local craftspeople—were confident that they could successfully collaborate to authenticate their goods and modes of production. Indeed, their initial collaboration produced certain strategic initiatives. First, *chocolatiers* at the national and local levels agreed on the necessity to incorporate an autonomous identity for their membership separate from that of pastry makers and confectioners. Second, they both espoused the dissemination of a new esoteric taste standard privileging dark, bittersweet chocolate. Third, and most significantly, they turned to the past as a means of grounding their claims of cultural authenticity. They selectively appropriated and reworked a number of different histories—craft, Aztec, local, and national—in the construction and re-presentation of a new history (compare Handler and Gable 1997). Yet, over the course of my fieldwork, strong tensions and disagreements emerged among all three groups. In spite of their consensus on goals, they could not agree on a suitable model of authenticity.

## Contested Histories

The search for such a model produced competing narratives of authenticity and contested histories of *chocolatier* tradition.

These contested histories and struggles over the meaning of authenticity were manifest in the incessant commemorations mounted by both groups and in the attendant silences produced by these very commemorations. The emphasis here on both silences and commemorations suggests new ways of conjoining anthropology and history in the analysis of craft culture and community in postindustrial settings (Sider and Smith 1997). It allows us to move away from the well-worn "invention of tradition" concept, with its persistent focus on the constructedness of history and on the resulting debates distinguishing a true from an invented past.[10] This is not to suggest that what really happened is unimportant or unknowable. Rather, the analysis of commemorations and silences centers not on the content or authenticity of historical affirmations so much as on the contests and contexts surrounding their making. It is the attempt to craft and commemorate particular pasts that commands our attention. The focus here is on a historical dynamic articulated in terms of the fractures, tensions, and contradictions that emerge as an integral part of the process of identity formation (Sider and Smith 1997, 10).

This contestation is a forceful reminder that authenticity is not a predetermined essence but an ongoing struggle whose meaning depends on the perceptions and practices of those who claim it. Authenticity is a social process in which multiple voices argue for their own interpretation of history and seek its validation by recognized authorities (Bruner 1994, 108). The production and authentication of history is also always an issue of authority and power (Rappaport 1998; Trouillot 1997). Claims of authenticity emerge in the struggles of groups with competing interests and unequal access to power. As a group often depicted as absent from or marginal to the history of postwar France, *chocolatiers* sought to empower themselves through the construction and the imposition of their own particular pasts—local, national, and folkloric (Friedman 1994).

The conflicts and disagreements among state officials, craft leaders, and local *chocolatiers* produced multiple histories that sometimes overlapped and often diverged. This was not simply a matter of three stories emerging separately but rather a dialectical process whereby some craft leaders came to share the view of state officials and many local *chocolatiers* articulated a counter history in opposition to the view of both their leaders and the state (compare Lamphere 1997, 263–283). It is a story not simply of hegemonic metropoles prevailing over weaker peripheries or of local cultural formations resisting the transforming effect of powerful centers but also of the mutual interpenetration of the local, national, and global in the making of craft and the stories told about it.

## Local Pasts

Both history and field research unfold in unexpected ways. I did not explicitly set out to do an ethnography in or of the margins (Herzfeld 1985, 1987; Nadel-Klein 1991; Parman 1990; Reed-Danahay 1996b; Rogers 1991; Wilson and Smith 1993). Rather, southwest France was suggested to me as a promising site for extended research because of its history. In the late sixteenth or early seventeenth century, the French Crown permitted Iberian Jews fleeing religious persecution in Spain and Portugal to settle in this part of France. They brought both cacao and the craft of chocolate making to the region. Bayonne and the surrounding area became and remained a vibrant regional center of chocolate production until World War II, when many local *chocolateries* closed permanently because of disruptions wrought by the German occupation of France. After the war, intensified competition from industrial manufacturers provoked the disappearance of most small-scale *chocolateries* as well as the subsequent restructuring of the craft.

By 1990, fifty years after the craft was radically disrupted and significantly reorganized, *chocolatiers* in southwest France were actively organizing commemorative rituals in order to impose their own record of chocolate tradition. This was a bold attempt on the part of a tiny craft to reposition itself centrally within the histories of the region and the nation. It claimed Bayonne, not Paris or the Versailles court, as the oldest site of continuous chocolate manufacture in France. In 1989 this was an audacious claim because few French people, or Bayonnais for that matter, knew the southwest to be the birthplace of French chocolate production. Indeed, the most frequently told history of chocolate in France centered on sophisticated urban metropoles like Paris and overlooked peripheral provincial centers like Bayonne.

These commemorations depicted southwest craft tradition as an unchanging set of work practices, skills, and associational rituals handed down and effortlessly reproduced through time by the family owners of craft businesses.[11] They celebrated local artisans as the true originators of a dark chocolate vogue and contrasted the time-honored taste preferences in the southwest to the rapidly shifting culinary fashions in Paris.

Thus, southwest chocolate was marketed to locals and tourists alike as a product both authentically local and distinctly French—a national symbol of culture and superior taste. This story of tradition was particularly useful for local *chocolatiers* trying to resist attempts by state officials and craft leaders to professionalize the craft and by European technocrats to "harmonize" norms of chocolate production.

At the same time, these commemorations produced elisions and silences on how local businesses are actually reproduced, how craft identities are adapted to a shifting regional political economy, how a local craft community is constituted, and how regional chocolate tastes change through time. Most significantly, the new history of chocolate told in the southwest relied on an aestheticized past that elided the early history of Iberian Jews, a complicated tale of both political sanctuary by the French Crown and sustained discrimination by Bayonnais notables. In addition, it completely silenced the much more problematic history of the persecution and deportation of Jews during World War II, as well as the stories of how certain *chocolateries* survived the repressive political and economic climate of the German occupation. In the few recountings told of this period, tales of collaboration and illegal marketeering were repressed in favor of those celebrating resistance and heroism.

## National Narratives

Craft leaders, for their part, also organized commemorations that focused on Paris as the dominant center of *chocolatier* traditions and highlighted the introduction of chocolate to French court society. These events, staged in the capital and covered by national media, effectively muted or reappropriated divergent histories of chocolate by reinforcing the continuing power of Paris to define and legitimate "true" French cultural production from craft and cuisine to literature and art.

Craft leaders also endorsed the presentation of chocolate as living tradition and historical patrimony. They actively collaborated with cultural tastemakers to stimulate demand for traditional candies reconceived as vintage chocolates. In the 1980s craft leaders attracted considerable attention from state officials and tastemakers through their repeated petitions for formal recognition of an autonomous craft identity. At a time when the value of professional credentials was rising and labor shortages in food crafts were intensifying, craft leaders sought the legitimacy of national training and certification procedures backed by the French state. However, their negotiations in the areas of training and certification relied on sending a clear message in the name of craft. Craft leaders drew on a resonant preindustrial guild model celebrating skilled craftsmen as exemplars of a traditional artisanal ethic grounded in honest work and high-quality goods.

Yet their celebrations and narratives also revealed contradictions and produced silences. The portrayal of *chocolatiers* as mere craftsmen was problematic in the 1980s because it conflicted with a prominent discourse of professionalization. State officials seriously considered *chocolatiers'* petitions only after exhaustively studying the craft. In a series of official reports published between 1987 and 1990, state representatives urged craft leaders to adopt a professional model and to confront the potentially hegemonic division of labor forthcoming in the "new" Europe. Craft leaders finally endorsed the state's professional model for training and muted their celebration of timeless tradition in favor of modernization. However, their attempts to persuade and mobilize local *chocolatiers* in the southwest to follow their lead were, in turn, substantially silenced and produced a number of unforeseen consequences.

This tale of chocolate is well worth telling because it situates both the craft and its artisans within history. It enhances our understanding of how minority groups in European centers make and assert their own particular histories and likewise reminds us of the powerful role historical consciousness plays in the formation of collective identity.

## How the Story Unfolds

The progression of this book mirrors my movement among multiple field sites in southwest France and Paris.[12] Whereas my fieldwork necessarily involved intensive participant observation and the collection of life histories, it also forced me to rethink my original methodology based on a narrowly circumscribed notion of "the field" (compare Gupta and Ferguson 1997). It challenged the ubiquitous conceptualization of craft communities as fixed, bounded entities. *Chocolatiers* formed a community of permeable, shifting boundaries constituted in numerous places over time. The creation of a community was dependent on continuous contact with and exchanges among locally situated as well as geographically dispersed members. These were exchanges of workers, goods, and knowledge, both empirical and theoretical. Tracing the connections among past and current owners, workers, and apprentices in local businesses took me away from the Basque coast and deep into the countryside, to a number of far-flung provincial cities and northern Spanish towns, and, also frequently, not occasionally, to Paris. During slack production periods I accompanied craftspeople to craft contests, shows, training seminars, and tours of famous *chocolateries* in Paris; to conventions in Beaune (in the Burgundy wine-growing region); and to induction ceremonies, lectures, chocolate tastings, and professional meetings in Pau (a city one hour east of Bayonne). I also interviewed state officials, sales representatives, cultural tastemakers, and French executives of firms that manufacture the raw materials used in artisanal workshops.

My tale begins with two chapters that introduce French chocolate as a historical and cultural commodity. Chapter 2 recounts the postwar transformations in French bread making and foodways and traces the multiple challenges facing *chocolatiers* even as they successfully mounted a prestigious national craft contest in Paris in 1990. Chapter 3 chronicles the collaboration between *chocolatiers* and tastemakers to create heightened social demand for French chocolates, recast as prestige goods, reinvested with both cultural authenticity and esoteric cachet, and associated with new symbolic meanings and uses. Connoisseur tastings and a gastronomic literature are examined in detail as the privileged media for "reeducating French palates" to appreciate the refinement of vintage chocolates.

Chapter 4 situates the Basque coast towns of Bayonne, Biarritz, and Saint-Jean-de-Luz within a historical and contemporary context marked by a changing regional political economy. It juxtaposes the historical claims made by local *chocolatiers* to a detailed examination of the profound restructuring of the craft and a concomitant redefinition of skill mastery. Chapter 5 investigates the sociological principles that inform the organization and performance of craft work in the short term, whereas chapter 6 examines the cultural logics underlying the intergenerational reproduction of craft businesses. Through a detailed examination of two local events, an induction ceremony and a craft contest, chapter 7 reveals how the local craft community was culturally imagined, socially constructed, and publicly represented.

Chapter 8 shifts its focus to Paris and centers on the evolution of the *chocolatiers'* professional organization and the recent initiatives elaborated at the national level to professionalize the craft. Chapter 9 looks at the local responses to Parisian initiatives and illustrates the tension between competing interests and identities based on craft. The detailed examination of French vocational education and apprenticeship demonstrates how national state policies are mediated and shaped by local cultural formations as much as the reverse (Sahlins 1989). Finally, chapter 10 broadens its focus to consider chocolate as a global metaphor for changing social relations in situations of great flux and as a device used in diverse media—from gastronomic texts and advertising to trade shows and art—to project and contrast orientalist images of a primitive Other (Said 1978) to occidentalist images of the civilized (French) Self (Carrier 1995b).

In the final chapter of Christian Constant's beautifully illustrated gastronomic text, *Le chocolat* (1988), one particularly arresting photograph depicts a golden brown brioche being slowly smothered in a stream of glossy, ebony-dark chocolate. This luxury bread treat constitutes a metaphor for contemporary consumer culture in France as well as the production of taste in Western prestige economies. It is also a suitably suggestive image with which to begin this story of bread and chocolate.

CHAPTER 2

# Bread and Chocolate

*As the independent artisans retire, bakery chains are springing up—but they are chains of gourmet bakers à la française that sell "country-style" loaves made from industrial mixes.*

Paul Rambali, *Boulangerie*

If France is known historically for a foodstuff, it is bread not chocolate.[1] An understanding of French bread culture is crucial because its very history will lead us back to chocolate and to the cultural elaboration that chocolate symbolizes. In the premodern era, bread was at the core of the material and symbolic organization of life, both private and public. France was a panivore civilization in which bread served not only as the principal staple food but as a preeminent emblem of the sacred. Throughout French history bread has been the food for the sacred ritual of the Eucharist and the basic metaphor for eating itself. Breaking bread signified mealtime in the home and in the workplace. The political, economic, and psychological power of bread in Old Regime France (prior to 1789) was revealed by the upheavals unleashed when it was scarce, overpriced, or poorly made. The scarcity of bread brought famine and provoked riot. The questions and anxieties surrounding its production and regulation—namely, the persistent monopoly of guild production—contributed to the outbreak of revolution in 1789 (Kaplan 1996).

The importance of bread resonates with a striking cross-cultural tendency for peoples to mark a particular food—often a single complex carbohydrate—as a metaphor for food itself (Mintz 1985). Rice defines food for the Chinese and Japanese (Ohnuki-Tierney 1993) in the same way millet did for the Bemba (Richards 1938), maize did for ancient Mayan and Aztec peoples as well as their descendants (Coe 1994), and bread still does for a number of Western peoples including the French (Mintz 1996b, 96–97).

The myriad linguistic phrases centering on bread conveyed salient notions of family, home, health, work, love, and sex—in short, the basic moral axioms around which much social life revolves. To take the bread out of someone's mouth *(ôter à quelqu'un le pain de la bouche)* was to deprive that person of her basic needs, and to suffer an interminable wait was like a day without bread *(long comme un jour sans pain)*. To sell things easily and quickly was to sell them like small rolls *(comme petits pains)*, not like hot cakes. To be the first to eat white bread *(manger le pain blanc le premier)* signified a promising beginning, whereas to be limited to a diet of dry bread *(au pain sec)* was to suffer a severe deprivation. Definitions of bread occupy considerable space in French dictionaries, in contrast to the few paragraphs accorded to chocolate. Moreover, chocolate's figurative meanings give pause because they conspicuously turn on the darker side of social life, such as deception, playing the fool, and even death.[2]

Today bread continues to reflect the structure of domestic ideologies and the logic of meals. A French meal without bread is inconceivable; and bread is still the subject of sufficient importance to be, in Mintz's felicitous phrase, "the basis of discourse" (1996b, 97). If 1996 was the Year of Chocolate, it was also a year in which the craft and standards of breadmaking became the subject of fierce debates (making headlines in French and American media) as well as the object of state intervention.[3] The state's decision to intervene in 1996 was designed to save the craft and to authenticate its products precisely because many lamented the progressive disappearance of artisanal bakeries and their bread products. Craft bread production has remained vital in France quite late compared to other Western nations; in fact, until the late 1960s it was the dominant mode of bread production. Since that time bread production has been steadily industrialized. The introduction of new machines and techniques—first fermentation accelerators and later cold leavening—reduced the time, skills, and costs required to produce bread (Bertaux, Dufrene, and Kersebet 1983). Accordingly, the number of craft bakers shrank from 54,000 in 1960 to approximately 36,000 in 1990. Over the same period, the per capita consumption of bread declined dramatically, and it became less of a staple and more of a complement at mealtime.[4] Yet this shift did not lessen the importance of bread in the French culinary imagination or the symbolic potency of the craft bakers who produced it. French observers—from consumers to gastronomes and bakers themselves—lamented the poor quality and taste of this industrial bread product: one journalist, Alain Schifres, even termed the 1980s the "era of bread shame" (*Nouvel observateur*, 25–31 December 1987, quoted in Kaplan 1996). Significantly, state intervention was finally prompted not by the ongoing proliferation of industrial bakeries but by the sale of loaves made from preprocessed, frozen dough in small *boulangeries*, the quintessential outlets for artisanal bread. Repeated state action since 1993 establishing a minimum price for the baguette as well as new guarantees that bread be made from dough prepared on the premises can only be understood in light of French breadways in the past.

The transformation of bread parallels important changes in French living standards and foodways during the thirty years of exuberant modernization and economic growth known as *les trente glorieuses* (Fourastié 1979). Fourastié's now famous comparison of one representative rural French village in 1946 and 1974 was a celebration of the attendant benefits of state driven development. It reflected the imperatives of a cadre of state technocrats who planned, implemented, and trumpeted a process they believed to have been long overdue in France (Kuisel 1993). Despite the pro-modernization ideology informing Fourastié's analysis, it provides a striking and accurate depiction of what compressed change could achieve in material terms.

In 1946, the village of Douelle had a subsistence economy dominated by noncapitalized family farmers toiling on small holdings. There was little cash for personal consumption, leisure, or durable goods, and three-fourths of the total family budget went for food. The local diet consisted mostly of bread, vegetables, and pork fat. However, by 1974, Douelle, like many other rural areas, was transformed and modernized, reflecting the overall changes in French life styles and foodways. Over this period the percentage of household expenses reserved for food declined steadily from 75 percent in 1946 to 20 percent in 1989 (Fischler 1990, 199). Diets diversified and broadened. Indeed, the emblematic measure of economic well-being shifted from the *gagne-pain* (breadwinner) to the *gagne-bifteck* (meat winner).[5]

The condensed postwar period of modernization and economic growth that transformed Douelle also enabled consumption to take place on a new mass scale. The postwar modernization tale told by French sociologists (Boltanski 1988; Bourdieu 1984) and historians (Nora 1984, 1–13; Prost and Vincent 1991, 9–49) centers on the rise of a French consumer culture and on the attendant reconfiguration of class structures. According to this tale, newly emergent urbanized middle classes—office workers, professional managers, service employees—embodying an individual ethos of accumulation based in consumption were progressively displacing the declining lower middle and popular classes—workers, farmers, artisans—marked by a collective ethos of mutuality based in production. The formation of a new postwar bourgeoisie composed of professional managers best exemplified novel class-based consuming attitudes. These managers initiated a break with traditional bourgeois cultural practices and explicitly positioned themselves within a modernity marked by a rhetoric of professionalization, a relaxed life style, modern home décors, and, above all, new consuming habits in food, clothing, and the pursuit of leisure (Boltanski 1988, 106).

For the first time, large numbers of French people were able to engage in a logic of consumption reconceived as both necessary and pleasurable, even liberating and self-fulfilling (Bourdieu 1984, 371). This logic of consumption was reimagined as immeasurably rich in goods and services and was enacted within new postwar venues—in Club Med vacations featuring unlimited food and wine in one all-inclusive price (Furlough 1993) and in the vast retail emporia for perishable and durable goods that have proliferated since the 1960s.[6] The refrigerator, car, highway, factory, and mass distribution super- and hypermarkets symbolized the reorganization and differentiation of social and work space, new leisure habits, higher living standards, and, in particular, changing foodways (Ross 1995).

Many social factors contributed to changing French foodways. A shorter work week, the progressive disappearance of the two-hour lunch and its replacement by the *journée continue* (continuous workday), the massive arrival of married women in the workplace, longer commutes due to urban- and suburbanization, and increases in adolescents' spendable incomes all reshaped the structure, composition, and timing of family meals. More meals were eaten outside the home, and family commensality was moved from the traditional lunchtime meal to a simplified evening dinner.[7] These changes in turn spawned the rapid growth of French agrobusiness conglomerates specializing in the processing and delivery of frozen and prepared foods to cafeterias in schools, at workplaces, and along highways. Increasing numbers of types of cheap industrially processed and frozen foods appeared, from instant coffee, bottled orange juice, and breakfast cereals to previously unknown imports such as avocados and kiwi. The introduction and popularity of new foods and drinks such as hamburgers and Coca-Cola within fast food chains announced a culinary Other, alternatively alluring and threatening.

Growing numbers of French restaurants adapted the fast food formula to the production and sale of traditional French foods, in particular bread. Indeed, French breadways perhaps best exemplified new consuming habits. The first successful fast food restaurants, the Brioche Dorée, were not American but French and sold bread-based snacks, not hamburgers or Coca-Cola.[8] The decreasing consumption of bread, the displacement of urban bakers, and the appearance of French fast food *viennoiseries* were emblematic of these and many other changes that coincided with the end of sustained economic growth from 1975 on. It is no accident that the 1989 creation of a National Council of Culinary Arts to preserve and defend the French "culinary patrimony" occurred at a time when fast food restaurants, both French and American, were expanding rapidly.[9] It is in the context of this transformation that bread comes to point the way to chocolate.

If the French were consuming fewer baguettes and less table wine, beer, and coffee, they were also eating more brioches, meat, fresh pastry, champagne, and vintage wines—foods previously consumed primarily in the context of ceremonial social occasions (Pynson 1987). However, in the mid-1970s, French consumption of chocolate—specifically, dipped chocolate and sugar candies, as well as molded figurines—exhibited striking similarities to those of the interwar period. This does not imply that consumption patterns were static or immune to changes in method or raw materials. It suggests merely that the symbolic properties and social uses of chocolate and sugar candies remained largely the same.

Artisanal chocolates were purchased primarily as gifts from small-scale *chocolateries* and *pâtisseries* and distributed to relatives, friends, and employees. The purchase of artisanal candies was inextricably linked to traditional seasonal and ceremonial occasions such as the rites of passage of baptism, communion, and marriage and religious holidays, especially Christmas and Easter. At that time, French customers mainly frequented locally or regionally known family businesses, purchased roughly equal numbers of dark and milk chocolate-coated candies, chose from a smaller selection of house specialties, and purchased only chocolate bunnies, bells, eggs, and chickens—no confectionery art or chocolate haute couture. Moreover, there were no specialized culinary guides with which to rate *grand cru* French chocolates.[10]

## *Meilleur Ouvrier de France* (Best Craftsman of France)

A series of developments in the late 1970s and 1980s coalesced to effect considerable change in the art, craft, and consumption of chocolate. To begin addressing these questions it is necessary to understand the context that stimulated change and to meet some of the social actors responsible for it.

The first public event I attended after returning to Paris in 1990 was the 30 October contest exhibition for the Best Craftsman of France award in chocolate and sugar candy production,[11] which was experienced by *chocolatiers* and reported in the mass media as a historic event. For seven years craft leaders had petitioned the Ministry of Education for the right to organize their first exhibition.[12] Five finalists had advanced to the national round from the regional contest held in February near Lyon. Over a three-day period immediately preceding the exhibition, they demonstrated their workmanship and stamina while being observed by a panel of judges. Working behind closed doors in contiguous work stations, they each completed artistic pieces in chocolate, molded figurines, various chocolate and sugar bonbons, and a signature candy creation (see chapter 8).

The exhibition presented a profusion of ebony black chocolate against a backdrop of elaborate multicolored décors: confectionery art and candies were arranged on rich fabrics and in trays and boxes also crafted in chocolate. Attendance was by invitation only, and the select audience included state representatives, craftsmen, workers, apprentices, journalists, food critics, leaders from companion food crafts, teachers, students, and administrators from the Parisian School for the Food Trades, which hosted the exhibition. I was among the several hundred guests who slowly filed past the exhibits. What struck me initially was the absence of the ubiquitous Parisian ennui often prevalent at exhibitions of this sort. Lay spectators were all breathless with admiration; professionals intensely debated the techniques required to craft the artistic pieces, which included a Belle Epoque chocolate lamp (see fig. 3), a chocolate writing desk, and a bronze (chocolate) sculpture of two playful cherubs.

Approximately one hour after the exhibition opened, the guests were

Figure 3. Chocolate lamp, designed and fashioned by Best Craftsman of France winner Jean-Pierre Richard, 1990.

invited to assemble around a raised podium. As I was juggling my camera and tape recorder, I heard a voice nearby say, *"Bonsoir Madame."* With this greeting, Alain Grangé, vice-president of the *chocolatiers'* professional association, owner of one of the oldest and most famous Parisian *chocolateries,* Foucher, and one of my first contacts and best consultants—made his way toward me in the crowd. Since a period of preliminary fieldwork in 1989, I had relied on his knowledge of French culture and chocolate as well as the critical distance he brought to both. He was one of the principal advocates of professionalization for *chocolatiers* and his steadfast involvement in trade-based syndicalism had been a family tradition since the nineteenth century. Although usually quite reserved in his personal manner, Grangé's pleasure at the audience turnout and their enthusiastic reaction was obvious.

Word had spread through the audience that the judges would publicly announce the contest winners, a departure from the usual procedure of written notification. There was a palpable sense of anticipation as the award ceremony began. The five finalists, attired in monogrammed white chef jackets and hats, lined up, faces tense from fatigue and anxiety. The president of the judging panel, Monsieur Boucher, a highly respected Parisian *chocolatier* who had devoted several years to organizing the contest, strode into the hall and, without ceremony, read the names of three out of the five. All of the contestants posed for a photo session, but one of the losers could not contain his disappointment and pain; he burst into tears.

A series of speeches followed in which craft leaders evoked a shared identity grounded in "love of work well done, perseverance, and competitive will." A past president of the *chocolatiers'* association celebrated the three contest winners as the "elite of our professionals . . . who in the tradition of the masters of old have worked, suffered, doubted, seeking relentlessly the originality and the aesthetic implicit in new creations." This leader warned that their spirit should serve as a lesson on the eve of the 1993 unification of Europe:

Being the best is the perpetual quest imposed on us by the impending opening of the European Community borders. Our citizens are tired of an overabundance that leads to uniformity and the lowering of product standards. For the family business with a human dimension, the solution is in the search for difference, originality, and know-how. The challenge for those who fight to maintain [our] civilization of taste is to compete by offering excellence.

Craft leaders also linked the imperative of excellence to revitalized recruitment and training programs for artisanal apprentices within the public educational system. They proudly noted their success in incorporating specialized training sections in artisanal chocolate making within state-run apprenticeship centers. Jacques Daumoinx, the president of the Confédération Nationale des Détaillants et Artisans-détaillants de la

Chocolaterie, Confiserie et Biscuiterie, took the floor to remind the audience of the need "to work on all fronts to revalorize manual work and a venerable French tradition of artisanship, [both of which are] indispensable to the balance of economic life in the nation."

Such discursive narratives by members of a tiny craft in an advanced capitalist society are important social texts. As texts, they tell cultural tales about craft, cuisine, and family entrepreneurship—potent, manipulable symbols of French culture on which numerous ideas are projected and validated. These narratives portrayed a seamless public image that celebrated French artisanship in general and *chocolatiers* in particular. They emphasized the "human dimension" of family entrepreneurship and the know-how of craftsmen in contrast to the bland "uniformity" offered by industrialization. They reflected the complex ideology of craft that is central to its practice in all postindustrial economies.

Narrative discourses actively capitalized on the enduring association between contemporary craftsmanship and the aestheticized image of premodern France. This association evoked a "simpler," "better" time when family workshops dominated the production of goods, both utilitarian and luxury. Family workshops were the backbone of guild communities premised on the notion of similarly skilled masters producing fairly priced, well-made goods. The prominent place accorded to artistic pieces in the contest recalled the masterpieces *(chefs-d'oeuvre)* completed as a necessary rite of passage in French craft guilds and journeymen brotherhood associations *(compagnonnages)*. The signature candies also invoked a renowned French gastronomic heritage based on refined taste and aesthetics. French *chocolatiers* were not only master craftsmen but also master chefs.

Yet this seamless public image concealed a more complex reality. First, the public image presented in the contest narratives belied a set of tensions at the core of French postwar society involving artisanship. Artisans occupy a highly ambiguous social category in contemporary France and are not always, to use Lévi-Strauss's famous phrase, "good to think." Moreover, *chocolatiers'* narratives on their work mirrored the tenor of wider debates on the central themes of French national identity. These issues included French competitiveness, economic power, political stature, and, especially, cultural autonomy in the new European and world orders. The Best Craftsman of France contest was staged in the context of mounting social and political upheaval in Europe and of heightened fears regarding the impact of the proposed European Community (EC) unification. For *chocolatiers,* as for many French people, 1993 brought the ominous specter of increasingly centralized bureaucratic regulation, intensified international competition, cultural homogenization, and the attendant loss of both national identity and French exceptionalism in domains as diverse as education, worker training, citizenship, and food—threats that for *chocolatiers* and other groups had become reality by 1998. Several features of the context surrounding the 1990 Best Craftsman of France contest deserve elaboration here.

First, 1990 was marked by sluggish economic growth and rising levels of unemployment in France. Of particular concern were the high levels of un- and underemployment among young people under the age of twenty-five. By citing the newly created training and certification programs in chocolate making and the jobs waiting to be filled in food trades, craft leaders raised sensitive issues for French politicians, educators, and business leaders. The craft contest was staged in the midst of widely publicized nationwide strikes by French secondary school students in the autumn of 1990. Their dissatisfaction with large class size, crumbling physical plant, outdated curricula, and diminishing job opportunities echoed public debate on the problems and lacunae of French public education. This debate resuscitated acrimonious exchanges dating back to the inception of secular public education in the Third Republic (1880s) relating to the prioritization of intellectual skills over pragmatic ones (Prost 1968). In the postwar period, repeated attempts were made to democratize and modernize the elitist nineteenth-century model of education according to a dominant postwar ideology of professionalization. In 1990, after nearly a decade of pressure by Socialist education ministers to increase lycée enrollments and baccalaureate degree holders, public education was being criticized for producing too many generalists with no applied skills or work experience and not enough skilled workers in trades and industry. Monsieur Daumoinx spoke to this issue directly when he admonished the French to "revalorize manual work" and invoked the young people without a lycée education. In fact, at that time vocational training programs were being scrutinized and compared to other European models, particularly German ones, in an effort to answer some hard questions. Would French workers be competitive in the "new" Europe? Could the French economy generate enough jobs to absorb the roughly 700,000 young people who leave the school system every year?

Second, the reference to a "venerable French tradition of artisanship" evoked a rich past of craft work, culture, and associational forms. Historically, France has been a preeminent nation of small manufacture, and the "civilization of taste" referred to by craft leaders was established largely through the design and worldwide export of luxury artisanal goods. From the preindustrial era to the present, the French state has had a long and complicated relationship with artisans representing a number of crafts. It has created, regulated, heavily subsidized, and, in some cases, assumed control of certain crafts. This strong interventionist role regarding artisanship has been emblematic of the state's management of the economy as well as its protection of business and industry. The overall shape of the pre–World War II economy reflected this; small-scale firms dominated business and trade in France until after 1945. Yet the thirty-year period immediately following the war saw the implementation of an ambitious plan of state-driven modernization designed to open and stimulate what had been a largely protected economy. It lifted some trade and price restrictions, encouraging competition and foreign investment both in France and abroad and promoting growth through an increasingly concentrated industrial sector.

Over this period, the small business sector shrank significantly (Parodi 1981). Artisans and shopkeepers under pressure periodically organized collective protests (for example, the Poujadist tax revolt of the 1950s and the defense of small independents led by Nicoud in the 1960s), but these were relatively ineffective in the face of the prevailing ideology favoring growth and modernization. Thus, over the period that gave rise to France's "economic miracle," artisanship came to represent an increasingly embattled idiom. In contrast, in the post-1975 period, the cumulative impact of economic and industrial change had a substantial effect on both public attitudes and state policy centering on artisanship. Traditional social groups like the vanishing peasant (Mendras 1970) and the disappearing artisan (Blasquez 1976) were recast as emblems of a modernizing process seen as temporally compressed and socially wrenching. Their symbolic potency in the national imagination meant that their passing engendered nostalgia for an idealized national past as it simultaneously created fears of an endangered social fabric. At the same time, center-right governments (1974–1981, 1986–1988, and 1993–1997) saw the small business sector as an important site of on-the-job training and a potential source of new jobs. This translated into shifting state policies designed to promote artisanal training models (such as apprenticeship), certification procedures, and cultural forms. The state decision to permit *chocolatiers,* a tiny craft threatened by increased competition, to organize their own Best Craftsman of France contest best exemplified this policy shift.

Third, during the award ceremony, craft leaders spoke on behalf of a unified national community of *chocolatiers* sharing a common craft ethos and identity. The successful staging of the Best Craftsman of France contest was only one of a number of collective initiatives undertaken by the Parisian leadership on behalf of its local membership. Over the preceding fifteen-year period, leaders had collaborated with state representatives and simultaneously worked through local activists to mobilize a grass-roots constituency. The initial goal was to authenticate craft producers with authoritative state credentials. As national craft leaders like Monsieur Boucher worked closely with state representatives intent on rationalizing craft apprenticeship training and certification, they adopted the modernizing state imperatives and worked to recast their traditional craft into a viable profession. However, local *chocolatiers* strongly contested the identity that their leaders fought so hard to professionalize.

Finally, the 1970s and 1980s were marked by continually evolving foodways and contradictory consumer trends. A prevailing French postwar discourse evident in the various contest speeches was highly critical of rampant mass consumerism and its incarnation in vast distribution outlets. Yet this discourse belied actual consuming habits. French consumers purchased increasing quantities of industrially prepared foods and shopped less frequently at open market stalls and artisanal shops in downtown urban centers and much more often at suburban super- and hypermarkets. Proliferating fast food restaurants like McDonald's embodied culinary danger and refigured the boundaries of the edible. French consumption of meals consisting of hamburgers, fries, and Coca-Cola violated a central tenet of French cuisine since the seventeenth century, which precludes mixing salty and sweet foods in the same course (Fischler 1990).

At the same time, the new middle classes embraced a novel culinary paradigm, *nouvelle cuisine,* which emerged during this period emphasizing a return to the authentic, natural products of the "regional soil" (*de terroir*). By October 1990, trends favoring French products with both cultural authenticity and esoteric cachet were supported, as we shall see, by state representatives and by *chocolatiers* who denounced the sheer volume and banality of industrial products both edible and durable.

The consumption of sweets—pastry, sugar candy, and chocolate in all forms—increased through the 1970s but exhibited diverging trends after that. French consumption of dipped confectionery products and dark chocolate became increasingly popular in the 1980s, whereas sugar candy consumption declined precipitously (Casella 1989). A dramatic restructuring of industrialized chocolate production also occurred during this period. By 1990 only eight multinational firms generated 80 percent of the total annual sales of chocolate products in France (Union of Industrial Chocolate Makers 1990). The five foreign manufacturers included three Swiss firms (Nestlé Rowntree, Lindt, and Jacobs Suchard France), the Italian company Ferraro France, and the American giant Mars. Only three of the eight were French: Cacao Barry, Cantalou, and Poulain Cadbury.[13] In the 1980s, artisanal *chocolatiers* occupied a specialized niche within a fully industrialized sector; they purchased industrially produced blocks of semi-finished chocolate and transformed them into a personalized line of candies and figurines.

An internal study completed by the Union of Industrial Chocolate Makers (1990) revealed, on the one hand, that French annual per capita consumption of chocolate (in all forms) had increased rapidly in the 1980s but at roughly 6.15 kilos was still low compared to 9 kilos for the Swiss, 7.9 for Norwegians, and 7 for residents of Great Britain. The gift nature of artisanal chocolate continued to limit its demand to ceremonial occasions. In contrast, the sales of mass-produced candies increased by almost 10 percent from 1988 to 1989.

In addition, from the early 1980s on, foreign franchise outlets specifically targeted the market for confectionery gifts by selling mass-produced chocolate candies in storefronts that closely replicated French artisanal boutiques. Although the franchise system of distribution and ownership was not then widespread, the appearance of confectionery franchises attracted immediate attention for several reasons. The high purchase price of a French *chocolaterie* combining a fully equipped workshop and well-appointed boutique costing $60,000–80,000, depending on its location stood in sharp contrast to the average price of $9,000 for a franchise license (Monassier 1991). Franchises provided not only products but a whole marketing program, including prefabricated displays, packaging, and sales training. Moreover, their mass-produced chocolates retailed for one-half to one-third the price of French artisanal chocolates. The franchise presence in the French confectionery market increased exponentially from 18 stores in 1983 to 673 in 1989; 79 percent of them were Belgian. Over a seven-year period (1983–1990), franchises captured 48 percent of the confectionery gift market (Mathieu 1990).

To enhance their successful marketing strategy, the Belgians systematically appropriated the presentational forms of French chocolates (sold in specialized boutiques that combined production and sales), their cultural value to consumers (linked to gifting relations and ceremonial consumption), and established French craft terms (used to distinguish among types of candies and to assign evocative names to them). Mass-produced for export along with prefabricated displays, these candies were sold by franchise owners who had little training and no contact with the family entrepreneurs of the local craft community.

The success of "the Belgians" touched a raw nerve in France. French *chocolatiers* were dismayed by the mounting popularity and market share of candies they judged to be in bad taste—both poorly made and repugnant in culinary terms. They were too large *(gros)*, too sweet *(sucré)*, and too full of butter and cream *(gras)*. Frustrated craftsmen and tastemakers discussed the success of these franchises and industrial chocolates in general by alluding to an overall assault on traditional French culinary taste. They compared this latest incursion of foreign foods with the rapid spread of the American fast food chain McDonald's, which had grown from 18 outlets in 1984 to 150 in 1991 (Fantasia 1995). Many bemoaned the fact that French palates had been "deformed" by exposure to candies mass-produced with too much sugar and milk and too little chocolate. In their award speeches, craft leaders targeted franchise outlets without specifically naming them when they decried the "lowering of production standards" in the market. The fabrication and display of exclusively dark bittersweet chocolate at the Best Craftsman contest marked them as distinctly French products, in contrast to the larger milk and white chocolates that, as Alain Grangé put it, one finds only *chez les Belges* (in Belgian shops).

In fact, in 1990, what counted as French taste in chocolate was not at all clear. This was true in the sense of both market segmentation and culinary identity. The Belgian incursion was made possible in part because French chocolates had a distinct market niche based on their mode of production—family and craft—and ceremonial purchase appeal, not exclusively on taste. Artisanal chocolates were consumed largely in the context of ritualized social occasions at widely spaced intervals. Unlike the culture of bread, there existed comparatively little knowledge, discourse, or standards concerning confectionery taste to distinguish meaningfully among different chocolates. It was deemed more important to exchange and circulate confectionery gifts that looked the part. Since French consumers shopped in businesses that usually sold roughly equal proportions of dark and milk chocolates, the appeal of milk, dark, and white chocolates in franchise outlets for half the price of French artisanal candies was too great. As Monsieur Daumoinx wryly observed, the surge in French per capita consumption of chocolate in the 1980s, from 3.2 kilos in 1982 to 6.15 in 1990, was largely due to "our Belgian friends, who developed the market." Nonetheless, the success of Belgian chocolates was particularly threatening because it represented an incursion into the sensitive French cultural terrain occupied by craft, cuisine, and family entrepreneurs. How could one speak of a distinctive artisanal French chocolate when consumers were just as likely to eat bars made by Mars or Lindt or to present gifts of bonbons made by Belgian franchises as they were to offer and consume French candies?

The allusion in the 1990 Best Craftsman of France contest to a "lowering of production standards" was also a veiled reference to recently proposed European directives. When I interviewed Monsieur Daumoinx in 1990, he expressed concern that the post-Maastricht harmonization of chocolate production norms would undermine existing French legislation. French law forbade the substitution of cheaper vegetable additives for the more expensive cocoa butter occurring naturally in the cacao bean. It defined chocolate according to the percentage of cocoa solids and cocoa butter, differentiating dark household or cooking chocolate (*chocolat de ménage*) with a minimum of 30 percent cocoa solids and 18 percent cocoa butter from a high-quality chocolate (*supérieur*) with 43 percent solids and 26 percent cocoa butter (Union of Industrial Chocolate Makers 1990).

The debate over additives other than cocoa butter dates back to 1973, when Britain, Ireland, and Denmark entered the European Union and obtained exceptions to a Europe-wide directive on chocolate manufacture instituted by the six founding member-nations. This original directive had stipulated that the label "chocolate" could only be used on products manufactured with cocoa solids and cocoa butter. Since then four other nations—Austria, Sweden, Portugal, and Finland, which use cocoa butter substitutes—joined the European Union and secured their own exceptions. The two-chocolate policy divided the seven "vegetable fat or MGV (*matières grasses végétales*)" nations led by Great Britain and the eight "purist" nations including France *and* Belgium, which require that chocolate be manufactured exclusively with cocoa butter.

Monsieur Daumoinx's position dovetailed with that of the French state, the French culinary establishment, and the Association of Cocoa Producers (led by the Ivory Coast) but diverged sharply from that of industrial manufacturers both French and foreign. The question of MGV was intimately linked to costs, profit margins, and competition.

Vegetable additives are divided into two basic categories. Cocoa butter *equivalents* exhibit the same physical and chemical properties, can be blended successfully with cocoa butter, and are processed in an identical manner to cocoa butter-based products. Cocoa butter *replacers* have similar physical characteristics but completely different chemical properties from cocoa butter. Because of the chemical differences, these replacers are largely incompatible with cocoa butter and require different processing methods. They are, however, significantly cheaper and easier to mass-produce (Minifie 1989, 101–109; Talbot 1994, 247–257). Daumoinx echoed widely shared French fears that a European directive permitting all member-nations to add MGV would radically alter chocolate taste, thus lowering overall quality, taste, and annual consumption.[14]

## Conclusion

We now return momentarily to the chocolate-covered brioche, which introduced this chapter. This luxury bread treat, constitutes a sort of metaphor for contemporary consumer culture in France. It stands for a culture in which consumption of a former staple food like the ordinary baguette is down but sales of previously fancy breads like brioche now mass-produced in fast food outlets and the new gourmet *rétro* baguette—hand-crafted with refined flour, a minimum of yeast and salt, and a slow, natural leavening process and retailing for twice the price of a normal baguette—are brisk.

It is a culture of consumption predicated on the primacy of individual expression, ostensibly obviating a language of class but preoccupied with the acquisition of goods that confer social status. It is, above all, a culture of consumption marked by rapid taste shifts and the proliferation of simulacra, of which Belgian franchise candies are but the latest example, but one that simultaneously longs to possess the old, the traditional, and the human, as a generator of a sense of self outside the sensory overload of consumerism (Harvey 1989, 292). It radiates nostalgia for local, culturally constituted identities, places, work practices, and commodities as a source of authenticity and distinction.

The craft commodities, both candies and art, proudly displayed at the Best Craftsman of France contest draw their power and value from their symbolic loading. In prestige economies marked by the production of volatility, craft commodities satisfy the nostalgia for and appeal of localized goods and modes of production associated with a traditional past. The very persistence of master craftsmen such as *chocolatiers* in these economies means that they can be absorbed and designated as unique manifestations of a unified national culture. They can be enshrined as part of the nation's historic patrimony, redefined as genuine, living cultural forms.

The Best Craftsman of France contest represented an important attempt to authenticate French chocolate and its producers. The promotion of signature candy recipes and confectionery art was a reassertion of French cultural integrity as it was manifest in the culinary arts, master craftsmanship, and aesthetics. Yet this contest was staged amid the uncertainty generated by the impending unification of the European Community. Mass-produced Belgian candies, marketed and sold as if they were freshly made, locally crafted French goods were particularly threatening because they represented an incursion into sensitive cultural terrain. They were also threatening because the Belgians like the Swiss have long-standing, internationally recognized traditions of excellence in the fabrication of high-quality chocolate. That they chose the French market for launching franchises selling inexpensive, mass-produced candies was galling. That these franchises proved to be so successful in the French confectionery gift market was intolerable. The task facing the French was to define and promote new criteria of connoisseurship in confectionery taste. All agreed on the imperative to reeducate French palates so that consumers could properly distinguish between authentic refined (French) chocolates and fake foreign substitutes. Sustained attempts to train French palates is the subject of chapter 3.

## CHAPTER 3

# Reeducating French Palates

---

*[A gift] of chocolates from an unknown* chocolatier *with . . .
a garish photograph printed on the top will not qualify you
as a person of good taste. Rather, elaborate packaging, a refined
design, and bittersweet candies made by a renowned* chocolatier
*will play greatly in your favor.*

Mariarosa Schiaffino and Michel Cluizel,
*La route du chocolat*

Two months after the October craft contest, an article titled "Artisanal *chocolatiers* Seek to Reconquer [French] Palates" appeared in the national daily, *Le monde* (20 December 1990). Although I had not personally seen it, the article proved impossible to miss. Several Bayonnais—both acquaintances and craftsmen—clipped copies for me, and it was reproduced and published by Guy Urbain in the *chocolatiers'* trade journal, *La confiserie* (Urbain 1991b, 66). Citing the troubled marketplace being flooded by Belgian franchises, the piece centered on "a profession that seeks every means of reinforcing its position." Messieurs Daumoinx and Urbain were cited, along with other artisans who agreed on the imperative "to reeducate French palates," that is, to reconquer them through a national campaign of communication and training. The article opened with a description of the satin robes and plumed Aztec headdresses of the Confrérie des Chocolatiers de France (Brotherhood of French Chocolatiers) and closed with a mention of the first Best Craftsmen of France contest. But what was left unsaid, *le non-dit*, like so much else in French public and private discourse, is the most revealing.

In 1990 a coalition of largely Parisian craft leaders and cultural taste-makers, with support from state representatives, was actively collaborating to increase demand for French chocolates by recasting them as prestige goods and reinvesting them with cultural authenticity. They sought to increase consumption by altering the culturally constituted uses and symbolic meanings of chocolate in France. Consumers were urged to eat more refined French chocolates not just on the ritualized ceremonial occasions traditionally associated with them but regularly, even daily. In other words, the French should consume not only their daily bread but, in the words of the oath sworn by new Confrérie members, their daily chocolate. These efforts relied centrally on the production of written, visual, and performative texts specializing in chocolate: culinary books, travel guides, newspaper pieces, television and radio interviews, craft contests, public induction ceremonies of producer associations like the Confrérie, guided tastings, window and counter displays in French boutiques—all to stimulate social demand for candies promoted as exemplars of a genuine chocolate haute cuisine, the work of French masters. The texts selectively drew on data from a variety of experts, including doctors, legal professionals, scholars, and marketers. It fell to both masters and tastemakers to initiate French consumers into the art of chocolate appreciation and to reeducate palates "deformed" by exposure to foreign fakes.

Both master *chocolatiers* and tastemakers were active in the elaboration of an esoteric taste standard informing the new chocolate haute cuisine. In contemporary economies, cultural tastemakers determine fashion and shape taste for prestige commodities. They collaborate and negotiate with producers to establish the principles that govern expert knowledge and refined taste. They place consumers in a game of constantly evolving criteria for consumption based on rarity and connoisseurship. Through their knowledge of the complicated consumption rules and specialized terminology, consumers demonstrate that they are worthy of "symbolically appropriating" the goods they possess (Bourdieu 1984, 279).

Several French *chocolatiers* were closely associated with the creation and promotion of this new standard. The first, Gaston Lenôtre, was a traditionally trained craftsman from Normandy who purchased a pastry business in Paris. He eventually expanded that business to a production facility employing 200 pastry chefs, *chocolatiers,* and caterers. By 1990 Lenôtre had built a gastronomic empire encompassing an international cooking school, which opened in 1971, two restaurants in Paris (the first purchased in 1976 and the second in 1984, a restaurant at Disneyworld in Florida jointly owned with chefs Paul Bocuse and Roger Vergé). Lenôtre authored numerous cookbooks, earning an international reputation for his pioneering creation of lighter mousse and bavarois desserts made with less flour and sugar as well as his promotion of the use of dark, bittersweet chocolate in both pastries and candies.[1]

One of Lenôtre's protégés, Robert Linxe, has been particularly effective in shaping national and international demand for the *grand cru* chocolates "made in France" that he produces in his chain of exclusive Maison du Chocolat boutiques. The professional trajectories of craftsmen such as Lenôtre and Linxe suggest a radical reconfiguration of the French culinary landscape tied to the worldwide expansion of gourmet cuisine as a new form of cultural consumption (Zukin 1991, 208–210). Traditionally, French *chocolatiers* gained renown in one of two ways. Either they established reputations as heirs to distinctive regional culinary traditions and continued to produce in situ (for example, the famous Bernachon house in Lyon or the Puyricard house in Aix-en-Provence), or they built Parisian houses that catered to the political, social, artistic, and literary elites of the capital. Despite the strength and repute of regional confectionery traditions, Paris still serves as a powerful magnet for the best practitioners in the food crafts.

The rapid and continuous taste shifts that accompany the globalization of markets in late capitalism and the creation of international demand for French culinary expertise has had important effects on chefs, pastry makers, and *chocolatiers.* Certain craftsmen who came from lower middle or working-class backgrounds and learned their crafts through the traditional mechanisms of on-the-job apprenticeships and long years' experience were integrated into a global organization of food consumption and propelled to positions of international prominence. The experience of both Lenôtre and Linxe suggests that the pinnacle of a professional career now requires global rather than regional or national recognition. Both Lenôtre and Linxe receive wide media coverage, write cookbooks that are distributed internationally, and travel around the world to promote in person the quality, cachet, and authenticity of their products. An international exercise of cultural authority and culinary power has become the new standard of excellence.

I met Robert Linxe in Paris on 18 October 1990, shortly before the Best Craftsman of France contest and my move to Bayonne. He had been invited to serve as a contest judge, but the November opening of a Maison du Chocolat boutique in New York precluded his participation. Given the constraints on his time, I felt fortunate that he agreed to an interview. When I arrived at his flagship boutique in the Faubourg St. Honoré, he was helping a customer choose chocolate candies for a gift purchase. This gave me time to assess how his boutique resembled or diverged from others I had visited. As I knew from six months of field-work in Paris in 1989, the organization and performance of work in artisanal *chocolateries* reveal the continuing salience of traditional forms of craft production and family entrepreneurship. Family members, both blood relations and in-laws, control daily business operations, which usually include two complementary and mutually reinforcing activities: sales and production. These houses, as *chocolateries* and *pâtisseries* are known, also adhere to a gendered division of labor whereby men generally produce goods in the closed, private space of the workshop and women sell them in the open, public space of the (often adjacent) boutique. Skill is transmitted largely through a model of apprenticeship predicated on knowledge as experience within a workshop and on learn-ing as ongoing participation within a community of practice (Lave and Wenger 1991). Craft work is organized hierarchically, according to skill and experience, under the authority of the craftsman-owner in the work-shop and the wife in the boutique.

In preparing for my interview, I discovered that Linxe had attracted considerable media attention when the Maison du Chocolat opened in 1977. Between 1977 and 1990, he conducted literally dozens of inter-views that had appeared in national and international media. Because of the importance of seasonal confectionery gift purchases in France and the high sales volume at those times (30–50 percent of annual sales are generated at Christmas), French *chocolatiers* are always showcased in print and visual media features during December and before Easter. At a time when most Parisian *chocolatiers* sold roughly equal numbers of dark and milk chocolates, Linxe proposed a house line of special-ties that included twenty-three dark candies and only four milk choco-lates (Champs-Elysées 1989). He also disdained the most popular type of chocolate candy center, the *praliné*, and privileged the *ganache*, which he insisted was "the true measure of the worth of a *chocolatier*."

The Faubourg St. Honoré boutique was likewise an innovation in design from its layout to its logo. In a departure from the pastel col-ors and enclosed glass cases of the traditional *confiserie*, Linxe's candies were invitingly displayed on open counters. The entire boutique décor recalled chocolate in its various hues: the dark granite floor, oak panels, cinnamon-colored swede wallpaper, and nougat-tinted marble coun-ters. The logo on house boxes and wrapping paper represented a *metate*, the curved stone on which shelled cacao beans were ground to make chocolate from pre-Columbian times in Mesoamerica up to the industrial revolution in Europe. Such a stone was displayed in the local ethnographic museum in Bayonne, Linxe's home region. Two saleswomen were present to wait on customers in the boutique, but Linxe, the master *chocolatier*, attired in monogrammed chef jacket, was a more commanding presence. At a time when most craftsmen remained in the private space of the family workshop, Linxe moved freely between the workshop and the public space of the boutique. He subverted and remade traditional work practices by taking a highly visible role in sales as well as production. He personally advised customers on the evaluation, choice, and proper consumption of their chocolates.

After finishing with his customer, Linxe invited me to follow him. When we were settled in a loft that doubled as storage and office, he waved the formal letter of introduction I had sent from the French embassy explaining my research and declared, "I would have talked to you without this. Just tell me what you want to know." "Tell me what is most important to know about you and your craft," I responded. "Well," he said, "then it's my life you want to hear about," and a life history is indeed what he began to give—a narrative device used by all the artisans I have interviewed or observed to celebrate an elaborate artisanal aesthetic (compare Kondo 1990):

You know that I am a native of Bayonne, in the Basque country, actually from Boucau, a working-class suburb north of Bayonne. I'm from a very modest background. My father worked for the railroad . . . a true autodidact, hungry for culture, an inveterate reader . . . [he was] crushed when I didn't stay in school, I did my business studies, I did well but I wanted a *métier*, so it was right after the war I went to Monsieur Carrère's house one or two years after they began, Port Neuf [medieval sector of Bayonne] . . . at seventeen I wasn't very young to start an apprenticeship in a *pâtisserie/confiserie* [apprentices started at twelve, thirteen, or fourteen years of age]. So my father said, "All right I'll help you," but it was a very hard *métier* in those days. I had to light the oven at seven in the evening, it was fueled by coal then and because I lived four kilometers away, I couldn't go home on my bicycle and be back on time to start work at two in the morning. So I stayed there and we worked all night until one or two the next day. In the morning we only had a short break, a *café* and a *pain au lait,* and then hop right back to work. But I worked hard, I was serious, and what a work ethic I had from my parents. So I did an apprenticeship with Monsieur Carrère, Fabrice's father, Simon's grandfather. I got on really well with *le patron* (boss), I really liked him, I was like a second son to him . . . I was more on the side of the *patron* than I was on the side of the workers, it was instinctive . . . my father who was a worker, who had never been a *patron,* how many years did he toil for others . . . so I stayed three years as an apprentice with Monsieur Carrère. . . . I had discovered the existence of an excellent school in Switzerland but it cost a fortune, 100,000F (old francs) a month in 1951, and at the end of my third year I was only making 4000F a month, you see. I had heard of a very good *chocolatier* in Biarritz and friends got me a place there but Monsieur Carrère was furious, he thought I would stay forever with him because he had workers who followed him [from the house in which he worked as head of production] when he got set up in business who had already been with him for years, some twenty years. I had other ambitions and I learned a lot from Monsieur Bourriet, who was from the north, he had other work methods, he was very demanding, he had been to Paris. I had to relearn everything I thought I knew about chocolate, like even the chocolate coating on *éclairs.* But I wanted to go to Switzerland, my parents didn't have any money so I left for Paris, found a good job in a *pâtisserie,* rue de l'Arcade, and though I earned more money, 18,000F a month, I still had to pay for lodging and food. Monsieur Carrère contacted me, he wanted me back and promised to pay me what I earned in Paris if I would return to work with him. I did, scrimping and saving on everything, a period of total sacrifice so I could go to the COBA school in Switzerland. So finally in 1952 I went, an era when the Swiss were the kings in chocolate. The director, Monsieur Perliat, really appreciated me, you see I was the only worker, the rest were the sons of *patrons.* I was the only one to have the privilege of remaining in Switzerland for a year to work with artisans. The only one, you see. I met my wife during that period, in Paris at a reception given for the baptism of a relative on my mother's side. We got engaged when I returned to France in 1953 and married the following spring. Return to Bayonne? a stifling provincial city where people don't make judgments on merit but on social connections. No, it was Paris, I immediately got a good position in a very good house, a *chocolaterie* in Neuilly [a high-class area]. My *patron* was an extraordinary man, he owned five restaurants, he had an eye, and he saw potential in me. He asked me what I wanted. In my naiveté, I replied that I wanted to start small, to rent and run a little business first and then buy one later. He laughed out loud. Listen he said you need to learn to be a chef, Parisians want food, you can't live on just chocolate, you'll have to be a caterer and pastry maker as well. So for two years with his help I learned to cook, you see it was really an apprenticeship but he paid me without letting it be known what I was getting as a chef *chocolatier* and then in 1955, at twenty-five, just twenty-six, I bought the Marquise de Presle, avenue Wagram in Paris and established myself as a *pâtissier, chocolatier* and caterer. My wife helped me so very, very much, you see she had a situation [dowry]. So I bought a house that was losing money, I was the fourth owner in the space of three years. For five years I ran in the red, I worked like a dog, getting up at two or three in the morning and never going to bed before eleven at night. Never. We had twenty Christmases in that house—we were enormously successful in fact so much so that Lenôtre bought me out. You see he wanted the boutique and the *bonhomme* [man] and got both in the deal. But working in his *laboratoire* [specialized term for confectionery workshop], do you realize that we were 200 at the time, did not suit my mentality. Of course I was his partner, I had my stock in the firm, I was part of management in charge of receptions and I put on the most beautiful receptions in Paris but at the end of three years I wanted a change. I wanted my freedom back and so I bought here [Faubourg St. Honoré], the Caves Cosette—interesting, isn't it, that in a store known for its vintage wines, I should create a *chocolaterie*. On 26 October it will be thirteen years since we opened for business. It was a risk, you see, at forty-seven years old to start over. In order to self-finance this operation, I had to use everything I owned, even more. I couldn't fail. I had one goal, I wanted to restore chocolate in all its nobility. Everywhere in France, I tasted chocolates, but without ever really enjoying any. Even in Switzerland things had gone downhill. I bet on the highest quality, believe me there wasn't much competition in that area. So four days after I opened the doors we were swamped. To give you an idea, I sold 2,500 kilos of chocolate in a year at the Marquise de Presle. So when we opened here I made 1,000 kilos for the Christmas/New Year period. Pure lunacy, they said. But in three weeks they were almost gone, this was the end of November! So between November and January, I had to make 3,000 kilos in unbelievable conditions . . . now there are three houses in Paris with a total of forty-five employees, half in production and half in sales, and the three stores have annual sales of 25 million francs [approximately $5 million]. You're surprised? Not bad for a small artisanal house. But on Monday we're moving to a new production facility, we are bursting at the seams here but you'll see what I mean in a minute when we visit the *laboratoire* in the cave.

Linxe's narrative was organized around the rites of passage that accompany movement through the main statuses of artisanal life: apprentice, journeyman, and self-employed master (Turner 1969). It accorded special attention to bleak, arduous periods of liminality marked by separation and sacrifice, when, for example, Linxe set out alone for Paris, then Switzerland, when he struggled to succeed as a new independent, or following his decision to quit the business partnership with Lenôtre to embark on yet another daring entrepreneurial venture. These descriptions were a necessary prelude to the triumphant story recounting his reincorporation within a community of full-fledged masters and his achievement of progressively higher status—first as a skilled worker, then as an independent master in his own right, not in a "stifling provincial city" but in Paris, and, finally, as one of the capital's preeminent *chocolatiers*.

The chronicle of Linxe's early years of apprenticeship that appeared in his 1992 memoir differed from the story I taped on 18 October 1990. In the written account, Linxe condensed a complicated experience into a homogeneous period of liminality and hardship with more dramatic effect because he was outside the freer and more associative realm of oral narrative. The life history in the book was also notable for the clever intertwining of personal, artisanal, and cultural histories of chocolate and for the space accorded to what I call chocolate testimonials by Parisian luminaries that validated his reputation as a master of the art (taste) and craft of chocolate.

Yet both of these celebrations of a work life produced significant silences, just as they elided the tensions inherent in the pragmatics of craft work and in the construction of craft identities in contemporary France. The celebration of artisanal success is always also a story of persistent status anxieties and established class hierarchies. Although Linxe readily volunteered his social origins, it is obvious that he suffered some of the hidden injuries of class. Given the importance of educational credentials as a key determiner of social class in France, Linxe began his life history by explaining his decision to leave school and to learn a manual craft. It is significant that he framed this decision as one freely chosen by him in contrast to his father's wishes. Yet the thematic thread of social origins and economic disadvantage is woven throughout his story. Given the importance of one's father's occupation as a key signifier of social status in France, Linxe keenly felt his status as the son of a worker, particularly when surrounded by the sons of bosses at the COBA school. This may explain his "instinctive" siding with the boss, as opposed to the workers, even when he was a young apprentice in Bayonne. Similarly, it helps us to understand his refusal to return to the southwest, where his modest background would never be forgotten. Finally, it may explain his emphasis on the mentoring and recognition he received from famous craftsmen such as Lenôtre, as well as the prominent place he accorded in his 1992 memoir to a description of his friendships with famous chocophiles such as the fashion designer Sonya Rykiel, conductor Daniel Barenboïm, and musician Etienne Watelot. The irony is, of course, that these "friendships" were established not through social connections but through commercial patronage. He got to know social elites because they were impressed first and foremost by his mastery of a manual craft.

Linxe emphasized, as do many artisans, that his resounding success was largely a result of his own work ethic and innate talent. He elided and minimized the critical start and financial help provided by Monsieur Carrère in Bayonne, which enabled him to go to Switzerland. He emphasized instead his Parisian mentors and famous customers. He cited the late social historian Jean-Paul Aron's summary accolade of his art, "Everyone knows that Robert Linxe is the best *chocolatier* in Paris . . .

he's an artist, on the level of goldsmiths and jewelry designers" (Linxe 1992, 100).

Linxe also neglected to mention, until I asked him directly, that the Maison du Chocolat was bought out by the industrial manufacturer Valrhona in the 1980s. Valrhona's parent company Bongrain financed the expansion of Linxe's new production facility and subsidizes or sponsors many other initiatives designed to promote French chocolate, including the Salon du Chocolat, the Gastronomy Show, the Pastry World Cup, exclusive chocolate clubs (Club des Croqueurs du Chocolat [Club of Chocolate Eaters]), cinematic festivals, sporting events, and the specialized training at the Valrhona cooking school.[2]

Linxe's elaboration of an artisanal aesthetic, like other celebrations of meaningful work in "solidary" communities, is a contested political terrain that masks the existence of similarly or less skilled workers (Kondo 1990; Rancière 1986). This narrative is at once gendered and exclusionary because it naturalizes the position of self-employed artisans at the summit of a craft hierarchy based on skill as it simultaneously obfuscates the important roles played by women—both Linxe's wife and sales help in the boutique—and the salaried artisans in the workshop.

Linxe had installed a complete workshop in what had been the wine cellar of the previous business. We descended a steep staircase and met his head of production, Pascal, a "fabulous worker," his "right arm," who was working on a batch of *ganaches.* Linxe pointed out the machines used for melting and tempering chocolate as well as those involved in grinding, mixing, and enrobing candy centers, now standard equipment in modern craft *chocolateries.* He compared the cramped space of this wine cellar to the vastly increased productive capacity of the new workshop in Colombes near the Defense, a western suburb of Paris. Linxe's estimates of daily production in the new facility were confirmed in his 1992 memoir: the daily average of chocolate produced was 300 kilos and the maximum capacity was 450.

As we climbed the stairs, I remembered a recent dinner party conversation at the home of Parisian friends. After the obligatory questions about my research work, one of the guests began to talk seriously about chocolate. In a conspiratorial tone she announced the arrival of a marvelous new *chocolatier.* "Tout Paris" was talking about him. Did I know the name? Having only arrived in September, I had to admit I did not. Undaunted, she added, "Well you will. He's a real artisan, he makes his chocolate in a workshop right behind his boutique, straight from the cacao beans." This exchange and many others I have had since reveal that, not surprisingly, in the case of chocolate, French consumers have ideas at odds with the realities of production, either artisanal or industrial. Few know, for example, that French artisans no longer select, blend, and process cacao beans in the fabrication of chocolate or that the skills associated with the production of chocolate from cacao beans had already shifted entirely to industrialized mass production by the 1950s.[3] Most remain unaware that nearly all *chocolatiers* purchase an assortment of chocolate blocks, *couverture,* produced from different blends of cacao beans, which they then transform into a personalized line of goods. Craft skills now center exclusively on the fabrication of dipped confections, both chocolate and sugar, preserved fruit, molded figurines, and, most recently, confectionery art. French consumers are also largely unfamiliar with the complex multi-step process undertaken in the large-scale industrial manufacture of chocolate.[4]

After our tour, we returned to the loft. Linxe looked at me over his reading glasses and announced that the best part had arrived—the tasting. I had fully expected and even anticipated a chocolate tasting, since I knew that Linxe had taken the lead in "reeducating French palates" and had conducted dozens of tastings. However, as I waited for him to present the chocolates, my palms began to sweat and I felt unruly butterflies in my stomach. At the time I was well aware of the new taste standard favoring dark chocolate that Linxe had helped to champion, and I knew that the upcoming tasting was designed to gauge my familiarity with new taste criteria and to test my judgment as a discriminating consumer of chocolate.

While in Paris in 1989, I myself had conducted some informal experiments in which I entered French boutiques and specifically requested sweet milk chocolates in order to observe and test the reaction of the salespeople. What shocked me now was my fear of failing the taste test as well as my eagerness to demonstrate my cultural capital in chocolate consumption. When Linxe returned bearing a silver tray with six chocolates, (four enrobed with dark chocolate and two with milk chocolate), I knew first off that I would never admit to liking sweet milk chocolate.

Before beginning, Linxe abruptly asked me, in a tone allowing only a positive response, "*Vous aimez le chocolat?*" Being assured that I liked chocolate, he described the experience as an "apprenticeship in taste allowing those palates which are receptive to learn to discriminate among different kinds of chocolate and to appreciate the best." Just then a saleswoman interrupted us saying that there was an important call for Monsieur. He hesitated, looked at me apologetically, and excused himself, urging me to begin on my own. He promised to question me on my preferences.

Left alone staring at the candies, my mind went back to a description of his house specialties I had read in *Le guide des croqueurs du chocolat*. It was published in 1988 and based on blind tastings of chocolates conducted by an exclusive club of Parisian chocophiles. Le Club des Croqueurs du Chocolat regularly organized chocolate-tasting soirées during which they rated chocolates from all over the country. Its founding members included gastronomes Claude Lebey and Sylvie Girard, wine connoisseur Nicholas de Rabaudy, Sonya Rykiel, and Jean-Paul Aron. Robert Linxe, the only *chocolatier*, was invited to serve as technical advisor to the club. Widely available in both specialty and mass distribution outlets and prominently displayed in the windows of French *chocolateries*, *Le guide* outlined the standard informing the ratings. It was the first systematic codification of the new taste criteria: "We want to make it perfectly clear that our taste leads us to favor dark chocolates over milk chocolate and . . . that we generally prefer candies with a high proportion of cocoa solids, which corresponds to the current taste standards of chocolate connoisseurs" (*Le guide* 1988, 5–6).

*Le guide* included definitions of basic confectionery terms, such as the different types of candy centers, and provided specialized oenological terminology for differentiating and evaluating high-quality chocolate. Like wine connoisseurs, consumers were urged to marshal their senses in the quest for vintage chocolates. They were advised "to look for a shiny coating, to smell the deep and powerful chocolate bouquet, to feel the creamy texture on the palate, and to taste the subtle combination of bitter and sweet notes in the composition" (9). It is important to note that the codification of the new taste standard occurred during a period beginning in 1985, when cocoa prices were very low.[5]

Reading *Le guide* for the first time, I had been struck by the inclusion of the newest Belgian franchises. It seemed paradoxical that a guide published to promote vintage (French) chocolates should even include cheap foreign imitations. However, Belgian candies served as a perfect foil to the highly rated candies produced by French masters and received the poorest ratings: "It is obvious that a certain public exists for these attractive sweets, which do not have much in common with the powerful subtleties of the Aztec cacao bean. In fact, one should really think of a name other than chocolate for these candies" (152).

As I sat facing the row of tiny, ten-gram candies, I remembered that Linxe was the only *chocolatier* to receive a rating of 19 out of 20. I tried without success to recall the descriptions his house specialties received in that review. I took several deep breaths and began slowly to sample the candies, mindful of Linxe's parting counsel to "allow the chocolate to melt slowly so that my palate could fully absorb it." Because French food tastings customarily progress from the common to the refined, Linxe had specifically admonished me to sample the milk chocolates first. Instead, because of nerves, I began with the dark chocolates and had only tasted two when Linxe returned.

He immediately took charge, briefly describing the basic ingredients and principal flavorings of the candies before I tasted them.

Here, you didn't taste this. It's a *ganache* made with caramelized butter, enrobed with milk chocolate, light as air yet not without body. But, of course, you've already started with the dark . . . this is Romeo, a very refined *ganache* flavored with fresh coffee. Let's go on. Here, this chocolate is a superb bittersweet ganache, a creamy dark center made with the freshest cream, butter, and finely ground morsels of pure, dark chocolate and then coated in dark chocolate. The center is delicately flavored with lemon. It's sublime, very long on the palate.

After each sampling, I had to cleanse my palate with sips of bottled water. After we finished, the analysis began. Which candy did I prefer? Could I say why?

I chose the first chocolate I had tasted, a *ganache* with a bittersweet dark center and dark coating, in part because it had left the most distinct gustatory impression. To my delight, and profound relief, Linxe emitted an appreciative "ah" saying, "Madame, I congratulate you on your taste. The candy you chose is my personal favorite, the Quito." He added, "Someone who knows how to judge good wine is also able to judge a good chocolate . . . a good chocolate is long on the palate, full-bodied, has the correct degree of acidity, a rich, balanced bouquet, and a wonderful finish."

At few months later, in February 1991, I attended another tasting organized in Pau (a city 106 kilometers southeast of Bayonne in the Pyrenean foothills) by the acknowledged regional head of *chocolatiers,* Jean Mourier. It was similar in nearly every particular to the tasting presided over by Monsieur Linxe. Mourier had decided to organize a tasting after attending the 1991 Paris trade show, Intersuc. He had received a list of specialized seminars scheduled in conjunction with the show and was particularly interested in one on taste offered by Matty Chiva, an eminent psychologist then on the faculty of the University of Paris at Nanterre (compare Chiva 1985). As it happened, Mourier had a scheduling conflict with that seminar, and since I planned to attend, he asked me to make a tape recording of Chiva's presentation.

Chiva began his seminar by describing his collaboration with the Tour-based International Institute of Taste directed by oenologue Jacques Puisais and their work in developing linguistic tools with which to distinguish different sensory experiences, in particular, food tastes. Chiva described the institute's collaborative effort with the French Ministry of Education in the design of presentations on "sensory alertness" (*éveil sensoriel*) conducted in French elementary school classrooms. In October 1990, a National Taste Day was organized during which professional chefs, caterers, *pâtissiers,* and *chocolatiers* were invited to introduce French third and fourth graders to the four basic food tastes, salty, sweet, sour, and bitter.[6]

This apprenticeship in taste had two goals: to enable youngsters to differentiate knowledgeably among taste sensations, and to arm them against the dangers posed by the banal uniformity of industrial foods and the (American) fast food chains then proliferating in France. According to him, judgments of taste and quality in food result from a multisensory "biological and cultural patrimony": "We appreciate one kind of food rather than another because of its texture, its temperature, its volume, the sound it makes when we bite into it, its color, and the memories it evokes." Chiva alluded to the unfortunate reality that in 1991 French consumers lacked a sufficiently precise, shared vocabulary with which to evaluate confectionery taste and to differentiate good chocolate from ordinary chocolate. Chocolate was a food in search of a patrimony, and the efforts of wine connoisseurs like Jacques Puisais promised to provide it. Although Chiva never mentioned foreign franchise outlets, the subtext of his presentation was a strong defense of French gastronomic traditions. It was no accident that his presentation was paired with a treatise on the superior taste of dark chocolate delivered by a representative of Valrhona, one of several industrial manufacturers (the others being Cacao Barry, Weiss, Callebaut, and Le Pecque) who in 1991 shared the artisanal market for chocolate *couverture*. The seminar on taste provided the inspiration for Mourier's tasting, and it was also the beginning of an ongoing collaboration between Mourier and Chiva in the education of French palates.

Mourier's tasting was patterned closely on Parisian chocolate tastings and borrowed from a Parisian physician's popular text published the year before, *Les vertus thérapeutiques du chocolat* (Robert 1990). Mourier received financial support from the Pau Savings Bank (8,000F, or $1,600, to subsidize the printing of promotional posters and personal invitations) as well as the donation of sixty kilos of chocolate samples from Cacao Barry and Valrhona. Representatives of local newspapers and radio stations covered the event, and Guy Urbain featured it two months later in the craft journal, *La confiserie* (Urbain 1991c, 29–32).

On 6 February 1991, at four o'clock in the afternoon, 250 people filled to capacity the conference room Mourier had reserved. Mourier and his *confrères* (comrades) in Pau invited almost 1,000 people to the conference, giving top priority to politicians from Pau, the surrounding municipalities, the department of the Atlantic Pyrenees, and the regional council. One of his primary goals was "to communicate the message about the selection of vintage cacao bean growths and the essential difference between industrial and artisanal chocolate." In addition to the tasting, Mourier arranged for local *chocolatiers* to sell an assortment of their solid chocolate bars and bonbons during the intermission and was pleased to learn that the sale proceeds yielded enough to treat conference presenters to dinner at a local restaurant.

After the lectures and an animated question-and-answer period, Mourier instructed his daughter-in-law (who worked full time in his business) and two other female workers to distribute the chocolate. I had positioned myself in the middle of the room so that I could judge the audience reaction. Silence fell over the room as the chocolates were circulated. A gentleman sitting in front of me provoked laughter by whispering loudly to his companion, "At last." Before Mourier allowed the audience to taste the first chocolate, he reminded them that a proper tasting required a specific apprenticeship and a certain ambiance.

The creator has given us five senses: sight, sound, touch, smell, and taste. We will interest ourselves principally with smell and taste, but the other senses are important as well. Sight permits us to appreciate the enrobing of the product, its color, texture, and size. Touch allows us to know if it is smooth or granular. Sound can also play a role. When you break a bar, it must make a clean, clear sound. Then comes the taste, placing the chocolate in the mouth.

At that point a number of people began to look impatiently at one another with their chocolates at the ready, but Mourier advised them, "Before the tasting can begin, there must be silence to allow for concentration, a smoke-free room so that the chocolate aroma can be fully appreciated, and a perfectly clear palate." He paused for dramatic effect and continued, "If one is to be a good taster, merely saying 'It is good' is not enough. No, one must have a precise vocabulary."

Mourier had the audience taste four different chocolates. As they sampled each one, he provided the specialized terminology and the expert judgment giving descriptive names for each of the four chocolates. The first was a sweet milk chocolate with 35 percent cocoa solids, and he labeled it "sweetness" *(la douceur)*. It was greeted by a loud chorus of appreciative comments from the audience that Mourier ignored. Speaking over the noise, he dismissed that chocolate as providing merely a "certain pleasure" *(un certain plaisir)*. He then proceeded to a semi-sweet dark chocolate *ganache* with 50 percent cocoa solids and described this family of candy centers. Although the audience reception to this candy was less enthusiastic, Mourier's commentary became more spirited. This candy he called "pleasure" *(le plaisir)*.

By the time they tasted the third chocolate—a semi-bitter dark chocolate with 62 percent cocoa solids—the audience's response was noticeably subdued. An elderly man sitting to my right registered an expression of distaste as the semi-bitter chocolate was fully absorbed on his palate, and he blurted out, "I liked the first one best." Looking around I judged that his response was not an isolated one. Mourier applauded the third chocolate as "sensual pleasure" *(volupté)* by reason of the "victory of dark chocolate over sugar." The tasting ended with a very bitter chocolate (70 percent cocoa solids). To prepare his audience for "ecstasy," Mourier told them to close their eyes and "to savor the delicacy of taste and the strong chocolate surge." He instructed them to block and unblock their noses, "a little insider's trick to allow the initial bitterness to give way to the sublime aftertaste." Although Mourier assured them that they had just experienced "ecstasy" *(l'extase)*, the audience reaction strongly suggested that the French consumers present preferred "a certain pleasure" to "ecstasy" in their chocolates.

These oenological encounters powerfully illustrate how taste is shaped and created for prestige cultural goods. As my fieldwork progressed, it demanded my personal investigation of chocolate taste—as aesthetic judgment, cultural standard, and sentient experience. My personal apprenticeship in taste, understanding of the craft, its practitioners, and the judgments distinguishing vintage French chocolates from foreign imitations demanded the education of my own palate. Through guided repetition, my "good taste" in chocolate was habituated and embodied. In the first case, however, the point is not that I was nervous in the company of native experts or that I finally acquired good taste in chocolate.

Nor, in the second case, is it to suggest that consumers in the southwest have bad taste. Rather it is to show how consumers, *chocolatiers,* and even anthropologists acutely aware of the processes at work can be drawn into mastering, displaying, and ultimately replicating taste protocols. The tastings *chocolatiers* organize and the gastronomic texts they publish are, as Linxe put it to me, "an apprenticeship in taste" meant to teach even resistant consumers to choose the "right" candies. Consumers, who internalize and reinforce the new taste standard by buying, eating, and offering bittersweet chocolates as gifts, can achieve some measure of social distinction. By virtue of their good taste they become more cultured and more French. It is significant that when Guy Urbain interviewed Monsieur Mourier for the craft journal article on the 1991 conference in Pau, Mourier reported a different audience reaction than the one I had observed, one more consistent with the craft leaders and tastemakers' expectations for consumer appreciation of bittersweet dark chocolates. Mourier indicated that 80 percent of the conference audience had preferred the semi-bitter chocolate (Urbain 1991c, 31).

## The Gentrification of Chocolate Taste

In France, the considerable interest in culinary arts is signified by a huge gastronomic literature, tourist guides, as well as regional and national exhibits. Cookbooks and gastronomic essays have played a particularly important role in providing consumers with comprehensive rules governing the choice of ingredients, appropriate utensils, correct preparation techniques, aesthetic presentation, and the ordering and consumption of different dishes. In postindustrial economies, cuisine defines a critically important area where the economic power and cultural authority of nation-states intersect. Nation building has, among many other things, precipitated the creation of national cuisines that collapse regional distinctions and subordinate them to a central culinary standard. French haute cuisine itself is an exemplar of this process (Mintz 1996b, 92–105). In an era of global markets and instantaneous linkages, chefs and cookbooks circulate globally, and the national cuisines they represent shape and are shaped by transnational culture and taste. Rising levels of per capita income, greater disposable income, and new structures of consumption have produced a broader, largely urban middle class of consumers whose financial means allow them to adopt a reflexive attitude toward the consumption of goods in general and food in particular (Zukin 1991). Their search for differentiation and authenticity in the consumption of food is reflected in the growing international demand for gourmet cuisine, a cuisine in which the latest French culinary styles enjoy a hegemonic position.

In what has been called the gentrification of taste, distinctive regional culinary styles and local foodstuffs are rediscovered and marketed by chefs, restaurateurs, and retailers (Bestor 1992). The appropriation and aesthetic presentation of regionally produced foodstuffs appeal to sophisticated urbanites who desire food with both cultural authenticity and esoteric cachet. Cookbooks and gastronomic texts target these consumers' search for authenticity and shape taste for culinary styles and foods identified as markers of distinction with a view to promoting the relentless expansion of demand. The formulation of a new epicurean standard in chocolate exemplifies the gentrification of taste. The new standard was codified and promoted in a new gastronomic literature centering on chocolate that appeared in the 1980s and continues to proliferate in France and abroad.[7] This literature reaffirms the gastronomic hegemony of France in global markets through the export of yet another manifestation of a French civilization of taste—*grand cru* chocolate. It also reveals the systematic construction of a luxury French chocolate cuisine in opposition to culinary Others. Gastronomic literature has a long history in France, having appeared as a distinctive genre after the 1789 Revolution. Gastronomes, like the famous Brillat-Savarin, have always played an important role as arbiters of taste and knowledge about food, although they were not themselves producers of it either as chefs or craftsmen in specialized food trades (Mennell 1996). However, the gastronomic texts that appeared in the 1980s were unique in several respects. First, they did not address food as a whole but centered on chocolate. Second, they were authored by cultural tastemakers *and* craft producers and were all directed at a general rather than elite readership, members of the rising urban middle classes.

The most striking characteristic of these texts is that they were not, for the most part, cookbooks, but rather gastronomic essays. Although most of these texts included a few recipes at the end, gastronomic, not culinary, issues were the central concern. These issues revealed themselves in the exhaustive detail given to the history of chocolate, albeit a peculiarly French version: its discovery in the New World and its reception in the Old; its cultivation on third world plantations and production in first world workshops; the different types and qualities of cacao beans used; and the new comprehensive set of rules governing the appropriate selection and consumption of refined chocolate. This taste standard borrowed its form from the specialized terminology and evaluation criteria of French wine connoisseurship. Furthermore, it drew its substance from the basic principles informing the nouvelle cuisine style of cooking that dominated the French culinary establishment in the 1970s and early 1980s.

We have already seen that *Le guide* borrowed from wine expertise in its attempt to codify chocolate consumption. That gustatory effort was considerably elaborated in the text published by Linxe (1992) in collaboration with gastronome Sylvie Girard and oenologue Jacques Puisais. An explicit goal was to extend the oenological model and to provide the public with "a more detailed, precise, and refined chocolate vocabulary." Indeed, twenty pages were devoted to tasting rules and terms. The sensory characteristics of chocolate were divided among seven categories accompanied by finely differentiated lists of adjectives—visual, olfactory, taste, tactile, chemical, aural, and thermal. For example, the visual presentation of chocolate could be described as: flat (unpolished), glossy (for chocolate bars), granular, shiny (for *dragées,* sugar-coated almonds, or chocolates), satiny, uneven (for example, for *rochers,* chocolates with crushed nuts in coating), powdery (for truffles coated with cocoa powder), or tinted (for *bouchées*). This could be further refined to indicate subtle shadings, such as earthy amber, burnt carmine, pinch of madder-root, red ochre, chestnut, tobacco brown, blood-red, or Etruscan red. Readers were invited to eavesdrop on an exchange between connoisseurs evaluating a *grand cru* chocolate with a "deep mahogany, purplish shade associated with Central American beans, a satiny finish, and exceptional nose with wood tones and noticeable tobacco accents" (Linxe 1992, 122).

If chocolate taste took its form from wine beginning in the 1980s, it took its substance from the nouvelle cuisine then dominant in the French culinary establishment. Formally codified by the gastronomes Gault and Millau in their guides and magazines, this style emphasized healthful eating habits, dietetic concerns (the elimination of heavy, butter-based sauces), radically simplified cooking techniques like steaming, the use of fresh, natural regional foodstuffs blended in idiosyncratic flavor combinations, and the intelligent incorporation of the latest technological advances in culinary material (Gault and Millau 1976, 154–157). In like fashion, the new chocolate cuisine mandated fresh natural ingredients, novel but simplified flavorings, and healthy, dark chocolates with less sugar.

These constructions have selectively built on distinct regional and national confectionery repertoires even as they have absorbed them within a new, culturally superior, French haute cuisine based on chocolate. Connoisseurs now insist that choice French candies be made from fresh regional products such as chocolate from the best cacao growths (see below), butter from Charente, cream from Normandy, and almonds from Provence, Spain, or Tuscany; that they incorporate exotic flavorings and foodstuffs of distant locales such as citrus fruits, coffee, tea, spices, and even chocolate itself. Mintz's recent distinction between cuisine and haute cuisine (1996b, 92–102) can be usefully applied here to the contemporary culture of French chocolate. In contrast to cuisine that is rooted in a social community and tied to local or regional foodstuffs, haute cuisine transcends geography, is class-based, relies on knowledgeable consumers and sophisticated cooks, and borrows eclectically from various regional cuisines, substituting rare foodstuffs for local ones. By conforming to this paradigm, chocolate haute cuisine spurns the chocolate of the masses. For one thing, it demands more expensive *couverture* with higher percentages of cocoa solids and less sugar. For another, it promotes one candy center, the *ganache,* made with heavy cream and the finest butter, versus the various dairy substitutions used in the past. It also rejects cheaper, tasteless California almonds (Linxe 1992) for more costly European varieties. It introduces novel spices like thyme into candy centers and rediscovers older ones like cinnamon.

Chocolate haute cuisine recipes include hot spiced beverages such as *le chocolat* (Constant 1988, 103) and dishes such as *langouste au chocolat amer,* or Mediterranean lobster in a spiced wine and chocolate sauce (125–126). They likewise favor the *ganache* made with myriad flavor combinations drawing on different culinary traditions, that is, Caracas, Quito, *cannelle* (cinnamon) (Linxe 1992, 111). Unlike the more coarsely textured and sweeter *praliné,* the smoother, creamier ganache offers diminishing contrasts and increasing variety, the hallmark of postindustrial cuisines (Mennell 1996). It provides the perfect medium for Linxe's confectionery innovation, as evidenced in his recent anise *ganache* creation or in the tobacco-flavored chocolate he planned to develop.

A second characteristic of these texts is their emphasis on the differentiation of authentic refined French chocolates (markers of distinction) from foreign fakes (in bad taste). The production of taste and the politics of demand surrounding vintage French chocolates involve a very complicated dialogue—sometimes competitive, sometimes cooperative—among cultural tastemakers, producers, consumers, and, in

France, state representatives. This dialogue entails a strategic manipulation of the gaps in knowledge that accompany the entry and flow of goods in national and global markets. These gaps intensify as the complexity of flows and the distance from cultivation to consumption sites increases, as exemplified in the description of the chocolate made from beans in a tiny Parisian workshop. The creation of demand for commodities like chocolate, which can be mass-produced, requires the considerable elaboration and management of the knowledge surrounding consumption—one need only witness the vastly complicated terminology and esoteric criteria based on wine connoisseurship. More complex knowledge about consumption in turn demands more detailed knowledge about production as a crucial means to authenticate French claims of superior quality and taste. One of the explicit goals of the gastronomic texts is to enhance consumers' knowledge about production, both industrial and artisanal. Consumers must be able to authenticate the rare craft version from the ubiquitous industrial one. However, this information about production remains incomplete and highly controlled. For *chocolatiers* like Linxe, the critical task is not to divulge the production process in all its complexity but to differentiate authentic hand-crafted chocolates sold in true family workshops from the inauthentic mass-produced candies retailed in storefronts masquerading as French artisanal boutiques. In contrast to foreign franchises, French artisans must make visible both the human labor embodied in the goods and a particular form of production: artisanship.

*Chocolatiers* make creative use of a craft model to manipulate adroitly consumers' knowledge of the myriad transformations chocolate undergoes between cultivation and consumption. Because craftsmanship links the conception of a product with its execution, *chocolatiers'* knowledge of and involvement in the productive process must appear to extend from the choice of the best vintages of beans to their transformation and presentation in the family boutique. *Chocolatiers* emphasize their possession of this knowledge in numerous ways. Before the chocolate tasting, Monsieur Mourier gave his audience a short lecture on the cultivation and harvest of cacao beans on far-off tropical plantations. Cacao beans and chocolate *couverture* were prominently featured in artisanal window displays and in the increasingly frequent workshop tours and live demonstrations of craft mastery performed in the boutique or urban spaces of French cities. *Chocolatiers* cultivate an artisanal mystique by emphasizing the manual component of production. Many have installed a glass partition between the boutique and adjoining workshop, offering a view of artisans attired in white jackets and toques hand-molding or decorating chocolates. During heritage days or promotional interviews, *chocolatiers* enact their skill as confectionery artists. In 1996, Bayonnais *chocolatiers* left their workshops to hand-dip chocolates and sculpt chocolate art in the medieval downtown pedestrian quarter. I photographed one young artisan who was fashioning a chocolate replica of the imposing Gothic cathedral in Grand Bayonne.

*Chocolatiers'* use of an oenological model lends them the authority of the internationally accepted reference standard of French wines along with a recognized national tradition of artisanship. Many chocolate texts address this issue directly. A *chocolatier* competitor of Linxe, also a former employee of Lenôtre, Christian Constant owns two exclusive chocolate boutiques, has traveled to cacao plantations in Venezuela and Trinidad, and has authored a popular book on chocolate, in which he laments:

Chocolate is still not the object of as much attention as wine. . . . Who knows today, for instance, that there are as many varieties, regions of cacao bean cultivation, good and bad years, and methods of preparation? How is it possible to appreciate the best vintages of chocolate without being aware of their existence? The true appreciation of great chocolate presupposes, as for any product of a particular art, an exact knowledge of the techniques required that governed its creation as well as its history. This knowledge alone serves as a corrective to the vagaries of taste. (Constant 1988, 10–11)

In a published interview, Constant described in oenological terms his plans for a "new line of luxury dark chocolate bars classified by plantation with a guarantee of the origin and growth of the beans . . . in order to establish the elite growths, *les grands crus,* of dark chocolate cultivation" (Pudlowski 1991, 26). Similarly, in Linxe's 1992 text, consumers are admonished to check the labels of chocolate bars just as they would the label on a bottle of wine. The label should state the percentage of cocoa solids, between 55 percent and 100 percent (the higher the better) and the origin of the beans: "aromatic Criollos from Ecuador, fruitier [Criollos] from Indonesia or more robust Forasteros from Africa" (1992, 122).

The establishment of esoteric criteria emphasizing the centrality of climate, soil, and varieties of beans in the production of good chocolates is integral to claims of craft and connoisseurship. Such criteria serve to categorize chocolates, objectively and authoritatively, separating them into a hierarchy of growths. Yet this categorization is hardly neutral. As we shall see, it selectively elides and naturalizes certain problematic historical circumstances. Ulin (1996) has demonstrated this phenomenon with wine production itself, showing that the standard classification of different growths masks the social construction of quality and taste as it simultaneously naturalizes the specific political economy that has long differentiated and privileged the owners of estate growths over local wine growers.

In the case of chocolate, the assertion of objective taste standards is complicated for a number of reasons. As noted above, French *chocolatiers* no longer make chocolate from cacao beans. All purchase blocks of chocolate, known as *couverture,* which are industrially produced from blends of three different varieties of beans. Master *chocolatiers* like Linxe and Constant, by virtue of their training and travel, do have direct experience with beans and knowledge of the taste differences among them. Linxe, for example, has served as a technical advisor to the industrial manufacturer Valrhona since the early 1980s. Many others do not have this empirical knowledge and in fact acquired familiarity with the bean varieties and geographical sites of cacao plantations largely from the marketing brochures and labels of industrial *couvertures* first sold by Valrhona in 1985.[8] The names of the cacao-producing regions were printed on these labels. Other industrial manufacturers such as Cacao Barry have adopted similar marketing strategies.

In 1986 Valrhona introduced luxury chocolate bars that featured location and/or bean variety, for example, Manjari, 100 percent criollo beans. The renewed focus on cocoa solids and on beans depends on a differentiation of bean growths and varieties. *Chocolatiers* clearly invoke a system for evaluating beans that closely parallels the system used to designate the highest-quality officially classified growths or estates (*les grands crus*) in the Bordeaux wine-growing region. No official classification of cacao bean plantations exists, and all industrial manufacturers use a blend of beans in most of the *couverture* they sell. French *chocolatiers* nevertheless assure consumers that they select only the best vintages of the finest varieties, criollos and trinitarios, from renowned domains in South America, the Caribbean, or South Asia. Recent guides cite the *couverture* used by producers in an effort to emphasize the source of cacao bean growths, but the results can be more confusing than revealing.[9]

The classification surrounding *grand cru* chocolates masks the realities of actual world production as well as the diffusion of cacao through European colonialism from its birthplace in Mexico to Africa, Asia, and the Pacific. Of the three varieties of cacao beans, the criollos, native to

Mesoamerica, are generally acknowledged to possess the most flavor and aroma, although the trees that produce them are more disease-prone and less productive. They currently constitute only 2 percent of the world crop even as they are cultivated in plantations around the world. The most common variety of cacao bean, the forastero, produced in former French colonies of West Africa, Southeast Asia, and parts of South America, is hardly mentioned in gastronomic texts but widely used by French industrialists who provision *chocolatiers*. Forasteros account for 80 percent of world production and appeal to industrial manufacturers because of their cheaper cost, resistance to disease, higher yields, and ability to thrive in many different parts of the world. A hybrid variety, the trinitario, combines the vigor of the forastero with the taste of the criollo but constitutes only 10–15 percent of world production. In the rush to reduce costs, plantations owners have in fact replaced the fragile criollo with the more productive trinitario. This happened, for example, in Venezuela after the trinitario had been introduced on its Caribbean coast (Coe and Coe 1996, 200).

The search for cheaper, more abundant raw materials that fueled colonialist expansion also prompted the seeding of cacao plantations around the world with cuttings from the more robust forasteros and trinitarios. The earliest cacao-producing nations in the Caribbean and in Central and South America, which provided the source of many of the names marketed by French manufacturers (such as Guayaquil in Ecuador), were gradually displaced as cacao spread steadily eastward in the nineteenth century via the Portuguese to São Tomé, the West African island of Bioko, and then to the Gold Coast (Ghana), Nigeria, and the Ivory Coast.[10] The Germans planted it in Cameroon, the British carried it to Ceylon (Sri Lanka), and the Dutch took it to colonies in Java and Sumatra. European imperialism continued its eastward march in the twentieth century with plantations in Oceania, New Hebrides, New Guinea, and even Samoa. In their recent history of chocolate, the Coes note the supreme irony of the fact that the West African nations that provided much of the slave labor for early European cacao plantations in the Americas have become the world's leading producers of cacao. In 1991, Africa was the source of 55 percent of the world's cacao, whereas Mexico, the birthplace of chocolate and of the word *cacao* provided only 1.5 percent (Coe and Coe 1996, 201).

A final characteristic of the gastronomic literature under consideration here is relevant because it speaks to a central concern in the anthropology of food, namely, taboos and prescriptions. These texts devote considerable attention to the moral and medical attitudes that adhered to chocolate in the past and continue to intrigue in the present. They all trace the controversies surrounding the incorporation of chocolate into European schemes of thought about food and drink—controversies centering on the religious requirements of fasting and the question of whether to classify chocolate as a food that broke the fast or as a drink that maintained it. These texts also detail the wildly differing medical opinions on chocolate firmly rooted in the humoral medicine that originated in classical antiquity and continued in the West until the advent of modern medicine two centuries ago.[11] The opinions of sixteenth- and seventeenth-century scientists, explorers, and courtly nobles are presented as amusingly archaic. One frequently quoted example is taken from the correspondence of the well-known chronicler of seventeenth-century French court life, Madame de Sévigné. At a time when hot chocolate was a part of court ceremonials, including the public morning ritual of the Sun King, Madame de Sévigné famously reversed her position on its salutary effects. In a 1671 letter to her pregnant daughter, Madame de Grignan, she implored her not to drink hot chocolate because "the Marquise de Coëtlogon drank so much when she was expecting that she gave birth to a little boy, black as the devil, who died."

The literature on chocolate does not limit itself to historical debates but directly addresses persistent popular beliefs concerning chocolate as a drug, aphrodisiac, and source of myriad ailments from migraine headaches, obesity, and high cholesterol to indigestion in its acute, peculiarly French, form of *mal au foie,* or liver complaint.[12] These beliefs remind us that food is never medically or morally neutral. The perceptions of its gustatory appeal are always linked to its implications for the health, status, and moral and mental equilibrium of the consumer (compare Appadurai 1988, 10–11). This is particularly true of chocolate. Both its persistent claim to divergent medical opinions and the very preoccupation with debunking the myths regarding its deleterious effects beg the question of why this should be so. A study of the social life of all commodities reveals that as they move along complex trajectories, both spatial and temporal, they are classified and reclassified into culturally relevant categories and invested with particular meanings, properties, and identities (Kopytoff 1986). Yet the fact remains that chocolate was and is distinguished by its semiotic virtuosity even as it has been consumed by the masses. Mintz's (1996a) persuasive explanation for this centers on the complex chemical composition of chocolate.[13] Unlike sugar and cocaine, chocolate and coffee cannot be refined into a "chemically pure (and therefore unmistakably standardized) product" (10–11). For this reason, chocolate and coffee are particularly susceptible to cultural elaboration and the fluctuating politics of demand.

If chocolate is thus imperfectly modern, according to Mintz, this cannot be merely a function of its chemical composition but also a function of its ritualized consumption. *Dragées,* both sugar-coated almond and chocolate centers, are the still the preferred gifts at baptisms, communions, bar mitzvahs, and weddings. Christmas and Easter remain the privileged moments for expensive confectionery purchases as gifts, both candies and figurines. Chocolate and champagne have replaced the bread and bouillon used in earlier periods and play a key if subversive role in *la rôtie,* a wedding night ritual documented in early modern France that persists to this day in rural Auvergne (Reed-Danahay 1996a). The purchase of chocolate is still treated as a moral and medical matter, one of managing the risks and obligations of human interactions in rites of passage; one of cementing social relations among kin and non-kin at important social occasions; one in which chocolate as remedy and pleasure does battle with chocolate as ailment and guilt.

The new gastronomic texts represent a sustained effort to reposition chocolate within a traditional moral and ritual matrix associated with prescription and taboo. They recast these prescriptions as consumption issues tied to confectionery etiquette and connoisseurship. Chocolate is presented as a food that appeals to the childlike hedonist within the consumer; it is promoted as a healthy and irresistible food to be eaten spontaneously whenever the urge arises. Dark, evocatively named chocolates such as Montezuma, Aztec, and Caracas evoke and invite new consuming passions; they suggest self-pleasuring, playful indulgence, and conspicuous leisure. French consumers are invited to join in the play and to follow the lead of accomplished masters and tastemakers in sophisticated urban centers who indulge their taste for *grand cru* chocolates.

## Conclusion

The reconception of French chocolates as culturally authentic artisanship and newly esoteric cuisine occurred at a unique time in the history of the craft. Both the anxiety associated with proposed European Community reforms and the swift proliferation of foreign franchises changed the terms of the dialogue between French consumers and artisanal *chocolatiers*. The issues of exclusivity that had informed this dialogue in the past, when chocolate was a rare and costly luxury reserved for elite consumption, gave way to the issue of authenticity (Appadurai 1986, 44). Authenticity in this context is determined by culturally elaborated judgments involving connoisseurship, taste, and correctness.

In contemporary prestige economies like that of France, discriminating consumers want goods that are both culturally authentic and esoteric. Yet in these economies the only way to preserve or recreate the elite resonance of commodities that can be mass-produced is to elaborate the criteria of authenticity surrounding them. Through the creation of an esoteric taste standard, French *chocolatiers* and cultural tastemakers seek to differentiate genuine French chocolates from foreign imitations. As *bricoleurs,* they adapted a number of relevant elements of French culture in order to transform traditional candies into dessert cuisine with enhanced value for both individual consumption and gift exchange. Informing the cultural authenticity of French chocolates are oenological criteria of connoisseurship in taste, a culinary discourse of purity, freshness, and aesthetics, and a long heritage of skilled artisanship.

The reconception of French chocolates as culturally genuine food occurred amid the uncertainty generated by the impending unification of the European Community. Attempts to forge Europeanness in the name of a universal culture were especially problematic given the existence of a notion of French culture also defined as universal and embodied in French cultural achievements from literature to cuisine. *Chocolatiers* sought to have their claims authorized and validated by state officials, social elites, and tastemakers. Here again Lionel Trilling's insight, that questions of authenticity arise when there is a pervasive doubt, is helpful. In chapter 4 we travel to southwest France, where struggles over conflicting claims to authenticity were projected onto the past. I will examine both the history of chocolate production there and the persistent claims made with respect to it.

# CHAPTER 4

# Unsettling Memories

## *The Politics of Commemoration*

---

*. . . to breathe in its fragrance, caress its fullness, exalt in its flavor, recognize the delicacy of its bouquet and its amber hue. And to remind ourselves that for four centuries in Bayonne, we have, without hesitation, surrendered ourselves freely to the power and poetry of a chocolate-memory, a chocolate-history and patrimony.*

The Year of Chocolate Commemorative
Lectures, Bayonne, 1997

The 1996 Year of Chocolate in Bayonne was an event through which local *chocolatiers* and municipal officials sought to construct and empower themselves by asserting and commemorating their own particular history (Friedman 1994, 118). Organized under the aegis of the city of Bayonne, the event involved a series of public lectures on the history of chocolate, with a special focus on southwest France. Almost a thousand people attended the three evenings of lectures given by two historians, an agro-engineer, a collector of chocolate memorabilia, a marketing representative from the French chocolate manufacturer Valrhona, and an anthropologist (me). The mayor, Dr. Jean Grenet, hoped to achieve, in his words, "a truly national audience" for the event by having a respected regional press, J&D Editions of Biarritz, publish the lectures in a special volume (*Chocolat, Bayonne* 1997).

Robert Linxe (see chapter 3) wrote the preface to the *Chocolat* volume and highlighted Bayonne as an important historical and contemporary center of artisanal chocolate production:

Since the seventeenth century, chocolate has been man's companion in his fabulous quest for olfactory and gustatory pleasure. . . . How satisfying to see finally a volume that had the intelligent ambition to focus on chocolate, not as a mere weakness of the gourmet, but as a true science, thereby establishing the ties that bind Bayonne to one of its strongest traditions: chocolate. Faithful to the demands of my craft, I fully endorse this passion for artisanal work, this legitimation of our Bayonnais traditions, this respect for the taste and the will of *chocolatiers* to perpetuate a rich savoir-faire.(vi)

The Year of Chocolate was only the latest in a series of initiatives designed to craft a new historical narrative on local chocolate. This event built on the 1994 creation of the Académie du Chocolat de Bayonne, the 1991 Pau Conference on the History of Chocolate, the 1991 Basque Coast Contest for Chocolatiers, and the 1988 creation of a new Bayonnais chocolate candy, *le chocolat de Bayonne*. Through the public enactment of craft rituals and the wide dissemination of texts—scholarly and popular—*chocolatiers* asserted their membership in an authentic local community of masters dating back to the original *chocolatiers*. The new history claimed Bayonne, not Paris or the Versailles court, as the oldest site of continuous chocolate manufacture in the nation. These rituals and texts constituted a historical narrative that commemorated and celebrated certain past episodes even as it elided and silenced others. This new historical narrative has been and continues to be used to market chocolates to a changing resident and tourist clientele. It was based on the creation of an aestheticized past that repressed profoundly unsettling events tied to regional and craft histories.

## The Creation of the Basque Coast

Today many people situate Bayonne on the basis of its proximity to two important tourist destinations in the southwest: Biarritz, the luxury Atlantic seacoast resort; and the Basque countryside located inland to the east that encompasses the three Basque provinces within French borders—Labourd, Lower Navarre, and Soule. Until the nineteenth century, however, Bayonne was intimately linked to its location on the Pyrenean frontier with Spain. Located astride the confluence of the Nive and Adour rivers just before they meet the Atlantic Ocean, Bayonne occupied what was historically a strategic position in the southwestern periphery of the Old Regime (pre-1789 Revolution) kingdom.[1]

Its location midway on a heavily traveled but sparsely populated corridor between Bordeaux and Spain has made Bayonne an important and necessary stop for wayfarers. The frequent successionist and territorial disputes in the southwest meant that troop regiments from England, France, and Spain either occupied or passed through the city at different points in time. Monarchs, nobles, and statesmen sojourned in Bayonne from the fifteenth century onward to seal alliances, assert their sovereignty, and resolve territorial disputes. Sailors and adventurers were drawn to the city during the seventeenth and eighteenth centuries as shipbuilding flourished and brisk trade was carried on with Spain, Holland, and the Antilles. Over the centuries the permeability of the Pyrenean frontier border made it an attractive trade route for smugglers and an escape route for outlaws, religious and political dissidents, and refugees. The latter included Iberian Jews escaping religious persecution by the Spanish Inquisition, Spanish refugees eluding the turmoil following the nineteenth-century Carlist wars and again after the twentieth-century civil war, Jews fleeing internment in French concentration camps and/or deportation to Nazi death camps, and, more recently, *pied noir* families repatriated to France in the wake of Algerian independence in 1962.

Over the centuries, retail merchants, hotel and inn keepers, restaurateurs, and artisans in a variety of trades have catered to the needs of these travelers. Indeed, the historic downtown neighborhoods of the city, Grand Bayonne, Petit Bayonne, and Saint Esprit, are still the site of hotels, restaurants, cafés, tearooms, and artisanal producers representing luxury crafts such as jewelers as well as a large number of food trades such as *chocolatiers,* confectioners, pastry makers, bakers, butchers, pork butchers, grocers, and cheese sellers.

In addition to seeing the continuous passage of travelers, Bayonne was also the site of ongoing exchanges between city and countryside as residents from the rural hinterland, Basque villages to the south and Gascon hamlets to the north, came regularly to sell and buy goods on market days. Migrants from those areas also sought work in the urban trades located in this commercial port center. Since the nineteenth century, successive waves of tourism to the Basque coast have transformed both the urban coastal landscape and the rural Basque hinterland and created a large service sector to cater to their needs.

## Bayonne and the Basque Coast

The 1852 coup d'état that reinstated a second imperial empire led by Napoleon Bonaparte's nephew, Napoleon III, after only a brief interlude of democratic government under the Second Republic (1848–1852) had an important impact on the southwest. It created a Basque coast regional economy dominated by luxury tourism and drew Bayonne into an ongoing urban dialectic with nearby Biarritz that persists to this day. Biarritz was a tiny seaside village accessible only by horseback until its "discovery" by the new aristocracy of the Second Empire. In 1854 the Empress Eugénie, the Spanish wife of Napoleon III, introduced her husband to the pristine beaches and rocky coastline of Biarritz. The following year construction began on an imperial summer palace there. This established Biarritz as a preeminently fashionable resort for a growing international elite, including European nobility, statesmen, and wealthy entrepreneurs. The demise of the Second Empire (1870) and consolidation of the Third Republic (1870–1940) brought new French political elites to Biarritz. A series of French presidents and prime ministers came to vacation and to take the cure—the special spa waters  available there. Queen Victoria's decision to spend a month in Biarritz in 1889 ensconced it as an unrivaled site for wealthy English travelers to spend the winter. In the aftermath of the upheavals associated with the Spanish Carlist wars, World War I, and the Russian Revolution, a high society community of expatriates, artists, painters, and literary personalities settled in Biarritz, adding to the upper-crust tourists who came yearly to spend the "season" on the Basque coast (Biarritz 1988). The arrival of these elites transformed the urban typography of Biarritz and its coastal landscape. The transmutation of Biarritz from a rustic fishing village to a cosmopolitan urban resort between 1854 and 1900 illustrates how essential the production of space is to the inner workings of a political economy (Lefebvre 1991). Ostentatious summer residences, luxury hotel-restaurants, sumptuous casinos, seaside gardens, elegant tearooms, gourmet groceries, and couturiers and jewelers from Paris and London remade an untamed seacoast into a self-consciously important urbanity marked by extravagantly eclectic architecture and frivolous social pursuits.

Bayonnais entrepreneurs and professionals invested heavily in Biarritz casinos and hotels while simultaneously adopting an oppositional stance with respect to what many saw as its garish ostentation and conspicuous leisure. They sought to capitalize on the luxury tourist market in Biarritz while maintaining a distinctively Bayonnais urban environment marked by commercial sobriety and a medieval patrimony. The conservative Bayonnais bourgeois who have dominated the municipal leadership since the Third Republic were intent on promoting Bayonne as a *ville d'art,* whose attraction consisted of historical landmarks and regional culture.[2] They virulently rejected a 1921 proposal to construct a luxury hotel and casino on the site of the medieval defensive fortifications. In the words of one municipal councilman, "Bayonne will never be a city of tango and roulette" (Hourmat 1990, 70). Instead, the city's public transportation systems were improved, a neoclassical public garden was constructed, the renovation of historical landmarks within the medieval city walls were undertaken, and two museums were opened, one devoted to high culture and fine arts and the other reserved for ethnographic artifacts and popular customs of Basque social and cultural life.

Beginning in the late 1930s, tourism on the Basque coast developed in quite a different direction, paralleling the overall expansion of mass tourism in France. After the Socialist Popular Front government of Léon Blum created the first paid vacations for French workers in 1936, the summer tourist population began to expand and democratize. This new brand of tourist had different spending habits and more modest financial means than the upper-crust clientele who had launched tourism in the region. This movement accelerated as successive postwar governments increased French workers' vacation from two to five weeks. Urban and coastal landscapes are a testament to the arrival and needs of a larger, middle-class tourist population in the postwar period. Some of the nineteenth-century luxury hotels in Biarritz were razed or converted to apartments. All along the coast, campgrounds, inexpensive tourist hotels, modest restaurants, and cafés opened. Since 1966, mass distribution outlets such as Carrefour have been opening in a newly rezoned commercial area linking Bayonne, Anglet, and Biarritz.

The 1980s witnessed an explosion of interest in the southwestern Atlantic coastline, still relatively undeveloped in contrast to the Mediterranean Riviera between Nice and Menton. Local mayors, such as the center-right mayor of Biarritz (1977–1991), Bernard Marie, strongly supported coastal development targeting an affluent upper middle-class clientele and oversaw the construction of an ultra-modern thalassotherapy center on the beach just north of Biarritz featuring sea baths, massage, exercise, and a healthy diet including dark, bittersweet chocolate.

In 1985, a venerable Biarrot institution, the elegant Bellevue casino, first constructed for the imperial nobility in the 1860s, was completely renovated and reopened as an international convention center. Marie's mayoral successor, Didier Borotra, undertook a costly renovation of the run-down municipal casino on the choicest piece of oceanfront property in central Biarritz.[3]

The father of the current mayor of Bayonne, Dr. Henri Grenet, also played an important role in promoting tourism in the southwest and Bayonne. When I interviewed him in April 1991, Dr. Grenet was in his sixth and last six-year mayoral term of office. Reflecting on his long mayoral career, Grenet emphasized the appeal of Bayonne as a tourist site and tourism's importance for the regional economy. In 1992, tourism represented 64 percent of the gross regional product and the total expenditures, of the 1.5 million annual tourists to the department exceeded $330 million (Pyrénées Atlantiques 1994).[4] Dr. Grenet promoted the city's status in tourist literature as a middle-size city (population 43,000 in 1990) that had escaped the disruptive effects of rapid urban growth.[5] He was particularly proud of the pedestrian zone created in Grand Bayonne, the oldest of three downtown neighborhoods. Both tourist guides and local residents direct visitors to the Port Neuf, a vibrant pedestrian street that cuts through the heart of Grand Bayonne, beginning across from the imposing nineteenth-century town hall overlooking the confluence of the Nive and Adour rivers and ending at the eastern flank of the massive Gothic cathedral that commands the medieval town center. En route, it wends its way past the popular tourist promenade where the city's oldest tearooms and *chocolateries* are clustered under a low, covered archway known as *les arceaux*.

## Bayonne, Ville de Chocolat

In 1988, two years before I began my fieldwork, the Bayonne Chamber of Commerce and Industry sponsored a contest in which Bayonnais *chocolatiers* competed to create a new chocolate candy, *le chocolat de Bayonne*. Most participants in the contest and many Bayonnais who attended the award ceremony and public tasting agreed that the initiative was not a total success. To most French and foreign tourists, Bayonne's best-known gastronomic specialty was a local pressed, cured ham, *jambon de Bayonne*, not chocolate. Moreover, the candy center chosen was a *ganache* flavored with cinnamon and enrobed with a dark, bittersweet chocolate. This recipe was meant to recall the spices used by the original *chocolatiers*. However, in 1988 the use of cinnamon in *ganache* centers was culinarily problematic. From the mid-nineteenth century on, Bayonnais *chocolatiers,* catering to their elite clientele, had adopted Parisian fashions in confectionery taste and had progressively abolished spices such as cinnamon and vanilla from their solid chocolates. When dipped chocolate confectionery appeared in the late nineteenth century, most candy centers were composed of a base of fruits, nuts, sugar, and/or chocolate; cinnamon was not used to flavor these centers. When Parisian *chocolatiers* such as Robert Linxe affirmed the superiority of the *ganache* and reintroduced spiced candy centers, local producers followed this trend. The problem was that this flavoring had quite literally been lost to local gustatory memory, so the initial public reaction to the *chocolat de Bayonne* was, I was told, mixed. Most importantly, since many *chocolateries* disappeared during or soon after World War II, younger Bayonnais had no knowledge or memory of chocolate making as a long-standing tradition in Bayonne and little appreciation for the history they were invited to celebrate.

Social memory plays a constitutive role in the formation and perpetuation of group identity and historical consciousness. Groups construct and make sense of themselves in the present by engaging in a dynamic process whereby the past is reworked and reshaped in order to explain dilemmas of the present and to guide collective decisions for the future. In the late 1980s, Belgian franchise outlets opened in the southwest and intrusive European Community reforms loomed, generating fears of increased cultural homogeneity and diminished authority in the areas of production, training, and taste. Because this period posed particularly acute problems of group identity and reproduction for *chocolatiers,* their memory work was intensified. It was this memory work that has proved so interesting to investigate and that still conditions my relations with the *chocolatier* community (see Terrio 1998).

## The French Cradle of Chocolate

In 1989 few people knew the southwest to be the historic cradle of chocolate production or linked chocolate making to the Portuguese Jews who sought sanctuary in France from the religious persecution of the Spanish Inquisition. Although famous tourist guides such as the *Guide Michelin* identified the Port Neuf as the site for "good chocolate," they reduced a complex and obscure history to one sentence: "Chocolate was introduced to Bayonne in the seventeenth century by Jews driven out of Spain and Portugal" (*Guide Michelin* 1989, 61). Parisian gastronomic texts alluded to the creation of an eighteenth-century guild for *chocolatiers* in Bayonne (Corporation des Chocolatiers)—the only one known to have existed exclusively for this craft in Old Regime France (Girard 1984; *Le guide des croqueurs du chocolat* 1988).

Local claims of historical authenticity were also explicitly made at the 1991 Pau Conference on Chocolate. One of the speakers, Dr. Toubon, was a retired Bayonnais physician and locally known chocolate aficionado, not a professional historian. Drawing on texts from the chocolate literature that I examined in chapter 3, he explained how chocolate arrived first in Spain and later entered France:

Chocolate came to Bayonne with Jews seeking refuge from persecution—terrible persecution from the Inquisition in Iberia . . . the three French ports offering sanctuary were Bayonne, Bordeaux, and Nantes. We have formal proof that the first artisans who fled Spain and brought with them the secret of making chocolate came first to Bayonne. It is a subject of satisfaction for every resident of the Atlantic Pyrenees department and in particular of Bayonnais, without chauvinism of any kind, it is a source of pride for us to know that chocolate came to France thanks to the warm welcome extended by Bayonne.

Just a few months later, in May 1991, these historical claims were reasserted in the context of a craft contest organized by a group of local university students in which southwest *chocolatiers* enthusiastically participated (see chapter 7). The public display of contest entries in the Anglet town hall was accompanied by a student-authored history of the local craft hung on the wall for visitors to read. This chronicle centered on the preindustrial guild:

In the beginning of the eighteenth century, the reputation of Bayonnais chocolate continued to spread. This was due to the quality of the cacao beans used and to its expert blending, according to the formulas brought from nearby Spain by Portuguese Jews. Long the only experts in this new craft, the Portuguese, who were unable to practice retail commerce, went to make chocolate at the shops of Bayonnais grocers and even took their tools to individual homes. Little by little, following their example, Bayonnais workers appeared who learned to make chocolate, and their numbers increased to the point that a new guild, that of *chocolatiers,* was constituted in Bayonne in 1761. This guild . . . sent a formal request to the mayor and municipal leaders in Bayonne to be recognized by the city. It demanded as well to restrict the production of chocolate to masters in the new guild who alone had the right to set up shop. This was an implicit demand for the interdiction of the Portuguese to produce chocolate in Bayonne.

Both texts celebrated Bayonne as the authentic cradle of chocolate production and related the role played by Iberian Jews in establishing the craft but elided numerous historical details. Dr. Toubon never provided, nor was asked to provide, the "formal proof" substantiating his claim that Bayonne, not Bordeaux or Nantes, was the true cradle of chocolate production. Nor did he mention the ongoing discrimination against Portuguese Jews once they settled in France. For their part, the students used one of the only accounts that chronicles in great detail the sustained anti-Jewish prejudice of Bayonnais officials (Léon 1893), but little of the author's exposé of this injustice appears in their account. Indeed, their historical narrative is unsettling precisely because the tale they tell describes the constitution of the guild as an almost inevitable, even natural, outcome of the diffusion of craft skills from Iberian outsiders to Bayonnais insiders. The emergent skill of Bayonnais *chocolatiers* seems to justify the demand for a protective guild. The mention of the discrimination against the Jews appears perfunctory—almost an afterthought. The students' account nonetheless raises the question of the systematic exclusion of minority others within state-sanctioned institutions and the question of the permanent integration of minorities within the French nation, then as now. Both of these accounts demand a fuller rendering of local history. The account I privilege here has itself been contested and, until very recently, has remained largely unknown except among local historians.[6]

Iberian Jews began to settle in France after they were expelled from Spain by Ferdinand and Isabella in 1492. Many sought refuge in France but hid their religious identity. In the sixteenth century, French kings issued a series of patent letters formally granting them asylum and authorizing them to live and carry on "trade and commerce" in certain southwest cities and towns, including Bordeaux, Bidache, Peyrehorade, and Labastide-Clairence as well as Saint-Esprit, the Bayonne neighborhood located on the opposite side of the Adour River, across from Grand Bayonne.[7] Iberian Jews came with the tools, the knowledge of transforming cacao beans into chocolate, and extensive contacts in the New World, but it is impossible to say exactly when they began to practice their craft in the southwest. In 1602, Henry IV specifically charged the powerful Gramont family, governors of the city of Bayonne, to provide the Jews with protection (Robert 1984). There was continuous tension between merchant/artisans in the Saint-Esprit Jewish community and Bayonnais municipal leaders across the Adour River in the neighborhoods of Petit and Grand Bayonne.

Although Jews were afforded sanctuary in parts of Old Regime France, they were not granted full citizenship until 1791, two years after the outbreak of the 1789 French Revolution. Until that time, restrictions on land ownership, profession, residence, and travel were imposed on them and they were subjected to special taxes. In Bayonne, a series of restrictive ordinances aimed at Jewish trade and commerce were instituted by Bayonnais municipal authorities over the course of the seventeenth and eighteenth centuries. These ordinances forbade Jews to own or rent commercial and personal property outside Saint Esprit or to live in the neighborhoods of Petit and Grand Bayonne. Indeed, Jews were required to quit the city every evening by sunset and to return across the Adour River to Saint-Esprit. In order to practice their craft and to sell their chocolate outside Saint Esprit, Jewish *chocolatiers* had to take their raw materials and tools to the homes of individual customers and to the shops of grocers, where they made their chocolate on the premises (Léon 1893, 19).

The chocolate tools that Saint Esprit Jews brought to Bayonne had changed little from those of pre-Columbian Olmecs, Maya, and Aztecs in Mesoamerica (Coe and Coe 1996). They included a roller, a concave granite stone *(metate à l'aztèque),* and fire. *Chocolatiers* ground the roasted, hulled cacao beans on the heated stone until they yielded a semi-liquid, homogenous mass to which sugar and various spices were added. The mass was shaped by hand and then allowed to cool. *Chocolatiers* charged their clients by the measure of a stone-full, or *pierrée,* of chocolate, roughly five pounds (Cuzacq 1949, 84). On the eve of the French Revolution, the cacao technology used in Bayonne and elsewhere in France was still virtually identical. A detailed engraving of eighteenth-century chocolate manufacture in Diderot and Jean d'Alembert's famous compendium of the sciences, arts, and trades, the *Encyclopedia,* shows *chocolatiers* grinding chocolate beans by hand on a heated stone (Diderot 1763).

In spite of local restrictions Saint Esprit Jews prospered. However, in 1681, their growing commercial success prompted municipal leaders to enact an ordinance limiting them to wholesale trade outside of Saint Esprit. It forbade them to engage in retail commerce by opening shops or selling goods directly to buyers in Bayonne (Léon 1893, 30; Nahon 1981, 107–108). A number of subsequent eighteenth-century ordinances designed to enforce the 1691 ordinance are proof that it was largely ignored. With the help, no doubt, of certain Bayonnais, Jewish traders and *chocolatiers* from Saint Esprit continued to flout the 1691 restriction by regularly retailing their goods within the city. By the middle of the eighteenth century, artisanal chocolate making had become an important commercial activity in Bayonne fueled by a brisk trade in cacao with the Antilles (Cuzacq 1949, 79). Craft skills had diffused to Bayonnais in the neighborhoods of Petit and Grand Bayonne as well as to Basque, Gascon, and Béarnais groups elsewhere in southwest France. Growing competition between Saint Esprit Jewish and Bayonnais *chocolatiers* increased hostility toward the Jews. In 1761 a group of Bayonnais *chocolatiers* of both French and Spanish ancestry attempted, once and for all, to wrest the production and sale of chocolate from their Jewish competitors. This group appealed to the mayor and city council of Bayonne for the right to create a guild *(corporation)*. One of the coveted privileges enjoyed by formal guilds in Old Regime France was the right to a craft monopoly in a specifically delimited, usually urban, space (Sewell 1980).

The Bayonnais *chocolatiers* argued that since other trades in Bayonne were organized into jurally recognized guilds with strictly enforced duties and privileges, artisanal chocolate production should be as well. They based their appeal on the need to regulate the craft in Bayonne because of the presence of a "multitude of foreigners who are inundating our city and infecting the public by the inferior quality and composition of the chocolate they sell there." They also charged that the intrusion of these foreigners had undercut their ability to provide even a meager living from their craft. "Deprived of work, [we] languish in a debilitating idleness" (Bayonne Municipal Archives n.d., HH 189, 435–446).

This appeal to a higher authority on behalf of a local craft community was a constant feature of life in Old Regime French cities and, as we shall see, can still be seen today. From the fifteenth century to the end of the eighteenth century, a succession of French monarchs had increased the centralized regulation of a number of manufacturing and commercial urban trades by mandating that formerly free trades be organized into jurally recognized bodies (Jaeger 1982). Disputes within the same craft and between companion crafts were ubiquitous and the source of constant strife and lawsuits.

The existence of craft guilds gave municipal authorities tighter control over both a skilled workforce and the manufacture and sale of goods deemed vital to the economic life of the city. Guilds were bound by complex written statutes registered with the law court in Bordeaux governing every aspect of the interwoven activities of production and sales: the type and quality of raw materials; tools and designs; the quantity of finished goods; the method of production; the length and content of apprenticeship; the skills required for the mastership; as well as the numbers of apprentices and journeymen permitted to work within a unit of production headed by a master. Municipal and royal authorities in Old Regime France attempted to regulate a moral economy by condemning speculation, hoarding, and excess profits, reducing competition from outsiders, and guaranteeing adequate supplies of comparable quality goods to the public (Coornaert 1968; Hauser 1927; Jaeger 1982; Sewell 1980). However, as this tale from Bayonne illustrates, the application of this labyrinth of rules could be very selective and was often politicized.

Bayonnais municipal notables strongly endorsed the *chocolatiers'* petition, in particular the guild statute that reserved the exclusive right to open a shop and to sell chocolates to "master *chocolatiers*," that is, the eleven founding members of the guild. The statutes were registered by the city of Bayonne in 1761 and by the Bordeaux law court in 1762. They effectively alienated Jews from the present and future exercise of the craft since the attribution of a mastership was reserved for Christian, French subjects of the Crown. The Saint Esprit Jews appealed to their patron, the Count of Gramont, whose influence provoked an investigation by the representatives of the king.

This intervention on behalf of the Jews provoked a furious reaction from the Bayonnais municipal authorities. In a 1763 letter, notable for its overstatement and bigotry, they defended their actions as an imperative mandated by the "public interest" given the growing commercial importance of chocolate. They advised the king's minister that its consumption was so commonplace that chocolate had become part of "the daily Bayonnais diet." They urged that more attention be paid to "the particulars of its preparation" and insisted that Jews "who habitually falsify what they sell should be prevented from making it" (quoted in Leon 1893, 70–73). In a classic piece of circular logic, they argued that the Jews had no reason to complain since "from time immemorial" they had been banned from working, living, and retailing chocolate in Bayonne. Jews could produce as much chocolate as they wanted "as long as they did so in Saint Esprit" (Cuzacq 1949, 79; Léon 1893, 72). City authorities ordered the seizure of the cacao bean stocks of Bayonnais merchant grocers who had continued to allow Saint Esprit Jews to produce chocolate in their shops.

A legal brief prepared on behalf of the Saint Esprit Jews was presented to the Bordeaux law court in 1764. It requested the annulment of the corporation statutes on the grounds that the Jews had long practiced the craft in Bayonne and that the creation of the guild was a blatant attempt to abrogate the rights accorded them by successive French sovereigns (Nahon 1981, 308–320). It is significant that these events coincided with the ascendancy to power of state officials who were sharply critical of the entire guild system. In a 1763 letter to the mayor and city counselors, a local representative of the king, de Moracin, reminded them that "for some time the views of the government tend toward unrestrained trade and it supports the position that all arts, commerce, and industry should enjoy it" (Léon 1893, 70). During this period they were attempting to reform and limit the power of craft guilds, not to enhance and extend them. This, more than the moral and legal issues raised by the Jews, may explain the lack of royal support for the *chocolatiers'* guild. Upon hearing the arguments of the Bayonnais authorities, another highly placed royal official, de Leverdy, rejected them and noted disapprovingly, "This is a new craft . . . as this craft does not bear on a necessity of life. . . . I would be of the opinion to revoke its statutes" (Léon 1893, 74).

Even the two Bordeaux lawyers invited to write opinions on behalf of the new guild were ambivalent. They concurred with the spirit of the guild but not at the expense of the "natural liberty" of "Bayonnais bourgeois" to choose freely their chocolate. Indeed, their support seemed to result more from deeply ingrained anti-Jewish sentiments than from their endorsement of the moral economy of guild corporatism.

We certainly believe that the production of chocolates by the master chocolatiers of Bayonne will be of a higher quality than that of the Jews; but if a bourgeois from Bayonne cares so little for his own self interest and is such an enemy of his own stomach as to prefer the chocolate of a Jew, why should one prevent him from having the Jew come to his home to make it? (Léon 1893, 73)

It took three years for the Bordeaux law court to render its judgment and, in 1767, it formally annulled the guild statutes.

Over the course of the nineteenth century the production of chocolate came to be dominated by families of Basque, Gascon, and Spanish ancestry in Bayonne and in the surrounding towns. Records from the Jewish Consistory of Bayonne reveal that Saint Esprit Jews were gradually moving their children out of chocolate making over the course of the eighteenth century. Following the grant of full citizenship to Jews in France in 1791 and the dismantling of the guild system in the same year, the number of Saint Esprit chocolate makers dropped sharply; by 1802, only two Jewish *chocolatiers* were listed in the Consistory records (Oukhemanou, 1995, personal communication). The number of specialized Bayonnais *chocolateries* increased over the course of the nineteenth and early twentieth centuries but experienced a progressive decline in the interwar period and then a dramatic drop after World War II.[8]

## "A Continuous Bayonnais Tradition from 1761 to the Present"

One of the persistent historical claims made about and by contemporary Bayonnais *chocolatiers* involved their status as direct craft descendants of the original artisans (*Le guide des croqueurs du chocolat* 1988, 45). Local craftsmen forged a myth of common descent with the first *chocolatiers* (compare Shore 1993). Instead of blood or biological ties, skill was the fundamental descent principle of the local community and as such replicated the logic of reproduction in confectionery houses, as we shall see. Contemporary *chocolatiers* claimed to inherit a shared patrimony of culinary and craft skill including recipes, tools, and secret techniques handed down in a direct line from the first *chocolatiers*. Old tools such as the *metate* were prominently displayed at the 1991 Pau Conference on Chocolate (see fig. 4), and "new" traditional tools were installed such as the hand-hewn wooden stick suspended from the ceiling with one end immersed in a copper basin of tempered chocolate in the special chocolate dipping room of the Dalbaitz workshop (see fig. 5). These claims bore witness to the craft as both historical patrimony and living tradition.

At Monsieur Mourier's 1991 conference, the *chocolatier* tradition was similarly represented as an unchanging set of work practices and associational rituals effortlessly reproduced through time. The concept of immutable tradition was symbolized by the display of a *metate* and roller and has been endorsed by some scholars, both historians and folklorists, French and foreign, who have written on the history of chocolate in southwest France. For example, two recent histories of chocolate contrast the radical technological innovations of the Protestant nations of Northern Europe with the static conservatism of the Catholic countries

Figure 4. Display of a *metate à l'aztèque,* Pau Chocolate Conference, 1991.

of the South (Coe and Coe 1996, 236; Schivelbusch 1992). Spain, Italy, and France all fall into the second category. The Coes use southwest France as an example of the "picturesque survivals of ancient ways of making chocolate" and note that in the 1870s, confectioners and pharmacists "still had their chocolates ground on *metates à l'aztèque* . . . by mostly Spanish and Portuguese Jews who traveled from house to house with their chocolate stones" (236). The Coes' conclusions draw heavily on work published in early twentieth-century French folklore publications (Aranzadi 1920; Blanchard 1909). Although their account supports localist claims of authenticity, it gives a misleading impression of the region as a static backwater and ignores the ongoing strategic adaptation of local *chocolatiers* to new technology and market conditions—including producers' astute use of chocolate historiography and folklore for their own strategic ends. It likewise neglects the restructuring of the *chocolatier's* craft, the redefinition of the skills required for mastery, and its tenacious persistence alongside the companion crafts of the confectioner and the *pâtissier.* One can best follow these changes through the

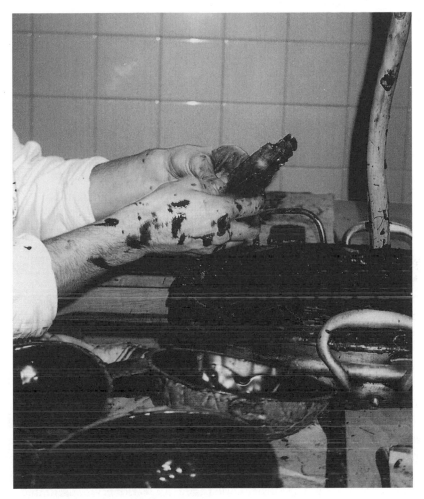

Figure 5. Chocolate dipping room, Dalbaitz workshop, 1991.

intertwined histories of two local confectionery houses and of the people who owned or worked in them.

## The Dalbaitz and Etchegaray Houses

The Dalbaitz house, currently an obligatory stop on the Port Neuf in Bayonne, was founded by Gaston Bernard Martin Dalbaitz and his wife in 1895.[9] Born in the Pyrenean mountain village of St.-Jean-

Pied-de-Port in 1870, Dalbaitz had come to Bayonne to apprentice in a pastry and confectionery business at the age of fifteen. After finishing that apprenticeship, he had found work in one of the most reputable *chocolateries* of the day, the Etchegaray house, on the rue Pannecau in the heart of Petit Bayonne.

Founded in 1815, the Etchegaray house, like others in Bayonne and the surrounding area, made its chocolate from cacao beans. When Dalbaitz worked there in the late 1880s, the house was in its fourth generation of family ownership and it specialized in the fabrication of solid, dark chocolate bars known as *billes*. Chocolate production was divided into separate processing phases involving steam-powered machines. There was a roaster *(torréfacteur)*, a hulling and winnowing machine *(tartare)*, a machine for heating and crushing the cacao beans to render a chocolate liquor *(moulin à cacao)*, another for blending it with pulverized sugar *(mélangeur)*, and a grinding machine *(broyeuse)* in which the cooled chocolate mass was ground to a finer, more homogenous consistency, and, then reheated and reintroduced to the blender *(mélangeur)* to make it smoother and more malleable. In a final processing phase, a machine *(mouleuse, boulineuse)* compressed, weighed, and channeled the chocolate into metal molds, where it was set by a vibrating mechanism *(tapoteuse)* that constantly removed air pockets from the chocolate, thus ensuring it would settle evenly in the molds.

Dalbaitz worked as a salaried journeyman until he had mastered the craft basics and saved enough money to realize his dream of setting up shop in Bayonne. Since self-employment in the provisioning crafts was (and remains) premised on the work of a married couple, the creation of a new business usually occurred simultaneously with marriage. Monsieur and Madame Dalbaitz founded their confectionery house immediately after their marriage in 1895. They rented a storefront on the Port Neuf and a workshop several blocks away. Monsieur Dalbaitz directed workshop production and his wife undertook sales in the boutique. Since a fully equipped workshop demanded a costly capital investment, the Dalbaitzs initially specialized in cookie and sugar candy confectionery production requiring only hand tools. After approximately six years in business, they purchased a confectioner's grinding machine, for the fabrication of their house specialty, *tourons*. They produced a full line of sugar candies and introduced a more limited line of dipped chocolate bonbons and molded figurines, purchasing their chocolate *couverture* from two industrial Swiss firms with branches in Bordeaux, Suchard and Tobler.

By the late nineteenth century, the skills required to roast, grind, and blend cacao beans were being gradually displaced from small-scale family manufacture to industrialized mass production. The technological innovations that transformed chocolate from a costly drink to a cheap food also made mass-produced products such as *couverture* more widely available. Over the course of the twentieth century, the invention of increasingly powerful and efficient industrial-sized machinery permitted the cost-effective transformation of cacao beans into more perfectly refined and flavorful chocolate products. Industrial manufacturers, Swiss, French, and Belgian firms, readily initiated strategies of selling small quantities of *couverture* to small and medium-sized producers in a number of food trades. The prices, sales terms, variety, and often superior quality of their products were more attractive to artisans than those offered by previous suppliers, small-scale family firms. Despite this competition from mass production, small manufacturers such as the Etchegaray house in Bayonne continued to thrive in the first half of this century by selling their finished chocolate bars, *billes,* and their own chocolate *couverture* to dozens of tiny retailers in the southwest and northern Spain.

In 1905, after ten years in business, the Dalbaitzs moved their business across the street after purchasing a four-story building in a choice location under the *arceaux* of the Port Neuf. Here they created an elegant Belle Epoque–style boutique and catered to a cosmopolitan clientele used to the latest Parisian taste fashions, most notably, dipped chocolate confectionery. Beginning in the 1890s, dipped chocolates became a more important part of local production, stimulated by elite tourist demand.

In the same period, a number of tearooms featuring hot chocolate opened in Bayonne and Biarritz. One tearoom adopted the name La Maison des Rois (House of Kings) because of its patronage by royals when the Basque coast boasted a clientele of "exiled kings and reigning princes" (Constantin 1933, 19). The owner of the Aguirre house, situated on the Port Neuf since its creation in 1854, traveled to Paris in 1890 to survey the most fashionable confectioneries there. After that trip, a tearoom was added and new house specialties were created, including *chocolat à l'ancienne* (hot chocolate) and dipped chocolate bonbons. In 1894 seven new candies were introduced at the Aguirre house.

In a decision that mirrored this trend, the owner of the Etchegaray house, Auguste Etchegaray, sent his oldest son, Georges, to Paris in 1919 to learn to make dipped candies. During the interwar period, Georges

Etchegaray oversaw the creation and sale of twenty different sugar and chocolate candies. Their candy centers included their most popular *praliné* (made from 50 percent caramelized nuts, both almonds and filberts, and 50 percent chocolate *couverture*), nougat, whole roasted nuts, marzipan, alcohol, and macerated cherry and raisin, as well as three flavored chocolate centers made with butter but no cream. They were hand-dipped in the dark chocolate *couverture* produced from beans supplied by a Bordeaux cacao broker, Touton.[10] Although it is impossible to know what kinds of cacao beans the owners purchased during this period, Michel Carré, an employee who worked there from 1940 to 1953, has indicated that during his tenure at the Etchegaray house only cheaper forasteros from the plantations of Ivory Coast, a French West African colony, were used.

The period immediately following World War I was one owners remember with great nostalgia in part because of their high-status clientele. The Dalbaitz house regularly sold exquisite Limoges porcelain and Lalique crystal containers filled with candies valued at $400 in Bayonne. Aguirre confectionery gifts were presented in boxes covered in fine leather and in baskets decorated with porcelain doll heads. The Dalbaitz and Aguirre houses counted French literary personalities, Spanish aristocrats, and, later, English nobles such as the Duke and Duchess of Windsor among their clientele. The Spanish monarch Alphonse XIII (1886–1941) came regularly to Bayonne to buy Etchegaray chocolates, each time snarling traffic because he insisted that his chauffeur double-park in the narrow street in front of the *chocolaterie.*

In spite of their success, the Dalbaitzes faced the dilemma of family succession as they approached retirement in the late 1920s. They had no family heirs able or willing to continue operation of the house and so put it up for sale. The Joliots, a craft family from Pau (a city in the Pyrenean foothills southeast of Bayonne) anxious to capitalize on the luxury tourist market in Biarritz, had purchased a store there in 1929 and, given its immediate success, the following year (1930) seized the opportunity to purchase the Dalbaitz house in Bayonne. In 1929, when the Joliots decided to expand their business to the Basque coast, they had a flourishing six-store business with one small production facility in Pau. The founder, Paul Joseph Joliot-Verges (1852–1912), was one of ten children born to a peasant family in a tiny rural commune in the High Pyrenees. He came to Pau and apprenticed first with a liqueur distiller and then with a confectioner (*confiseur,* or sugar candy maker), where he learned to make preserved fruits, jams, marzipan, caramels, and hard sugar candies. He created a confectionery business in his home immediately after his marriage in 1880. He and his wife sold goods through a first-floor window before they were able to build a separate workshop on an adjoining property.

The Joliots had three sons, Louis, Ulysse, and Raymond, born in 1884, 1886, and 1891. Their business expanded rapidly, and as their three sons came of age, they were trained on the job in the family workshop and progressively drawn into the business. In 1911, one year before the death of the founder (1912), the family purchased a choice commercial property in downtown Pau and a second just a short walk away in 1914. In the decade following the founder's death, all three sons married, in 1913, 1915, and 1919, respectively. Their wives began a lifetime role in the business, each assuming primary responsibility for one of the three sales boutiques in Pau. The organization of production in the workshop was directed by the brothers and the operation of the boutiques by their widowed mother and wives. In 1919, with the family succession assured, the Joliot brothers purchased a new expanded production facility. In the excellent economic climate of the 1920s, the family also expanded their outlets, acquiring two stores in the Pyrenean mountain spa town of Cauterets (1921, 1924), a boutique in the pilgrimage city of Lourdes (1929), and, as we have seen, the Basque coast stores and workshop in Biarritz (1929) and Bayonne (1930). Beginning in 1919, they produced both sugar and chocolate candies *(confiserie, chocolaterie)*. These crafts were often practiced simultaneously in the southwest since they required mastery of certain common ingredients—sugar, nuts, and fruits—and shared similar production rhythms determined by the seasonal and ceremonial nature of confectionery sales. The Joliots purchased their *couverture* from the Swiss firm, Tobler.[11]

As in other confectionery houses, a structural hierarchy placed fully skilled workers in a superordinate position relative to less-skilled workers and apprentices. However, in contrast to the pastry businesses of the period (see Clavel 1962; Zarca 1987), confectionery workshops employed both men and women in production. Work tasks were gendered and work stations separated so that women rarely worked next to men. The main area of the workshop was devoted to the preparation of chocolate and sugar candy centers, and twelve workers were employed there. Craft families like the Joliots recruited salaried workers, both men and women, from rural farming and working-class families when they were young and unskilled. They provided them with on-the-job training, molding them to the particular rhythms and ethos of the family workshop. They sought to identify and retain a cadre of workers in both the workshop and the boutique whose trustworthiness was unquestioned and, ideally, whose personal circumstances precluded their departure to become small independents (and future competitors) in their turn.

Young men recruited in their early teens began by performing the unskilled, repetitive tasks of preparing raw materials—pitting, shelling, sorting—and delivering finished goods. They advanced slowly over time to the mastery of the multiple transformations of the basic raw materials (sugar, nuts, fruits, and chocolate *couverture*) from grinding, mixing, flavoring, and cooking to shaping and cutting. Their full line of sugar candies included toffees, caramels, hard sugar candies, marzipan, marshmallows, and medicinal lozenges, as well as chocolate-dipped *praliné* and liqueur centers.

In the Joliot workshop, as in other artisanal *chocolateries* and pastry businesses, there was little division of labor. Even though the workshop was divided into specialized work stations, workers often rotated from one station to the next at regular intervals so they could master all aspects of production. Indeed, a full-fledged artisan was, and still is, expected to possess the skill required to perform all the basic operations subsumed within the craft. However, this did not mean that all workers were equally experienced, skilled, or hardworking. In fact, full-fledged artisans were ranked according to skill and experience as the first *(le premier)*, the second *(le second)*, and so forth. It was generally assumed that the most experienced craftsmen were also the most skilled. Exceptions to the rule tended to confirm it.

In the main area of the Joliot workshop, the most skilled and valued work station was the stove, which involved the metamorphosis of sugar and chocolate into candy syrups, sugar creams, preserved fruits, and caramelized nuts for *praliné* centers. When the grandson of the founder, Maurice Joliot, began his apprenticeship in 1938, in addition to the family owner, his Uncle Raymond, there were two senior workers, each with more than twenty years' experience, who worked primarily at this work station. Maurice Joliot recalled how one of them initially refused to divulge what he knew because he feared that doing so would compromise both his workplace position and his authority. Other accounts of artisanal work during this period reveal that in some workshops only the family owner or the head of production had access to the original house recipes. Sometimes the owner would arrive in the workshop before the workers to measure out and prepare the basic ingredients himself. Many artisans in the southwest and elsewhere described how they had to find clever ways to "steal" craft secrets in order to acquire the empirical knowledge needed to become fully skilled (Blasquez 1976; Coy 1989; Kondo 1990; Perdiguier 1977; Zarca 1987).

Maurice Joliot's detailed description of the family workshop began with and centered on the main workshop area—a work space associated with the skilled work of male workers. It was only later in the interview that he described two additional work stations staffed by women. In a small room located next to the furnace, women tempered and hand-coated chocolate centers, which, after being allowed to set, were carried to a third station on the second floor of the workshop where *plieuses,* or women wrappers, hand-packaged them.

The work women did was specialized and limited to one facet of production—the tempering and dipping of chocolate. The proper tempering of chocolate requires considerable skill and is critical because it determines the sheen, texture, and taste of the finished candy. The women tempered chocolate without the benefit of thermometers, relying instead on a purely empirical understanding of the heated raw material. After providing a detailed description of the crystallization of cocoa butter fat that is at the core of the tempering process, Maurice Joliot dismissed the women's skill as purely experiential: "You see, they could never explain what they were doing. As for my apprenticeship, I was just told to be quiet and watch." The *chocolatières,* as they were called, developed an intimate sensory mastery of the material by smelling and feeling the heat of the chocolate mass against their skin, by visually measuring the final result for a brilliant gloss, and by tasting the cooled candy for the cleanest bite under the teeth and the smoothest consistency on the tongue.

Although their skill was acquired experientially over time like their male counterparts, women were not considered skilled workers—artisans—in the same sense. This became apparent to me when I asked for the total number of workshop workers in the 1930s. Joliot counted twelve. Puzzled, I asked if that included all three stations. He paused and replied, "Of course not, I mean the [main] workshop [not the chocolate dipping room]." Joliot had counted only those positions in the main area, occupied by men, which held out the potential, if not the certainty, of becoming fully skilled. The positions in the dipping room were semi-skilled, involving specialized tasks; those in the wrapping room required virtually no skill. In the mid-1930s the Joliots purchased a machine to do the time- and labor-intensive work of wrapping the individual candies, thus limiting the number of *plieuses* to two.

Both the workshop acquired in Pau in 1919 and the one purchased with the boutique in Bayonne in 1930 were equipped with only coal-burning furnaces, stoves, hand tools, and very few machines. In response to increasing sales, family owners preferred to hire more workers rather than to mechanize their workshops. Maurice Joliot and other owners pointed out that in France, until 1936, there was virtually no labor legislation mandating paid vacation, length of work week, or overtime compensation or regulating shop floor routines and management–labor relations. Similarly, the comprehensive social security system providing health, retirement, disability, and unemployment protection for all workers was not legislated until after World War II. Labor costs were so low that it was often cost-effective to increase the workforce and have work performed manually rather than invest in expensive machinery, even when the technology was available. Moreover, *chocolatiers* and confectioners faced no competition from mass distribution outlets or industrialized producers of dipped chocolate candies.

By 1938, when Joliot began his apprenticeship, the retail business had developed sufficiently to permit the wholesaling of candies to pastry makers and confectioners in Pau and the outlying villages. The family had made the important decision to make its own chocolate from beans and had acquired the necessary machinery. The inventory of machines provided by Joliot was virtually identical to those in the Etchegaray workshop in Bayonne. Unfortunately, just as they were ready to begin production, France declared war on Germany and the accompanying disruptions precluded this planned expansion.

The outbreak of the war and the German occupation of the entire Atlantic coast dealt a severe blow to the regional economy. The French state, led by Marshall Pétain's collaborationist government in Vichy, was forced to ration basic foodstuffs such as bread, sugar, and pasta beginning in September 1940, and to extend rationing to all other foods including chocolate in 1941. As a staple of the diet, the bread ration for adults in 1940 was 350 grams a day; in contrast, the chocolate ration for the same category was 250 grams a month (Azéma 1979, 160–165).

Professional associations such as the Union of Industrial Chocolate Makers had the responsibility of delegating regional representatives to oversee the distribution of rationed foodstuffs within their respective areas. The head of the Etchegaray house, Georges Etchegaray, was responsible for distributing both cacao beans to manufacturers of chocolate (there were sixteen on the Basque coast in 1941) and semi-finished chocolate products to pastry makers and *chocolatiers* like Dalbaitz who specialized in dipped candies. The distributions of cacao and chocolate were based on proof of the volume of production during the preceding three years. All foodstuffs became scarce as the war wore on, and there was enormous pressure for both individuals and businesses to resort to both barter and the underground market.

The World War II Vichy period remains an enormously problematic and charged topic of discussion in France. One French historian produced a pathbreaking book, *Le syndrome de Vichy de 1944 à nos jours* (Rousso 1990), which centers on memories and representations of the war. Rousso plotted successive phases in which the French have constructed memories of this painful past. He argued that during the first phase, at the 1944 liberation, the bitter wounds of defeat and occupation could not be confronted or healed by a collective remembering and mourning because of the deep ideological divisions in the nation. Despite this "failed mourning," a new national consensus was forged in the early 1950s around a useful fiction. Both Gaullists and Communists, representing the main political currents of postwar France, succeeded in imposing a history of the universal French resistance to Nazi tyranny. During this second phase, painful memories of collaboration and persecution of Jews, Freemasons, and leftists were largely repressed in favor of remembrances celebrating only French resistance and heroism throughout the war. Numerous postwar politicians perpetuated and institutionalized this myth of universal resistance in official state commemorations from the liberation of Paris in 1944 to the early 1970s.

In a third phase that began in the early 1970s and continues to swell in intensity (see Conan and Rousso 1998), a plethora of films, documentaries, historical texts, and personal memoirs have extensively examined the Vichy period and postwar commemorations of it in an important effort to deconstruct the Gaullist myth and to reconstruct a different history. The new historiography of this period privileges collective and personal memories as a critical means to reestablish a more objective and truthful chronicle of it. Indeed, the field of memory has received the most systematic attention from those historians whose work examines the Vichy period.

Georges Etchegaray's niece, Madame Rénaud, and an Etchegaray employee, Michel Carré, remembered chocolate production during the war years. This remembrance is important because it was the only detailed discussion of the war years that I was ever able to conduct with or without a tape recorder. The sequel to Rousso's first book (Conan and Rousso 1998) seeks to refute the widespread notion that the French are still covering up their wartime past. However, my field research suggests strongly that the memories of *chocolatiers* who lived through the war could only be evoked in the most elliptical fashion. I reproduce this segment in some detail because of what it reveals, suggests, and elides. Carré began by describing his arrival at the Etchegaray business and alternatively addressed his narrative to his former employer's niece, Madame Rénaud, to her husband, and to me.

I came to work on the 11th of March 1940 at the age of fifteen, with my mother because in those days when you began a job your parents formally introduced you to your new employers. [Turning to Madame Rénaud] Your uncle needed help in the office because he had just been chosen the union delegate for *chocolatiers* in the southwest and that meant regular trips to Paris. When I came to work, they were selling chocolate for 13F a kilo, but soon the government set the price at 16F a kilo so that was already a good bonus for us.

Madame Rénaud interjected:

Yes, my uncle [Georges Etchegarary] used to say that chocolate manufacturers made money during the war.

To which Michel Carré responded:

Yes, but I must say, obviously, cacao shipments diminished as the war wore on, I don't know why the Allies allowed cacao shipments to get through, but we did have cacao during the entire period. . . . We even continued to make bonbons but with bizarre concoctions made of pumpkin and fig centers. Also your uncle set up a special rationing list for his friends, and I can tell you that new friends were sprouting like mushrooms [laughter].

He paused and continued on a more serious note:

[turning to me] There were so many people who really suffered from the food rationing . . . we had to put up a sign in German that said the *chocolaterie* was producing chocolate only for the French population.

Madame Rénaud:

Everyone suffered from the rationing, especially the lack of bread rations because we ate so much bread in those days, now consumption [of bread] has fallen to nothing.

Michel Carré:

to 150 grams a day.

Madame Rénaud:

Yes, but then we ate an enormous amount of bread. Now there are other things to eat.

Carré:

But I want to thank you as a representative of the Etchegaray family because throughout the entire war we only had enough work for one full week a month, maximum, but no one was ever laid off and everyone received full monthly wages. When the Germans came looking for workers [to conscript as laborers in German factories], we'd get word and start up the machines just as they entered so they wouldn't take any of our workers. Not everyone was that honest. One thing *chocolatiers* did . . . [turning to me]. You see in normal times, the winnowing machine hulled and separated the roasted beans from the shells and the seeds and then these were discarded. But during the war, some dishonest *chocolatiers* took the seeds and a part of the shells and added them back to the chocolate mass. You see the union set rigid production standards and we were allowed 20 percent total loss during the roasting of the beans and 3 percent on the chocolate mass, so by adding in the shells and seeds, they could get an additional 2 percent gain . . . as things got worse, the underground market price for chocolate soared, it was worth a 1000F a kilo at that time.

Madame Rénaud interrupted, addressing her comments to both Carré and me, insisting:

My uncle never had anything to do with the black market, we didn't earn a cent from the black market. I admit that for shoes, for instance, it happened that we would exchange chocolate for a pair of shoes, or give a little of our wine for a liter of milk, but that was the barter system *(le troc)*, it wasn't dishonest . . . but it is true that there were people who earned a lot of money during the war.

Michel Carré's story of the war years is a contradictory one that was constrained and shaped by its telling in the presence of a family member of his former employer as well as a foreign ethnographer. On the one hand, it gives voice to a master narrative on the occupation as Carré recounted the honesty of the Etchegaray family, their unswerving protection of their workers, and their courageous resistance to German occupiers. Indeed, my attempts to elicit talk about the war years from other *chocolatiers* prompted them to recount similar but truncated tales of unimpeachable conduct in the face of terrible adversity.

On the other hand, Carré's story subverts this narrative in a number of ways. His effusive thanks to the "family representative" for their honorable wartime behavior is telling because it suggests that this behavior was exceptional. His detailed knowledge of the process whereby chocolate was adulterated for profit strongly implies that such dishonest production practices were not uncommon. Similarly, his recounting of his employer's plan to provide his friends with chocolate reveals the fiction of a strictly equitable rationing system.

This tale was also the attempt of a salaried worker to remind both his former employers and a resident foreigner of the privileged position and tidy profits that some business owners enjoyed during the war. Carré had to work in 1940 because his dream of continuing his formal education had been thwarted by illness and what he described in the beginning of the interview as his family's poverty. His wartime chronicle thus conveyed a clear picture of how the rationing and pricing system put in place by the Vichy government actually enabled some *chocolatiers* to make money. His mention of the price of chocolate on the underground market may also have been intended to correct the myth that few people engaged in such practices. The temptation for owners to sell their chocolate on the black market for 1000F a kilo versus the official government price of 16F a kilo must have been great indeed.

The wartime conduct of small family entrepreneurs, particularly in the food trades, has attracted considerable attention. Many fictional and historical accounts center on their mercenary exploitation of the underground market to turn a wartime profit. Salaried workers and city dwellers often saw farmers and shopkeepers such as grocers, butchers, bakers, and dairy food sellers as selfish profiteers who abused the public trust. Because of their control over scarce foodstuffs, they were "feared, respected, and as a whole, scorned and, even, envied" (Azéma 1979, 156). In an enormously popular life history entitled *Grenadou, paysan français* (Grenadou, French Peasant), the protagonist unabashedly described his many illicit activities (Grenadou and Prévost 1966, 204–205). The equally popular novel, *Au bon beurre* (The Good Grocers) (Dutourd 1952), made into a 1992 Claude Berri film, focused on the insatiable greed of the married owners of a Parisian grocery store who amassed a personal fortune by selling rationed foodstuffs on the underground market.[12] Salaried workers were often at the mercy of small shopkeepers. As Carré and Madame Rénaud rightly emphasized, many French people without the connections or the financial means to supplement their food rations suffered great deprivations during the war.

In the southwest, as elsewhere in France, young men were conscripted to work in German factories or sent to youth work camps run by the Vichy government. Others fled in order to escape the forced conscriptions of the Compulsory Work Service and lived in hiding in Pyrenean villages on the Spanish side of the border. Maurice Joliot and his younger brother Henri were conscripted and spent the entire war in Germany, but their cousin Paul Joliot escaped forced conscription. As a result of wartime disruptions many *chocolateries* closed their doors permanently. Others shifted their productive capacity. During the immediate postwar period family owners who had continued to make their own chocolate from beans reassessed their businesses' prospects in light of the intensified competition from industrialized mass production. Faced with the necessity of investing large sums in updated machinery and of continuing to purchase adequate supplies of cacao beans at highly unstable prices, eventually all of the sixteen producers on the Basque coast ceased production of chocolate from beans. In Pau, immediately after the war, the Joliots sold all their unused machinery at a considerable loss and reverted to making candies from industrially produced *couverture*. In 1953 the Etchegaray house closed after 138 years of continuous family operation. Of the seven Bayonnais *chocolateries* listed in the 1936 commerce and trade register in the archives of the Bayonne Chamber of Commerce and Industry, only two specialized *chocolateries* still operate: the Dalbaitz and the Aguirre houses.[13]

The postwar transformations of the Joliot and Dalbaitz workshops in Pau and Bayonne illustrate the ongoing evolution of the craft in a political economy marked by mass tourism, changing confectionery habits, new technology, and increasingly high labor costs. When the Joliot family purchased the Basque coast businesses in 1929 and 1930, it was decided that the eldest son, Louis, would move permanently to Bayonne with his wife and family. Shortly before the outbreak of the war in 1939, Louis's only son Paul took his place beside his father in the workshop after completing training at Tobler, the Swiss *chocolaterie* in Bordeaux. In the late 1940s, with the end of rationing, the Joliots looked to increase their workforce. One woman, Dora, who entered the Dalbaitz workshop in 1948 at nineteen years of age and labored at the same work station for thirty-eight years, described how fully skilled family owners presided over a tiny semi-skilled female work force permanently assigned to specialized work stations. The Joliots recruited young, unmarried women from rural Basque communes, from which there has historically been a large outmigration, and hired young women from working-class families settled around the industrial iron works north of Bayonne at Boucau, the birthplace of Parisian *chocolatier* Robert Linxe.

It was difficult to collect life histories from retired female workers because the owners always insisted on being present. In spite of this presence, Dora, like Michel Carré, found subtle ways to assert her voice as a worker and to critique the practices of her employer. Although she defended the Dalbaitz workplace, insisting, "We were more like family, it wasn't, you know, the boss wants this and the boss wants that." She continued in a semi-facetious tone, "We worked such long hours in those days . . . you know it was forbidden to be sick, you couldn't be married, children were forbidden too [by employers]. You know, Monsieur Paul was very close with his money and every week he would call us individually into his office to pay us—he gave us our overtime in cash."

Dora advanced to share the important task of tempering and hand-coating the candy centers with "Monsieur Paul" only when an older worker fell ill and left work. Even when the Joliots built a new workshop in 1960, they did not mechanize their workshop, preferring instead to perform the work manually. In the early 1980s, when Paul Joliot's son-in-law, Patrick Sarlate, was trained in the family workshop, there was still no hot water heater, specialized hand tools, or machines except the vintage 1901 grinding machine that Louis Joliot acquired with the business in 1930. The production pace of the late 1940s had remained the same. Family owners and workers began Christmas production in late September and toiled six days a week. As December approached the work days steadily increased from eight to twelve hours. During the week before and after Christmas, work began at eight and proceeded until all the orders were filled, even if it meant several consecutive fourteen-, fifteen-, or sixteen-hour days.

Control of the Joliot business in Pau shifted to Odette and Maurice's daughter and son-in-law in the early 1980s, and in Bayonne to Paul's daughter and son-in-law, Patrick Sarlate, in 1986, when Paul Joliot died unexpectedly. The 1980s business climate was considerably different from that of earlier periods. Comprehensive legal reforms were undertaken in the 1960s and 1970s that had the effect of drawing artisan entrepreneurs into standard business, fiscal, and labor codes as well as establishing uniform mandatory training and certification programs in public educational institutions for artisanal apprentices. As a result, artisans enjoyed added legal protections but also faced higher operating costs as well as increasing pressure to comply with state-mandated labor, management, accounting, and training regulations. The appearance of new craft technology and an increased middle-class tourist clientele in search of less costly but "authentic" hand-crafted gifts also had an impact on the organization of production and the definition of skill. The demand for chocolate gifts in costly crystal containers or in luxury gift boxes (*boîtes*) declined in favor of candies less extravagantly packaged (in *ballotins*). Over the last fifteen years, the chocolate has become as important as its presentation.

Since 1986, Patrick Sarlate has directed production and progressively mechanized the workshop, bringing in efficient, small-scale machines for shelling nuts, pitting cherries, grinding chocolate, sugar, and nut mixtures, mixing candy dough, and tempering and coating candy centers. One machine, the *enrobeuse,* has had a dramatic impact on production since it appeared in an artisanal size on the French market in the early 1970s. This is the machine used to temper the chocolate *couverture* and to enrobe candy centers. It enabled *chocolatiers* to coat the same number of centers in six hours that had required two weeks to hand-dip.

These machines permitted the mechanization of the most repetitive and time- and labor-intensive aspects of production. They allowed fewer workers to increase production while working shorter hours. In the Joliot workshop in Bayonne in 1991, three workers plus the family owner now work only four and a half days a week, in contrast to the seven employed in 1948. This pattern continues except at Christmas, Easter, and the peak August period, when by intensifying the pace of production, working longer hours, and taking on temporary help—frequently kin or part-time workers are hired to perform unskilled tasks—the necessary quantities of goods can be produced within a shorter period of time. For instance, the production of Christmas chocolates now begins one month later, in late October.

The recent promotion of *grand cru* chocolates has put an added emphasis on high-quality ingredients and the rapid turnover of freshly made stock. As we have seen, Parisian *chocolatiers* such as Linxe and Constant privilege increasing varieties of fragile *ganache* centers. For the last ten to fifteen years, local *chocolatiers* have been increasing the flavor assortments and the quantity of goods. Between 1951 and 1986, the Dalbaitz house line scarcely changed; there were twenty-one Dalbaitz house specialties—virtually the same assortments of candies as those produced by the Etchegaray house. Between 1986 and 1991 six new candies, all *ganaches,* had been created and a seventh was being perfected. It is not uncommon for *chocolatiers* to produce a regular line of thirty-five to forty-five different kinds of candies. Some *chocolateries* boast up to seventy different house specialties.[14]

Another change in the workplace has involved the gradual replacement of the semi-skilled female workers by the new artisanal machines and male workers with specialized training. When Dora retired in 1986, she was replaced by Francis, a worker who had completed a formal apprenticeship and earned a specialized state diploma in chocolate and sugar candy production. Although two women work full time, they specialize in the production of the house specialty, the *touron;* Francis and Patrick Sarlate are the only fully skilled workers. In Pau, the Joliots had installed a new, fully mechanized workshop and employed only male producers in their workshop.

The rapid disappearance of *chocolateries pures* has not meant the local extinction of the craft. Rather, the recent demand for high-quality dark chocolates has prompted a number of established *pâtisseries* to incorporate the craft by hiring *chocolatiers* (all of whom are also confectioners) and/or by training their full-fledged *pâtissiers* in chocolate production. A number of factors have facilitated this process. First, the skills required to produce chocolate and sugar are closely related to and overlap with those acquired in the companion craft of pastry production. The use of chocolate in the fabrication of fresh pastries has increased sharply along with the demand for dark chocolate over the last twenty years. Second, the appearance of artisanal machines for tempering and coating chocolate centers has accelerated the adoption of this craft within *pâtisseries* and even within some bakeries. Without these machines, it took Patrick Sarlate two years to master the craft, including what he described as long and frequently frustrating hours next to Dora learning to temper the chocolate. Now that precision machines automatically temper and maintain the chocolate at the appropriate temperature for coating candy centers, mastery of this skill requires less time. Full-fledged skill centers on the creation of individualized artistic creations, in taste, in the form of signature recipes, and, in aesthetics, in the form of chocolate sculptures, paintings, pottery, and lamps.

The adoption of chocolate making within *pâtisseries* has also had the effect of reinforcing the traditional gendered division of labor in the food crafts: only male artisans produce. This in turn mirrors what many saw as the remarkably clear rules regarding the appropriate familial and strictly gendered division of labor among craft family owners, with the owner in the workshop and his wife in the boutique.

In 1991 most Basque coast pastry makers produced a supplementary line of chocolate and sugar candies. Some pastry makers had switched their primary production to chocolate and sugar while continuing to produce pastries, whereas some *chocolatiers* in Biarritz and Saint-Jean-de-Luz had added a supplementary line of pastries. Indeed, it was common to see two and sometimes more companion crafts included in one business and rare to see a business that limited its productive activity to only one.

## Confectionery Consumers and Markets

The market for confectionery goods was inextricably linked to culturally valued seasonal and social occasions. These included public celebrations such as local festivals, state holidays, private rites of passage such as baptism, first communion, bar mitzvah, engagement, and marriage, and religious observances such as Christmas and Easter. These celebrations continue to be clustered within a seasonal cycle—Christmas in winter, Easter at the onset of spring, Labor Day and communions in May, weddings in early summer and fall, National Independence Day (Bastille Day) and the Festival of Bayonne in July—resulting in an annual cycle of peak and valley production phases.

When asked about the market for confectionery goods, the family owners did not speak in terms of market share, market segmentation, or consumer demographics. Rather, they differentiated among two main groups of consumers who together constituted roughly equal parts of the market for their specialties: local residents (including those who live elsewhere but return regularly on holidays) and vacationing tourists. Among both groups, *chocolatiers* marketed the esoteric cachet of their goods priced in 1991 at 220–300F a kilo. They attempted to increase the numbers of what they call "good" customers among both a local and tourist clientele. Yet they readily acknowledged that a "good" customer meant something altogether different in 1991 than it did during the interwar period, when resident and tourist elites were their primary patrons.

Good local customers were said to be loyal to one business over time and, even, over generations. They were discriminating, demanding personalized service and high-quality goods freshly made on the premises. They eschewed the cheap, mass-produced chocolates sold in the two Belgian franchise outlets that opened in the mid-1980s in Grand Bayonne. They never patronized the convenient hypermarkets located outside the city, which offered abundant parking and longer store hours and sold candies mass-produced by both French and foreign manufacturers for one-half the price of artisanal candies. Good customers were those whose financial means and attachment to tradition meant that they marked important social occasions with confectionery gifts that were both tasteful and abundant. For instance, Madame Abeville and her mother before her always purchased their Christmas gift boxes of assorted candies at the Dalbaitz *chocolaterie*. Now a grandmother herself, Madame Abeville remembered each of her five grandchildren at Easter with the traditional hand-molded chocolate bells, roosters, chickens, or rabbits worth approximately $10 each. Madame Abeville preferred the traditional assortment of Easter figurines at the Dalbaitz house and has noted somewhat disapprovingly the proliferation of an eclectic mix of new figures "borrowed from everywhere," such as the Japanese Ninja turtles featured at a house in Saint-Jean-de-Luz.

Madame Courtois, too, was both a loyal and demanding customer. When planning the first communion celebration of one of her children, she insisted on ordering the traditional individually prepared boxes of sugar-coated almonds *dragées* for each of her guests as well as a center-piece festooned with the candies, worth $200. She appreciated the care artisans took to produce Christmas specialties such as sugared chestnuts *(marrons glacés)*, truffles, and dipped liqueur-macerated cherries. In addition to individuals, private and public-sector businesses were good customers. Indeed, business gifts at Christmas and New Year's constituted an important part of sales because they involved annual orders of gift boxes offered by employers to all of their employees.

Craft families defined the core of a local clientele as bourgeois—middle and upper middle class. Most local customers, young and old, still purchased candies as gifts. However, increasing (although still small) numbers of customers in their thirties and forties were purchasing chocolates for their own consumption. These were established, educated consumers from business and professional backgrounds who prided themselves on their refined palates. They were increasingly aware of chocolate as a product with deep regional roots and were receptive to new cinnamon- and ginger-flavored *ganaches.* They sampled and shared chocolates and cakes with their friends at dinner parties. These were the customers who sometimes ordered extravagant, customized pieces of confectionery art or purchased the pieces featured in boutique window displays such as the huge chocolate chicken coop sold by one local house in 1991 for $250. In addition to this clientele, *chocolatiers* also noted that customers of very modest means also purchased gifts at important religious holidays like Christmas and Easter. For example, there was Madame Leclerc, who cleaned the Anglet town hall for the minimum wage but purchased a $35 Christmas gift box of chocolates for the elderly aunt who raised her.

In contrast to a local clientele, *chocolatiers* also catered to a large, more anonymous middle-class tourist clientele who vacationed on the Basque coast during the summer months of July and August. These were months craftspeople regarded with ambivalence because hotels and campgrounds were full, local roads were clogged with traffic, parking was impossible, and the area was mobbed with tourists. On the one hand, tourists made smaller average purchases than they did before World War II, but their sheer numbers demanded a frenetic work pace. Saleswomen complained that both Parisians and foreigners were demanding and arrogant. On the other hand, heavy tourist traffic, particularly in August, provided owners with their third best sales period after Christmas and Easter.

## Conclusion

Over the past 150 years, the craft of chocolate making was profoundly restructured. The skills required to roast, grind, and blend cacao beans were displaced from small-scale production to industrialized mass production. After the disruptions caused by World War II, many specialty *chocolateries* closed permanently. New technology appeared, labor costs soared, confectionery consumption evolved, and tourism expanded. These changes provoked the increased mechanization of family *chocolateries* and the progressive disappearance of semi-skilled female producers from artisanal workshops. This reinforced a gendered division of labor that separated male producers from female sales help and redefined a hierarchy of skill based on constant innovation in taste, technique, and aesthetic design. This displacement of skills had the effect of drawing companion crafts together within the same workshop—*chocolatiers,* confectioners, and pastry makers.

Basque coast *chocolatiers* have responded to consumer demand for genuine regional chocolates by actively engaging in heritage tourism. Their claims of cultural authenticity have been grounded in the construction and celebration of a new historical narrative surrounding Bayonne as the birthplace of French chocolate, a repository of unchanging craft skills, and a refuge for persecuted minorities. This narrative has relied on several key historical events—the documented arrival of Iberian Jews and the incorporation of the only *chocolatier* guild in Old Regime France. The affirmation of Bayonne as a historically genuine center of chocolate production was contingent upon the suppression of the problematic particulars of that history as well as the virtually total elision of the war years from *chocolatier* craft and personal histories. This was a period when political dissidents and religious minorities—in particular,

Jews—were rounded up, interned, and deported by German and French forces. The international publicity surrounding the 1998 trial of the Vichy functionary operating in southwest France, Maurice Papon, and his conviction for wartime crimes against French Jews over fifty years after the fact reminds us that Vichy is an ever-present past for the French.

From historical claims, we shift our focus to the organizing principles that informed the performance and representation of work in contemporary confectionery houses. In contrast to the selective representation and celebration of a craft life, such as the one provided in chapter 2 by the Parisian master *chocolatier* Linxe, we explore the complex, everyday realities associated with gendered work in less well-known businesses on the Basque coast.

# CHAPTER 5

# What's in a Name?

One of the first things Michel Harcaut showed me when he invited me into his workshop was the dipping fork he used to hand-coat chocolate. He immersed a candy center in the tempered chocolate mass and then carefully positioned it on a customized aluminum sheet that imprinted the house name, Harcaut, on the bottom. I noted that even when he coated his chocolates by machine, he still instructed his apprentice to stamp the house name on the bottom. At first I assumed that this practice was linked to his ongoing effort to make himself known in a town dominated by well-established *pâtisseries* and *chocolateries*. He and his wife Michèle often complained that they had little name recognition since theirs were the newest *pâtisserie* in town. It seemed normal that they would give their name to both their business and their house specialties. Selling house chocolates as signed creations appeared to be a logical, even astute, marketing strategy.

Around the same time I interviewed one of the owners of the Aguirre house. The house name, Aguirre, was also stamped on their candies. Having just heard the house history I was struck by the significance of the house name. It was not that of the current owners, although they have owned the house since 1934. Rather, it was the name of the founder, a shadowy, distant figure about whom the owners knew little. Indeed, since its creation in 1854, the Aguirre house had been sold several times to different craft families and all had retained the founder's name.

## The Confectionery House

Soon after I settled in Bayonne, I paid a visit to the Carrères, the first craft family I had met in 1989. When I asked the owner, Fabrice Carrère, about his house and family, he showed me an article that had appeared in the local newspaper before my arrival. Entitled "Family Businesses," the article featured a large photograph of Fabrice Carrère, his wife, Fabrice's son Simon, and his eight-year-old grandson Benjamin. It described them as a model of the "dynastic spirit" of confectionery houses. At the time I was seduced by the photograph and by Fabrice's obvious pride at having achieved a family succession. Only later did I understand the photograph to be an expression of a cultural ideal, achieved with difficulty and accompanied by conflict. Fabrice Carrère and other *chocolatiers* used the text as a strategic device, like the speeches at the Best Craftsman of France contests, to suppress the contradictions and elide the tensions associated with the everyday operation and intergenerational transfer of confectionery houses. Craft families employed myriad representational strategies to cultivate and project a seamless image celebrating artisanship and familial continuity over time. However, this public image was often belied by their lived practices and the many tales they told themselves and the ethnographer concerning the rise and fall of confectionery houses and the survival of the family name.

*Chocolatiers* worked in and passed on commercial property referred to as the house *(la maison)*, as in the House of Lanvin. Confectionery houses were created by, named for, and traced back to a founding craftsman and his wife. The founder gave his patronym to the business as well as a distinctive stamp to the line of house specialties he developed over the course of his professional life. The model confectionery house was an indivisible unit that existed intergenerationally and comprised a craft family and a commercial property. This property included the name and good will of the business, the workshop machinery and tools, the boutique displays and furnishings, the stock and raw materials, the commercial lease necessary to operate in a given locale, and, on rare occasions, the building(s) in which the goods were produced and sold. Although confectionery houses were closely associated with a particular urban place, such as the Port Neuf in Grand Bayonne, and their commercial value derived in large measure from that location, they could and sometimes did change location. Nonetheless, confectionery houses were designated by family names, not place names, and only survived as long as the patronym perdured.

I came to understand the house as a corporate family unit that held commercial property (ideally) in perpetuity rather than a kinship unit based on lines of descent. The house was a unit of production encompassing the dual roles of enterprise and household. In each generation, a married couple had to be recruited as permanent heads of the house and the family to ensure the continuity of both through time. Since this couple held the family property in trust, they were responsible for increasing house assets in the present and transferring them intact to the next generation. This couple not only controlled but also participated in daily business operations. These included two complementary and mutually reinforcing activities, production and sales, which were organized by gender and skill. Thus male owners oversaw production in the family workshop and their wives supervised sales in the boutique. This arrangement gave the family control over the two basic spheres of business activity and, in theory, ensured the smooth liaison between them. It was inconceivable, except in extraordinary and temporary circumstances, for the male owner to sell goods in the boutique or for his wife to produce them in the workshop.

The inflexibility of this rule regarding the artisanal couple was constantly reinforced for me. For example, I attended the weekly practicum classes for both apprentices and salaried artisans at the Bayonne Chamber of Trades. Salaried workers were following a demanding two-year schedule of evening courses leading to the rigorous examination for the master artisan's diploma *(brevet de maîtrise)*. In 1990 this credential was in theory a state requirement for artisans who wanted to create or purchase and then head their own businesses.[1] Although the class was legally open to both male and female producers, the vast majority of those who actually received this credential were men (Bayonne Chamber of Trades Archives 1991). In 1990 one of the fourteen workers enrolled in the course was female. She explained that she had earned her entry-level vocational diploma and was working at a local *pâtisserie*. When I asked how she got the job, she explained that it was the result of a misunderstanding. The house owner had assumed that she was seeking the sales position he had advertised and did not look carefully at her work papers. When she arrived dressed for the workshop, he was flabbergasted but allowed her to stay. When I met her she had been on the job for six months. She admitted that it had been "very hard" and had made her see all the practical problems of becoming self-employed one day. She dropped out of the course only a few weeks later. One of her male colleagues remarked on her absence. "Did you notice that she didn't return? You see, it was a bad idea because it just doesn't work."

A few months later Monsieur Mourier (see chapter 3) related a story he had heard over dinner with colleagues. They were preparing the succession of their house but had a dilemma. They had two teenagers, a son with no interest in the craft and a daughter with a passion for it. Their daughter had earned the entry-level state diploma and wanted to take her permanent place in the family workshop. Although this couple recognized their daughter's talent, they were reluctant to give their consent. Mourier advised them to send her to an advanced training course in Paris, where she could meet and fall in love with a *pâtissier* or *chocolatier*. They could get married and then both enter the business, he in the workshop and she in the boutique. I asked Mourier why it would not be possible for their daughter to produce and for her mother to handle the boutique. He responded emphatically, "Do you think she would have any authority with the [male] workers? What happens when her mother retires? You mustn't think that she could hire an outsider to take her place! No, she can't be in two places at once, and her place is in the store. There her production knowledge would be a real asset."

The difference between a confectionery house and true kinship-based groups emerged clearly when the issue of succession was examined (compare Kondo 1990, 121–137). Because the house was a corporate group established in perpetuity, the critical issue was its continuity. The one absolute imperative was to identify and recruit two successors to a lifetime role in the operation of the house. However, the rules used to accomplish this goal allowed for considerable flexibility. This was so because confectionery houses were organized according to a set of positions in a structural work hierarchy, not according to a set of kinship relations. The recruitment of kin, in the sense of blood relations, was an ideal only if other requirements were satisfied. It was by no means the only possible or even the most desirable solution to the dilemma of succession.

The mechanisms used to recruit suitable successors were not absolute rules but rather ranked preferences that could be readily modified according to economic and social circumstances. These mechanisms privileged sons over daughters, kin over non-kin, craft skill over managerial competence, and experiential training with craft masters over formal courses with schoolteachers. Permanently recruiting a skilled son and his capable wife was a cultural ideal. Failing that, a talented daughter and her artisan husband was a highly attractive prospect. However, a family could have a son who had no interest in or talent for the craft. Alternatively, a family could have a son who was interested and talented in both but they might encourage him to pursue a different career path because the local business outlook was poor. Or a family like the Dalbaitzs could have three daughters all of whom married men with established professions and no interest in learning the family craft. In such cases, families usually turned to a skilled outsider or to a trusted apprentice as a possible successor. Conversely, in a prosperous economic climate, the general rule limiting successors to two could be suspended. The three Joliot brothers and their wives were all incorporated as permanent members because sustained business growth permitted the creation of separate Joliot house branches over which each couple had control.

A major goal for owners, like other systems based on the house, was the preservation of family property through impartible inheritance (Flandrin 1979, 79). Unlike the Pyrenean model (Assier-Andrieu 1981; Douglas 1988), which designated houses by the place name, the confectionery house was always identified with its patronym.[2] Indeed, the identity and reputation of the house remained ineffably linked to the founders who gave it their patronym. The problem was that confectionery houses frequently outlived a particular household and even the founding family itself. A house was often owned by several different families over the course of its life. However, owners avoided patronymic discontinuity between successive households because it changed irrevocably the identity of the confectionery house. For this reason, when a house was transferred or sold to successors with different patronyms, such as a married daughter or an outside couple, they usually retained the founders' name. Six of the eight houses investigated in detail here had been sold to new families at least once over the life of the house. All but one of the owners retained the name. Confectionery houses perished if the name was not passed on. Alternatively, they could be reborn and acquire a new identity when successors provoked a radical disjuncture with the past by renaming them.

The family name provided the house with a unique identity just as it distinguished one confectionery house from another. To have value, it had to be constantly reproduced through the fabrication of the individualized line of specialties that established the house reputation. Like the house name, individual candies and cakes were inextricably linked to the founders. For example, sixty-one years after the Dalbaitz house was purchased by the Joliots in Bayonne, some customers still referred to the original house specialty, *tourons,* as "Dalbaitz" candy. House specialties were also baptized *(baptiser)* with individual names that remained constant over the life of the product. While *chocolatiers* and *pâtissiers* generally denied that names were bestowed with any ritual, I participated in one apparent exception to this rule. I was invited to Sunday dinner at the Harcaut home and was advised that Michel was intending to test a new house specialty on his wife Michèle, their three children, a family friend, and me. At the end of the meal there was an exchange of significant looks as the new dessert—a variation on a *charlotte aux poires*— was proudly displayed along with a bottle of champagne. I exclaimed, "Champagne! What's the occasion?" Michèle responded with a twinkle in her eye, "It's a baptism." When I looked perplexed, she smiled and replied, "The cake . . . what do you think about the name 'Susan'?" I stammered something about being honored and we drank to the "birth" of Michel's newest "addition" to the house line, christening it *le (gâteau) Susan*.

The naming of house specialties served a number of purposes. Named candies were a potent semiotic device linking the production of local houses with a shared historical, geographical, and literary patrimony. Southwestern specialties like the Empress's Kiss, the Rock of the Virgin, *pelote basque,* and Rostand recalled, respectively, the glamorous past association of royalty and Biarritz, the enduring natural beauty of the rocky Basque coast shoreline, a popular regional sport, and one of a number of national literary personalities who lived (however episodically) in the area. *Chocolatiers* also chose names that connected their candies to the aristocratic culture of Old Regime France and to the high cuisine created and conspicuously consumed at court. Candies with names such as *Le Marquis, Le Petit Comte,* and *Dauphin* were meant to connote high status and social distinction. Individual names also played on exoticized visions of the origins of chocolate in distant lands, especially Central and South America, and consciously recalled commonly used tropical flavorings such as coffee, tea, and citrus fruits, as well as ground chocolate itself, for example, Caracas, Moctezuma, Guayaquil, Brazilian, and *Jasmin*. These names also linked candies to the gifting relationships that called for their purchase and exchange. Some reflected innocent courtship rituals and love—Caprice, Shepherdess's Heart, and Intoxication—while others evoked eroticized desire and seduction— Temptation, Bacchus, and Don Juan. House specialties were sometimes named for family members. For example, the Harcauts created cakes for each of their three children. In this way both the house, which took the family patronym, and the candies, named for individual family members, remained connected to the founders. If the house outlived the founders, its name and distinctive ethos would survive that household and be reproduced in the line of individualized specialties crafted there. The names of family members, too, outlived them and perdured in the sweets crafted for the social occasions that marked passage through the life cycle. Even ethnographers could achieve a measure of immortality in house product lines. One Bayonnais acquaintance laughed heartily when I suggested he sample my "namesake" at the Harcaut *pâtisserie*. "I'll think of you when I order and eat that cake," he exclaimed.

The Harcauts' house illustrated well this naming principle. After purchasing the Dominguez house in 1982, they dropped the name of the founder. Their predecessors had developed a poor reputation in their later years and the business was sorely rundown. When the Harcauts purchased it they completely redesigned the boutique interior with updated appointments such as rich wood paneling, customized temperature-controlled display cases, and the abundant use of mirrors and glass shelving. They replaced the earthen floor of the workshop and, most importantly, introduced a wholly new product line. When the Harcauts baptized the house with their name, the business created in 1936 by the Dominguez ceased to exist. The Harcauts had little name recognition because they had in effect created a new house. Compared to other house heads in Bayonne, the Harcauts were in the same structural position as the Dalbaitz family when they opened for business in 1895. They were no longer salaried workers but independents. Their place within a craft community composed of self-employed craftsmen could only be established with time.

## Succession of Confectionery Houses

Given the clear preference for achievement through skill and motivation over ascription by birth or marriage as well as the imperative to preserve house integrity intergenerationally, the preparation of the house succession was a constant preoccupation. Once the succession was decided, its implementation was always seen as fraught with potential problems. However, the nature of the problems engendered by the transfer of houses depended on a number of factors: the age and reputation of the house, kin versus non-kin successors, and the socioeconomic climate. For example, the transfer of a house to a son and his wife or to a daughter and her husband could be as or more problematic, although in different ways, than its sale to skilled outsiders.

## Recruiting a Son and Heir

When a son or daughter was identified and accepted a life-time role in workshop production, two pressing issues presented themselves: training and marriage. The challenges posed by the training and marriage of a son are discussed in detail because this succession represented an ideal to be achieved. When a son was recruited as heir, the first priority was his training. Even though he had been born into the craft, he might need to acquire basic training. Alternatively, he might have some familiarity with the basics but need to perfect his command of the family craft(s) or to acquire new, complementary expertise in a companion craft. An ideal scenario involved sending him out of the family business to receive at least part of his training with other craftsmen, either former masters or established agemates of his father. Increasingly popular options were the training courses taught by master artisans in the private culinary schools run by professional organizations and subsidized by the French state.

Gaining experience with different masters before permanently settling into the family business was desirable for a number of reasons. Given the pronounced regional gastronomic diversity in France, working elsewhere permitted exposure to different craft techniques as well as other product lines. Moreover, it was felt that unrelated masters were better able than kin to instill the necessary discipline and work ethic. At the same time, masters were carefully chosen for both their expertise and their ties to the heir's family. It was expected that heirs work hard—just like everyone else—but also receive special attention precisely because they were heirs and future house heads. In cases where heirs could not be sent out of the house, the critical task of training was delegated to experienced workers rather than to their fathers. This situation replicated to some degree the advantages afforded by training outside the house. When sons-in-law were recruited, their position as outsiders largely obviated the necessity for them to train elsewhere. Indeed, as with in-marrying women, the imperative for owners was to neutralize their potential for disruption as outsiders by binding them to and integrating them within the business. The overriding concern was that they learn the craft(s) as uniquely practiced within that house.

When an heir returned to the family business after training elsewhere, he had to reconcile a number of contradictions. He entered a workshop where craftsmen were ordered by experience and skill. Fully skilled craftsmen stood in a superordinate position to less skilled and experienced workers. Apprentices were subordinate to everyone. Despite his status as heir, the son held a subordinate position to more experienced workers and was ranked below his father or father-in-law. The senior craftsman was the master and occupied the summit of the structural hierarchy by virtue of his position as independent owner and as (theoretically) the most skilled practitioner in the workshop. The hierarchical structure of the workshop was encoded linguistically in the forms of address used. The senior craftsman often addressed the craftsmen in his employ with the familiar *tu* form as he did members of his own family. This was almost always the case with craftsmen of long standing or those who began as apprentices in the house. Owners used the *tu* or the polite *vous* form of address with craftsmen whose full-fledged skill and experience made them structural equals. Workers responded with the *vous* form connoting respect as well as their subordinate position. This pattern was replicated at each level down as workers generally used the *tu* form among themselves as equals and to apprentices as inferiors while apprentices responded with the *vous* form. The ambiguity of the son's status in the house was also revealed in language. The senior craftsman used the *tu* form with his son but so did the most experienced workers who had known him as a child and trained him in the basics. On the other hand, workers sometimes eschewed this familiar form with the heir as a sign of the social distance separating them from the future workshop head. Some heirs, such as Serge Mathieu, insisted that workers use *tu* with him. In so doing he signaled his status as a skilled worker just like them and simultaneously reinforced a hierarchical ordering of the workshop based on ongoing practice.

Ordinarily, a senior craftsman was expected to remain the head of the enterprise and household by maintaining an active role in production. The French expression for this, *avoir la main dans la pâte,* is illustrative because its literal translation is "to have a hand in the dough." His influence and authority increased with the number of years he spent working in the house. Until he relinquished control of production to a designated successor, the house head usually retained exclusive power within this sphere. The incoming heir had to accept his authority and to adopt existing workshop practices as well as the established product line. This was what made the house successful and guaranteed the continuity of its name and operations over time. On the other hand, the heir learned or perfected his skill in different houses or by training with well-known masters at culinary schools. This outside experience gave him a new perspective and heightened awareness of the necessity of knowing how to adapt and change. Safeguarding tradition and encouraging innovation was a difficult balancing act in confectionery houses given their hierarchical structure. Heirs often had to work alongside their fathers, deferring to their authority and resistance to change for many years before they were in a position of control.

Monsieur Mourier's own business is a case in point. His son had worked full time in the house since he completed his military service in 1962. In 1990 he turned fifty and his father celebrated his seventieth birthday. Although officially retired, the elder Monsieur Mourier still retained total control over the workshop and business operations. The transfer of authority was always difficult, and the struggle for control often continued even after titular responsibility for the house had passed to the heir. Regardless of who really controlled the workshop and house, producers were distinguished by their rank in age order, namely, Monsieur Mourier, *père* (father) or *fils* (son). It was a ranking system that explicitly referenced and implicitly privileged the older man as pater familias of the house for as long as he lived. The following story traces one house across two generations and illustrates both the possibilities and the problems involved in the transfer of a house to a son and a daughter-in-law.

The Carrère house was the oldest *pâtisserie* in Bayonne and occupied a prime location on the Port Neuf in Bayonne. Louis Carrère and his wife went into debt in order to purchase it in 1944. During the twenty-two–year period of their headship (1944–1966) the house prospered and earned a reputation as one of the best in Bayonne. The Carrères purchased the building in which the house was located, renovated the boutique, creating a tearoom employing five saleswomen, and not only modernized but also expanded the workshop, increasing the number of salaried workers from one to eight. Louis Carrère was a well-known public figure in Bayonne and played an active role in the local craft community. He understood the imperative to innovate. He initially built the house line around the bread and pastry doughs that were his specialty but later broadened it to include fancy confectionery products. Louis Carrère insisted that his only son Fabrice enter the house but master the crafts of confectioner and *chocolatier*.

Fabrice apprenticed in the family workshop for four years before completing his military service and departing with another Carrère worker, Robert Linxe, for the COBA Confectionery School in Bale, Switzerland. He completed an intensive two and a half–month course in choc-olate fabrication and confectionery decoration. In 1952, at twenty-two years of age, he began as a full-time worker in his father's house special-izing in decorative cakes and candies. At his father's insistence he also entered and won numerous regional and national craft contests, earn-ing renown as a confectionery artist. Despite this recognition and the special workshop niche he monopolized, he was, in his own words, al-ways closed up *(enfermé)* in the workshop, with no internal say in house operations and no public role in the local craft community. When Louis Carrère died suddenly in 1966, his son Fabrice finally assumed the posi-tion as house head at age thirty-seven. He had worked under his father since he was fourteen and felt completely overwhelmed by the myriad house responsibilities he had never been trained to shoulder. He con-fessed that it took him years and a Dale Carnegie course in personal pre-sentation to feel secure as house head. In spite of his uncertain begin-nings, everyone agreed that Fabrice Carrère had distinguished himself as an artisan and manager of the business. He was exceptionally proud of having presided over a period of unprecedented profitability for the house. The number of craftsmen in the workshop increased to ten and the net profits to 10 percent of the annual sales turnover.

My fieldwork coincided with the culmination of a prolonged period of tension and conflict between Fabrice and his only son Simon that was ostensibly resolved by the official transfer of house control to Simon in March 1991. Only twelve years after assuming control, Fabrice faced the matter of succession in a particularly acute form. His son had earned a secondary-level baccalaureate degree but had not distinguished himself in school and did not have any specific career plans. Simon spent two years (1976–1978) working part time for his father and requested a per-manent role in the business. Monsieur and Madame Carrère agreed and financed three years of training for him in the best Parisian confection-ery houses, including a nine-month apprenticeship at Robert Linxe's Maison du Chocolat. When Simon returned to work full time in the fam-ily workshop in 1981, problems began almost immediately. The 1980s were marked by a stagnating economic climate, higher operating costs, and a substantial decrease of net profits (from 10 percent of total sales in 1980 to 3.5 percent in 1990). Simon and his father agreed on the ne-cessity for change but disagreed on how to effect it because their views concerning craft work and business management differed greatly.

Simon resisted his father's and the senior workers' authority and, de-spite his lack of experience, attempted to cultivate a more egalitarian ambiance in the house based on his understanding of modern management. He insisted on his right to private personal time and routinely took long lunches at home or indulged his passion for hunting in the fall. He also refused to maintain a full-time presence in the workshop. Instead, he spent more time in the office than the workshop and was perceived as a manager rather than a craftsman. Although he enthusiastically promoted his own gifts as a master *chocolatier,* his true passion seemed to be marketing and public relations. When he did produce in the workshop, he was chronically late and easily distracted. I well remember one November morning when I had been invited to observe Simon make a batch of his signature *ganaches.* He had, on several occasions, reminded me that he was the creator of the winning recipe for *le chocolat de Bayonne.* I waited with Roland, the worker assisting Simon, for ninety minutes because he was on the phone with customers. He finally burst into the workshop flushed with excitement and anxious to share the details of the lucrative order he had just landed. His father became angry and Roland totally exasperated when barely twenty minutes later Simon left again to accept another phone call. When Simon and his father were safely out of earshot, Roland loudly remarked, "I don't know what will happen to this house the day Monsieur [Fabrice] Carrère and his wife retire." As it happened, Fabrice Carrère's failing health gave Simon the necessary leverage to gain control of the business just a few months after Roland's comment.

Many of the people I knew in Bayonne were pessimistic about the change in headship and critical of Simon Carrère because his behavior struck at the very organizing principles of the confectionery house. On the one hand, his refusal to authenticate his craft skill through long hours and positive results in the workshop compromised the respect and authority a master craftsman and house head must cultivate among employees, both artisans and saleswomen. His ongoing conflicts with his father and stubborn rejection of structured and ranked work relations seemed to have the paradoxical effect of subverting them among some younger employees within the Carrère house but of reinforcing them for older workers, members of the craft community, and clientele alike.

## Integrating a Daughter-in-Law

Embedded in the problem of recruiting a skilled heir for the workshop was the imperative that he find a wife willing and able to assume a lifetime role in the retail side of the business. In a confectionery house, the marriage of a designated heir was critical but implied some interesting paradoxes. On the one hand, house identity was inextricably linked to a particular craft family and its lifelong commitment to the business. On the other hand, house continuity depended on the permanent recruitment of an outsider to the household and to the enterprise. Moreover, the gendered division of labor in the house meant that outsiders occupied and controlled the crucial *public* sphere of the boutique. The demanding public nature of their work demanded that they embody the house's good name as they sell the products that carry it on.

Artisanal wives were required to assume sale and merchandising responsibilities that were complex and varied. They involved the cultivation of highly personalized customer relations among a demanding local clientele, the management of a more anonymous but equally demanding tourist clientele, the knowledge of merchandising and marketing techniques, the authority required to manage employees, and the physical stamina needed for long retail hours. Most importantly, artisanal wives had to have an outgoing personality and the ability to relate (at least superficially) with all kinds of people.

Wives also balanced multiple roles related to work and family and were obliged to embody two conflicting cultural ideals. They had the primary responsibility for managing their households (encompassing both the private space of the home and the public space of the boutique) and for raising children. On the one hand, their marketing of elegance and the elite cachet of their goods required that they embrace and project a French bourgeois ideal associated with domestic order, family values, well-raised children (who might take their place in the house), and well-managed, tastefully appointed boutiques. This bourgeois model was characterized by strong familial traditions stressing women's critical role as the principal organizers of a domestic ideal (Le Wita 1994). This ideal stressed their primary duties as cultivators of private space and life style in the home and as authorities in the vital realm of their children's upbringing. Bourgeois women increasingly pursue careers outside the home, but their financial means, educational credentials, and extensive social networks provide both professional rewards as well as the flexibility to oversee personally their children's upbringing. Artisanal wives did not share the same flexibility. Since they usually worked full time alongside their mothers-in-law, they had to delegate the critical responsibility of child rearing to public day care or private caregivers. Although a wife proved her devotion to the house through her work as well as the children she bore, her public role in the boutique often superseded her private role as mother and housewife.

On the other hand, most artisanal wives were not from a bourgeois social milieu, and few had completed the full cycle of secondary education culminating in a baccalaureate degree. Instead, they became part of a particular craft family and were associated with petty bourgeois entrepreneurship. The very nature of craft work required that they adopt the work ethic implicit in small-scale commerce. They could not passively accept their role but had to embrace it enthusiastically, promoting craft work and independent entrepreneurship through their success at performing it. This meant long hours over weekends and holidays, hard work, and very little time for their own children, natal families, or themselves. They could not accompany children to and from school, stay home with them when they were sick, personally oversee their homework, or fully participate in family celebrations at important holidays such as Christmas and the New Year in France. Indeed, their busiest work times coincided with the leisure and holiday time of their customers and their own children.

Many artisanal wives invoked the metaphor of the boutique as theater either directly or indirectly to describe the specific public presentation demanded by their work. During one of my weekly visits to the Parisian *chocolaterie* of Francis and Christiane Boucher in 1989, Christiane made a remark that illuminated the peculiar skills demanded by her work. That morning her husband was beginning fabrication of his Easter figurines—six differently posed chocolate elephants adapted from Jean de Brunhoff's famous character Babar. I greeted her and we chatted for a few minutes before I turned toward the adjoining workshop. With a mischievous smile, she said, "Now you are leaving the stage of the theater *(la scène)* and going behind the scenes, into the wings *(dans les coulisses)*."

I thought little of her comment until I settled in Bayonne in 1990. During my first visit with Madame Carrère she drew explicitly on a theatrical metaphor to describe the skills demanded by work in the boutique:

We are actresses *(comédiennes)*. When we are in the boutique we are on stage and we must play a role, we create a mood. Regardless of how we feel inside we must always be pleasant and attentive to the customers, we must remember their names, important details about their families, their work, their health, their lives . . . events like baptisms, communions, engagements, degrees earned, grandchildren visiting from Paris, trips abroad. . . . We rarely have a script but must be adept at improvising. For example, you may have ten customers in twenty minutes, at a very fast pace, and then a demanding person will come in and you will have to give her fifteen minutes of your time. You must know to avoid certain topics but to always broach others. Some days customers' problems don't interest you because you have a sick child at home or their complaints seem unreasonable to you, all the more so because you have a headache, but you have to feign concern, to listen attentively, and always, always to appear interested.

Michèle Harcaut even suggested that I could only really understand her work (without disrupting it) by observing her exchanges with customers from behind the "curtain," the one-way mirror that separated the boutique from the workshop. The theatrical dimension of women's work in confectionery houses involved a number of skills. These included sustained emotional labor, difficult class negotiations, and the ongoing integration of work and family activities, as well as aptitude in sales and merchandising. However, the demands of work in the boutique have intensified because competition from industrialized mass production and foreign franchise outlets has placed increased importance on customer service and focused attention on modern marketing approaches (see chapter 9).

## Managing Feeling

The essential skills women were required to develop were those of presentation. They described themselves as actresses, their boutiques as the stage complete with props, costumes, and special lighting, and the workshop as the stage wings. Like theatrical performers their production was talk and their audience was live. Like performers their work required intense emotional labor (compare Hochschild 1983, 35–55). In order to fulfill their roles convincingly, women could not act "as if" they had feelings toward their regular customers. Regular customers were adept at recognizing and criticizing commercialized feeling; mere surface acting earned reproaches of indifference and superficiality from them. The owner of the Aguirre house recalled her hurt feelings when a customer of long standing noted her "put-on smile" *(son sourire commercial)* one particularly busy afternoon in the tearoom. Women were obliged to develop and project true feeling for the parts they played. They had to learn deep acting skills that utilized their own emotional memories and experiences.

Artisanal wives experienced daily the strains of putting private emotions to commercial use, of investing public display with personal feeling, and of selling family values in a business setting. Yet many women successfully acted from the heart and took pride in their success at cultivating sincere, personalized relations with a local clientele. Like hostesses in their own homes, they expended great effort to welcome regular customers—remembering names, personal events, and product preferences. They not only spent considerable time advising regular customers on product choices and family celebrations but also assumed the obligations associated with friendship and kinship by willingly providing extra services. They made deliveries, did personal errands for elderly or sick clients, and acted as empathetic confidantes to those with personal problems. For example, Michèle Harcaut was a sensitive listener to heartrending accounts of domestic abuse, family breakup, and widows' loneliness, to bawdy stories of illicit affairs, and to cautionary tales about ungrateful children and tyrannical parents involved in family inheritance disputes. On numerous occasions, she also had to play the role of informed but politically neutral social commentator in response to local, national, and international events such as the Gulf War in 1991.[3]

In order to perform persuasively this emotional labor, artisanal wives drew on a number of strategies. They used the emotional arts expected of them in their roles as mothers and wives within the home. Their work in the confectionery house replicated to a great extent the domestic roles of women as nurturers, family organizers, and social managers. These roles helped to prepare women to accept uneven exchanges as part of the job. Customers could bare their souls, place or cancel orders at the last minute, take fifteen minutes to make a tiny purchase, or complain loudly when dissatisfied. Women, on the other hand, had to suppress their anger or frustration and manage both their own emotions and those of their clientele. Members of craft families and many French customers alike agreed that women's control of the boutique was "normal" given the attributes of *le beau sexe,* the beautiful sex. They were "naturally" at ease with people, tactful in difficult situations, nurturing, patient, and adept at enhancing the well-being of others and had "innate" flair with window dressing and "natural" dexterity with product packaging.

Women employed deep acting and the sense of "as if this were true" in the course of dealing with their clientele. They used numerous stage props not only to influence the clientele but to reinforce their own commitment to transform commercialized customer relations into personalized ones and to provide service that was real. Women arranged the front stage of the house, their boutiques, to set the mood and to guide the reactions of customers when they entered. They promoted feelings of both intimacy and exclusivity by creating interiors that evoked the privacy of the eighteenth-century salon as well as stylized décors of the French court. They projected high-status images of rarity and distinction in their elegant yet inviting boutiques, in their fashionable yet understated personal appearance, and in the merchandising of their fancy confections.

Boutiques were designed with warm woods, decorated with ornamental columns, delicate corniches, and abundant use of mirrors, and illuminated with both indirect lighting and crystal chandeliers. Pictures of Old Regime aristocrats indulging in courtly pursuits such as the hunt were displayed alongside porcelain and crystal vases and figurines (see fig. 6). The prestige cachet of the candies was suggested by their arrangement in window and counter displays that resembled precious jewels from distant sources. Like jewels they were packaged in customized gift boxes, the most lavish of which were bound in rich fabrics and tied with satin and velvet ribbons. The intimacy of the private salon was evoked in some Bayonnais boutiques by a departure from the common practice of showcasing products in enclosed glass display cases. Chocolates were invitingly arranged on open counters and sold by women who projected a bourgeois class image through the dress and hairstyles they adopted. Madame Carrère summarized it succinctly for me: "I never wear expensive jewelry, lipstick, or nail polish. I dress for the boutique as I would for an afternoon outing. I'm not one to wear fancy clothes and put on furs. One must present a uniform image to the clientele, the same image inside and outside the boutique."

As Arlie Hochschild has noted for service workers, to the extent that hearts are successfully managed and emotions kept in check, "something like alchemy occurs" (1983, 119). Civility and well-being were enhanced and women derived great satisfaction from their work. This was particularly true for women who left behind low-status, salaried jobs to create new houses or to marry into craft families. As artisanal wives they were self-employed and enjoyed greater status, financial rewards, and control over their work than workers on a fixed wage. However, the training of feeling in the service of institutions, even small family-run businesses, had social costs. Women's work was time- and labor-intensive, and their very success at creating a salon ambiance recalling the intimacy of home and the joy of celebrations often occurred at the expense of their own relations with children, extended family, and friends. Women enacted traditional roles in the boutique that, for lack of time and en-

Figure 6. Confectionery boutique, Dalbaitz house, 1990.

ergy, were largely denied them in the home. Commercialized customer relations took priority over personalized familial ones, and the demands of the customers and the boutique often overwhelmed those of the family and the home. Those who worked in confectionery houses often said that the work of wives became their life and the boutique their home.

The use of a salon analogy was vulnerable from a number of points of view. First, the salon was a closed, private space that *habitués* (regulars) or selected guests were invited to enter on the basis of shared interests and a common class background. The confectionery boutique was a public space open to all, not just to well-known regulars but increasingly to a democratized and expanded tourist clientele. The tourists who crowded downtown Bayonne during the summer and on holidays had less interest in slow, personal service than in fast, efficient service. Indeed, selling gifts to a whole busload of tourists who have one hour on the Port Neuf involved a dramatic speedup of service and little contact time between saleswomen and customers. This increased stress and made it impossible—even undesirable—to deliver the required emotional labor. It complicated the management of estrangement between the self and feeling and between the self and display (Hochschild 1983, 131).

Second, the salon analogy relied on the projection of high-status images of confectionery boutiques, products, and the persons of women. Yet these images were belied by women's own class position and a personal life style of hard work. They were merchants of elegance and promoters of refinement in taste. They sold fancy confections that provided social distinction but could claim little of this social status for themselves. Many artisanal wives were from lower middle-class backgrounds and had only an abbreviated vocational track secondary education yet interacted with a local clientele that was educated, middle- and upper middle-class, and largely female. Advising customers on the appropriate etiquette surrounding confectionery gift purchases demanded considerable tact and a constant class negotiation (compare Gimlin 1996).

The French place considerable importance on the preparation of high-quality foods as well as on their aesthetic presentation. Thus, the choice of gift items at rites of passage and family holiday gatherings was taken very seriously, and purchases were usually made only after several consultations between the *patronne* (artisan's wife) and a customer. These bourgeois women regarded themselves as exemplars of culinary taste within their own milieu and prided themselves on their status as discriminating (*exigeante*) consumers. However, most demonstrated very little actual knowledge of the composition of confectionery products. My observation of sales in the Harcaut and Dalbaitz boutiques in 1990 and 1991 revealed that most customers could only differentiate between dark and milk chocolates, solid and dipped candies, *praliné* and non-*praliné* centers, cream and chocolate-filled centers, and candies flavored with or without alcohol.[4] Few were able to define or distinguish among the different types of candy—*ganaches, gianduja,* marzipan, and *pralinés* made with hazelnuts versus almonds—but most refused pre-packaged gift boxes and insisted on personally choosing their own candy assortments.

In situations like these, wives and/or their sales help were obliged to give lengthy explanations of product ingredients and to wait patiently as consumers debated the merits of one candy over another. They induced customers to buy by engaging the symbolic battles for status that were waged through confectionery gift purchases among bourgeois consumers. "You might try our new specialty made from a recipe of Lenôtre," or "Madame X [the wife of a prominent municipal council member] purchased this assortment as a gift for her son's music professor," or "Did you know that Monsieur Mitterrand [movie celebrity and relative of then French President Mitterrand] is here in the southwest and paid us a visit? He really likes our ginger-flavored *ganache* and purchased a whole box of them."

Skill at customer relations also had to be accompanied by an aptitude for merchandising. Women prepared, priced, and displayed merchandise, keeping detailed records of the production dates and product shelf life of goods. They also performed the time- and labor-intensive work of designing and executing innovative window displays. These changed with the seasons and reflected the creative stamp of the artisanal wife. They were important in creating and conveying the prestige cachet of the house and its products to a larger public. Women also handled the elaborate packaging of gift purchases and took considerable time and pleasure in choosing the personalized boxes and labels, paper, and ribbons used to wrap their candies. This packaging sends a specific message to the recipient of the gift item. It is intended to reflect the good taste of the giver and the exclusive image of the house.

Women's skill also involved the celebration of an artisanal aesthetic based on highly developed skill and quality production. Women linked the good taste of house candies to the consummate art of the craftsmen in the workshop. They actively promoted artisans' possession of the current emblems of craft mastery. These included prestigious craft contest titles, both local and national, membership in elite producer associations such as the Confrérie des Chocolatiers de France (Brotherhood of French Chocolatiers), and mentoring relationships with masters. These relationships allowed local artisans to appropriate as their own a part of the cultural capital and repute attached to famous masters. Women played an important role in publicizing their husband's or son's training under famous Parisians such as Robert Linxe or Gaston

Lenôtre. For example, Madame Carrère reminded customers that her son Simon learned his skill with chocolate by working with Linxe in Paris. Madame Mathieu promoted her son's training at the Lenôtre school in Paris, and Michèle Harcaut displayed the certificates her husband earned "at the most exclusive confectionery school in France," the Ecole Nationale Supérieure of Yssingeaux. Immediately after he was inducted into the Confrérie in October 1990, she had new house cards printed that mentioned his membership in that organization.

Michèle Harcaut's situation illustrates both the opportunities and conflicts occasioned by her work. Her move into self-employment and association with a valued craft was a move up from her parents' work and social class. They were family farmers who acquired a modest land holding in a tiny village outside Bayonne after years of agricultural wage labor. Their home had electricity but no indoor plumbing until the early 1960s. They cooked food from their own farm over the hearth fire and brought water from a well. They had no car and trips to Bayonne were rare. Since "they didn't worry about providing daughters with an education," Michèle left school at the minimum leave-taking age after earning a vocational diploma in home economics. She had a series of un- or semi-skilled jobs as a live-in maid (earning 11F, or $2, a day for twelve hours of work six days a week) and a stitcher for the minimum wage at a local shoe factory. After the factory closed, she did a variety of odd jobs cleaning homes and working part time for her paternal uncle, a baker in downtown Bayonne. Until she married her husband, she had had no experience with fancy pastries, and when they purchased the Dominguez house, she was unprepared for the demands of her job, although this was something she did her best to hide from customers and colleagues: "I was overwhelmed at first. The first year [1982] was so bad that we both lost 10 kilos [laughter] . . . there was extra room in the bed I can tell you. I found myself all alone in the boutique, I didn't know how to display the products, how to package them, and I knew nothing about how to dress."

Although Michèle Harcaut learned quickly (she participated regularly in the training workshops offered by the local Centre féminin d'études de la pâtisserie [Confectionery wives' association, hereafter, the center]) and developed an excellent reputation for her customer relations, her interaction with her bourgeois customers demanded a dificult negotiation. They took her advice on confectionery gifts, recognizing both her product knowledge and personal charm, but asserted their superior class position and cultural capital through their language use, aesthetic judgments, and intellectual knowledge. Some customers employed literary allusions that escaped her, some touted their social connections, one retired high-ranking civil servant routinely lectured her on various topics including local history, philosophy, and world religions, and one executive mocked what he thought was her garish taste in Christmas decorations.

This incident occurred just after she had decorated her boutique for the holidays. In contrast to the more understated decorations in other confectionery boutiques, she had created a winter scene with artificial snow, icicles, and a rotund, red-suited Santa Claus resembling less the religious Saint Nicholas commonly associated with European Christmas celebrations than Clement Moore's American creation in *'Twas the Night Before Christmas*. She was obviously pleased and phoned to invite me to see the result. I was in the boutique with my camera when a male customer arrived to pick up a cake ordered by his wife. He entered, examined the display slowly and deliberately with raised eyebrows, then stared pointedly at her and announced in a haughty tone, "Madame, your Father Christmas is very red." She was visibly stung by both his remark and affect but maintained her composure and responded, "If he is red, Monsieur, that is because it is the holiday season."

The inverse of Michèle Harcaut's situation obtained in some cases, such as the Dalbaitz and Aguirre houses, where women who saw themselves as middle-class were drawn into a permanent role in the family boutique. Bourgeois women who had earned secondary-level baccalaureate degrees such as Hélène Sarlate experienced difficulty being associated with a manual craft and accepting the public demands of retail sales work. Madame Sarlate sought to distance herself from both the manual work and customer contact while maintaining the presence and authority of the *patronne*. One of the ways she did this was to delegate sales and packaging to sales help and to intervene only at the point of sale. Madame Sarlate relied on a saleswoman trained by her grandmother who had twenty-two years' experience in the Dalbaitz boutique. She also spent mornings and early afternoons working at home. She came daily to the boutique but usually stayed only several hours in the late afternoon. She claimed to enjoy the boutique accounting, ordering, and merchandising because it "amused her," not because she had any professional investment in it. She never participated in the training seminars and social events organized by the local artisanal wives' association, the center, and likewise never considered the possibility of any social contact with other artisanal couples. When Madame Sarlate was in the boutique, she remained almost exclusively behind a cash register located squarely in the center back of the boutique, a focal point for all customers entering and leaving.

Houses could not survive without wives to oversee the boutique, but their recruitment by marriage meant that it was impossible to know how they would measure up to the heavy demands made on them. An inappropriate marriage could produce the same result as no marriage at all: irreparable damage to the house. Because most women entered confectionery houses through marriage, they had little or no preparation for the responsibilities in retail sales and management awaiting them. This problem was compounded by the fact that many of the women in this study were trained for and already employed full time in other positions when they met their future husbands. In contrast to sons who were sent out of houses to train, families insisted that in-marrying women (and men) train within the house. This meant that women in established houses received the foundation of their training on the job from the wife of the senior craftsman or older saleswomen. The progressive and often conflict-ridden incorporation of a son or son-in-law into the family workshop controlled by his father or father-in-law was mirrored by the integration of his wife into the boutique. Young women had to take their place as subordinates in a structural hierarchy commanded by their mothers-in-law or their mothers. This hierarchy paralleled that of the workshop, where salaried saleswomen were ranked as the first, the second, and so forth, according to experience and aptitude. All were under the authority of the senior wife, who had the last word in merchandising and sales decisions, handled special orders herself, and managed the house finances, in which personal and business assets were usually merged. The daughter-in-law, like her husband in the workshop, found herself in the painful position of being ranked below both her mother-in-law and all the experienced sales help. Whereas fathers, sons, and daughters were identified by their blood relation, in-marrying women were distinguished from their mothers-in-law not by their first names but by their links to their husbands. This categorization emphasized their recruitment by marriage as well as their precarious status as outsiders to the house and to the family.

The boutique hierarchy was encoded in the forms of address and relations between the *patronne*, her family members, and the salaried sales help. Those in a superior structural position spoke more familiarly to subordinates, who in turn responded using the polite forms of address that connote respect, authority, and distance. Although they were part of the same family, it was common for the *patronne* (and indeed for many French mothers-in-law) to use the polite form of address with her new daughter-in-law (compare de Singly and Lemarchant 1991). It signaled both the formality of an unproven familial relationship and the uncertainty of a crucial but unknown work relation. The daughter-in-law chose this form of address with her mother-in-law because it both indicated her position as stranger and reflected her deference to the older woman's rank.[5]

All participants in confectionery houses agreed that women were vitally important yet potentially very disruptive. The relationship between mothers-in-law and daughters-in-law was perceived as particularly problematic (compare Bringa 1995, 48–50; Rogers 1991, 87–88) although in different ways by different house members. From the vantage point of subordinates, both salaried employees and daughters-in-law, mothers-in-law were frequently depicted as autocratic. This view has been vividly rendered in ethnographic and historical accounts of artisanal businesses (Blasquez 1976, 45; Darnton 1985, 74–104). From the perspective of their sons, husbands, and agemates, mothers-in-law were seen as tirelessly steadfast and necessarily authoritarian given the troublesome nature of women (and the unruly nature of journeymen). For everyone, in-marrying women were the *pièces rapportées*. This expression is taken from dressmaking and refers to a contrasting piece of cloth stitched onto an existing garment (compare Le Wita 1994, 47). Daughters-in-law represented a potential threat because it was uncertain whether they would blend in and become an integral part of the house, thereby ensuring its survival. The biggest fear was that a daughter-in-law would undermine her husband's allegiance to his father's house and convince him to leave it.

Families attempted to neutralize this threat in a number of ways. In-marrying women were expected to devote themselves entirely to the house and craft family by reducing their contact with their natal families. At the same time, craft families encouraged their sons to choose spouses who came from a similar class milieu and had equal amounts of education. Such spouses were expected to understand the demands of work in a family business and to harbor no dangerous ambitions for social mobility. Moreover, they were more likely to accept the constraints of a long apprenticeship to their mothers-in-law in the boutique because of the hope of one day achieving the higher status and authority as senior wife. In older houses, heirs, both sons and daughters, sometimes married with marriage contracts excluding their spouses from ownership of family property. This kept the commercial property in the family in the event of death or divorce while guaranteeing the dependence of the in-marrying spouse on that family.

A daughter-in-law's entry into the family boutique usually occurred immediately after her marriage and was a delicate matter given the public nature of retail sales. She had to depend on the presence, knowledge, and largesse of her mother-in-law for her integration into the house and the craft. It was a process greatly colored by the personality of both women and by the family's feelings about her suitability as a spouse and lifetime participant in the business. The requirements of the retail boutique demanded that the vulnerability and inexperience of young women be masked by their mothers-in-law. In the best of scenarios, daughters-in-law were progressively incorporated into the management of the boutique and the handling of customer relations. Since they worked side by side with their mothers-in-law for many years, some developed very strong bonds. This was the case in the Salinas house in Saint-Jean-de-Luz, where the heir's wife and his mother evolved a mutually satisfying division of labor and maintained a close working and personal relationship until the latter's death.

However, it was all too common for conflicts to occur. For instance, in the Dalbaitz house, an irreconcilable tension developed between Madame Joliot and her daughter-in-law. At the time of Paul Joliot's marriage in 1942, his mother had managed her boutiques in Bayonne and Biarritz for thirteen years and was widely acknowledged to be an exemplar in the myriad requirements of her public role. The Joliots insisted that Paul marry with a contract, and Madame Joliot made it clear to her husband and son that her new daughter-in-law would have no role whatsoever in the flagship boutique in Bayonne. Instead, she drew her two unmarried daughters into the business and managed her boutique (over a fifty-year period) until her retirement in 1980 at ninety-one years of age.

Even when a workable arrangement was achieved, the chain of command in the boutique was clear. A daughter-in-law had to defer to her mother-in-law's authority, proving her loyalty to the family and her devotion to the house over a number of years before she enjoyed any authority. The transfer of power from a mother-in-law to her daughter-in-law or from a mother to daughter occurred only when the senior woman reduced her participation in the boutique or officially retired from her public role. Women played a pivotal role in the succession process. Wives frequently outlived their husbands and worked longer in confectionery houses than did their husbands. Thus they provided an important generational bridge after their husbands retired or died and before heirs were in a position to assume full control, when they were single or newly married. Given her vital role in ensuring the continued success of the house as well as the long years it had taken her to achieve a measure of authority, relinquishing control was difficult if not impossible.

## Recruiting Outsiders

When a house was sold to outsiders, the new artisanal couple worked alongside the previous owners in the workshop and in the boutique. This arrangement sometimes lasted for many months and gave the desired impression that a "true" family succession was in progress. New owners replicated the original product line of the founder as well as the distinctive retailing skills of his wife. They had to preserve the continuity of the house name through its established product line and personalized relations with customers. Only by first merging their family line with the distinctive ethos of the existing house could they cautiously begin to innovate. Only with time could they complement and individualize the product line, fashioning it in the image of the new master craftsman. The Bourriet business illustrated this process.

The Bourriets came to Biarritz from northeastern France after World War II, creating a *pâtisserie* on a prime piece of real estate one block from the ocean. They built a national reputation among the high-status clientele of the immediate postwar period. Over the years many young journeymen came from all parts of France to work under the supervision of Monsieur Bourriet. For example, Francis Boucher, the president of the Best Craftsman of France judging panel, spent a season in the Bourriet house before establishing his own *chocolaterie*. In 1978, when Monsieur and Madame Bourriet were sixty-six and sixty-one, respectively, they were looking for a successor. They were childless and had no kin or employees who were able or willing to purchase the house. Although they had not advertised the sale, they were approached by an established couple, the Bergerons, owners of a *pâtisserie* in a small town in the neighboring department of Lot-et-Garonne. The Bergerons had acquired a foundering bakery business in 1967 by assuming the flour mill debts of the previous owner and turned it into a sound business. They were ambitious and anxious to sell that business and to acquire a house on the Basque coast with access to a more sophisticated clientele. The Bourriets, in their words, "took a gamble on the Bergerons," agreeing to lower the sales price and to allow them to pay part of the purchase price in cash and the remainder in monthly payments continuing until their death *(rente viagère)*.

After the sale was concluded, the Bergerons worked alongside the Bourriets for a month. Monsieur Bourriet introduced his successor to suppliers and members of the local craft community. Meanwhile, his wife presented her successor to customers in the boutique and to local shopkeepers. As it happened, these two women looked remarkably alike, so many Biarrots and tourists assumed that they were mother and daughter and that Mademoiselle Bourriet had had the good sense to marry a skilled craftsman. The Bourriets never disabused their clientele of that notion. This impression was further confirmed as the two families developed close ties and the Bourriets enthusiastically assumed the role of surrogate grandparents for the Bergerons' only daughter. The Bergerons maintained the original line of pastries that made the house reputation before progressively switching to the production of chocolate and sugar candies for which the Bourriet house and Monsieur Bergeron currently enjoy a national reputation.

## Conclusion

The meaning of the house name was linked to the sociological principles that informed the performance and representation of gendered craft work in confectionery houses. It was likewise closely connected to the cultural logics underlying the intergenerational reproduction of confectionery houses and the complex motivations for undertaking craft work in contrast to modern work. Chapter 6 examines these questions in detail: What made craft work worth doing in spite of its many demands? What were the motivations for creating or purchasing houses and for selling them once they were established?

# CHAPTER 6

# "Our craft is beautiful . . ."
## — Guy Urbain

The narratives in chapter 5 beg the question of motivation. What makes craft work worth doing? Why was the ownership of confectionery houses attractive to couples in the 1990s? Data from older established and newly created businesses suggested that house ownership had a strong cultural value and appealed for a number of reasons. It conferred a social identity based on personal initiative, satisfying labor, and economic independence. It provided the freedom to be one's own boss and implied inclusion within a group of *les petits* (small independents) in opposition to *les gros* (big business) and *les fonctionnaires* (salaried civil servants) in the huge French state bureaucracy. Craft families defined themselves as small producers with personalized customer relations in contrast to the anonymous and, therefore, suspect relations of mass distribution. They emphasized the modest size, local character, and handicraft production of their businesses. Guy Urbain put it this way: "The French artisan . . . is by definition small, limited to his own labor power *[les bras]* and his immediate environment. His number one enemy is big business, shopping malls, and speculative capital." This emphasis gives voice to received popular notions of family artisanship while eliding the contradictory realities of contemporary entrepreneurship: virtually all houses relied on salaried labor and many were not craft businesses defined by the state as employing ten or fewer workers but medium-sized business with ten to fifty salaried employees.

Artisans said that they did honest work and sold their goods for a reasonable price.[1] They saw their mode of small-scale entrepreneurship as an antidote to the excesses of unbridled capitalism. Unlike huge corporations, artisanal producers were family entrepreneurs who made their own products and stood behind them. They engaged in what one owner called "humane business practices," insisting that, unlike mass distribution outlets, customers knew with whom they were dealing when they shopped at confectionery houses and could expect excellent service there. As Michèle Harcaut angrily reminded her husband one particularly busy Saturday morning when he chided her for not having restocked her display cases by noontime, "I am not here just to take people's money and say good-bye. I have to give each person the time required."

Craft families also asserted an identity based on personal initiative in opposition to salaried work. In particular, they targeted public sector employment, which they saw as safe but stifling. This was certainly an oppositional identity in a nation with a proclivity for big government and a passionate attachment to costly public services as well as secure public sector jobs. The public sector makes up well over one-third of the economy, and the state employs 5 million civil servants (five times as many as in the United States for a population roughly one-quarter the size). Public sector employment provides a large variety of privileges, such as retirement at fifty-five, five to six weeks' paid vacation, and lifetime job security (in exchange for low pay). Small business owners such as craft families did not automatically enjoy these benefits and felt particularly vulnerable when discussing job security. Yet most insisted that craft work attracted them precisely because of their desire for personal control and freedom from both the coercion of bosses and the boring predictability of salaried work.

The adjective *artisanal* was used to connote a positively valued notion of personal or group autonomy. For example, the French editor of *Esprit* described it as a tiny "artisanal business." *Esprit* was artisanal because it no longer received financial subsidies or editorial directives from its former parent publishing house, Seuil. Thus, the editor could describe it as "an independent publication from an intellectual and financial point of view" (Fassin 1991, 82–83). This attachment to independence was evident in artisans' predilection for financing expansion and mechanization out of house profits rather than obtaining costly credit from banks. They were particularly wary of the onerous conditions attached to commercial bank loans.

In addition, an equally important motivation lay in the possibility for personal creative input in the performance of work. The adjective *artisanal* was used in French as a synonym for the ability to mark one's work with an individualized stamp. In a recent interview, for example, Michel

Sardou, a popular French singer, was asked who arranged his music. He responded emphatically, "I do. I'm an artisan." Artisans derived particular personal satisfaction from the exercise of crafts with an elaborate aesthetic dimension approaching art, such as jewelry, wood sculpture, glass making, leather working, and the food crafts *(les métiers de bouche)* such as *pâtisserie, glacerie,* and *chocolaterie* featuring confectionery art. This had to do in part with the cultural value placed on aesthetics in French culture. It was also connected to the negative depiction of artisans in the postwar sociological literature because many left school at fourteen years of age to do apprenticeships and earned only culturally devalued vocational diplomas. Their ability to earn recognition for pieces that resembled fanciful art rather than functional craft helped to reduce the persistent stigma associated with manual versus mental work.

I also asked Guy Urbain to describe the most common motivation for young people to become *chocolatiers.* His reply: "Well, of course there is an increasing demand for up-scale chocolates and a shortage of skilled artisans to make them. But most of all our craft is a beautiful one. Oh, it may not guarantee him [the *chocolatier*] wealth, but he will practice a craft with dignity and humanity. His independence will provide a deep sense of professional accomplishment."

In fact, as we have seen, the exercise of the food crafts could be very lucrative. However, to focus exclusively or primarily on financial rewards would be to miss the point. Compared to many industrial crafts that are noisy, dirty, or even dangerous, the craft of *chocolatier* really is a beautiful one. Some *chocolatiers* described themselves as "dream merchants" and enjoyed immensely the fact that their work consisted of what they called "the preparation of pleasure for others." *Chocolatiers* presided over the important task of crafting the highly valued, aesthetically pleasing sweets synonymous with the special social and religious occasions that called for their consumption. Over time they became an integral part of the fabric of their local communities; their houses became intimately associated with the wedding cakes, baptismal *dragées,* and communion centerpieces they made for rites of passage, the chocolate-covered cherries and *tourons* they sold at Christmas, as well as their Easter and high season confectionery art recalling larger historical and current events.

Ownership of confectionery houses carried implicit assumptions about the character and backgrounds of the craft families who operated them. It was expected that house owners were exceptionally hardworking, honest, and upstanding (compare Kondo 1990, 130–133). The public nature of work in confectionery houses required that families project an outward image of absolute moral rectitude while maintaining a specific style and elegance in the presentations of themselves, their boutiques, and their products. These positive associations were heightened if a house was owned and operated by the same family over several generations. When that happened, it was valuable social capital that families profitably exploited in the representation of their craft and modes of entrepreneurship to both customers and a larger public. For example, when Monsieur Mourier conducted public tours of his workshop, one of the first things he told visitors was that "the family succession of this house was recently assured when my youngest grandson joined my son and me in the workshop." He introduced his wife, son, daughter-in-law, and grandson to visitors, announcing, "Three generations of this family now work here." Similarly, Patrick Sarlate in the Dalbaitz house welcomed busloads of tourists by presenting himself as a *chocolatier* "with a pure pedigree" since he formed part of a family (his wife's) that had been continuously involved in the production and sale of confectionery products for five generations.

However, the status of dream merchants necessarily masked a number of tensions and conflicts related to the performance of craft work. Since these artisans were an intimate part of the city in which they practiced the craft(s), both their personal lives and families were subject to particular scrutiny. Their management of adversity was expected to confirm the moral attributes necessary for success: honesty, determination, steadfastness, and strength. As one artisan noted bitterly, this meant that "we don't have the right to get sick, to miss work, to have problems, period." One artisanal wife told of receiving a call from an angry customer in her hospital room just two days after surgery. The customer was incensed that when she unwrapped an expensive gift of chocolates arranged in a black lacquered duck, part of the finish came off with the scotch tape.

Because of their name recognition and the very success of their houses, craft families faced jealousy and prejudices based on negative stereotypes of the petite bourgeoisie. Although craft families were expected to be exemplars of family values, they were also suspected of shady business practices such as giving customers less merchandise than they paid for or skimping on high-quality ingredients. As Michel Harcaut's son put it, "People have the impression that money is easy to earn, that small business owners cheat, and that, as a result, they are very rich." The owner of a prominent *pâtisserie* in the neighboring town of Anglet described how her daughter had been stopped for speeding by a policeman. He seemed more inclined to flirt with her than to write a traffic ticket until he read her identity card. "Are you the daughter of Monsieur Clouseau? Well, he can afford to pay the fine. Here, give this to your father." Another woman recounted with disgust how her daughter had nearly failed the end of the year lycée exam. "Her professor hated her from the moment he knew who she was, daughter of a business owner." She gave voice to a general view that many lycée professors embraced leftist politics and openly disdained the owners of capital in any form, industrial or petty.

Like all other families, owners of confectionery houses periodically faced serious problems such as grave illness, obstreperous children, marital conflict, spousal infidelity, abuse, and alcoholism. However, the preservation of a good name that was intimately linked to the craft family necessarily meant projecting a positive public image and hiding opprobrious house secrets. The De Closet house provided a particularly poignant example.

The Bonbonnière is a tiny confectionery boutique located on a busy commercial street in downtown Biarritz. In 1947 it was purchased from a seller of funeral crowns and transformed into a candy store by Madame Bonnet, the mistress of Monsieur Pierre LeBlanc. Monsieur Le-Blanc was born in Grenoble in 1899, and because he was an orphan the state placed him in an apprenticeship at age thirteen with the owner of a well-known *pâtisserie*. He apprenticed for three years, worked for two more years, and performed his military service as a cook in the French army during and after World War I (1917–1919). After the war he got a job at one of the most reputable confectionery houses in Grenoble, La Confiserie de Milan, married, and had two sons. He worked sixteen years before he and his wife had enough money to create their own business in 1936. Near the end of World War II he fell desperately in love with a woman who worked in their *confiserie*. They had a secret affair until his mistress announced that she could no longer tolerate that situation and left Grenoble to start over in Biarritz. He intended to remain and do his duty but was so despondent after her departure that, just a few months later, he abandoned everything and followed her to Biarritz. Since he was a *pâtissier/confiseur*, her customers assumed they were married, and when they called him Monsieur Bonnet, no one corrected them. Thus began what his son described bitterly as a clandestine life that continued until his father's death in 1964. His father never divorced his wife or returned to Grenoble.[2]

Monsieur LeBlanc fell gravely ill when he was seventy-five and sent for his youngest son Max and his wife. He did so at this point in his life for several reasons. His mistress held title to the business, and a sale to outsiders would have revealed the truth of her personal circumstances to the local community. Monsieur LeBlanc proposed that his son purchase the business for a very modest price and pay his mistress a monthly income. Since she was only sixty-one, a family succession was intended to protect Madame Bonnet's reputation and to provide a pension for the duration of her life. The low price of the business was meant as a peace offering as well as an opportunity for Monsieur LeBlanc's youngest son to obtain his own business. His eldest brother was in line to inherit the confectionery house in Grenoble. Max LeBlanc and his wife had worked in the family business since 1952 and agreed to the elder man's request. They worked alongside Madame Bonnet for several months before the succession was complete. Giving the impression of seamless familial continuity was excruciatingly difficult for Max LeBlanc. He described his father's mistress "as the woman *(la bonne femme)* whose company my father preferred to my own mother."

Owners of confectionery houses had to conceal not only family secrets but the toll their work exacted over time. The public nature of their work devoted to the preparation of celebrations for others often belied a life style of hard work, sacrifice, exiguous rewards, and the continual stress that accompanied the balancing of multiple, conflicting roles. Children whose parents owned and worked in confectionery houses frequently had a store of unhappy childhood memories linked to their parents' work and frequent absences.

One of the reasons Simon Carrère was so insistent about spending time with his own children was directly related to his childhood and the succession of hired helpers who raised him. He repeated the same story several times:

I never saw my parents when I was young, not on my birthday, especially not on holidays. All they ever did was work and when they weren't working they were talking about work. They have nothing else in their lives. Take my father, he can't understand why I want it to be different with my children. He can't believe that I insist on going home at lunch and playing with them instead of resting so I can be in good shape for work in the afternoon.

In-marrying spouses endured great tensions and conflicts. These conflicts, combined with the imperative for artisanal wives to celebrate family entrepreneurship in the privileged public space of the confectionery boutique, made it very difficult to elicit the reality of their work lives. The narrative that follows, told by Madame Carrère, wife of Monsieur Carrère *père* (senior), is exceptional in this regard both in its truthfulness regarding the incentives and disappointments of craft work and in the insight we gain on gendered relations and hierarchies within confectionery houses. It was painful to hear and to reconstruct in detail here because it reflected the extraordinary strain under which Madame Carrère performed her work during the period of my fieldwork.

I formally interviewed Madame Carrère shortly after my arrival in Bayonne and regularly observed her role in the house during my weekly visits. At the beginning of my fieldwork she recounted a story that emphasized the important role she played within the house and the public visibility she earned as an advocate for Bayonnais family merchants. Her husband enthusiastically joined in the telling of her story, describing with pride both her artistic talent (she had studied at the local School of Fine Arts) and inexhaustible energies. Madame Carrère played a leadership role in the initiative to create the Grand Bayonne pedestrian zone and noted mischievously that Mayor Grenet had labeled her a tigress because of her tenacity. Madame Carrère mentioned problems with her mother-in-law, but she assured me that over time they became close and even used the familiar *tu* form of address with one another. After Louis Carrère's death in 1966, she had invited her mother-in-law to live in her home. However, I noted that it was Monsieur, not Madame, who described his mother's tireless devotion to the house and her extraordinary work ethic. Madame Louis had continued to work (at least a few hours daily) until one month before her death in 1983.

As my fieldwork went on, Madame Carrère appeared to be under considerable pressure and worked less often in the boutique, delegating her role to hired sales help. I learned from her husband that, in addition to the succession problems preoccupying them both, she had a crisis in her natal family. The last time I spoke at length with her, Madame Carrère told quite a different story. This narrative was distinctly shaped by its telling in the context of the official transfer of the business property in 1991 and the intense pain it caused her. The narrative she reconstructed was necessarily rhetorical and highly selective (White 1978). It reflected both her personal experience of the succession and the dialogical nature of her encounter with an American ethnographer. My presence in Bayonne and interest in her work gave her the opportunity she had previously been denied to tell her story publicly. Her choice of the family boutique as the forum in which to recount her narrative was strategic. Her timing of a meeting after the morning rush was even more so. She intended her story to be heard by house employees, her husband, son, daughter-in-law, and me, not by the house clientele.

I knew of the arrangement whereby business control had passed to

Simon Carrère in return for a monthly cash payment to supplement his father's retirement pension. Fabrice Carrère's frustration with his son had steadily mounted over the course of the year, and he confided to me that he had had to ask for this payment. "Do you know how he reacted? Well, he balked, and I had to insist." I wanted to ask Madame Carrère for her view of things. When we first met, she had explained with some bitterness that she never had juridical status in the house as an owner or a salaried employee and would receive no pension. In late April 1991, at her suggestion, I arranged to meet her in the boutique and found her with her sister and two full-time saleswomen. After she finished with a customer I moved toward one of the back tables where we usually chatted, but she motioned me to the center front of the tearoom. We sat down and I began by asking her some biographical details about her family but noticed that she was distracted and upset. Her sister hovered nearby and persistently but gently corrected her on her facts. Madame Carrère waved her away impatiently and interrupted:

Those are details. . . . What Madame [me] has to know is how I arrived in this house. You see I first worked here for a season as a salesgirl when I was fifteen. I was in school but returned to work during the summer. Did you know that I studied at the School for Fine Arts? Well, I came into this house immediately after our marriage [in 1956], and it was expected that I would work in the boutique along with my mother-in-law. You know they [her in-laws] thought I had married above me [her father was a butcher and ran a successful business in Grand Bayonne] and insisted on a prenuptial contract [excluding her from family property and assets]. I entered as a mere employee, I had no privileges, no access to the cash register, no access to checks, no personal cash, no salary. I had to ask her [her mother-in-law] for everything. She alone controlled the money, she did the accounting, all the purchasing for the boutique, she took care of the clientele.

She paused, caught sight of her husband entering the tearoom from the workshop doorway, and resumed her narrative:

In those days we didn't have the equipment for freezing that we have now. Everything had to be made fresh. My father-in-law gave us a room and a toilet upstairs over the workshop. He would knock on my door at five o'clock in the morning and during busy periods we would work until eleven at night. At that time people from the whole Basque countryside came to Bayonne to buy Carrère products. People had huge baptismal and communion celebrations at home and then there were the lines after each mass on Sunday morning.

Monsieur Carrère approached and reminded his wife that he had an appointment, and as he turned to go, she sarcastically suggested that he might need his car keys. As he retrieved them from a cabinet just off the tearoom, she continued defiantly:

It was so hard because right from the beginning, they cut me out [of house ownership and assets]. My father-in-law used me for all I was worth. Things improved greatly after my son was born [in 1958]. Of course I played up to my father-in-law and tried to improve my own position. I became his favorite (*chou-chou*). You see he and his wife led very separate lives. He had his mistresses and she had financial control. Of course, I had a completely different personality from my mother-in-law. I had excellent relations with the clientele, also I was very strong, I could handle the grueling pace, I didn't need much sleep, I had a very good memory. I wasn't afraid of people in new situations. I had nerve and he liked that . . . but from the time my son was born they demanded that I stay and work. I didn't have the right to raise my son. Oh, I had domestic help at home, but I didn't have the right to raise my son. I had furs, jewels, clothes, went to the hairdresser when I wanted but I always had to ask.

She paused and I was acutely aware of the stunned silence that had descended on the boutique. Her husband had left with an embarrassed backward glance at us, and her sister's face registered both embarrassment and worry. I remarked that she was no doubt a huge asset to the house. She continued wryly:

Oh yes, at that time I was somebody, I was a lady, Madame Carrère and I led a very rich life. But now Madame Carrère doesn't mean the same thing. I have a title that in present circumstances is worthless. I should have demanded a salary and assured my own financial independence. I have spent my whole life here. . . . I did it to assure a future for my son. I sold part of my inheritance [from the sale of her parents' business] so he could build a house and now I have nothing. I have to work in this store on Sunday afternoons in order to have the money to buy stockings and go to the hairdresser.

Her eyes filled with tears and her voice trembled with emotion. I knew that I should get up and leave but instead I could not keep myself from asking the question that was so often debated among the house employees—whether her daughter-in-law would be working in the boutique now that their son was in control. In 1981 Simon Carrère had married the daughter of a well-respected family of jewelers [with a marriage contract] but his wife had never worked full-time in the boutique. There was agreement among house employees and family members that although that situation was highly unusual it was necessary. As Simon Carrère put it, "sparks would fly if those two tried to work together." Madame Carrère's face hardened and she responded:

I told my son I could not work with my daughter-in-law. She is too independent and headstrong. You don't really know her, she is the kind to come in here and take over. Now, if you will, I have become the mother-in-law. I've been working in this house since I was married and only got control over the boutique when my mother-in-law died [in 1983]. You know of course that my son is going to take over and I have been cut out again. For the fourth time I've had to sit in front of a notary and watch the property transfer without a provision for me. My husband is [seven years] older than I am. If something happens to him what will I do? How will I live? I'm very unhappy and I cry a lot.[3]

Suddenly she stopped because she saw a regular customer enter the boutique. She quickly brushed the tears from her cheek, collected herself, and put on a beautiful smile. She had assumed once again her role as *patronne,* a role that she played well as she greeted older workers with the traditional kiss on both cheeks, engaged regular customers in conversation about their children and grandchildren, took charge of large customized orders, or packaged the Easter eggs she hand-painted herself.

As it happened, that was the last time I talked with Madame Carrère before leaving France at the end of May 1991. When I returned to Bayonne in 1995, I was not surprised to see Monsieur and Madame Carrère *père* still playing an active role in the house. Both they and Simon described his latest plan—the creation of an up-scale restaurant in nearby Biarritz. I left before the restaurant opened and was saddened to hear when I returned one year later that it had lasted barely one month. In 1996 the once proud Carrère house was still in business but much reduced. I remembered then a long conversation I had had with Fabrice Carrère in January 1991 concerning the net profit figures for 1990. As we compared the lean years of the late 1980s with the 1960s, 1970s, and early 1980s, he confessed that he would have sold the house long ago if he didn't have a son.

The principles that informed the organization and performance of craft work made it difficult to sustain and reproduce intergenerationally. House ownership could provide the economic capital necessary for children to stay in school and to obtain the academic credentials for more culturally valued intellectual careers in professional or white collar work. When owners reached the end of the work cycle without family heirs to succeed them, their businesses could be sold to outsiders yielding a cash supplement to retirement pensions and/or an inheritance for children or grandchildren. When this occurred, owners attempted to sell their houses to artisans whose skill and capacity for hard work were known, such as former apprentices or skilled independents. This was one means of preserving the continuity of the house name as well as its value as a piece of commercial property. On the other hand, when children like Simon Carrère exhibited little interest or talent in school, or when the opportunities for securing more valued work were limited or unavailable, ownership of well-run houses could offer a lucrative means of livelihood over the course of the work cycle. The Bonbonnière illustrates the range of alternatives considered by family owners as they approached and planned for retirement.

Max LeBlanc was ready to retire in 1988 when he was approached by the De Closets. They were anxious to get set up in business and knew that he was looking for a successor. Monsieur LeBlanc explained:

When we took over in 1964, I never cared about making a lot of money so the business stayed a modest size. We had one son who was really bright and we encouraged him to stay in school. He prepared a doctorate in physics, and the day he defended his thesis he was offered an excellent public sector job. However, if he hadn't been interested in school I would have drawn him into the business and today I would have two boutiques in Biarritz, one for him and one for me. The day he was established professionally (*casé*) I retired mentally and I decided to sell. I waited five years for the right couple to appear, and when I was approached by my successors, the De Closets, we made a deal and shook hands on it in one afternoon.[4]

Independent entrepreneurship provided the means of establishing or solidifying a personal and professional patrimony not normally within reach of workers on an hourly wage. Independent status appealed equally, although for different reasons, to lower middle-class family owners and to owners who saw themselves as "bourgeois" by virtue of their education, acquired wealth, and leisure pursuits. On the one hand, for the newly self-employed like the Harcauts, the move out of rural, artisanal, factory, or clerical salaried work and into self-employment was a step up. It afforded the possibility for lower middle-class, working-class, and farm workers to achieve social mobility (see Bertaux and Bertaux-Wiame 1978; Lequin 1986; Mayer 1986; and Zarca 1986, 1987). Artisans employed over a lifetime regretted that their status as skilled workers, as opposed to self-employed masters, precluded them from acquiring commercial property and accumulating assets that they could pass on to their children. On the other hand, purchasing or inheriting an established business like the Dalbaitz house conferred status in an area like the southwest, where a commercial bourgeoisie has always predominated among local elites.

Successful houses provided the economic capital necessary for family members to create and/or increase their social and cultural capital and to pass it on to their children. This economic capital could serve a number of different purposes. First, it provided the financial means for children to move out of craft work. Although artisanship enjoyed a positive resonance in post-1975 France, it has frequently been castigated as a backward, anti-modern mode of entrepreneurship. This has been especially true during periods when modernization was perceived to be a priority. Although artisanship connoted personalized commercial relations, satisfying labor, and high-quality goods, it also carried the stigma associated with manual labor in France. This stigma was attached to manual versus intellectual work, although it was mitigated somewhat in crafts with a pronounced aesthetic dimension approaching art, such as jewelry, wood sculpture, glass making, leather working and, to a lesser extent, the food crafts, especially cuisine, pastry, sugar candy, and chocolate making.

## Newcomers

For first generation entrepreneurs, the ownership of confectionery houses provided the opportunity to earn a more lucrative living and to establish an inheritance for their children. Yet the costs associated with creating a new house or purchasing an existing one made it difficult for young workers from lower middle-class, working-class, and farm backgrounds to become self-employed. The economic climate ushered in following the oil crisis of the 1970s exacerbated these difficulties. Inflation drove up the commercial value of established commercial property and the leases on business real estate. Business loans for artisanal independents remained scarce and difficult to obtain (Auvolat 1985). The start-up costs for new businesses, including machinery for the workshop, display cases, and boutique furnishings, increased. Similarly, as the commercial value of existing houses rose, so did closing and notary fees tied to the purchase price.[5] In many cases, prosperous established houses became and remained too expensive for young workers to afford and too costly for older, more experienced workers to buy and amortize over the remainder of their professional lives. Only successful independents seeking to trade up by selling a first business in order to buy a larger or more valuable one could afford this type of commercial property. In the early 1990s newcomers often attained self-employment by purchasing inexpensive houses that needed renovation, had few machines in the workshop or outdated appointments in the boutique, and/or suffered from declining sales for other reasons like poor management and staffing or personal problems. However, even run-down houses in exceptional locations commanded huge prices. One such commercial property, a tiny, old-fashioned *pâtisserie* located in the pedestrian zone of Grand Bayonne, was on the market for $170,000 during the 1990–91 year.[6]

Michel Harcaut had to work for many years as a salaried worker before he was able to realize his life-long ambition to become self-employed. He completed a three-year apprenticeship, earned a vocational diploma (CAP, or *certificat d'aptitude professionelle*) in pastry production in 1964, and worked in a number of Basque coast houses. He spent eighteen years (nine in the local Mathieu house) as a salaried worker before he and his wife were able to purchase the Dominguez house in 1982. Although the physical plant was completely outdated, the house is situated on a prime location opposite the medieval cathedral in Grand Bayonne. Because of its location, the asking price of over $100,000 was still very high. However, the Dominguez's accounting practices caused problems when it came time to sell their confectionery house. French notaries handle commercial real estate transactions and require verification of the sales price with records of annual sales and income tax receipts. Like many artisans of their generation, the Dominguez paid state income tax based on a system of estimated earnings *(le régime forfaitaire)* and routinely declared only approximately 50 percent of their actual sales. Thus, they were forced to reduce the asking price to $50,000, and the Harcauts were able to afford the business. They combined a cash gift from Michel's mother (who ran a successful fish business with his brother in the neighboring department of Lot-et-Garonne) with a short-term bank loan to cover the purchase fees as well as the renovation costs.

After 1982, the Harcauts more than doubled the annual sales figures of their predecessors. Yet in describing their future prospects they sounded a pessimistic and contradictory note. They predicted the imminent collapse of artisanal food crafts, blaming labyrinthine state fiscal and labor regulations, competition from mass distribution outlets, and lowered taste standards evidenced by the popularity of cheap, mass-produced confectionery products. They saw this "crisis" in artisanship as resulting from the dearth of young people being trained in manual crafts and from the growing numbers of unemployable baccalaureate degree holders. Yet they urged all three of their children to stay in school and to prepare these academic degrees. As their son explained, "At a certain point in my adolescence I would really have liked to take over the family business, but to do that it would have been necessary to learn the craft and especially to want to practice it with the same passion and the same flair as my father." Another son explained, "It was my father who decided for me by insisting that I study and do well in school." In fact, the decision to stay in school was, for many children, a decision to leave the craft behind.

## Established Houses

The decision to transfer business property to family heirs or to sell it to outsiders was always complicated by the impact of shifting social and economic circumstances. Family owners faced different challenges and opportunities with regard to craft work in the 1918–1939 and 1945–1980 periods, in contrast to the last decades of the century. For different reasons, craft work was difficult to maintain and reproduce in both periods.

Life histories taken from craftsmen whose careers spanned the 1939–1980 period revealed the intensive work rhythms and extensive manual component to craft work, often described as slavery. Until the early 1960s, there were no industrial producers of fresh pastry products, few large-scale producers of dipped chocolate and sugar candies, and no competition from mass distribution outlets. During this period craft families prospered and earned substantial profits. They shielded themselves from what they considered to be onerous government tax burdens by routinely declaring only a portion of their earnings and sought to provide retirement income by investing profits in real estate, both commercial and land holdings, jewelry, and furniture. Many families actively recruited sometimes reluctant heirs during this period. The Joliots in Pau and Bayonne provide an example.

Louis Joliot and his wife had a son and two daughters. Their son Paul (1914–1986) earned a baccalaureate degree as well as a university degree in law studies at a time when few young people pursued a secondary and university education. As Paul was nearing the end of his studies in 1939, the expiration of a fifteen-year legal partnership among the three Joliot brothers followed by the sudden death of Ulysse Joliot provoked a rapid restructuring of the business. Louis got ownership of the stores in Bayonne and Biarritz, and the remaining business property was divided between his brothers' families in Pau. At age fifty-five, Louis was anxious to have an heir in place in the workshop. Both of his daughters had problems that precluded their designation as heiresses of the house. In the stagnating economic and deteriorating political climate of the late 1930s, Paul Joliot was pessimistic about a law career and bowed to his parents' desire that he enter the family business. He received training in the family workshop and in Bordeaux, continuing an active role until he died in 1986.

Shortly after World War II, the Joliot family in Pau faced a crisis. Ulysse Joliot's sons, Henri and Maurice, took their deceased father's place in the workshop upon their return from work camps in Germany. Their mother remarried and continued her active role in the family boutiques in Pau. Maurice stayed single, but in 1947 his brother Henri married a shopkeeper's daughter from Pau. Henri and his wife had a two year old and were expecting another child when disaster struck. Henri was killed in a gas explosion in the workshop in August 1950. The likelihood that these potential Joliot heirs would be removed from the family and the house through the remarriage of their widowed mother threatened house continuity at a delicate juncture. The possibility that she might bring a new husband to work in the house alongside a blood relation recruited as heir was even less palatable. The only solution that made sense involved a levirate marriage between the deceased heir's widow and his elder brother, Maurice.

In contrast to other house systems in the southwest such as the Aveyronnais *ostal*, where brothers- and sisters-in-law are not thought of as relatives, and levirate or sororate marriages are seen as a logical solution to the premature death of an heir or heiress (compare Rogers 1991, 93–94), owners of confectionery houses were far more circumspect about such marriage strategies. They were keenly aware that the Catholic church, custom, and a bourgeois family model proscribed such practices. Although Hélène Sarlate told me in a disapproving tone about the marriage of her uncle and aunt, none of her Palois cousins mentioned it. When Maurice's wife described her entry into the house, she referred only to her 1947 marriage. However, when her daughter quoted 1951 as the date of her parents' marriage, I questioned Madame Joliot about the discrepancy when we found ourselves alone. She said, "There is something I have not told you, Madame.

My husband Henri was killed in a workshop accident when Sylvie was only two and I was three months' pregnant with our second child. I always liked my brother-in-law and you know he adored his brother and our children. So we married and I told him I would be willing to have more children if he wanted but he said no. Things have worked out. It was the best solution because in that way everything stayed in the family.

During the 1960s and 1970s, a number of factors reinforced the cultural predilection for moving children out of craft work and into white collar jobs. Legislative reforms during this period brought independent craftsmen under standard business, fiscal, and labor codes. Small independents enjoyed added legal protections but also higher labor and operating costs as a result of at least partial compliance to state-mandated labor, management, accounting, and training regulations. Comprehensive educational reforms broadened access to secondary and university programs and created new degree options in general and professional studies. In addition, rapid economic growth from 1945 to 1975 increased career choices for young people. For these reasons, children were encouraged to stay in school. Their parents were hopeful that they could pursue white collar or professional careers. However, their hopes were sabotaged by a shifting socioeconomic climate.

The family craftsmen who were preparing to retire in the late 1970s and the 1980s were faced with a dilemma. Established confectionery houses were becoming too expensive to sell to outsiders. Inflation and high interest rates along with scarce small business loans and the high value of houses as commercial property conspired to put them out of reach of most salaried craftsmen. Pressure increased on elderly owners to sell outside the craft and have their houses die or to draw young kinsmen back to preserve continuity. At the same time, the sluggish economy and mounting unemployment among young people in France during the 1980s conspired to make a permanent entry into other careers problematic for their children in spite of their advanced education.

For example, in 1981 Paul Joliot was sixty-eight years old and ready to retire. Like the Dalbaitz owners, his three daughters had married men with university educations, and two of their husbands were well established in professional careers. He and his wife decided to sell the business to outsiders. Given the location of the boutiques in Bayonne and Biarritz, the clientele and the large workshop, the price was high and there were no takers. The following year Paul Joliot asked the husband of his eldest daughter, Patrick Sarlate, to enter the business. Patrick Sarlate's version of how the offer was made and accepted has been told the same way in countless public interviews, including the one I recorded on 8 November 1990 in the Dalbaitz workshop:

My in-laws came to our home for Sunday lunch and I made a chocolate cake. I love to cook by the way. My father-in-law really liked it and just asked me straight out if I would consider coming into the business [to produce]. I said I would think about it and two weeks later spent a whole day with him at the workshop. When I was leaving, he asked if I had made my decision and I said, Why not?

In fact, there were a number of excellent reasons for Patrick Sarlate to accept the offer. Hélène Joliot Sarlate had received a baccalaureate degree and trained at a secretarial school in Paris, but her job was not satisfying. Moreover, she was affected by her parents' dilemma and conscious of the setbacks her husband had suffered. After spending two years preparing the entrance exam for advanced graduate training in the humanities at the Ecole Normale Supérieure, he was not accepted. He then completed a degree *(licence)* in history at the University of Bordeaux, hoping to pass the national secondary teacher examination (CAPES). He failed that exam twice. During this period he became involved in local politics. His patron, the mayor of Biarritz, Bernard Marie, secured him a position in the tourist office. In 1977 he was elected to the municipal council in neighboring Anglet, and this election made it imperative that he have a secure professional position.[7] His job at the local tourist office was not sufficiently remunerative or prestigious, linked as it was to political patronage. Although he was married with a marriage contract, Monsieur Sarlate made his acceptance contingent upon payment of a good monthly salary and the time to pursue his political interests. The position as head of production, if not the legal owner, of a well-established confectionery house was a very attractive prospect.[8]

## Conclusion

Houses were created by, named for, and traced back to a founding craftsman and his wife. Even when the house was transferred to one or a series of different owners, the name was immutable and through time became inalienable (Mauss 1990). The reproduction of confectionery houses was assured through discourses of skill and authenticity. Houses were reproduced by a continuous line of craft families whose skill and training authenticated French chocolates and differentiated them from the inauthentic goods sold in mass distribution stores and foreign franchise outlets. Handicraft skill and family entrepreneurship were what gave the name its value and made the oldest houses so desirable and costly as pieces of commercial property.

The continuity of the family name through time gave the appearance of a system of biological reproduction based on a patriline. In reality it was a system of craft inheritance based on skill. The reproduction of the name and its goods depended on the recruitment of an unbroken line of craft families, skilled craftsmen in the workshop, and qualified women in the boutique. *Chocolatiers'* practices revealed that the transfer of houses could not be left to biology. Suitable and willing heirs were made, not born, and the recruitment of successors was always fraught with problems. Yet *chocolatiers'* discourses belied their lived practices. They actively cultivated the image of house transmission within the family and masked the actual system of reproduction based on skill. Written and visual texts, like the newspaper article on Bayonnais confectionery houses featuring the Carrère family photograph, implied continuity with family systems in the southwest and with received popular notions concerning the transfer of houses from father to son. They allowed *chocolatiers* to assert a collective identity and to claim a history with cultural resonance. The seamless image of familial continuity also served to conceal the social mobility that was a critical feature of the system whereby salaried craftsmen achieved independence by creating or buying their own houses. The positively valued image of the confectionery house also masked to some extent the ambiguous class status and negative images associated with artisans and petty bourgeois entrepreneurship in contemporary France. Close study of houses revealed that actual ties of descent only confirmed a system of reproduction based on outsiders. Although it was depicted as a model of intergenerational reproduction, the Carrère house had been sold numerous times over its life and had been owned by the present family only since 1944. Family ties were conflated with and added to an inheritance grounded in skill. For this reason, recruiting a son or son-in-law into the workshop was seen as an ideal scenario.

Whereas the work identities of artisans were tied primarily to skill in production, the work identities of women were connected to social presentation and emotional arts, skills used in their roles as spouses and mothers. These skills underlay and reinforced a gendered division of labor whereby tasks were assigned according to the "innate" attributes of women. This rationale effectively masked the social construction of skill as it naturalized women's control of sales based on gender characteristics. Since women were expected to be adept at juggling multiple tasks, it was judged to be normal that they manage their boutiques, run their homes, and oversee their children. As more than one artisan put it, "I just don't have the head for that." Since it was natural for women to manage people and sales given their natural aptitudes, it was unnatural for men to do so. Despite their obvious manual skill, male artisans insisted that they just could not tie those intricate knots and bows on packages or deal with demanding customers. It was also unnatural for women to produce goods and to manage male workers and therefore acceptable to exclude them from production. The question of both salaried status and formal business ownership for artisanal wives in confectionery houses was a matter of considerable concern not only to Madame Carrère but to craft leaders and state representatives alike in 1991. A majority of artisanal wives in her generation found themselves in a similar situation and were, as a result, particularly vulnerable when the legal transfer of business was considered (Zarca 1986).

For their part, women internalized and reinforced this discourse based on a natural division of labor. They naturalized their place in the boutique through their own discourses of skill. For many the move into family entrepreneurship was an abrupt and difficult one for which they were unprepared. In contrast to artisans' narratives that emphasized, even celebrated, the slow and arduous acquisition of skill through apprenticeship and lifelong participation within communities of practice (Lave and Wenger 1991), women's public narratives concealed this difficult transition by describing their skill as an innate gift. When women were complimented on their window dressings, house packaging, and boutique interiors or asked how they mastered this aspect of the job, many replied that one simply had to possess a natural sense of taste.

At the same time, the construction of identities based on social presentation, emotional labor, and family artisanship was fragile at best in a context marked by an increased emphasis on white collar work and professionalization in sales. This emphasis meant that there were increasingly complicated exchanges among local and national craft leaders, business consultants, tastemakers, state representatives, industrial chocolate manufacturers, and family owners. Craft families in general and artisanal wives in particular faced increased pressure to rationalize management procedures and to modernize their sales techniques.

Chapter 7 moves the object of focus from individual families to the construction, representation, and reproduction of a local craft community as it was enacted within the context of two publicly staged craft rituals—the creation of a southwest chapter of the Confrérie des Chocolatiers and the mounting of a local craft contest. It examines how family owners and salaried workers performed and perceived craft work and what constituted craft mastery. How did craftsmen define, display, celebrate, and transmit this skill in the workshop?

CHAPTER 7

# Craft as Community,
# Chocolate as Spectacle

The third weekend in October 1991, thirteen elders of the
Confrérie des Chocolatiers (Brotherhood of French Chocolatiers) traveled to Pau from Paris, Bordeaux, Avignon, Grenoble, Rouen, Limoges,
Lyon, Pont-Audemer, and La Charité-sur-Loire to create a new chapter. On Sunday, 20 October 1991, Confrérie elders assembled in full re-
galia in downtown Pau. They were resplendent in ankle-length brown
satin robes accented with gold ribbon and fur, their plumed headdresses
glimmering with the effigy of the serpent god Quetzalcoatl, a deity
about whom local spectators were justifiably curious. The elders piqued
their curiosity, adding a titillating air of mystery, by describing Quetzalcoatl in radio and newspaper interviews as the Aztec God of Chocolate.[1] This costumed procession was headed by the Confrérie master
of ceremonies, who brandished proudly the official banner emblazoned
with a crowned cacao bean pod. The procession wended its way slowly
through the main streets toward the site of the main ritual event, where
twelve new members were to be inducted.

The induction ceremony was held in the historic Parliament of Navarre, site of the royal law court in prerevolutionary times. Confrérie elders solemnly filed in, forming a line at the back of the council chamber
beneath an immense portrait of Pau's most famous native son, Henry,
King of Navarre (1562–1610) and of France (1589–1610). The grand master and master of ceremonies summoned each new member individually to swear a public oath of loyalty. As they acknowledged the "noble
matter" with which they were entrusted and swore "faithfulness to the
spirit of French chocolates," "promising to eat them each day," the craft

medallion—an imitation cacao bean pod suspended on a gilt-edged ribbon—was ceremoniously placed around their necks. Twelve craftsmen were inducted—five from the Basque coast (Messieurs Mathieu, Sarlate, Bergeron, Harcaut, and Santoro), five from Pau, one from Peyrehorade, a small town between Bayonne and Pau, and one from Jarnac in the department of Charentes. A sounding of trumpets from a tape recording provided by the Confrérie signaled the formal incorporation of the twelve within the membership ranks.

Created in 1986 by members of the *chocolatiers'* professional organization, the Confrérie had expanded to include sixteen chapters by 1991.[2] The organizers' goal was to increase consumption of French chocolate and to celebrate the master craftsmen who produced it. Monsieur Mourier had hosted the sixth Confrérie chapter in Pau in 1988, and flushed with the success of the February 1991 conference, he immediately began to plan for the opening of a new chapter in the southwest. Since only Palois *chocolatiers* were inducted in 1988, Mourier was intent on sponsoring Basque coast artisans.

At the same time, Mourier was deeply concerned about the results of a Basque Coast Craft Contest held the previous May. The contest was the first of its kind on the Basque coast and elicited the enthusiastic participation of craftsmen from all over the region. The contest exhibition received coverage in the local press and was well attended by the general public, and the award ceremony was presided over by municipal notables. However, the contest results generated considerable debate within the craft community. The piece that drew the most attention and acclaim, a magnificent antique (chocolate) phonograph crafted by Monsieur Bergeron, owner of the Bourriet *chocolaterie* in Biarritz and the premier confectionery artist of the entire region, had been disqualified on a technicality. The first prize had been awarded to what many saw as a less deserving piece crafted not by the owner of the house in question but by an unspecified number of skilled workers employed by him. In the wake of this dissension, Mourier deemed it crucial to organize an event that would reaffirm a sense of regional community.

Confrérie membership was possible only through a system of sponsorship (*parrainage*), whereby existing members proposed new members in two categories. First, only self-employed artisans or young heirs (with at least five years' experience) were inducted with the rank of *commandeur*. Second, well-known local personalities in business, political, and artistic circles were welcomed as honorary members. Although their induction was promoted in news media coverage on the basis of

their discriminating palates and preference for refined (French) chocolates, in reality it had more to do with their social status and cultural
capital as an important source of cachet for the Confrérie. This is what
earned them the privilege of membership alongside the craft producers
who formed the core of the Confrérie.

Although the criteria for membership as *commandeur* seemed
straightforward enough, the actual choice of individual producers
proved to be both difficult and political. Decisions about who did and
did not belong revealed a complex politics of sponsorship as well as the
allure of membership in producer associations. Since I lived in Bayonne
and made weekly rounds to Basque coast workshops, Monsieur Mourier talked to me frequently about the member list for the new chapter.
His plans seemed to change daily. Initially I felt very uncomfortable being placed in the role of expert consultant or resident spy, particularly
when he questioned me closely on production in particular houses.
Ultimately, however, the many conversations I had with him over the
three-month period during which he reworked the list permitted me
to understand the salient mechanisms through which a local craft community was created and sustained. These mechanisms included (1) the
hands-on acquisition and public display of skills intimately linked to
the celebration of an artisanal aesthetic, (2) collective craft rituals such
as the Confrérie induction ceremony, (3) mentoring relationships between masters and apprentices, and (4) subcontracting relationships
among house owners. These same mechanisms both engendered a local
community and, because they posed a constant potential for conflict,
also threatened its continued existence. Whereas the May 1991 craft contest created conflict among local craftsmen, the Confrérie ceremony was
intended as a celebration of a solidary and similarly skilled craft community. It was a social drama that "fused disparate elements, glossed conflicts, and provided a sense of individual and collective continuity in the
course of mounting a bold and original fiction" (Myerhoff 1992, 133).

Craft communities, like national communities, are culturally imagined and socially maintained. A salient feature of artisanal identity involves the establishment of a boundary between members of a particular craft and other work groups (Coy 1989, 8–9). Incorporation within
the ranks of a community of skilled practitioners is often accomplished
through formal or informal rite-of-passage tests and ongoing learning
and participation within a community of practice (Lave and Wenger
1991). Cross-cultural accounts of contemporary artisanship (Blasquez
1976; Bradburd 1995; Cooper 1980; Coy 1989; Moeran 1984; Nash 1993;

Zarca 1979a, 1986) and historical studies centering on France (Auslander 1996; Coornaert 1966, 1968; Kaplan 1996; Lequin 1977; Perdiguier 1977; Reddy 1984; Scott 1974; Sewell 1980; Sonescher 1987; Truant 1979) reveal the complex patterns of alliance and cooperation in recruitment, training, and production that exist among producers within the same craft. These patterns of alliance are often crucial to the short-term maintenance and long-term reproduction of a craft. Given the received wisdom on craft in advanced capitalism, there is little documentation of how craft communities are constituted and reproduced intergenerationally.[3]

Like any drama, the extended planning and backstage events that preceded the Confrérie ceremony were highly instructive. The decision to extend or withhold the privilege of membership revealed local power relations, established craft hierarchies, and the nexus of class and craft, as well as the tensions and ambiguities that underlie the construction of artisanal identities. When Monsieur Mourier first mentioned his plans for the induction ceremony and described the candidates at the top of his list, I was confused. His first list included Monsieur Bergeron in Biarritz, Messieurs Mathieu, Harcaut, and Carrère in Bayonne, and Monsieur Clouseau in Anglet but not the owners of the Aguirre and Dalbaitz houses in Bayonne or the Salinas house in Saint-Jean-de-Luz—all three owned and operated by the same family for at least three generations. The candidates for membership included family heirs as well as newcomers, owners who directly participated in production and those who functioned more like managers, as well as a mix of established and new houses. Why did Mourier include Monsieur Harcaut, the newest independent in Bayonne but exclude Monsieur De Closet, the newest *chocolatier* in Biarritz? Why did Mourier decide not to invite the owner of the Aguirre *chocolaterie* in Bayonne, a house widely promoted in national culinary and tourist guides for its hot chocolate? What was his motivation for including Simon Carrère and Serge Mathieu—both of whom took a limited role in workshop production—and excluding Monsieur Sarlate, who had learned the craft from the bottom up and produced regularly? Careful examination of the shared backgrounds and work experiences of the top candidates will illuminate how artisanal identities were linked to the construction, reproduction, and public representation of the local craft community.

What did the top candidates all share? To begin with, all of the craftsmen on Mourier's first list were from working-class or lower middle-class families. French society is still very much stratified on the basis of educational attainment (Bourdieu 1984), and the value of mental work has intensified in the postwar period through the burgeoning of a service sector and a concomitant ideology of professionalization coupled with rapid modernization. Despite their possession of (in some cases considerable) economic capital, these artisans' lack of social and cultural capital—most had left school at fourteen and held only devalued vocational certificates—relegated them to an intermediate, highly ambivalent, lower middle-class status. They were themselves keenly aware of the contradictions French artisans embody based on their dual functions of skilled worker and independent entrepreneur. Although highly skilled and self-employed, craftsmen were still manual workers and petty entrepreneurs in a context where intellectual work has the most cultural value and where business proprietorship confers less social status than liberal professions, civil service, or management positions.

Indeed, their ambiguous class position directly informed the narratives they recounted concerning work, skill, family, and community. These owners were all guardians of an artisanal aesthetic grounded in self-realization, meaningful work, and aesthetic participation in the material world (compare Kondo 1990, 229–244). Their narratives drew on an idealized discourse of artisanship as a vestige of "true" France—a France characterized by a traditional work ethic, family values, community cohesion, and the noncompetitive practices of the small business sector. They created and enacted an identity depicting artisanal work and identities as living tradition and historic patrimony. These owners' narratives and performances of selfhood celebrated a similar craft ethos predicating skill as the necessary condition for community membership—its acquisition through guided practice and its display in public places. Through their active mentoring relationships, management of salaried workers, participation in craft rituals, subcontracting arrangements, and patterns of sociability, they produced and reproduced a local craft community.

## Narratives of Skill

All of these craftsmen had undergone traditional hands-on apprenticeship in the workplace, and most had perfected their skill by working in other houses or training in specialized courses under recognized masters. They saw their skill as inextricably linked to a community of practitioners with whom they could and frequently did have alternating cooperative and conflict-riven relations. Although the corpus of skills required for mastery of a given craft changed over time in response to new technology and market demands, they acknowledged and used it as the standard by which to position themselves within a structural hierarchy in the present and against which to measure progress over time within the workshop and the individual craft itself. They agreed that all artisans defined themselves as skilled practitioners of a manual craft—regardless of the level of skill they actually attained—and pursued the goal of entrepreneurial independence, although many did not reach it.

For them, craft skill was predicated on knowledge as experience and on learning as ongoing participation within a given community of practice (Lave and Wenger 1991). It could only be properly acquired through an apprenticeship combining both observation and practice. For these owners, a period of routinized, low-level participation in the workplace was necessary to lay a foundation of implicit understandings as a prelude to mastering the more complex aspects of the craft. Apprenticeship training was necessarily extended and sometimes arduous because it involved the slow, progressive acquisition of craft skill. A repertoire of collective dispositions, including precision hand and arm movements, stance, work rhythm, terminology, and ways of interacting were imprinted through repetition and rehearsal. Through guided practice, apprentices developed both empirical mastery and cognitive understanding of the chemical properties that governed the transformation of their raw materials into a finished product. Learning proceeded through participation in the daily and seasonal routines of the house. The tempering of chocolate and the preparation of candies could not be separated from the hierarchical ranking of the workshop, the proper greetings exchanged among house members, the sixteen- to eighteen-hour workdays at Christmas, the constant flirtations and bawdy exchanges between saleswomen and artisans, the mid-morning coffee break, specialized vocabulary for the workshop *(laboratoire)* and craft tools such as the dipping fork *(fourchette),* as well as the goofing off, work slowdowns, and pilfering of bonbons when the *singes* (here, "owners," literally, "monkeys") were not around.

In their view, apprentices had to learn the craft from the bottom up and should, therefore, begin by stacking and storing finished goods, cleaning, and making deliveries. They should advance slowly to learn the beginning and end parts of production, preparing raw materials, cutting and machine coating prepared candy centers before learning to measure, mix, flavor, and grind, to temper the chocolate, and to cook candy centers. Innovation in product conception, elaborate aesthetic presentation of goods, and confectionery artistry came last and were deemed signs of the most advanced skill. They saw advanced skill as the active interplay between the hands and the head. When asked to define fully fledged craftsmen, these artisans echoed the views prevalent in other French crafts by insisting that "the head functions as much as the hands."

They acknowledged the importance of physical knowledge or learning with the body and, watching them rapidly hand-dip chocolate candies or produce an entire tray of identical truffles from a pastry tube in under two minutes, it was obvious that certain techniques had been committed to muscle memory (see fig. 7). However, in contrast to Japanese confectioners, who stressed exclusively physical idioms of technical expertise over cognitive ability and referred to an artisan's skill as his arm (Kondo 1990, 238), French artisans' discourses privileged a cognitive model of skill in which the most accomplished practitioners understood both empirically and intellectually the chemistry and geometry of chocolate—that is, the optimum temperatures at which to work it and the forms it could be made to assume. True masters' cognitive understanding allowed their heads to guide and direct their hands and thus enabled the mastery and artistic elaboration of unruly media like chocolate and sugar. Indeed, the measurement of skill after apprenticeship or in craft contests often included both empirical tests such as the crafting of a masterpiece and written exams to certify theoretical knowledge of the craft medium (compare Blasquez 1976). Theoretical and empirical understandings of the raw material were judged to be inseparable from a sustained attention to aesthetics in the fabrication of both candies and confectionery art. Through the conception of pieces whose appeal was primarily aesthetic, functional craft was elevated to decorative art and artisans became more like artists. The brilliant chocolate sheen and impeccably smooth surface of molded Easter eggs was as important as the placement of two perfectly formed pale pink sugar roses as contrast against the dark chocolate background.

All of the craftsmen on Mourier's first list would have identified with Michel Harcaut's apprenticeship experience. In 1961, at fourteen years of age, he began an unpaid three-year apprenticeship. He routinely worked twelve- and fourteen-hour days six days a week with a day off in the middle of the week. On one slow February morning in the Harcaut workshop, Michel produced his apprenticeship contract and read parts of it out loud to me. The language of the contract spoke powerfully to the multidimensional nature of training. It mandated an unspecified amount of professional classes "to acquire the requisite theoretical

Figure 7. Hand-crafting chocolate truffles, Harcaut workshop, 1990.

knowledge"—knowledge he learned in the workshop because the formal classes were held at the Chamber of Trades in another city. It included not only training in the special physical skills and the economics of craft production but the inculcation of the structured social relations of craftsmanship (compare Coy 1989, 1–4). Casting a dismissive look at his two apprentices, Harcaut said emphatically, "Things were completely different then. Listen, you see the apprentice owed, and he read verbatim from the contract, 'loyalty, obedience, respect to his boss, to other workers [in a superordinate position to him] . . . to conform to the present and future workshop regulations, to help his apprenticeship master to the extent of his abilities and strengths, and to observe the rules of courtesy, demeanor, and dress with the house clientele.'" The master was enjoined "to behave toward him [the apprentice] as a good head of the household *(père de famille),* to teach him methodically and completely the profession of pastry maker" (Chamber of Trades, Lot-et-Garonne, 13 October 1961).

When I interrupted to ask how he had begun his apprenticeship, he exclaimed, "How? Bah! With a load of dirty dishes and a mop." Like so many craftsmen trained before the 1970s, little by little Harcaut was taught to make different doughs and batters for bread, croissants, brioche, pies, and cakes. He stole minutes from his work to observe the owner's son (who had trained, like Robert Linxe and Fabrice Carrère, at the Swiss COBA School) crafting chocolate bonbons and art. Harcaut went on, "I would wolf down my lunch and rush back early to the empty workshop to practice some of the techniques I had observed. I couldn't wait to get back to work." Later, as he distinguished himself by his seriousness, discipline, and skill, his master gave him more time explaining and sharing his own tricks of the trade. By the time his contract ended, he had learned the basic skills and was eighteen and ready to leave for military service. A few weeks later, I was invited to a dinner at the Harcaut home and Michel dug out old photos taken during his apprenticeship and his military service in Abidjan. His three children teased him mercilessly, and we all laughed heartily as we compared the handsome, cocky soldier to the gawky, immature apprentice looking hopeful but unsure as he stared into the camera. Harcaut paused, and on a more serious note he mused, "Well, I had become a man." His attainment of adulthood paralleled the gradual internalization of the craft; it signified both social maturity and a work identity.

Harcaut and other owners contrasted their own difficult experiences to those of the pampered apprentices they saw in the year 1990–91.

They depicted this personalized training as a quintessential rite of passage and described their own apprenticeships as a series of trials marked by the stressful ambiguity of their outsider status. All were overworked, some were ridiculed or ignored, and a few were mistreated physically. They readily acknowledged the past exploitation and sometimes abuse of youngsters by masters in the form of grueling hours, little or no pay, and harsh living conditions. Indeed, tales of cruel masters were rife—a number of artisans specifically admonished me to read a autobiographical novel based on the apprenticeship of a young *pâtissier/chocolatier* in the late 1930s. His master Monsieur Pétiot not only overworked, underfed, and housed his apprentices in unheated, flea-infested quarters but also physically beat the novel's protagonist because his uncle, a leftist labor activist, dared to complain to the Labor Inspection Office about the working conditions (Clavel 1962). Yet they insisted that hardships were necessary in order to provide young people with the mental discipline and physical stamina demanded by house ownership. They felt it was entirely appropriate, indeed necessary, that apprentices accept the structural ranking of a community of skilled craftsmen and their position at its base.

Craftsmen agreed that this shared experience, in both its positive and negative aspects, created a collective identity among a community of similarly skilled practitioners. Apprentices could only attain full membership in the community by successfully passing an empirical and theoretical test of their mastery of craft skill. This test could be formal or informal, but its results had to be certified by a self-employed master. Serious craftsmen considered this rite of passage as only the first stage in a longer process that would include ongoing training with masters in different settings, from family workshops to culinary schools. As young artisans aspiring to independent ownership, they knew they must perfect their mastery of all aspects of the craft. What they described was a Tour de France modeled on the journeys undertaken by young artisans in preindustrial journeymen brotherhood associations *(compagnonnages)*.

Many artisans and French people in general saw these *compagnons,* or journeymen, as craft exemplars whose devotion to traditional workmanship standards and techniques was elevated to a calling. One retired *chocolatier,* whose great-grandfather left his home to begin a Tour de France organized in bakery production by a brotherhood association in 1850, contrasted the traditional notion of craft work embodied in his Tour with that prevalent in many contemporary work settings: "Now all people say is, 'I have the legal right not to do such and such.'. . . In those days they said, 'It's our duty.' Even if the journeyman did not agree with his boss, it was his duty to master his craft and to do all that was required. He had to pick up stakes and go on to the next position in another city."

The mystique associated with journeymen's relentless pursuit of perfection in their work was said to afford all true artisans an idiom of distinction that legal rights and officially defined occupational categories could not. For those who organized a personal Tour de France before becoming self-employed and even for those who could not, the arduous and mystery-shrouded journeys of *compagnons* throughout preindustrial France in search of skill constituted a resonant metaphor for the slow, halting process involving sacrifices and deferred rewards required before craft mastery could be achieved (Zarca 1979a, 1979b). Given the pronounced differences in regional and national confectionery cuisines, working for a month, a season, or a year in a number of houses in France and abroad or combining work experience with professional courses was deemed essential training for future independents. The founder of the Bourriet house in Biarritz described it this way:

You see I didn't have the mentality of a skilled worker trying to earn a living. No, I was only interested in gaining experience in as many houses as I could. After my apprenticeship (1926–1930), I worked in five different houses in the north and east of France where my father had contacts. I would stay as long as it took me to master a particular work station—the oven *[four]*, bread and sweet rolls *[tour]*, cakes and desserts *[entremets]*, or ice creams *[glacerie]*—and then move on. Also, during the *drôle de guerre* (1939 1940) I also met a Swiss *chocolatier* stationed nearby. My father befriended him and he taught me the art of chocolate.

In 1991, sixty years after Monsieur Bourriet's Tour de France, a young heir described his experience in the Clouseau house in the same way: "I'm not working there to earn money [he was making the minimum wage]. . . . This house is a school and you go there to learn."

## Mentoring Relationships between Masters and Apprentices

In their narratives, these artisans attributed both their initial passage into a community of skilled practitioners and a nascent attachment to the craft to a workshop mentor. They described the strong and enduring bonds that emerged between them and a master or head of production. Michel Harcaut maintained a close relationship with his master from the conclusion of his apprenticeship in 1964 until his master's death in 1991. He also had a similarly intimate relationship with Philippe, an apprentice he himself had trained. When Harcaut and his wife Michèle went on short trips to Paris for trade shows or to Lyon for training courses, Philippe was always the one he left in charge. Although Philippe was employed full time in the Salinas house, he agreed to rearrange his schedule there or to work double shifts in order to accommodate Monsieur Harcaut.

The usually taciturn and often irascible Monsieur Motte, an instructor at the Bayonne Chamber of Trades, was in an expansive mood one late November afternoon when an unhappy first-year apprentice asked him about his own apprenticeship. As Monsieur Motte brought the chocolate to the right temperature for the hand-dipping of truffle centers, he shared the following story:

I was my master's twelfth apprentice, but over the eight years I worked with him [three as an apprentice and five as a worker], I became like a son to him. He bought me my first car, paid for me to get my driver's license, and created a job for me after I returned from my military service. One day we had a terrible fight. I left his house in a rage and did not go back or speak to him for years. However, when the time came for him to retire, he contacted me through an intermediary—he had his pride after all—to tell me he wanted me to buy his business.

This story is powerful because it links the personalized mentoring relationship between masters and apprentices to the reproduction of craft communities. It also suggests the tensions always implicit in that relationship, tensions that reveal its fragility, threaten its breakdown, and imperil the reproduction of houses. The reproduction of the house name, its goods, and ultimately the craft depended upon the recruitment of an unbroken line of skilled craftsmen to carry on production. The longevity of confectionery houses and the craft was contingent upon the training of apprentices who would one day become independent masters and reconstitute the local craft community in their turn. Within the house the master supervised the recruitment and training of the apprentices and journeymen who came for a number of years, months, or a season to learn the craft or to perfect their mastery of it. Those who were particularly disciplined and talented were kept as permanent workers and cultivated as possible heirs.

As the renown of a house grew, so did its attraction as a place in which to train and work. Reputable houses attracted motivated apprentices and serious workers. Learning or perfecting one's craft skills in the house of a respected master greatly facilitated the movement into permanent, salaried work and, ultimately, self-employment. For heirs, work experience in the houses of celebrated masters in other regions, and particularly in Paris, augmented the standing of their natal confectionery houses by demonstrating their connections to a national, even international, community of master *chocolatiers*.

Over the years the owners of the Bourriet and Carrère houses trained many apprentices and journeymen. Robert Linxe apprenticed in both these houses before training at the Swiss COBA school and creating his own house, La Maison du Chocolat. When it came time for Simon Carrère, the grandson of Linxe's master Louis Carrère, to learn the craft, he embarked upon a three-year Tour de France that included nine months with Linxe. The Carrère family adroitly marketed the start they provided to Linxe and their close relations with him, as well as the valuable social and craft capital acquired by Simon while training with him. In turn, Linxe acknowledged both houses in his 1992 memoir.

Both apprentices and skilled workers were closely identified with the houses in which they trained and worked. For example, instructors at the Bayonne Chamber of Trades never introduced apprentices and workers by their names but by their association with a particular house. For instance, when visitors stopped by, Monsieur Motte identified his apprentices by saying, "This one is with Carrère, these two with Mathieu, this one with Harcaut, that one at the Bourriet house," and so forth. Whether they performed well or acted out in class, the same association was evoked. One afternoon Monsieur Motte had repeatedly scolded a particularly obstreperous apprentice from the Carrère house for his sloppiness, incessant chatter, and dirty work clothes. When the youngster nearly dropped a baking pan full of cake batter, Monsieur Motte took the pan and, in a tone of controlled rage, fumed: "What a fuck-up you are! The day you open a business of your own, Monsieur Carrère will tear his hair out." On the other hand, those apprentices who finished their basic training, perfected their skill, became owners, and earned recognition as accomplished masters in their own right were a continual source of credit to their master and his house. As masters they identified and cultivated gifted apprentices, imparting a distinctive craft ethos to them.

Workers, too, differentiated themselves by their affiliation with individual houses but, more importantly, divided themselves into two groups composed of sons of owners *(fils de patron)* and sons of workers *(fils d'ouvrier)*. This categorization was used most prominently by heirs to mask the social, cultural, and economic capital they had inherited or to naturalize their superior talent and skill on the basis of an exceptional work ethic or better motivation. Heirs used this categorization and a discourse of ownership as a means to distance themselves from unruly workers whose behavior confirmed their class status or to laud worthy workers whose discipline set them apart.

One evening close to Easter, the president of the Chamber of Trades, Monsieur Arnaudin, stopped by the master artisan class to express his displeasure at the dwindling class attendance of the young artisans working overtime in preparation for the upcoming holiday. Arnaudin singled out one young artisan from the Clouseau house for particular reproach. As he turned to leave, that young man muttered, "Asshole *[con]*," loudly enough for the other workers to hear. Christophe and Philippe, two other *fils de patron* who were also working at the Clouseau house, noticed my surprise and pulled me aside. "He's a son of a worker," Christophe explained. "He'll never make it [as an independent master] because he doesn't have the mentality or the discipline. You see we grew up knowing what it takes. Our parents made us toe the line *(ils nous ont mis au pied du mur)* from the time we were kids, so we work harder and better as a result."

## Managing Workers

This discourse on workers was mirrored by owners, for whom the construction of community and reproduction of houses depended vitally on the successful management of salaried help as well as the mentoring of heirs. Most owners saw non-kin workers as costly and unpredictable. They insisted that only family members could be counted on to be hardworking and honest. They justified this distrust with stories recounting the misdeeds of apprentices, workers, and saleswomen. A consistent theme involved employees caught red-handed stealing candies or cash, or workers who stole house recipes, craft secrets, or equipment, created their own houses, and then competed directly with their former masters. Variations on this theme included tales of the irresponsibility and laziness of hired help who quit without notice, came late, or performed poorly. Owners developed a number of strategies that allowed them to manage and control the outsiders they employed.

They made astute use of a familial idiom in the organization of the house, where craftsmen and saleswomen ranked by experience and skill worked under the authority of the owners. The symbolic incorporation of salaried help within a family hierarchy served to imbue work relations with the moral imperative inherent in personalized, authority-based family relationships. Inclusion within a fictive, patriarchal family structure, which evoked the preindustrial organization of households, and the cultivation of a work ethic grounded in self-employment were devices meant to temper the inclination of outsiders to pursue their own self-interest rather than the collective good of the house.

Family owners were highly selective when they hired outsiders. After the creation of a confectionery house, owners frequently relied on apprentices because they were less costly and generally more pliant than fully skilled craftsmen.[4] Later, to hire full-time, skilled workers, they sought former apprentices whose motivation, skill, and honesty were proven, or they hired workers recommended by trusted local craftsmen or respected Parisian masters. During peak production periods, they also hired craftsmen on temporary work contracts. These contracts provided considerable flexibility to small-scale producers who needed temporarily to expand or contract their salaried workforce in response to shifting economic circumstances. Families attempted to find and keep a cadre of workers whose trustworthiness was unquestioned and, ideally, whose personal circumstances precluded their departure to become small independents in their turn. This system permitted the circulation of skilled labor among confectionery houses, giving owners a pool of workers that allowed them to balance the need for dynamic, motivated heirs with the demand for docile, subordinate labor.

The close working proximity between owners and workers, the creation of a metaphoric family structure, and the ambition of craftsmen to become independents all created a specific work ambiance hostile to trade unionism. Owners often eschewed the state labor codes regulating management and labor relations and invoked instead a set of traditional work practices. Family owners appealed to salaried workers to forgo some state-mandated benefits such as yearly wage increases, overtime pay, contributions to retirement pensions, and paid vacations that were renegotiated annually for each trade and industry by representatives of the state, the trade, and the unions. Workers often exchanged these concessions for guarantees that included access to training under the guidance of a regionally or nationally known master, job security in cases where independent ownership was not possible, flexible work schedules, or, in some cases, an opportunity to acquire ownership of the business.

During slow periods, workers were sometimes asked to work for the family directly by cleaning or refurbishing work areas or undertaking time- and labor-intensive tasks such as the crafting of confectionery art. Owners viewed the willingness of workers to come early, stay late, and expend effort beyond normal levels as a sign of seriousness and commitment to both the craft and the family. It was seen as evidence that workers were capable of shouldering the enormous responsibilities inherent in becoming their own bosses. The readiness with which workers took on extra tasks represented their recognition and acceptance of the special character of family entrepreneurship, namely, that work in family businesses, their own or the houses they aspired to own, spanned any arbitrary divide between personal and professional tasks.

A plan put forward by the owner of the Mathieu house in 1990 generated much discussion among the workers enrolled in the master artisan classes. In return for significant monthly salary raises, the workers were asked to give up all overtime pay and to accept restrictions on their yearly paid vacations. By early March 1991 all but one of the workers, François, had accepted the plan. François was the labor representative (*délégué du personnel*), and because he took his responsibility seriously, he had gone to the National Labor Office and calculated that he would make much more money under the legal system. One Monday evening when the class pace was slow, I asked him why he had not accepted the owner's offer. He became agitated, exclaiming, "I don't like getting screwed. I'm not like other workers who are totally ignorant of their rights and blindly trust the boss. If I'm there it's because I like my craft and I do it for the satisfaction." One of his co-workers, Nicholas, who had already accepted the pay plan, overheard our conversation and retorted, "Yes and you also do it for the money. Besides, it's a good house and it means something to work there." And turning to me he added, "He's like me. His wife is a teacher and won't go into business. Besides where else will he work? So, just as the boss predicted, he'll end up accepting the offer."

## Subcontracting Relationships

In addition to the recruitment of capable heirs and manageable workers, house owners affirmed and sustained membership within a regional and national craft community by entering into intersecting, mutually beneficial sets of subcontracting relationships. These relationships allowed them to maintain high-quality, small batch production of a large selection of goods without assuming the burden of producing all of them on the premises. Most family owners produced extra quantities of candies for resale to other independents and in turn purchased small amounts of candies from them or other craftsmen as well as from selected industrial suppliers of goods such as *dragées* and solid chocolate bars. Most purchased goods were renamed, repackaged, and sold under the buyer's house name. This preserved the artisanal mystique but only if the purchased goods were the same quality as those produced on the premises. For this reason owners were very careful to establish subcontracting relationships with owners whose production methods resembled their own. All of the members on Mourier's first list were connected to one another through subcontracting relationships. Some like Monsieur Mourier himself and Monsieur Bergeron supplied their candies to large numbers of independents in other departments.[5]

## Finalizing the Confrérie Membership List

In light of these mechanisms sustaining the local craft community, Monsieur Mourier's refusal to sponsor the owner of the Salinas house in Saint-Jean-de-Luz was not surprising. Monsieur Salinas had eschewed any active role in the community, had no social relationships with Basque coast or Palois houses, and maintained only one subcontracting relationship, with the De Closets. Furthermore, in 1991 the succession and, therefore, the future of the Salinas house was in doubt.

I was initially puzzled when Monsieur Mourier refused to consider the De Closets in Biarritz. He had suggested that I include their tiny *chocolaterie* in my study and had played a mentoring role with Monsieur De Closet, urging him to join the Confédération Nationale des Détaillants et Artisans-détaillants de la Chocolaterie, Confiserie et Biscuiterie in Paris, sharing information on the latest machines, and suggesting ways to better promote his new business. Mourier was intent on helping him so "his products would be a credit to the craft" but disqualified him on the basis of insufficient years of professional experience and house ownership. However, there were a number of more serious strikes working against Monsieur De Closet. First, De Closet had never undergone an apprenticeship in a confectionery house. Instead, he had taken a course in industrial chocolate manufacture offered for engineers and supervisors at the German confectionery school in Sollingen and had supervised production in a local factory that produced low-end chocolate bars for mass distribution outlets and the French armed forces. His ongoing conflicts with the factory owner were the motivation for becoming self-employed, not a desire to practice the craft. Moreover, his choice of a confectionery business was serendipitous; it was one of the few affordable, centrally located businesses for sale in downtown Biarritz.

Perhaps the most damning factor was Monsieur De Closet's training and work experience as a butcher in his parents' business. Artisans acknowledged a hierarchy among crafts, ranking those with a luxury clientele, a pronounced aesthetic component, and/or ceremonial consumption above those oriented to daily consumption such as bread making and butchering. A set of negative associations with the pollution of animal blood, viscera, and offal put butchering near the bottom of this hierarchy (Vialles 1994). This hierarchy also determined what constituted companion crafts as well as the movement among them based on overlapping skills. Many *chocolatiers* were also confectioners and pastry makers just as butchers of red meat *(bouchers)* also sold poultry or the foods commonly found in the shops of pork butchers *(charcutiers)*. However, for most people it was inconceivable for butchers to practice chocolate making or for *chocolatiers* to become butchers. Since the De Closets were newcomers to the craft and outsiders to the region—they were *pieds noirs* (descendants of European settlers in French colonial Algeria) who had settled in Biarritz after repatriation to France following Algerian independence in 1962—few craftspeople and residents knew them. Many questioned me about them after learning that they were included in my study. They were routinely shocked to discover that he had been trained as a butcher.

The question of inducting the owners of the oldest Bayonnais confectionery houses—the Dalbaitz and Aguirre houses—initially proved to be more puzzling. Monsieur Mourier refused to invite the owners of the Aguirre house, although they were always among the first to be interviewed by journalists and gastronomes. In spite of the house's national reputation, Mourier and other craftsmen were unimpressed with the quality of their chocolate and sugar candies, although most agreed that their hot chocolate was excellent. The owners had continued to insist publicly that they made their own chocolates directly from cacao beans in their family workshop. Most craftspeople I knew dismissed this claim as ridiculous.

The senior Aguirre craftsman, Monsieur Larosière, who had spent over forty years in the family workshop (1948–1991), had firmly refused any role in the local community and avoided all contact with his craft *confrères*. In fact, he adopted what many considered to be an obsessively secretive manner by categorically refusing access to the workshop and declining to participate in the creation of the *chocolat de Bayonne* even when directly approached by the Bayonne Chamber of Commerce and Industry and the Mayor's Office. In recent years, local craftspeople had been actively cultivating an artisanal mystique that included public tours of the workshop and free product tastings. In light of these trends, many were suspicious of the owners' attitudes and concluded that "something was wrong in the Aguirre workshop."

At the same time, the local sales representative of Valrhona told Mourier that the Aguirre owners were attempting to sell a grinding machine *(broyeuse)*. Since these machines are indispensable for the production of candy centers, Mourier suspected that the owners were no longer producing at least a portion of their goods on the premises. In early 1991 the ownership and management of the Aguirre house passed from Larosière and his sister to their second cousins. These heirs were both well-educated bourgeois who intended only an indirect role in house production and maintained the same aloof posture with regard to members of the local craft community. Since Mourier had met with a cold refusal when he invited them to his February chocolate conference, he declined to sponsor them for membership.

Monsieur Mourier's attitude toward the owners of the Dalbaitz house was also revealing. The senior craftsman, Monsieur Sarlate, seemed a logical choice for sponsorship, particularly when he was compared to the owners of the Aguirre house. In the year 1990–91 he divided his time between mornings in the workshop handling managerial tasks and participating directly in production and afternoons in the Anglet town hall discharging his duties as assistant mayor for culture, communication and twinning. Mourier initially refused to sponsor Monsieur Sarlate, saying he didn't practice the craft full time—a fact that automatically disqualified him from membership in the Confrérie.

This reasoning seemed paradoxical in light of Mourier's decision to sponsor Monsieur Mathieu and Monsieur Carrère, who took similarly limited roles in production. When I raised this issue, Mourier insisted that "it wasn't the same thing at all." Both Mathieu and Carrère had inherited the houses they managed from their fathers and like their fathers took an active role in the local craft community. They had both completed an extended apprenticeship in confectionery houses and had augmented their skill through specialized courses at the Lenôtre culinary school outside Paris. Although Monsieur Mathieu no longer personally directed workshop production, he personally managed house operations and still crafted confectionery art. Simon Carrère, too, participated in production, albeit irregularly, and had taken great pride in introducing a new line of cakes and *ganaches* to the existing house line.

Mourier objected to Sarlate mainly because of his refusal to identify himself as a skilled practitioner of a manual craft and, most importantly, because of his bourgeois class status and graduate history degree. These facts alone made Mourier doubt Sarlate's abilities. When I protested that I had repeatedly witnessed Sarlate's craft mastery, Mourier scoffed, "Bah, he is not an artisan, he just does it for the money, his heart is in politics." Mourier distinguished Sarlate from other owners who actively asserted their membership within the craft community in a number of ways. They were involved in local craft associations, which included a significant social component such as evenings of dinner and dancing. Most actively sought the peer recognition afforded by titles earned in craft contests, membership in producer associations, and leadership positions in employer associations. Although Sarlate supported collective initiatives on behalf of Basque coast *chocolatiers* and marketed an artisanal mystique, he was acutely uncomfortable being depicted as a master craftsman and delegated that role to Francis, the young artisan he had hired and trained to head workshop production. In interviews with journalists, he always mentioned his university education and predilection for high cultural pursuits. He insisted that although he had mastered the craft completely, this amazed him "since he was not good at manual tasks."

Although Monsieur Sarlate would reluctantly don the master's garb of white chef jacket to hand-dip chocolates for promotional events, he took no interest in the aesthetic dimension of the craft, instead encouraging Francis to perfect his skill. Although the Sarlates belonged to the *chocolatiers'* professional association and regularly attended their annual show in Paris, they steadfastly avoided any of the social events organized in conjunction with it. Bourgeois by virtue of their education, social connections, acquired wealth, and leisure pursuits, they cultivated friendships exclusively among local arts, business, and political elites.

The politics of sponsorship were further complicated for Monsieur Mourier by the social relations among the wives of house owners. When I wondered if this were really a crucial criterion given the Confrérie emphasis on producers, Mourier retorted emphatically: "What do you mean? Not consider women?? Impossible!! Believe me, if they don't get along they can wreck everything." Neither Monsieur Sarlate's wife nor Fabrice Carrère's wife were on speaking terms with Madame Clouseau, the wife of a prominent pastry maker and owner of a flourishing business in nearby Anglet—one of the artisans at the top of Mourier's first list. In the past the Sarlates and the Clouseaus had engaged in a fruitful subcontracting relationship, whereby the Clouseaus purchased certain chocolate candies from them and the Sarlates ordered pastries and hors d'oeuvre platters for receptions at the Anglet town hall. However, a rift had developed between them. On one occasion Monsieur Sarlate was embarrassed and angry when Clouseau goods had arrived half-frozen at a municipal reception he was hosting for visiting Parisian dignitaries. Monsieur Sarlate complained, but when the Clouseaus denied freezing goods in advance, he stopped ordering from them.

Meanwhile, the Carrères and the Clouseaus had had a similar falling out. The Carrères were smarting from the increased competition from the Clouseaus. Monsieur Clouseau belonged to the elite pastry chef organization Relais Dessert, and Madame Clouseau had assumed the presidency of the local Centre féminin d'études de la pâtisserie, a position Madame Carrère felt she did not deserve given her recent arrival in the area. As a result, Madame Carrère had stopped attending the center's seminars. Mourier was concerned that this animosity would poison the atmosphere of the ceremony or even provoke a refusal to participate on the part of one or the other. Privately, he was immensely relieved when the Carrères' financial problems and Monsieur Clouseau's health problems precluded either artisan's induction.

Thus, in spite of his initial decision not to sponsor Monsieur Sarlate, Mourier had to consider the social costs involved in not doing so. Sarlate was not only an assistant mayor—an office carrying much more prestige in France than the United States—but also very active in the community. He served as a district council member and sat on the boards of the Bayonne Conservatory and the Basque Coast Orchestra. Since assuming control of his in-laws' business, he had improved the variety and quality of the goods produced there. He had also promoted artisanal chocolates by organizing well-publicized public tours of the workshop. In 1988 Mayor Grenet and members of the municipal council visited the facility. Sarlate bought expensive advertising space in the Sunday section of a national daily newspaper, *Le Figaro,* at Christmas time.

Although Mourier did not recognize Sarlate as a craftsman, in the end he compromised and sponsored him as a Confrérie member, insisting, "It is important to promote a public image of craft solidarity." For his part, Sarlate selectively celebrated his own artisanal skill and supported local initiatives with the best media potential for enhancing the Dalbaitz house renown. Therefore, when Mourier offered to sponsor him, Monsieur Sarlate accepted the invitation with pleasure.

## The Basque Coast *Chocolatier* Contest

Public displays of skill have served to affirm membership in craft communities since the preindustrial era, when the right to head one's own unit of production was contingent upon the attribution of a mastership based on the crafting of a masterpiece. Although the guild system was dismantled during the French Revolution, significant vestiges remained. For example, self-employment was still equated with mastery (whether it corresponded to reality or not) since it was assumed that only fully skilled artisans could and should head their own houses. Thus, self-employed artisans, not salaried workers, constituted the core of the community.

Public displays of skill retained a strong salience among contemporary artisans because they provided the preeminent medium through which established owners affirmed and sustained membership in the craft community. Displays of skill could be cooperative endeavors—such as the creation of the *chocolat de Bayonne*. Or they could be competitive, even agonistic, tournaments of value, in which *chocolatiers* were pitted against one another in a contest for rank, prestige, and power within the local community (Appadurai 1986, 21). New independents and ambitious workers also used these competitions both to contest and to challenge established owners' dominance within the community.

Competitive displays were evident in the enormous investment of time devoted to the design and execution of individual pieces for window displays, promotional events, and, in particular, craft contests. Window displays were the hallmark of *chocolatiers* at Easter and during the summer tourist season. These pieces included objects that masqueraded as the functional, such as musical instruments, as well as objects that served as souvenirs of the public, the monumental, and the historical (Stewart 1984, 136–151). For instance, in the Dalbaitz house, Francis crafted part of the Bayonnais historic district—a block of distinctive five-story medieval dwellings clustered along the Nive River—for a summer window display. *Chocolatiers* also brought the world into the boutique through pieces that commemorated or parodied the history of great men. In 1988, Robert Salinas created a scene from the French presidential campaign of that year. Using the puppet caricatures of national personalities satirized on a popular television program, "The Bébête Show," he portrayed presidential contenders on the left and the right scrambling to beat one another to the summit of a marzipan mountain. Craftsmen also used chocolate and sugar to evoke nostalgia for French regional customs and the use value of objects associated with the preindustrial village economy, such as the hearth, spinning wheel, chicken coops, and horse-drawn wagons.

Competitive displays of skill were most vividly demonstrated in the pieces submitted to craft contests. In May 1991, four students from the Bayonne professional lycée hit upon the idea of organizing a craft contest as an independent study project required for their business studies degree.[6] This contest bore witness to the importance of public displays of skill but also to the dynamic tension within the craft community between Palois and Basque coast *chocolatiers,* between house heirs and the newly self-employed, and between owners and workers.

The student organizers were surprised but gratified at the enthusiastic response since the contest was the first of its kind and did not have the aura associated with more prestigious titles. With the help of local craftsmen, the students formulated contest rules, chose music as the theme, obtained a sponsor for the first-, second-, and third-prize trophies (the French industrial manufacture of chocolate *couverture,* Cacao Barry), drew up a list of contestants, solicited original entries of chocolate art, and, based on *chocolatiers'* recommendations, constituted a judging panel. Monsieur Sarlate offered them free space at the Anglet town hall to display the contest entries and to hold an award ceremony.

The solicitation of entries and the constitution of a judging panel revealed much about the dominance of established owners within the community. The student organizers started with the names of local producers best known largely because of their astute self-promotion in local media and craft events. These producers recommended craft colleagues in an order that replicated a craft hierarchy of closely connected activist owners. At the top were owners who served as powerful patrons to newly self-employed or lesser-known craftsmen. Some owners could be relied upon to play this role consistently, while others did so only when it furthered their own self-interest. They sent business to newcomers or included them in craft events as a means of widening their own networks and consolidating their own power.

The Clouseaus and Bergerons were at the top of the students' list. They recommended other well-established owners in Bayonne and Biarritz as well as Monsieur Mourier. Monsieur Mourier took charge of soliciting entries from selected Palois houses and recommended Bayonnais such as the Mathieus, the Carrères, and the Tolbiacs, a bakery and pastry house that employed a *chocolatier*. The Carrères mentioned the Dalbaitz and Aguirre houses, who in turn suggested the Harcauts. Messieurs Bergeron and Mourier advised the students to have professionals constitute at least half of the judging panel. Bergeron suggested Monsieur Santoro, a Bayonnais pastry maker active in the Basque coast pastry makers' association to whom Bergeron supplied his chocolates, as a judge. Three weeks before the contest, when the students were searching for an additional craftsman for the judging panel, they returned to see Monsieur Clouseau, who suggested Monsieur De Closet. They had contacted Monsieur Harcaut weeks after the most well-established owners, and he was so angry at being one of the last to be invited that he declined to participate, saying he was too busy. Another Biarrot house owner, Monsieur Dudet, declined to participate because, "If I enter I have to win. I can't risk even being in second place."

In the end, artisans from eight houses in Bayonne, Biarritz, Pau, and Peyrehorade crafted thirteen pieces of chocolate art, including musical instruments, composers, performers, and scenes from three Mozart operas. Entries in a special category for apprentices were submitted by the Pau and Bayonne Chambers of Trades as well as individual pieces made by Monsieur Mourier's grandson and Monsieur Bergeron's apprentice. The contest exhibition opened on Friday, 3 May, and was covered in the Basque coast edition of the regional newspaper, *Sud-Ouest* (3 May 1991). The article's headline, "If Music Softens Manners, Chocolate Excites Gourmandise and Originality Attracts Visitors," appeared above a large photograph of entries with the caption "Masterpieces in Chocolate." Both Messieurs Mourier and Bergeron urged the student organizers to hold the award ceremony before the public exhibition because of the possibility that entries would get damaged. They had also strongly suggested that the pieces not be identified in order to protect the integrity of the judging process. However, since the award ceremony could not held until 5 May, the students yielded to pressure from both the artisans and the public, who complained that the pieces should be labeled. The students assigned numbers to all the entries the morning of the award ceremony, but everyone, including the judges, knew the houses in which they had been crafted.

That morning I arrived at the same time as the student organizers, who had graciously invited me to attend the deliberations of the judging panel. Since we were the first to arrive, I had the opportunity to photograph all the entries. I had seen some pieces in various stages of development in family workshops and heard about others from the workers I saw weekly at the Chamber of Trades classes. The smaller, less imposing pieces, submitted by both Basque coast and Palois *chocolatiers,* were arranged on two tables near the entrance to the Festival Hall and evoked the long-standing rivalry between these two geographical areas. Monsieur Mourier had entered a grand piano crafted in white chocolate on a black and white tile floor. Mourier loved the aesthetic dimension to the craft and looked forward to Easter, when he designed his signature half-meter–high eggs, hand-painting them with different scenes and figures from his beloved Pau. He was equally enthusiastic about the contest, spending many hours on his entry because as he put it, "If I enter this contest it's because I want to win."

Mourier's entry and that of his grandson—a set of chocolate musical instruments from the Ivory Coast—called to mind the heated discussions of the April meeting of the Club of Palois *chocolatiers* I had attended in which Mourier exhorted his colleagues "to defend the honor of Pau." He insisted that the apprenticeship instructor in Pau have his students enter the contest and that his grandson craft an individual piece. He also supplied the block of white chocolate that one of his colleagues carved into a bust of Mozart. He was very pleased that a young heir of an established Palois house had entered a piece entitled "jazz ensemble" featuring a group of dark chocolate musicians performing on the bass, piano, drums, and clarinet.

The pieces displayed at the back of the festival hall recalled the rivalry among the owners of the best-known confectionery houses. The modest proportions and less-polished workmanship of Mourier's piece stood in marked contrast to the superb antique phonograph crafted by Monsieur Bergeron (see fig. 8). The wood-grained base, turntable, circular stylus, and immense horn speaker were incredibly lifelike. Its placement next to the Clouseau entry hardly seemed accidental. The Clouseaus and the Bergerons were friendly competitors because each was judged to be among the most active and skilled practitioners within their respective crafts on the Basque coast: Monsieur Bergeron in chocolate and Monsieur Clouseau in pastry. Moreover, it was common knowledge that Monsieur Bergeron was an accomplished chocolate artist, whereas Monsieur Clouseau's passion was producing excellent doughs and innovative

Figure 8. Chocolate phonograph, Basque Coast Craft Contest, 1991.

cakes. I knew from attending the master artisan class that Clouseau workers had crafted the piece submitted in his name for the contest. It was a pipe organ with an enormous—six-by-four-foot chocolate back-drop—that dwarfed all the other entries.

As I surveyed it I became aware of Monsieur Santoro, a contest judge, who was officiously measuring all the entries to assure that none surpassed the dimensions specified in the contest rules.[7] Messieurs Santoro and Mourier had also arrived early, and after greeting them I had asked if the judges would strictly apply the rules on size since both the Clouseau and Bergeron entries seemed too large. Although Monsieur Mourier himself had advised the students to specify the size, he stared at me with surprise and annoyance, exclaiming, "But no, Madame, that is not important. What counts is the finished product, and it's clear that the phono is by far the best piece in the contest—from every point of view." Monsieur Santoro hesitated and then announced that, since the rules were the rules, he would measure each piece.

The grandiose entries of the Clouseau and Bergeron houses were flanked by pieces crafted by workers in the Bergeron and Dalbaitz houses, originally labeled not with the name of the individual craftsman but with the name of the house in which they were crafted. Next to the phono was an impeccable white chocolate saxophone (see fig. 9) crafted by Bergeron's head craftsman, and opposite it was the piece submitted by Francis of the Dalbaitz house. These pieces evoked the tensions and conflicts among a community of independent masters and the skilled workers they employed. Owners asserted their place at the summit of the craft hierarchy by virtue of the social power and economic means afforded them by business proprietorship. The owners of established houses were privileged in this hierarchy because, if properly managed, a confectionery house accrued value that increased with its intergenerational longevity. Moreover, an owner's authority and reputation were maintained by the hierarchical ordering of work relations and the asymmetrical power relationship existing between him and his workers—a relationship predicated on the owner's superior skill. That relationship had the potential of being transformed into progressively symmetrical relations over time, yet the potential for change was itself a paradox. The worker became more valuable as his skill increased; yet this ability brought him closer to his dream of independence and a position as a potential competitor with his former master (Buechler 1989, 32). Given the high costs of creating new houses and purchasing established ones, many gifted workers without financial means had to settle for permanent, salaried employment and a lifetime position as a structural subordinate.

Owners retained their dominant position within the workshop and the craft in a number of ways. First, they recounted a master craft narrative, defined and controlled by them, based on precision workmanship and artistic competence, which presumed originality. Late twentieth-century French masters asserted their place at the summit of a skill hierarchy by their ability to advance the craft through innovations in tech-

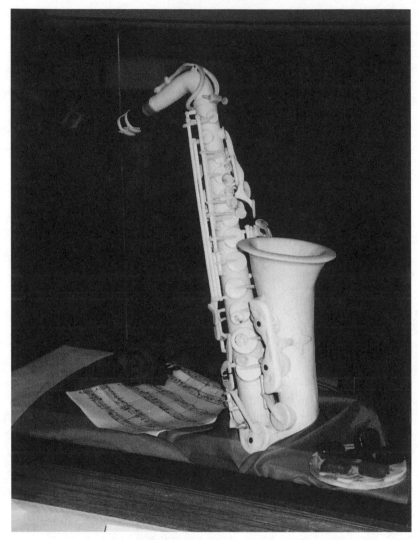

Figure 9. White chocolate saxophone, Basque Coast Craft Contest, 1991.

nique and taste. The celebration of superior skill served as an effective
exclusionary device because it aggrandized the status of a small elite of
independent masters and elided the contributions of other, sometimes
equally skilled owners and salaried workers. In their workshops, owners
had to strike a difficult balance between sharing their expertise with talented, ambitious workers, enabling them to become self-employed in

their turn and protecting the production techniques and social capital that enhanced the reputation of their own houses. Thus, some owners guarded production secrets, while others appropriated the technical expertise of skilled workers as their own.

If owners were the guardians of an artisanal aesthetic, then workers too told their own counter narratives in which their bosses forged an elaborate mystique of artisanal skill both to mask their own inadequacies and to appropriate the expertise of workers more skilled than they. These were cautionary tales centering on the theme of rapacious owners who took credit for the goods and art crafted by their workers and, in some cases, their own sons. Journeymen recounted stories of the clever ways they found to steal craft secrets, the renown they earned at the expense of their masters, and the anonymous labor they performed not for pecuniary reward or professional recognition but for the love of the craft.

During the six weeks before the craft contest, I had regularly visited the Dalbaitz workshop in the afternoons when Francis worked alone because I wanted to observe the creative process at work. One day I found him depressed and upset, pacing back and forth in front of his unfinished entry. He had completed the scene from the first Mozart opera Monsieur Sarlate had chosen, *The Abduction from the Seraglio,* but was stymied by the depiction of Don Juan. When I remarked how difficult the process must be, Francis agreed:

It's really hard. You know I have the *certificat d'aptitude professionelle* [in chocolate] and a passion for chocolate but I don't have that much experience . . . this is only my third house. You understand I realize that I am fortunate to have found this [permanent] position but I really regret not having done a Tour de France and gained experience elsewhere. I'm so isolated here, I'd like more contact with other [full-fledged] craftsmen. [In the Dalbaitz workshop only Francis and Monsieur Sarlate were fully skilled.] Monsieur Sarlate, you know, he knows what he's doing but his heart's not in it. He just wants to develop the commercial side of things.

I knew from conversations with other workers—particularly those who had worked for his father-in-law—that Monsieur Sarlate was considered to be a fair and generous boss. When he had taken over in 1986, he ended what he described as "the archaic paternalism" of his father-in-law, who had only declared 70 percent of his business earnings, kept worker salaries below or at the minimum wage, and distributed overtime salary in cash to reduce his employer costs. Sarlate scrupulously observed the letter of labor law and worked hard to cultivate good relations in the workshop by addressing all workers, even Francis, whom he described as "a younger brother," with the polite *vous* form of address. He brought croissants and prepared coffee himself everyday for the workers' mid-morning break. Sarlate had a particularly close relationship with Francis, and Francis repeatedly sought his advice on personal decisions and help in familial crises. Sarlate fought for and obtained the special title of manager for Francis (entitling him to certain tax and pension benefits) and ensured that he received generous bonuses at Christmas and Easter and for the summer tourist season. When I mentioned this Francis retorted:

Of course you're right and I appreciate all that but you know what my wife says? "So you're a manager, big deal, you only have the title, what kind of a manager earns a [monthly] salary as low as yours [slightly higher than the minimum wage]?" Besides, I don't really run things, he does. He insists that I enter these contests and then he tries to tell me how to do it! We had a fight about it this morning because he makes impossible demands . . . he doesn't understand what can be done in chocolate art.

Since Monsieur Sarlate had told me that he and his wife hoped to transfer ownership of the Dalbaitz house to Francis one day, I reminded him of that. He scoffed at the suggestion: "Do you really think so? A house worth what this one is? Besides it doesn't belong to him but to his wife and her family. They will be the ones to decide."

Here as in other houses, the use of a familial idiom was vulnerable in a number of ways. Despite Monsieur Sarlate's obvious fondness for him, Francis was always acutely aware of his position of structural inferiority. His decision to leave school at fifteen to complete an apprenticeship and his marriage to a hairdresser also put him into a different social class than the Sarlates. Although Francis and Monsieur Sarlate shared confidences and complaints, their social worlds were entirely separate. Like other French bosses and, in contrast to American companies and Japanese firms, Monsieur Sarlate never socialized with workers—or other craftsmen for that matter—even at important ceremonial occasions. Francis also understood that Monsieur Sarlate's promises regarding ownership were well intentioned but unreliable. Although he drew a very comfortable salary and directed house operations, he was married with a contract excluding him from house ownership. He thus had no authority to make assurances concerning its future.

I had just finished photographing the pieces at the back of the hall when I felt someone tugging at my arm. I looked down to see Béatrice, the six-year-old daughter of the De Closets, smiling up at me. Close by were her parents and grandparents—Monsieur De Closet's mother and father—all attired in their Sunday best. Although I knew from conversations with him and his wife how pleased they were to be participating, I also knew that De Closet's lack of experience and outsider status made him feel unsure. On several occasions, he had asked me pointed questions about the techniques other contestants used. He had also pushed quite hard to establish friendly relations with me, insisting too early in the relationship, by local standards, that we all use the familiar *tu* form of address. Several weeks earlier he and his wife had invited me to dinner, and as he escorted me to my car he asked if I would meet him at the festival hall the day before the judging so we could compare notes on the various entries. I used humor to rebuff his request but worried about the judging process.

By this time the hall had filled with the other contestants and their families, the apprenticeship instructors from Pau and Bayonne, and the sales representative from Cacao Barry, as well as municipal notables. Soon after I joined the judging panel, which was beginning its deliberations on the second floor of the town hall. Once we were settled upstairs, De Closet raised the issue of size and asked about the Clouseau and Bergeron entries. "After all," he said, "we have to apply the rules the same to everyone." To my astonishment, Monsieur Santoro argued that since the pipe organ was detached from the huge, eye-catching backdrop, how could they disqualify it? On the other hand, since the phonograph was one piece and clearly in violation of the size specifications, the rules had to be applied. The Bergeron piece would not be judged. Monsieur De Closet acquiesced without further argument, and the third judge—a music professor at the Bayonne Conservatory—who had entered late raised no protest.

The music professor spoke forcefully for adapting coherent judging criteria, suggesting "originality with the respect to the musical theme of the contest." He used "number eight," the Dalbaitz piece, and its creative adaptation of three Mozart operas as a perfect example of originality. Only later did I realize that his opinion may have been colored by the fact that Monsieur Sarlate was an ardent supporter of the Basque Coast Orchestra and served on the Bayonne Conservatory board. The fourth judge—a culinary critic at the local newspaper—entered late, as the professor was making his case for the Dalbaitz piece. He cut quickly to the chase, conceding the importance of creativity in confectionery art but expressing his unconditional admiration for the pipe organ. "It should be first," he proclaimed. A few days after the contest, I learned that here too the judge in question may not have been totally impartial; he was a devoted customer of the Clouseau business.

In a valiant attempt to introduce some professional expertise into the deliberations, Monsieur De Closet admonished the others to consider technique. "Originality is important, as you say, but we must remember that it is easier to make artistic pieces from molds than it is to shape and sculpt them from a block." Everyone pondered this remark until the journalist turned to both professionals and asked, "As professionals, then, which pieces have been molded?" Monsieur De Closet spoke up, repeating what I had, in an unguarded moment, revealed to him several weeks earlier about Francis's piece. "Well, it is obvious that number eight could not have been molded. Just consider the pillars, the steps, the stage curtain—all the product of hand workmanship." He paused, and since neither he nor Monsieur Santoro ever crafted any confectionery art, he was at a loss to say more about molding. He explained later that although he had initially favored the saxophone for the first prize, he allowed himself to be swayed by the journalist and voted for the pipe organ. In fact, since De Closet knew that the influential Monsieur Clouseau had suggested him as a judge, his decision may have been one way of expressing appreciation. Just then a student organizer appeared and urged us to hurry since we were behind schedule and the crowd below was restless. On a secret ballot, each of the four judges voted for their first-, second-, and third-place choices and the results were rushed downstairs.

I took my place in the crowd as Monsieur Sarlate opened the ceremony—in his capacity as assistant mayor—and introduced the municipal dignitaries in attendance. He prepared to announce the prize winners beginning with the third prize, which was awarded to the entry from his own Dalbaitz house. Monsieur Sarlate made a special point to identify Francis as the craftsman before announcing that the second prize went to the entry from the Bourriet house. It was not the phonograph designed by the house head Monsieur Bergeron that had been honored but the saxophone crafted by his worker. Finally, Monsieur Sarlate read out the name of the first prize winner—the pipe organ submitted by the Clouseau house. Madame Clouseau was the only one present, and she accepted the award on behalf of her husband—too busy in the workshop, she explained, to attend. Immediately after, Monsieur Mourier took the floor. He had fashioned a number of commemorative medals in chocolate and took the opportunity publicly to acknowledge and thank the students organizers of the contest as well as the resident anthropologist for their "actions taken on behalf of the craft."

As the crowd began to disperse, I caught sight of Monsieur Bergeron, who was attired, like the other contestants, in a white chef jacket. He was standing alone staring straight ahead, his face a peculiar shade of gray. At the front near the microphone, Madame Clouseau, a pretty and loquacious blonde, was making the most of the first prize award, engaging local journalists in lively conversation as they took her picture beside the trophy. Monsieur De Closet seized the opportunity to ingratiate himself with Monsieur Sarlate, who, annoyed at having to congratulate Madame Clouseau and suspicious about De Closet's presumed leftist leanings, coldly rebuffed him. I also saw Monsieur Mourier's whole family—his wife, son, and daughter-in-law—gathered around his grandson congratulating him for winning in the apprenticeship category. Only later did I learn the depth of Mourier's anger that Bergeron had not won a prize. A few minutes later, Monsieur Santoro approached Bergeron, who, I learned later, registered his shock and demanded an explanation. His surprise gave way to disbelief and then anger upon learning that his piece had been disqualified. Santoro scoffed, "Maybe it's not such a bad thing because if you had won, it would have given you the perfect excuse to raise the price of your chocolates again."

The Basque coast contest was an occasion for owners to attempt to affirm a craft hierarchy privileging well-known houses and to enhance their own individual reputations. However, these efforts were partially muted by the rivalries opposing Basque coast and Palois craftsmen, on the one hand, and those dividing competing owners, on the other. In the end, all of the winners were skilled workers, not house owners. The disqualification of a piece most saw as exemplary of a craft ideal—combining precision technique with decorative art—could be interpreted as an attempt to level the local playing field by humbling a craftsman whose national reputation earned him not only the respect and patronage of Parisian masters such as Linxe (who, it was rumored, actually purchased his caramels from Monsieur Bergeron) but also dramatically increased the value of his business property. The Bergeron house was by all accounts one of the most valuable and best known on the Basque coast. In using size as a justification for disqualification, the judging panel, composed of clients and competitors from other houses, implied that Bergeron was *démesuré*—ostentatious in the display of his art, and therefore, his success. As a customer of Bergeron's, Santoro suggested that Bergeron was also greedy in the pricing of his goods. What better way to embarrass him than to award prizes to his own worker and to his main competitor?

It could be argued that workers used the contest to challenge and subvert the local craft hierarchy and to create a reputation in their own names. However, this would not be a correct interpretation. The workers had entered the contest at the behest of the house owners and knew only too well who would get credit for the entries they crafted. They understood that anonymity in workmanship was often the norm until and if they headed their own houses. The contest entry labels paid tribute to confectionery houses and, therefore, their owners, not to the individual workers who produced them. In cases where a worker was personally recognized, such as Francis in the Dalbaitz house, the press reported only the house in which he worked. Even the humiliation suffered by Monsieur Bergeron was softened when, several weeks later, Monsieur Mourier organized a special exhibition in Pau and featured his *vieux phono*. Moreover, when it came time for the public induction into the Confrérie, it was Messieurs Bergeron and Sarlate, not their skilled workers, who received the attribution of membership.

## Conclusion

The 1991 Confrérie induction ceremony had a critical social role to play for organizers, participants, and consumers. It authenticated both the southwest as a center of chocolate production and the master *chocolatiers* who produced there. Local elites, news media, and the public were all invited to witness the celebration of membership within a craft community sharing an ethos rooted in independent entrepreneurship and skilled workmanship. The creative reinvention and public enactment of craft rituals drawn on a resonant French preindustrial guild model conveyed a sense of authenticity, rightness, and emotional power to the event. The use of the term *confrérie*, a separate annex of the preindustrial guilds charged with important religious and charitable activities, was strategic because it connoted the all-encompassing role of the artisanal community as a devotional, social, and economic entity (Sewell 1980, 33), recalling the corporate ceremonial events enacted by craft communities in the public spaces of preindustrial French cities. These events included both quotidian and festival observances such as collective attendance at mass, distribution of alms to the poor, and colorful costumed processions with craft banners on the occasion of the feast of the guild's patron saint, the attribution of the mastership, and municipal ceremonies honoring the passage of royal persons through the city.

Brotherhood associations have been continually reworked since the preindustrial era. Since the 1930s in the southwest, for example, brotherhoods associated with particular crafts and industries have been revived to promote local and regional gastronomic specialties such as Bordeaux wines, Armagnac brandy, and Bayonnais ham. These brotherhoods adopt a similar guiding principle—the induction of new members—in the staging of ritual events. The elaborate staging, costumes, craft symbols, and varied speech acts used in these inductions are all attempts to resolve the difficulty of mounting new rituals that are both moving and convincing in complex secular contexts (compare Myerhoff 1992, 132). Indeed, the 1991 ceremony involved alternating recurrent ritual acts such as songs and oaths with more open-ended productions such as unrehearsed speeches, which permitted the organizers to convey meaningful but unique messages.

The trumpets sounded at the beginning of this chapter marked the end of the scripted, ritual acts of processing and oath taking at the induction ceremony and the beginning of more improvised events such as speeches. A sumptuous banquet followed in the town hall, hosted by the deputy mayor of Pau, André Labarrère. Three hundred guests attended the buffet, including new members and their families, local elites, and journalists. The deputy mayor praised *chocolatiers* for their dynamism and high standards. He drew specific attention to the eldest practicing *chocolatier* in the southwest, Monsieur Blasco, calling him "a symbol of fidelity to tradition and quality," and to Monsieur Mourier, "whose fervor, energy, and faith ensure the enduring vitality of the craft." The president of the Chamber of Trades, Monsieur Arnaudin spoke next:

If it is true that the department of the Atlantic Pyrenees was the place where the production of chocolate from Spain developed, I am happy to say that this tradition is not in danger of dying out. . . . The Chamber of Trades contributed financial and technical support for this ceremony . . . in order to reward a craft which gives a strong and convincing image of artisanship. These artisans, united to better preserve the cultural and gastronomic patrimony that is French chocolate and to transmit their skill to the next generation, are proof that the artisanal sector today plays an essential role as an economic actor and agent of growth, innovation, and jobs.

Monsieur Mourier's creation of two Confrérie chapters was noticed by the craft leadership and reported in *La Confiserie*. Confederation leaders were intent on institutionalizing a distinct craft identity for artisanal *chocolatiers*. To gain local support for their collective initiatives they worked simultaneously through state representatives in Paris and activists in French regions. In chapter 8 we travel to Paris and examine Confederation leaders' attempts to develop an appropriate model by which to authenticate the skill of French *chocolatiers*.

# CHAPTER 8

# From Craft to Profession?

In the final moments of the October 1990 Best Craftsman of France contest ceremony, Madame Lombard, president of the judging panel, took the podium to thank the contest organizer, Monsieur Francis Boucher, for his "countless hours" of work.[1] After reminding her listeners "of the seven years of effort needed to persuade and to mount this contest," Madame Lombard turned to the presiding state representative, Monsieur Baudo, the secretary general of the National Work Exhibits, and said: "Seven years—the age of reason. [But] Monsieur Baudo did not wait for us to attain the age of reason before supporting us, helping us, advising us. Please accept our deepest thanks, kind sir, for having immediately believed in the excellence of our craft and in the men who perform it." After thanking the principal of the Paris School for the Food Trades, Mademoiselle Sauvage, for graciously agreeing to host the event, Lombard paused and suddenly sounded a somber note. She evoked "the miserable state of apprenticeship in this country," adding:

How can I not address this problem? We are desperately short of masters and apprentices in all manual crafts. There is a pact of silence regarding this training which now allows young people to prepare baccalaureate degrees just like those awarded in the academic track [of secondary school]. The only difference is that *we* do not train young people for the unemployment line. We have a CAP [certificate of professional aptitude] and a master artisan diploma, and are now fiercely intent on continuing in this path, with one objective: to attain level IV [equivalent to the final three-year cycle of secondary-level study in the lycée].

She had finished her thanks and invited the audience to enjoy the reception prepared by chef apprentices when Confederation President Jacques Daumoinx unexpectedly jumped onto the podium and grasped the microphone: "I must also express our concern in the face of the relative discredit with which children and especially their parents regard manual labor in France. Eighty percent of the young now get the baccalaureate degree, and we consider the twenty percent who don't to be failures, hardly even capable of performing manual work. We have to work on all fronts to revalorize manual work . . . indispensable to the balance of economic life."

I begin with a discussion of the Parisian activists within the confederation who staged an event "of historic importance for the profession."[2] They not only enact policy on behalf of the national membership but, given the highly centralized structure of this organization, also represent the membership in myriad national and international venues. The troubled tenor of the statements quoted above contrasted sharply with the generally exuberant tone of the speeches delivered by both state representatives and craft leaders. These statements spoke directly to a set of challenges faced by craft leaders in the postwar period.

Although the training of future *chocolatiers* had emerged as a problem in the early 1970s in the wake of shifting economic circumstances and state imperatives, the threats posed by foreign franchise retailers added renewed urgency to the problem. Craft leaders and the state representatives to whom they appealed agreed on the necessity to develop an appropriate model with which to authenticate French *chocolatiers* and to revalorize craft labor. Both groups believed that the creation of a model of authenticity should center on the institution of national recruitment, training, and certification procedures for future *chocolatiers*.

At a time when the value of professional credentials was rising and labor shortages in many food crafts were intensifying, craft leaders sought the legitimacy and support that would come from formal state certification of craft producers. Craft leaders petitioned state officials despite the state's position as a competing authority in the areas of training and credentialing. For their part, state representatives aimed to modernize what had been a largely decentralized and locally regulated apprenticeship system by incorporating it into national labor codes and public institutions. They sought to standardize and professionalize the artisanal sector as a means of preserving it.

Yet state attempts to construct and impose a professional model of artisanship were neither uniform nor hegemonic. The responses and initiatives these attempts elicited among craft leaders were both inventive and contradictory. The collaboration between craft leaders and state representatives had important, unintended consequences for the training of *chocolatiers,* for the construction of a confectionery aesthetic, for claims of membership within the craft community, and, ultimately, for the recruitment and reproduction of artisanal labor.

These speeches evoke the reality of complex, often tense negotiations on the subject of apprenticeship and professionalization that were then in progress among state officials, craft leaders, and local producers. The tensions and ambiguities surrounding these issues are evident in the apparently conflicting priorities espoused by Lombard and Daumoinx. Madame Lombard admonished craft producers to acquire professional credentials in state vocational schools, whereas her colleague, Monsieur Daumoinx, celebrated chocolate making as a manual craft *(métier)* with both economic value in the marketplace and sociocultural worth for the body politic.

In the 1980s and 1990s, apprenticeship received renewed attention in European debates on workplace training, new technologies, and global competitiveness. In a corpus of books published by French civil servants, academics, and business leaders, apprenticeship was linked—as both problem and solution—to such potent themes as national security, youth unemployment, and *insertion sociale,* or integration within the social body.[3] Although apprenticeship is not a statistically significant mode of training—in 1991 only 8 percent of a given school-age cohort underwent apprenticeship training—it remains an ideologically charged social category (Céreq 1994). Both the high expectations projected onto a reformed apprenticeship system and its continuing failure to meet these expectations reveal much about craft, class, educational capital, and social reproduction in contemporary France.

In order to understand the initiatives craft leaders elaborated with regard to worker training in the postwar period, it is necessary to situate the evolution of apprenticeship training and vocational education as well as the postwar history of the confederation within the social and economic histories of nineteenth- and twentieth-century France.

## Public Education and the Politics of Training

Before the 1789 French Revolution, craft apprenticeship was subsumed within a guild system. The 1791 Le Chapelier law dismantled guilds as well as the training of apprentices and the attribution

of masterships that they controlled. Following the deregulation of urban crafts in the nineteenth century, there was a consensus among
many observers that apprenticeship was in a perpetual state of crisis (Lequin 1986.) The crisis was blamed on the massive changes—proletar-
ianization within crafts and the beginnings of urbanization—start-
ing to transform an entire social order. In the industrializing context
of the nineteenth century, a number of French crafts such as garment
making, jewelry, furs, building, and shoemaking underwent a long, progressive devolution in which the division of labor increased, skills were
diluted, and some phases of production were put out to rural home
workers or to workers assembled under one roof, where mechanized
production partially or completely replaced hand workmanship (Sewell
1986, 51).

The deskilling of artisans and the decline of craft work generated intense debates on the nature and pace of large-scale change and likewise
focused attention on how to train a skilled workforce within an emerging industrial order. In the early part of the nineteenth century, social
reformers' writings on apprenticeship were part of a moralizing project
that celebrated venerable craft practices such as personalized hands-on
training within family workshops. These writings sought to revive and
preserve craft apprenticeship as a means of forestalling the "degrada-
tion" wrought by deskilling and of reclaiming a growing, "morally prof-
ligate" industrial working class. By the late 1880s, the view of craft apprenticeship had changed radically. Social reformers documented the
rampant abuse of young apprentices as a source of cheap labor and used
this as a powerful argument for eliminating or radically reforming craft
apprenticeship (Lequin 1986).

The Ferry laws, passed into law from 1879 to 1886, created compulsory secular elementary education in France. A 1881 law created the legal
framework for vocational schools in contrast to workplace apprenticeship (Prost 1968). It exemplified two competing and basically antitheti-
cal notions for training a skilled workforce. Apprenticeship signaled personalized, guided practice at the workplace by masters of a corpus of skills
encompassed within discrete crafts. Vocational training was defined at
the same time as compulsory, and free public education was institutionalized. It presupposed the increasing fragmentation of the labor process
in an industrializing context. Vocational training was conceived as a
means to realize the pragmatic goals of training skilled workers in industrial trades while providing the basic literacy skills and civic precepts
required to consolidate the newly created liberal, democratic Third

Republic (1870–1940). In contrast to the guild model informing craft apprenticeship, vocational training espoused a professional model that called for general educational preparation, standardized work routines, and shorter periods of narrow, on-the-job training for the majority of workers, on the one hand, and longer institutional education for highly skilled specialists, on the other (Buechler 1989, 32). This is a model predicated on learning as individualized assimilation of specified knowledge domains leading to state-sanctioned credentials.

In the wake of the Ferry legislation, the appropriate role of public vocational education was intensively debated. In 1887, a national commission was convened to examine the merits of craft apprenticeship in the workshop versus vocational training in the public schools. The testimony heard by the commission reveals a tension, which persists to this day, between a more highly valued, intellectually oriented curriculum and a less prestigious, practically oriented one. (Prost 1968, 318). Although very few state vocational schools were actually created until after World War II, state representatives nonetheless voiced a strong ideological preference for vocational training complemented by general education within public schools as opposed to craft apprenticeship training on the job. Apprenticeship remained largely locally controlled long after vocational education was formally brought within the purview of the French state.

During the interwar period, debates surrounding apprenticeship generated sporadic calls for its standardization and regulation—in 1918–1919 and again in 1937–1939. These debates reflected national fears surrounding shortages in a skilled labor force and raised the larger issues of national security, worker productivity, and the nation's place in a changing world order (Prost 1968). The rise of a national artisanal movement in the 1920s, a period of socioeconomic upheaval in many crafts, led to the passage of the 1925 Courtier law (Zdanty 1990). The Courtier legislation created the Chamber of Trades, a corporate institution grouping masters and journeymen and with a mandate to organize and conduct apprenticeship on the departmental level. Yet Courtier did not specify the exact powers of the Chamber or how recruitment would be used to control entry into specific crafts. Despite this legislation, apprenticeship continued to be organized without the benefit of a written contract. Independent masters and the apprentice's family or guardian agreed on the length and cost of the training. The family bore the cost of the training, room, and board. The matter of a salary, spending money, working conditions, hours, and the quality of the room and board were entirely the prerogative of the individual master (compare Bertaux and Bertaux-Wiame 1978; Blasquez 1976).

At the end of the 1930s, economic crisis, political polarization, and the military threat posed by Nazi Germany again exacerbated French fears concerning the dearth of a skilled labor force and focused renewed attention on worker training. Passage of the 1937 Walter-Paulin law was significant because its authors sought to reshape and institutionalize traditional notions of craft training and definitions of skill. It resuscitated a professional diploma, the CAP, created in 1911 to certify both basic literacy and skill mastery in manual crafts. The law's sponsors also recommended the creation of a master artisan diploma, the *brevet de maîtrise,* to be awarded after advanced training in craft skills, technology, and management. This training was designed to be conducted entirely under the aegis of the Chamber of Trades, not the Ministry of National Education. Thus, the Walter-Paulin law perpetuated the divide between vocational training provided by state-certified teachers in public institutions and apprenticeship training conducted in family workshops and certified by a corporate body outside the mainstream educational system (Zdanty 1990).

## Artisanship in Vichy France

Following France's swift defeat in 1940 and the installation of the German-sanctioned Vichy regime led by the World War I military hero, Marshall Pétain, artisanship served as a potent ideological device in the service of right-wing political propaganda. Some of Pétain's advisors attributed the crushing German defeat to punishment for France's departure from the craft and peasant values that had provided economic balance, social order, and a glorious past (Paxton 1972, 268). Pétain dedicated his regime to a "national revolution" that sought to make small independent producers, both artisans and peasants, the basis of a national and cultural regeneration steeped in preindustrial values (Faure 1989). Pétain's regime invested Chambers of Trade with new administrative powers and authorized the reorganization and unification of the virtually defunct preindustrial journeymen brotherhood associations *(compagnonnages).* His regime celebrated artisanal skill and the ennobling qualities of manual labor through a plethora of craft contests, radio programs, and film documentaries and in 1941 created a school, patterned after the most prestigious public universities, to prepare the future artisanal elite (Faure 1989).

## Schooling for a Modernizing Economy: *Les Trente Glorieuses*

Although many of the institutions created under Vichy ended with the liberation of France in 1944, this regime prefigured the specific role of the centralized state in the planning of the postwar economy and in the comprehensive reform of French public education (Prost 1997, 156–184). During this period, Western European countries in general, and France in particular, experienced sustained economic growth and industrial concentration lasting from 1945 to the first oil crisis in 1973—*les trente glorieuses*, "the thirty glorious years." This growth was accompanied by state-driven modernization that encouraged both the emergence of a new entrepreneurial business culture and the reform of existing vocational programs.

The emergence and popularization of new approaches to entrepreneurship began with the substantial economic aid provided by the United States' Marshall Plan. American reformers sought to rebuild the shattered French economy and to transform what they saw as a flawed business culture. They decried what they saw as the low productivity of French firms, the pervasive ignorance of management science, a strong resistance to investment and mechanization, conflictual relations between employers and workers, and little concern for market research, fiscal planning, or sales training. They made economic aid conditional on the creation of training programs designed to produce a new class of French industrial managers well versed in American-style management science, marketing, and human engineering (human relations, social psychology, group dynamics) (Boltanski 1988, 99–103).

The goals of Marshall Plan reformers dovetailed with those of high-ranking civil servants who were the architects of the postwar modernization initiatives. In the 1950s and 1960s, the combined efforts of Marshall Plan administrators and a French reformist avant-garde shaped and popularized a new model for French business defined largely in opposition to family entrepreneurs, who formed the backbone of what they saw as "the old-fashioned, Malthusian, Poujadist, and reactionary" petite bourgeoisie (Boltanski 1988, 104).[4] This effort spawned a plethora of business publications, management consulting firms, market research companies, training courses in human relations and the psychology of sales, a vast new literature on organization theory, and, ultimately, the establishment of study programs and universities devoted to business science.

In addition to the creation of a new entrepreneurial ethos, the expansion and concentration of French industry depended on both a well-trained labor force able to adapt to rapid technological transformations and a large supply of cheap, unschooled, and flexible labor willing to accept unskilled manual jobs. Because of low birth rates throughout the interwar period and serious labor shortages after World War II, French capital increasingly recruited (im)migrant and female labor to fill the least skilled positions in the labor structure (Noiriel 1990; Raissiguier 1994).

The French state—through public schools—had to regulate the process of skilling/deskilling while at the same time meeting increased social demand for education. The reform of vocational education was crucial to this project. Educational reforms included raising the school leave-taking age from thirteen to sixteen, creating common tracks for all children in public middle schools *(collèges)*, and expanding secondary education through the establishment of new vocational programs. These reforms ensured greater access to education at all levels, and, indeed, enrollments in secondary and postsecondary education increased five- and sixfold between 1948 and 1991 (Raissiguier 1994, 31).

Despite a significant broadening of the social base in the educational system, pronounced inequities remained whereby middle- and upper middle-class students dominated the most prestigious academic tracks and students from lower middle- and working-class backgrounds were disproportionately represented in the low prestige vocational tracks. The composition of these tracks reflected an enduring bias in favor of the knowledge and sociolinguistic practices associated with the dominant bourgeoisie. Vocational schools recruited students whose ignorance of class-based codes and weak academic performance precluded their upward advancement in the more valued academic track in the long cycle of secondary education (lycée) leading to university studies (Prost 1997, 108). Even as vocational education was expanded with the creation of new programs designed to parallel existing general educational programs at the middle, secondary, and university levels, a sharp divide separated it from the general educational system. Despite the theoretical possibility of movement from the vocational to the academic track, in reality each level still leads from the educational system directly into the job market or upward within the vocational track, rarely upward within the academic track.[5] In contrast to vocational education, apprenticeship training remained completely outside the mainstream public educational system until the 1970s. When it was partially moved from the workshop into the public school following the 1971 reform law, it supplanted existing vocational education at the very bottom of the academic hierarchy (Durand and Frémont 1979).

For state planners, both apprenticeship training and the artisanal entrepreneurs who employed apprentices emerged as a problem in the 1960s. French legislators passed a series of laws focusing specifically on artisanship between 1962 and 1973 that reflected the dominant postwar ideology of modernization and a pervasive discourse on professionalization. These laws redefined the artisanal sector, reorganized apprenticeship training, and consolidated the Chambers of Trade (Bachelard 1982). A 1962 law redefined artisanship in order to integrate it more closely within standardized legal and fiscal codes and to align it with a set of professional job descriptions used by the state to track and evaluate sectoral shifts in the workforce (Desrosières and Thévenot 1988). This law exemplified the postwar concern for promoting unrestrained economic growth and facilitating broadened access to independent crafts and trades (Zarca 1979a, 1986). It also signaled the seeming eclipse of an older categorization of work by independent occupation *(métier)* associated with undivided labor and the personal ownership of the means of production, be it skills or property.

This legislation de-emphasized the traditional links between craft and skill in the definition of artisanship and established an occupational category based exclusively on self-employment, the size of the workforce (first limited to five and later increased to ten salaried employees), and the nature of the firm's activity. It fixed the parameters of a category encompassing a heterogeneous group of independents including skilled artisans such as masons, cabinetmakers, and bakers as well as semi- or unskilled independents like building painters, taxi cab drivers, and window washers (Zarca 1986).

The 1971–1973 legislation extended standardized state protections to the small business sector in the form of social security benefits, investment incentives, and new forms of limited liability partnerships. It regulated apprenticeship in accord with French labor law providing a minimum guaranteed wage, paid vacations, and social security benefits. It also gave the Chamber of Trades the exclusive authority to approve ap-

prenticeship masters, establish mandatory written contracts, and organize examinations certifying craft skill. It raised the minimum school
leave-taking age for apprentices from thirteen to sixteen and mandated
that a shortened two-year period of training combine alternating periods of hands-on experience in the family workshop with formal academic and practical instruction in newly created state apprenticeship
training centers (*centres de formation d'apprentis*). These centers provide practicums and specialized classes in technology, management, and
labor and commercial law, as well as general educational preparation in
mathematics and French. At the conclusion of the two-year training period, apprentices take a written and practical state examination and, if
they pass, are awarded the entry-level professional diploma, the CAP.

The preparation of the CAP, in contrast to the simple skill-based
test previously administered at the conclusion of training (*examen de fin
d'apprentissage*), became more common as school officials consistently
urged apprentices to prepare the state diploma. Yet this decision depended on the existence of a CAP in the apprentice's craft. In 1971, no
such specialized training programs or diplomas existed in chocolate or
sugar candy production. *Chocolatiers* who had relied on informally training apprentices in their workshops suddenly found themselves without
a formally sanctioned means to train and certify them at a time when a
postwar ideology of professionalization was making state educational
credentials more important (Zarca 1986). How did the confederation
respond to these challenges? Who took the initiative to formulate these
strategic responses?

The confederation responses to these challenges were formulated
by a cadre of dynamic Parisian business owners.[6] Alain Grangé, Francis
Boucher, Madeleine Lombard, and Guy Urbain were the first craft leaders I interviewed in 1989, and over the ensuing years of my fieldwork
they maintained a continuing presence on the confederation's executive board. Alain Grangé owns Foucher, one of the oldest and most prestigious confectioneries in Paris, and he served as confederation vice-
president for many years before his election as president in 1995. Francis
Boucher, owner of a small but reputable Parisian *chocolaterie,* served
several terms as confederation treasurer, worked closely with state representatives to codify the bases of the craft, and coordinated the organization of the first Best Craftsman of France contest. Madeleine Lombard is the owner of a centenary confectionery business in Paris and
comes from a family well known for its involvement in employer syndicalism. She served as confederation president from 1977 to 1990 and in
1986 became the first woman to be elected vice-president of the execu-

tive board of the powerful Paris Chamber of Commerce and Industry. In 1990 she was named a Knight in the French Legion of Honor for her contribution to her profession.

Guy Urbain is the grandson of a founder of the confederation, and his family has played a prominent, some say even dominant, role since its creation in 1920. Urbain created the Center of Confectionery Studies in retail sales in 1950, assumed the editorship of *La confiserie* in 1955, and in 1958 oversaw the establishment of an annual show for small business owners in the food trades. He served continuously on the executive board from 1955 to 1997, served as a consultant on marketing and sales, led numerous study trips to visit colleagues in France and abroad, and assumed public relations responsibilities, giving interviews with journalists and academics. In 1991 Urbain presided over the creation of the Université de la Confiserie, an advanced center for confectionery studies. When I last saw him in October 1996, he insisted that he was planning to retire after more than forty years on the confederation executive board. However, I was not surprised to see him quoted in a Washington *Post* article (7 January 1998) devoted to France's "bitter chocolate battle" over vegetable additives, or to learn that he was elected president of the Confederation in 1998.

Urbain's wife regularly assisted the paid clerical staff at the confederation headquarters, and one of his sons, Alain Urbain, managed the annual trade show, Intersuc, which grew from a two-day event involving 70 exhibitors and 3,016 visitors in 1958 to four days in 1997 during which 168 exhibitors drew 22,197 professionals from six crafts, including confectioners, *chocolatiers*, pastry makers, ice cream makers, bakers, and caterers (Urbain 1997b, 17).

Confederation initiatives were informed by the massive scope of change occurring during *les trente glorieuses*. Numerous articles in the craft journal centered on the quickened pace of industrialization, the exodus from rural to urban areas, and the arrival of mass distribution outlets in France beginning in the late 1950s. Articles in the 1950s and 1960s centered on the new rationalized, scientific business practices. Craft leaders internalized and reproduced hegemonic ideas about the backward practices of family entrepreneurship. It is significant and ironic that they—members of the archaic group presumably destined to disappear—were avid readers of the new literature and, through their journal, introduced their membership to this American business model.

Urbain led a delegation of French family owners to the United States in 1961 and became a proponent of American-sponsored training seminars in sales, management, and marketing. In the 1960s and early 1970s, he and other board members urged their members to abandon some of the traditional practices favored by the small business sector. These were cast as old-fashioned and ineffective and included a French selling style characterized as too stiff and overly ceremonious. The leadership criticized the practice of displaying goods on or behind counters, which created a rigid division of the store into a public and private space. Leaders also decried traditional merchandising because it neglected new advertising techniques that attracted customers through the artful display of goods and the spatial rearrangement of boutique interiors permitting both freer movement and browsing. Older approaches discouraged browsing and buying on whim by barring entry into a store unless a purchase was made. Indeed, it is still assumed that customers enter a shop only if they intend to buy. Leaders encouraged small retailers "to specialize and streamline" their product lines, abandoning the traditional large assortments of house goods, to lower costs by banding together to make collective purchases, to search actively for export markets, and to adopt rationalized management and merchandizing techniques.

In 1966 Guy Urbain published a survey conducted on the future of the artisanal food crafts (*La confiserie* 1966, 29–31). A majority of those polled expressed pessimism and blamed their negative outlook on the increased competition from mass distribution outlets. The following year Guy Urbain captured this ambivalence in a journal article:

Who are we? How are we recruited? Are we the new soldiers of a forward-looking profession or the rear guard of a stagnating one? For the most part we are self-made and self-trained. Without much technical preparation in school we assume important business responsibilities. . . . We need to know our weaknesses, to play courageously the card of continuing education, professional exchanges, and rigorous self-improvement. This is all the more imperative because we are entering an era of mobility where . . . stability and the solidity of an acquired position will be thrown into question. We are involved in a commercial revolution, in a perpetual struggle for sales outlets. . . . Where are we going to fit in this competition? Can we act to find positive solutions?

The leadership also developed strong linkages to crucial public and private sector officials. They cultivated relationships with the representatives of municipal governments, key national ministries, and public bodies such as the Ministry of Commerce and Artisanship, the Ministry of National Education, and the Permanent Assembly of the Chambers of Trades (which all have authority in the area of artisanal training). Craft leaders developed contacts among the industrial producers of chocolate products who not only supply craft producers with *couverture* but also sponsor events like craft events, trade shows, and chocolate tastings. Leaders also established relationships with members of the various commercial and trade organizations they deemed vital to the interests of their businesses. Key private and public sector personalities were also invited to preside over the official opening of Intersuc or to address the annual meeting (*convention*) in September as well as the national convention (*assises nationales*) held every four years.

## Certifying Professional *Chocolatiers:* The *Trente Glorieuses* End

From the creation of the confederation in 1920 until World War II, the membership had been dominated by the family owners of gourmet groceries (*épiceries fines*) and confectioneries (*confiseries*). From the end of the war to the present, the proportion of *chocolatiers* in the confederation has grown from a small minority to 50 percent of the total membership. The arrival of small-scale *chocolatiers* was motivated by three important changes. First, the interests of industrial and small-scale producers diverged sharply in the 1970s. Alain Grangé reduced his participation in the Union of Industrial Chocolate Makers, which had included a section composed of small- and medium-sized *chocolateries*. It was a difficult decision because both his father and grandfather had held leadership positions in that organization. He explained: "They [industrial producers] were primarily concerned with the procurement of raw materials, product pricing, and state regulatory policies aimed at large-scale manufacturers. They had little interest in issues of great importance to us: training, professional certification, product development, export markets for luxury confections, marketing and advertising techniques. . . . In short we felt that our interests were better served by the confederation."

Second, the 1973 oil crisis marked the end of rapid economic growth in France and ushered in a period during which additional pressures were exerted on artisanal food producers. There was a scarcity of business loans from banks and government lending institutions while inflation was driving up the purchase price of business property. These developments coincided with the arrival of franchise outlets, which, as we have seen, made a swift incursion into the confectionery gift market.

Third, craft leaders recognized and seized on a shift in the national mood in the 1970s away from a modernist attraction to the future and toward a nostalgic evocation of a traditional past (Rigby 1991, 9). This shift nurtured a longing for a national heritage of artisanal workmanship and the family entrepreneurship that had predominated in France until the postwar period. Although the leadership continued to advocate modernized business practices, they articulated two marketing strategies designed to differentiate clearly their products and houses from mass production and distribution "by playing the card of quality and marketing the exceptional," in the words of Guy Urbain. On the one hand, they began to exploit an artisanal mystique drawn from the past. This craftsman ideal relied heavily on the revival and celebration of a traditional guild idiom in the training and performance of skilled work and on the aestheticization of confectionery taste and consumption. It was a strategy that coincided with the global spread of gourmet cuisine, one marked by the hegemony of French culinary arts. On the other hand, they sought to authenticate their craft and goods through professionalization.

From the mid-1970s on, confederation leaders focused on securing the markers enjoyed by other professions such as state diplomas and national collective labor agreements. One of their first organized initiatives involved the creation of the CAP in chocolate and sugar candy production. They assembled an internal commission charged with formally codifying a corpus of basic craft skills and, subsequently, petitioned Education Ministry officials for the right to create a CAP.

Their efforts were complicated by what Guy Urbain termed "internal corporatist rivalries among companion crafts." Disputes over claims to specialized skill among companion crafts are a ubiquitous feature of contemporary France just as they were in preindustrial French cities. These disputes were exacerbated by the existence of a plethora of employer associations representing the owners of food craft businesses such as the National Confederation of Pastry Makers, the National Confederation of Bakers and Baker-Pastry Makers, and the National Confederation of Ice Cream Makers. When confederation leaders petitioned the state for their own CAP, leaders of the National Confederation of Pastry Makers registered a stiff protest. They argued that the skills of the *chocolatier* and confectioner had long been subsumed within their own craft and were adequately addressed by the state diplomas in pastry production.[7] The 1979 confederation request was denied.

Two years later, in 1981, continuing lobbying efforts under the leadership of Madame Lombard resulted in the approval of the CAP. Once institutionalized, the confederation's CAP became a crucial component in subsequent state decisions to recognize, defend, and ultimately promote the autonomy of the craft. Lombard and her executive board moved quickly to consolidate their gain. In the same year, 1981, they collaborated with the hotel management profession to open a private apprentice training school, the Paris School for the Food Trades. In 1982 the confederation leadership lobbied state representatives for the right to organize its own Best Craftsman of France contest (also strongly opposed by the National Confederation of Pastry Makers) and to define a corpus of advanced craft skills. Their goal was to provide a complete professional trajectory by creating the highest craft credential—the *brevet de maîtrise,* or master artisan diploma. In 1984 the state approved the first national collective labor contracts for salaried workers in the craft.[8]

Meanwhile, this period was marked by economic recession and restructuring in France and Western Europe. There was a rapid loss of unskilled jobs in the industrial sector, rising levels of under- and unemployment, and a concomitant burgeoning of service sector jobs requiring more formal education. Successive education ministers emphasized the link between economic strength and a highly skilled French workforce. For example, Jean-Pierre Chevènement, named minister of education in 1984, stressed the need for rigorous technical training in order to prepare French workers for high technology production sectors (Prost 1997, 194). Chevènement also argued that for France to be competitive globally, 80 percent of an age cohort should complete the full secondary educational cycle in the lycée, thereby reaching, in his words, "the level of the baccalaureate degree." In order to accomplish that goal and to curb mounting unemployment among young people aged sixteen to twenty-five, he launched initiatives to expand the vocational track. For example, in 1985, new vocational baccalaureate degrees *(baccalauréat professionnel)* were created along with special professional lycées.

Chevènement's call was heeded. In the school year 1982–83, only 35 percent of a given age cohort had reached the level leading to the baccalaureate examination; by 1990–91, 80 percent had entered the full secondary cycle and 55 percent had continued on to the final year in the lycée. Due to this increased pool of young workers with more education, those with no or low-level vocational diplomas increasingly found themselves locked into long-term unemployment alternating with cycles of temporary employment (Prost 1997, 209). By 1989 only 30 percent of youth without a diploma had a stable job three years after leaving school (Raissiguier 1994, 43). However, it also became clear that the possession of a baccalaureate degree was not a guarantee of job competitive-

ness or security. In 1988, fully 30 percent of baccalaureate degree holders were unemployed one year after leaving school (Prost 1990). It was
this shift—increased numbers of young people preparing the long cycle
of secondary school and a concomitant resistance to craft apprenticeship—that Jacques Daumoinx lamented in his contest speech. Madame
Lombard, too, contrasted the shortage of skilled workers for the un-
filled jobs in the food trades and the unemployment line for those with
higher education levels.

The perceived need to address the lacunae of an educational system
criticized for not preparing students for economic and workplace transformations produced the 1987 apprenticeship law. The law's sponsors
aimed to recast and revitalize an apprenticeship system that attracted
low numbers because of the widespread perception among teachers and
parents that it was the exclusive preserve of academic failures eliminated
from more culturally valued academic tracks (Lebaube 1990, iv). Legislators bemoaned the progressive decline in the numbers of apprentices
over the preceding twenty-year period; the drop from 318,700 apprentices in 1966 to 220,000 in 1991 was widely reported in the mass media
over the course of my fieldwork (Betbeder 1991).

The 1987 law attempted to bridge two divides: one between the short
and long cycles of secondary education, and the second between vocational schools and apprenticeship centers. It sought to bring the logic
of mainstream education to apprenticeship by allowing trainees in apprenticeship centers to prepare degrees previously available only in vocational high school and university programs. Similarly, it attempted to
professionalize vocational training in secondary schools and universities
by sending trainees into the workplace for longer periods of on-the-job
training.

In 1986 preliminary plans for the reform included proposals for the
elimination of a number of specialized CAP diplomas, such as the one
in chocolate, which attracted only small numbers of trainees. When
state representatives approached the confederation leadership, Madame
Lombard and her executive board flatly refused to relinquish their newly
created CAP. Their refusal stunned state representatives and prompted
the first of three studies commissioned by various state ministries between 1986 and 1990 to study "the problem of French chocolate production and training." These studies reveal that state officials moved
from merely acknowledging the existence of a distinct craft identity to
facilitating and controlling the implementation of specific strategies intended to consolidate it.

Commissioned by the Ministries of Education, Employment, and Social Affairs, the author of the first study (Descolonges 1987) acknowledged the low numbers of apprentices preparing the new diploma (an annual average of only thirty-two since its creation) as well as the reluctance of youth and their parents to choose a craft offering only basic-level certification. Yet he strongly recommended not only the retention of the CAP but the creation of additional credentials, such as the master artisan diploma. The study raised the issue of international competition and evoked the "imperatives dictated by the impending unification of the European Community." Citing the steady expansion of Belgian franchise outlets, it noted the crucial role that professional training would play in the "struggle" to prevent the absorption of a French "art of chocolate production" in a rapidly advancing and potentially hegemonic European division of labor. It warned that if French artisanal *chocolatiers* disappear because no specialized training exists, "a French culinary art goes with them and subsequently a French standard of taste —developments detrimental to artisanal and industrial producers alike" (5). The author also painstakingly outlined the corpus of basic skills and collective dispositions constituting what he termed a "traditional craft habitus," yet simultaneously admonished artisanal *chocolatiers* to conform to the professionalizing imperatives of a rapidly changing European and global market.

The professionalization theme sounded in this study was echoed and amplified in the one that followed (Casella 1989). This study urged *chocolatiers* not only to rely on artisanal skill and craft culture but to seek a broader preparation encompassing studies in marketing and management. Empirical handicraft method should yield to rationalized "scientific" pedagogies and formalized certification procedures. The craft (*métier*) of chocolate making should become a true profession (*profession*). It concluded that "the prerequisite of a true profession . . . was the implementation of an education at "level four." Professional *chocolatiers* should have "legitimate" educational degrees such as the new professional baccalaureate degree, as opposed to the specialized vocational diplomas like the CAP, because this would ultimately enhance their competitiveness at home and abroad (73).

Craft leaders worked closely with then director of artisanship, Jérôme Bédier. As soon as Bédier assumed his duties in 1986, the confederation leadership contacted him. Most of the executive board members were enthusiastic. Alain Grangé explained: "He is young, an *énarque* [graduate of the most prestigious public university training high-level civil servants], and really interested in artisanship." Bédier accepted an invitation to attend the confederation convention held in Corsica that same year, 1986. Bédier offered to finance a third study (Mathieu 1990), and four years later, in 1990, he personally presented it at the confederation convention in Saint Tropez.

Bédier explained that the study was intended to develop a market for French chocolate while preventing further loss of market share to franchise outlets. He advised those attending the plenary session that "training, communication, and quality are at the root of our strategy": "We can say that there is in France an overall underinvestment in training of artisanship which is absolutely frightful. Until 1987, we equated artisanal training with the acquisition of a CAP. It was a terrible misjudgment. . . . It is imperative to create training tracks which are adapted to [job market] demands, that is, say, degrees at least at level four [full secondary cycle]." Bédier reminded his listeners that a craft credential such as the master artisan diploma was not recognized by the Ministry of Education until 1987: "What was it three years ago? Then, we awarded in the whole country only 850 master artisan diplomas for 850,000 artisans. . . . There were only a few particularly worthy and impassioned craftsmen who got their master artisan diploma." He hastened to emphasize that in the three years since the 1987 reform, the diploma promised "growth," "dynamism," and, most importantly, cultural capital equaling mainstream educational degrees: "The CAP was not motivating enough. But, if in the apprenticeship center there is a CAP class and a professional certificate or professional baccalaureate or a master artisan diploma, the families' attitudes change completely. . . . The young person will complete the same classes as in the lycée, in addition he will be in a business and he will be paid."

Bédier addressed the frustrations of confederation leaders whose repeated petitions for a master artisan diploma had been denied. He assured them that the new diploma revived by the 1987 reform would have "a fantastic appeal" and ended by announcing:

I know where your profession is now. You have your CAP. I understand that you want to put in place very quickly, through the master artisan diploma, a diploma at level four, and I encourage you strongly to do it. Indeed, I am now ready to create with you a master artisan diploma [in chocolate and sugar production] so a section can be opened in fall 1991. It's a title which can be perfectly adapted to your profession.

In spite of his support, Bédier sounded a cautionary note and urged the creation of higher-level degrees such as the professional baccalaureate and a technical university degree, the BTS, earned after two years of university study.

In the question-and-answer period that followed, one *chocolatier*, Monsieur Lalet, asked a question that resonated strongly with the audience. In 1990 the only training centers offering the CAP in chocolate and sugar were in Paris and Nancy, in northeastern France: "I'm in Bordeaux [southwestern France] and we have trouble getting apprentices because we have to send them to Paris. How can we improve this situation?" Bédier did not directly answer him but made an ardent plea for reformed apprenticeship training—not the old informally organized and locally defined model but one newly recast and closely articulated according to a professional model in which on-the-job training was subsumed within educational programs implemented and overseen by the Ministry of National Education in Paris. By citing the national importance of apprenticeship, Bédier also linked *chocolatiers'* concerns to a national issue widely reported in the mass media, namely, as one commentator put it, "what future for our young people?" (Agulhon 1994).

In the fall of 1990, there was increasing debate about the mounting social fragmentation engendered by a stagnant labor market and the potential unemployability of young people. Unemployment rates for those between sixteen and twenty-five hovered at 25 percent. The dearth of jobs posed acutely the problem of the procurement of permanent, full-time employment. A 1990 poll conducted among this age group revealed that many of them had only experienced full-time work as a succession of low-level, temporary positions in a number of different workplaces. A majority yearned for satisfying work providing financial stability and social advancement, yet, given the dismal job market, had abandoned any hope of finding such work (Capdevielle, Meynard, and Mouriaux 1990).

Bédier ended his session by urging *chocolatiers* to implement other state recommendations, namely, the creation of a craft symbol as a marketing tool.

## The Craft Symbol

At the same convention, the confederation leadership planned a session on future initiatives. Based on the 1990 Mathieu study, it recommended modern communication strategies designed to market the cultural value embedded in family artisanship. Confederation leaders had received an advance copy and had distributed a questionnaire proposing twelve new initiatives. The creation of a craft symbol received the strongest endorsement (89 percent) among respondents. Despite this consensus, there was instant disagreement as to what a collective symbol would signify in terms of craft identity and who would have the right to purchase and display it. The renewed emphasis on training and certification had heightened a tension within the membership between retailers and producer/retailers that emerged strongly during discussions on the craft symbol. In 1990 the confederation membership was evenly divided between retail merchants (50 percent) and small and medium-sized firms that produced and retailed goods (50 percent).

The confederation leadership hired Jean-Luc Pinson, a marketing consultant, to lead the discussion. He began:

What is our identity? Should the symbol be available to everyone? What should it communicate to consumers? If you create a system of recognition whose objective is communicating to the masses, then it's merely a sign . . . it doesn't say quality, brand, name of the professional, or one's predecessors. The media message is simply, "You can get some here." Nothing else.

This introduction provoked immediate protests. One person insisted that the symbol be given only "to the French." It was not clear whether he meant to exclude the French owners of Belgian franchises, the French owners of French franchises, the Belgian owners of French and Belgian franchises, or all of the above. Moreover, it was also unclear which confectionery Other was being opposed to the French: American, Swiss, or Italian mass-produced chocolates? The newly arrived Belgian franchise outlets such as Léonidas versus the older Belgian firm Godiva? French franchises? Madame Lombard took the floor to emphasize that the symbol should indicate merely a confectionery retail outlet. Another member strongly disagreed: "If we are creating a symbol as a means of distinguishing ourselves as *chocolatiers,* then how can we give it to everyone?" A majority of the board members initially supported Lombard's position. At Pinson's insistence they took a vote on whether the symbol should indicate primarily a sales outlet. Of those present, 71 percent overwhelmingly seconded the leadership's view.

Pinson urged participants to consider what they were selling through the use of this symbol. Pierre Cluizel, heir to a prominent *chocolatier* family, suggested that just as French hotels are differentiated by the attribution of stars, so too should *chocolatiers* "move toward a system of internal differentiation." His view was seconded by others, and in a number of successive votes participants reversed their initial vote and overwhelmingly supported a symbol that would signify not merely a specialty outlet but one selling high-quality products. The symbol most participants envisioned was, as Pinson suggested, "the medieval emblem [hung outside preindustrial workshops to signify the exercise of a particular craft] presented in a high tech form."

When Pinson turned to the specifics of design, cost, and implementation, the questions of identity and membership were posed with renewed intensity. Who should pay for the design of a costly symbol? Who could benefit? Could the symbol be used as a means to augment the confederation membership? What message would its display convey to consumers regarding the composition of a national craft community? Could businesses that merely retailed candies produced elsewhere have the right to purchase and display it?

Both Pinson and Jacques Daumoinx skillfully directed the debate away from this divisive issue and centered it on the logistics of creating a symbol. Daumoinx's son, Gilles, recommended the establishment of a budget of $50,000, and a number of owners pledged seed money for the first phase—hiring a well-known Parisian marketing firm to design and test-market a symbol.

## The Best Craftsman of France Contest

Six weeks after the convention ended, the contest award ceremony was held. The contest's success owed much to the dedication of Francis Boucher, who undertook the long, painstaking process of codifying a corpus of advanced craft skills so that the contest rules could be formulated.

Francis Boucher is the owner of a highly successful *chocolaterie* employing one full-time worker, two apprentices, and a full-time saleswoman to help his wife Christiane in the boutique. I knew the Bouchers well because I had visited their boutique and workshop weekly for a six-month period in 1989. Boucher had followed a traditional craft trajectory (before the 1971 legislation was enacted) by leaving school at fourteen, completing a three-year apprenticeship, earning a CAP in pastry production, and working to perfect his skill in a number of confectionery houses before becoming self-employed. Boucher married, created a business in his native Normandy, sold it, and with the prof-

Figure 10. Frog designed for Go Voyage travel by Francis Boucher.

its purchased business property in Paris. When I met the Bouchers in 1989 they had been at their fifteenth arrondissement location for thirteen years and their confectionery house was grossing approximately $350,000 a year. Boucher had earned an excellent reputation for his chocolates and chocolate figurines (see fig. 10). Boucher was often featured in newspaper and trade journal articles and interviewed on French radio and television. He was an active and well-respected member of the executive board and connected through his brother André to a national network of celebrated *pâtissiers*. His brother held the title of Best Craftsman of France in pastry and, in 1990, had just sold his business to accept a position as head of new product development at the industrial chocolate manufacturer Cacao Barry. André Boucher played an integral role as advisor to his brother when Francis Boucher was appointed to serve as the president of the judging panel.

When I arrived back in Paris in September 1990 to continue my fieldwork research, my first stop was the Bouchers' *chocolaterie*. During the three weeks I spent in Paris before moving to Bayonne, I went there often so Francis Boucher could catch me up on all that had happened since May 1989. The preparations for the contest were a central preoccupation for him because he had spent dozens of hours in difficult negotiations with Ministry of National Education representatives. State officials had to balance the confederation's petitions with the stiff opposition registered by the pastry makers.

Moreover, Francis Boucher worried about the success of the final round. The preceding February a pall had been cast over the semi-final round when one of the contestants, a well-known *pâtissier* and holder of the Best Craftsman of France title in pastry production, had been caught cheating and was eliminated from the competition. At a dinner organized to honor the five finalists, he had made a public scene denigrating the finalists' work as "shit" and later registered a formal complaint with the Ministry of Education alleging "improper contest management."

Partly because of the pastry makers' opposition, Francis Boucher spent considerable effort constituting a judging panel of big names in the three categories of evaluation: work technique, taste, and aesthetic presentation. I knew him to be a meticulous worker with an optimistic outlook, a passion for his craft, an inexhaustible capacity for both work and conversation, and a ready sense of humor, but during the final weeks before the contest, accumulated stress took its toll. His wife Christiane confided to me that he suffered from chronic insomnia. As I was leaving the workshop early one evening after the workshop help had gone and Christiane was already in their upstairs apartment, I noticed how tired he looked. Instead of closing so he could go up to dinner, he lingered. I quipped that instead of organizing the contest, he should have entered it because he would have no difficulty earning the title. He smiled, obviously pleased by the compliment, paused, and replied, "Bah, I'm too old. . . . I am in a very awkward position serving as president of the judging panel." When I wondered why he felt that way given the success of his house and the reputation he had earned, he replied in an uncharacteristically impatient tone, "But it's obvious. I have state officials to confront at every turn and I have to defend our [confederation's] position and what do I have as a credential? A primary level certificate *[certificat d'études]* and a CAP in pastry production."

During my next visit, Boucher was pleased that he had secured the participation of some eminent craft figures and state representatives including Monsieur Ponée, then head of the Lenôtre culinary school and former teacher at the Swiss COBA school, Robert Linxe, and Jérôme Bédier, among others. He showed me the contest rules explaining that finalists would be required to complete ten different kinds of classic chocolate candies, two sugar candies, a caramel candy, three molded figurines (one in chocolate and the other in marzipan), and an original piece of chocolate art in keeping with the theme of Saint Valentine's Day. In addition to preparing well-known chocolate and sugar candies, contestants would also create two signature recipes and two pieces of original confectionery art using no internal support structures or nonedible materials. The rules stipulated that the piece completed during the contest be a smaller replica of a larger entry executed before the competition.

We had talked for nearing two hours in the office when the salaried worker Jean-Marie asked Monsieur Boucher to take a phone call. Jean-Marie has spent nearly his entire professional life with the Bouchers, and in addition to being an excellent craftsman with command of both pastry and chocolate, he was loquacious and good-humored. He also had an exemplary working relationship with the Bouchers. That afternoon he had been supervising the first-year apprentices in the hand-dipping of delicate candy centers. As soon as his boss was safely out of earshot, Jean-Marie said to me with an air of disgust: "Well, Suzanne do you want to know how I feel about this MOF [Best Craftsman of France contest]? It's a show *[ils font du cinéma]*. The guys who go for a title like this are so affected!" When I registered a look of surprise, he added: "Now don't get me wrong. I admit that there are people who are truly gifted—artists—people who start in [the School of] Fine Arts in drawing and then go into the profession. That is art they do. But I can't stand these pretentious snobs. I prefer people who work hard, who know how to exercise their craft, and who do it with modesty." I had little time to digest Jean-Marie's remark because just then Francis returned to the workshop. Several visits later, on 18 October, I stopped by the Boucher workshop in the morning before my scheduled interview with Robert Linxe. It was a day when both apprentices were working, a situation in the tiny workshop that made for tight quarters and short tempers. Moreover, the morning had begun badly when one apprentice had prepared the wrong kind of chocolate *couverture* to coat an entire batch of candies. When I arrived Jean-Marie was supervising the apprentices in the fabrication of a *gianduja* and complaining about having to keep a constant eye on them. Francis was concerned because both Robert Linxe and Jérôme Bédier had withdrawn from the judging panel (Linxe to attend the opening of his New York boutique and Bédier because of a professional conflict) and he had just over one week to find suitable replacements.

Just then representatives from the company committee of the neighborhood hospital stopped by to place their annual order for the employee Christmas gift boxes.

By the time the Bouchers finished with the order, I had to leave for my appointment. I did not have the opportunity to speak with them until the day after the award ceremony. Since only the ceremony and the exhibition were open to the public, I was very anxious to know what had happened behind the scenes.

I learned that in twenty-eight hours over a three-day period the five finalists labored under rules specifically delineating spatial, temporal, and material requirements. They worked behind closed doors in contiguous work stations under the constant gaze of the judging panel. Contestants were assigned work space by drawing lots, and a central location was crucial in order to ensure constant visibility. Judges circulated continuously requesting explanations and evaluating technique, technology, organization of work space, use of allotted time, and the performative presence exhibited by finalists. One of the winners, Jean-Pierre Richard, the co-owner of a medium-sized *chocolaterie* known for the designer chocolates it produces and distributes in Paris and New York, drew the best location and impressed all the judges with both his rationalized organization of work space and his adaptation of the techniques and tools of woodworking to chocolate. He fashioned the shapely base of a Belle Epoque lamp from a block of marbleized dark and white chocolate with the aid of an electric lathe and a chisel (see fig. 11). Other contestants crafted a miniature chocolate writing desk, a molded "bronze" (chocolate) sculpture, chocolate replicas of black and white photographs, delicate pink marzipan roses, and a pair of young confectionery lovers.

The criteria and categories of evaluation, the value assigned to these categories, and the actual objects produced reveal that more is at stake than merely the identification and celebration of superior craft skill.

Figure 11. Jean-Pierre Richard demonstrating technique, Intersuc, 1991.

The choice of contest winners illuminates the politics of cultural production, authentication, and display as well as the tension between art
and craft, between autonomy and standardization, and between innovation and tradition. Contest entries were judged according to three
categories of evaluation: aesthetic presentation, gustatory appeal, and
work technique. Contest winners were expected to demonstrate control
of the bases of the craft as well as the superior skill required to advance

it through innovation. Technical expertise and confectionery taste were intimately linked to both individualized expression and a highly elaborated aesthetics in the overall categories of evaluation. Out of a total of 200 points, 80 were given for presentation: design, color, contrast, and arrangement of goods. Of those 80 points, the two artistic pieces represented 50 points, whereas only 30 were reserved for all of chocolate and sugar candies.

In their evaluation of the confectionery art, judges were asked to assign points in finely differentiated categories such as faithfulness to the contest theme (Saint Valentine's Day), artistic worth, creativity, originality, and technical merit. The category of taste was deemed almost as important and represented 70 points of the total. Here again the internal differentiations among candies were revealing. Judges assigned one overall score for all the classic candy centers they sampled but were asked to provide detailed commentary on contestants' signature candies, noting gustatory appeal, creative flavor blends, original couplings of centers and coating, texture of candy centers, cleanness of bite under the teeth, and palate quality. At first glance the weight assigned for taste and presentation versus the 50 points accorded work technique seemed curious. However, from the point of view of Francis Boucher and his brother, who designed these criteria, this did not mean that technical prowess was subordinated to aesthetics. It was rather an integral part of its successful realization. Moreover, this category included not only mastery of the medium represented but also the organization of work and the correct handling of craft tools.

The contest emphasis on aesthetics is emblematic of the "art culture system" (Clifford 1988), which perpetuates the hegemony of conventionally appropriate high art categories. This system provides the basis for discounting craft as lesser popular art or folklore and celebrates individualized creations that imitate high art (Bright 1995, 1–18). Best Craftsmen of France contestants seek acclaim as artists, not mere artisans. Contest winners must demonstrate originality and aesthetic mastery of a material medium—be it metal, wood, leather, clay, glass, cloth, ice, pastry sugar, or chocolate. In the kinds of objects produced, contestants both contest and reproduce hegemonic notions of French artisans as producers whose "art" is inspired by an aesthetic defined and validated by their social betters, whether state representatives or bourgeois consumers.

On the one hand, *chocolatiers* contest their representation in scholarly and popular media as members of the declining petite bourgeoisie whose low cultural capital makes it impossible for them to appreciate or reproduce the cultured classes' disinterested aesthetics based on pure form. Indeed, food is one of the privileged arenas of French consumption in which the opposition between form and substance exemplifies the polarity of high culture and popular culture (Bourdieu 1984, 193–199). In order to earn the title of confectionery artists, *chocolatiers* must privilege form, originality, and aesthetics over function, tradition, and pragmatics. They must demonstrate the technical competence that allows them to master and transcend the constraints of a highly demanding and unstable medium—sensitive to climatic changes and subject to decay—such as chocolate. To have the edible masquerade as the functional in the form of chocolate vases, pots, lamps, and desks is to indulge in a higher form of abstract play. To create decorative chocolate art such as photographs, paintings, figurines, and sculpture that will never be tasted or eaten is to perform an aesthetics divorced from function. To create candies whose flavor combinations radically challenge the palate is to affirm discerning taste and invite expert judgment. Thus, signature candies and confectionery art challenge and subvert received art taxonomies in which the artist is cultured and the artisan is traditional. The artist's work acquires an aura of authenticity dependent upon its originality in contrast to the artisan's craft, which is authenticated by its conventionality (compare Babcock 1995, 124–150; Bakewell 1995, 19–54).

On the other hand, *chocolatiers'* attempts to demonstrate their cultural capital by performing a disinterested aesthetics based on form only reproduce the hegemony of high art dictates. Moreover, when they enter the contest, *chocolatiers* surrender a significant measure of interpretive authority concerning both art and craft to state representatives and culture brokers interested in promoting French chocolate nationally and internationally. The globalization of markets and the spread of transnational culture have made the processes of national cultural production both more complicated and strategic. In a context of intensified international competition, the status of competing national cultures within a historically produced and constantly shifting hierarchy of nations is critical to establishing or maintaining claims of cultural authenticity. The ability to be recognized in international arenas is critical because it affects the validation of cultural forms within national arenas. Similarly, the historical continuity of particular cultural forms within national arenas is helpful to the defense of claims of authenticity promoted internationally. For example, France's historical reputation as a preeminent nation of luxury crafts and culinary arts lent considerable weight to the authentication of French chocolate.

In France there is a long tradition of state control over the determination of which cultural forms are labeled as genuine and then subsequently identified as high culture or even national traditions. As *chocolatiers* petitioned state representatives to recognize their distinct craft, they confronted the state's own civilizing process (compare Herzfeld 1997) as a condition for the authentication of French chocolate. Shifting international circumstances only intensified the long-standing impulses of a historically powerful national center to domesticate and control the designation of mastership in chocolate. Thus, issues of authenticity came to the fore in the judgment of both signature and classic candies; these issues are intimately connected to expert knowledge, aesthetics, and originality. As in art, the copy, the forgery, and the fake can have no place (Baudrillard 1981, 103). Hence, the necessity for contestants to produce under the constant gaze of a plethora of experts—producers, gastronomes, state functionaries—and the instant disqualification of those who use unauthorized tools, materials, or methods.

Although contest winners claim the status of confectionery artists, these claims are vulnerable from several points of view. First, the enduring division between art and craft is reflected in French museums, where the politics of art, culture, and display are performed (Karp and Levine 1991; Karp, Kreamer, and Levine 1992). Confectionery art is most often displayed in the ethnographic and decorative arts museum or special exhibitions devoted to craft culture, rarely in the art gallery or even less in national (high) art museums. This division is perpetuated by the French state and revealed in the long and complex relationship the state has had with artisans, beginning with the trade guilds and royal manufactures of the Old Regime. It has created, regulated, subsidized, and controlled a number of French crafts. In the preindustrial era, the French crown oversaw the completion of masterpieces and the attribution of masterships within guilds but exercised a conservative influence on crafts by mandating standardized tools, methods, and skills. In contrast, in modern times the state has legislated craft innovation through the creation of small numbers of national artisanal schools and contests. Created in a 1923 context marked by great upheaval in many trades, the Best Craftsman of France rules were written to promote both modernization and quality in artisanal production as a means of forestalling the definitive disappearance of endangered crafts. Thus the demand for originality in both design and technique demonstrated by contestants and celebrated by craft leaders was generated not from within the community but by various ministries of the French state.

Second, reactions to the confectionery art produced by the contes-

tants highlight the linkages between art categories and cultural boundaries. Despite the audience admiration for the chocolate art and candies
exhibited at the award ceremony, all of the French intellectuals to whom
I showed the pictures of the exhibition admired the craft technique but
dismissed the art as kitsch. These reactions suggest the ways in which
"high" art circumscribes popular art forms to reinforce existing class and
social hierarchies and the ways "low" forms seek critical validation from
experts (Bright 1995, 5–6). State recognition of the craft engendered respect for chocolates newly recast as prestige goods and for *chocolatiers*
as master artisans and, even, chefs. However, their "art" was still linked
to the exercise of a manual craft, and it did little to improve their ambivalent social status or to resolve the tensions they embody as workers
and petty bourgeois entrepreneurs.

Finally, the designation of the first generation of master *chocolatiers*
reveals much about craft and community. Through their discursive narratives, confederation leaders presented a seamless view of a solidaristic
community united in the pursuit of common goals. Madame Lombard
depicted the contest winners as the "best of our professionals . . . who
in the tradition of the masters of old, worked, suffered, doubted, seeking relentlessly the originality, aesthetic . . . implicit in new creations."
Yet the celebration of superior skill exemplified by contest winners masks
the hierarchies of domination and the politics of membership within the
craft community. Lombard suggested that ancestral tradition and a craft
work ethic alone suffice as sources for the aesthetic creativity demanded
to earn the title. Although the contest is theoretically open to everyone,
in reality, the stiff competition, enormous time investment, and financial resources required privilege participants from well-established confectionery houses. Indeed, despite significant differences in age and professional experience, the five finalists shared important commonalities.
They were all sons of house owners *(fils de patron)* who were born into
the crafts of pastry or chocolate and skilled through workplace experience. All but one were heads of or heirs to their own houses at the time
of the contest. The one exception, a title winner, Pascal Brunstein, was
a salaried instructor at the prestigious private culinary school of Yssingeaux, located near Lyon.

The Best Craftsman of France contest represents a crucially important "tournament of value" (Appadurai 1986, 21) because it is a complex,
periodic event (held every three years since its 1990 creation) that is removed in a culturally defined way from the routines of craft economic
life. Such a tournament is an instrument of status contests involving

competitive, even agonistic, displays of skill in which select *chocolatiers* strive to assert and maintain a prominent position within a national craft community. In a similar but more striking way than the Basque coast contest, the Best Craftsman contest works to aggrandize the status of a small elite of largely self-employed artisans while preventing salaried workers from gaining access to the techniques, resources, and cultural capital those artisans monopolize. It also effectively masks the skill, knowledge, and importance of sometimes similarly or more skilled salaried workers. In this case, the organizers and contest winners all relied on salaried producers in the workshop to assure the continuity of production. They were also heavily dependent on the support and willingness of their wives to assume extra responsibility before and during the contest. Monsieur Boucher's salaried worker, Jean-Marie, understood only too well that it was his subordinate position in the workshop hierarchy and lack of both social and economic capital, not necessarily inadequate skill, that precluded his participation in such a prestigious contest. His critique of "pretentious" masters was directed less at the contest itself than at the group of powerful independents who were the primary guardians of an artisanal aesthetic. His critique reminds us that celebrations of ancestral skill and craft solidarity are contested political domains. They elide and silence the tensions between independent masters and skilled workers that inhere in the construction and celebration of hierarchies of skill privileging both taste and art. They also suggest the many ambiguities and problems attendant upon attempts to professionalize craft work and empirical training models.

What was at issue for *chocolatiers* in this 1990 tournament of value was the authentication of a distinct identity for the craft as well as rank, reputation, and potential pecuniary gain for individual masters and houses. The contest title itself is highly coveted and is displayed on storefronts, monogrammed chef jackets, product labels, house cards, and promotional literature on training. The conflation of skill and nation in the contest title is particularly powerful. Hand-crafted commodities and their makers satisfy the nostalgia for and appeal of the localized goods and modes of production associated with a traditional past. The very persistence of master craftsmen and family modes of entrepreneurship in these economies means they can be absorbed within and designated as unique manifestations of a unified national culture. They can be enshrined as part of the nation's historic patrimony and redefined as authentic, living cultural forms. In a context marked by an intense preoccupation with French regional and national identity, *chocolatiers'* texts and tournaments of value—public rituals, contest speeches, published memoirs, oral histories, and gastronomic essays—are a crucial and eminently political medium for a minority craft to proclaim its products as distinctly French and aesthetically superior. National contest titles that symbolize the skills, goods, and pasts of artisans become resonant—and marketable—cultural commodities. As Francis Boucher reminded me, some immediate benefits for contest winners would be to raise the prices of their goods, to offer seminars, to act as consultants to industrial manufacturers, and to enhance the renown of their houses.

One year after the Best Craftsman Contest, in September 1991, the confederation's annual meeting was held in Lyon. The leadership had chosen a craft symbol from thirty-nine prototypes designed by a Parisian marketing firm and selected by a representative sample of French consumers. They unveiled it in a ceremony designed to resemble the presentation of a commemorative piece of art. Once again, the symbol prompted heated debate. The display of an emblem recalling preindustrial producer guilds was fraught with difficulties. Guild traditions remain closely intertwined with artisanal production in public memory; they evoke the image of small family workshops in which similarly skilled artisans produce high-quality goods. Moreover, the display of a collective symbol suggested most cogently a shared craft identity that did not exist. The leaders, most of whom owned Parisian businesses catering to a local, national, and international clientele, were preoccupied with issues related to sales and market share in rapidly shifting circumstances. They wanted a symbol that would serve primarily as an effective marketing tool. For artisans outside of Paris catering to local and regional markets, the evocative power of a publicly displayed collective symbol resulted from the link necessarily created in consumers' minds between contemporary craftsmen and a traditional producer ethos. Given these associations, how could a business that merely retails candies produced elsewhere display the symbol? Could the owners of pastry and bakery-pastry businesses who produced only a supplementary line of seasonal chocolates have it? Most importantly, would the French owners of Belgian franchise outlets be entitled to the symbol? These were some of the questions repeatedly raised after the 1990 convention. I remember asking Francis Boucher what he would do if the confederation offered the symbol to franchise owners. "I wouldn't take it," was his emphatic reply.

Jacques Daumoinx presided over the debate that ensued. However, when he reiterated the position favored by the executive board of allowing all specialty confectioneries to display the symbol, he was greeted with resistance and a loud, angry retort from an artisan on the floor. "Well if the Belgians get it I won't take it." My return trips to Paris in 1995, 1996, and 1998 revealed that ongoing internal division among the membership over the symbol's meaning precluded its adoption as an unambiguous emblem of group identity. When I interviewed Alain Grangé in 1998, he admitted that the campaign to create and promote a craft "totem" begun so enthusiastically in 1990 had ended in failure.

## Conclusion

Both the contest speeches by confederation leaders and state ministers' addresses evoked themes central to French national identity and cultural authority but increasingly problematized in the current context. The lack of economic growth and unacceptably high unemployment levels among young people were a challenge to the social fabric of the nation and the traditional French right to work. Jérôme Bédier's warning about the lacunae in vocational education echoed long-standing historical debates on schooling.

In a context of rapidly shifting international circumstances, the leadership recognized the importance of marketing the cultural cachet of French chocolate. They pursued a complex politics of authenticity designed to certify their cultural pedigree in production, entrepreneurship, aesthetics, and taste in contrast to foreign "fakes." They saw the necessity of promoting genuine French chocolates made by state-certified craft producers. They ended by internalizing and reproducing hegemonic discourses on professionalization and actively collaborated with state representatives to transform a traditional experiential model of apprenticeship.

The formal recognition of an autonomous craft identity reveals the important role of the French state in the protection and promotion of valued forms of French culture such as cuisine and craft. The fear of the loss of a French, albeit new, tradition of chocolate production prompted state representatives to intervene actively. Like the signature recipes created and circulated throughout the world by French chefs, the esoteric cachet of French chocolates commands a high price on the international market. Yet this state recognition had a number of unintended consequences. First, in a professional model, control over the definition, transmission, regulation, and certification of craft mastery passes from local practitioners in family workshops to state bureaucrats. Through the disciplines of organized curricula and structured classes in vocational schools, state examinations combining theoretical and practical knowledge, professional certification, and formalized craft contests, the state acquired a new role and power in the identification, regulation, and reproduction of the *chocolatiers'* craft.

Second, confederation leaders established the first state training programs in chocolate production, but their initiatives were caught in the cultural logic of the French educational system. High status and class position are dependent on the possession of rarefied cultural knowledge and intellectual skills certified by academic credentials. Vocational diplomas such as the CAP, and even the master artisan diploma, are at the bottom of a hierarchy grounded in academics; they are still associated with low status groups and limited occupational opportunity. Thus the attempts to attract new recruits and to revalorize a form of labor debased in the intimately linked processes of industrialization and professionalization seem problematic at best. It is significant that such ardent advocates of manual training in state programs as Daumoinx, Guy Urbain, his son Alain Urbain, Alain Grangé, and the two authors of the collective labor contract for *chocolatiers,* Benoît Digeon and Christophe Chambeau, never underwent apprenticeship training themselves, took no direct role in production, and function more like managers than artisans.

Nonetheless, confederation leaders sought to persuade and mobilize local practitioners to embrace and implement national initiatives. As we shall see, small independents in the southwest challenged the collective identity affirmed in Paris and asserted their own particular notion of craft. In chapter 9 I examine how local family owners, both male producers and their wives, responded to national initiatives.

# CHAPTER 9

# Defending the Local

A few weeks after the Paris craft contest, Jacques Daumoinx traveled to Bordeaux to preside over a meeting of *chocolatiers* from the entire southwest region. Monsieur Mourier from Pau and Monsieur Bergeron from Biarritz both attended that meeting. The most important item on Daumoinx's agenda concerned the ongoing "problem" of apprenticeship training and the implementation of a CAP (certificate of professional aptitude) section in chocolate production in the southwest. Daumoinx reminded his listeners that almost ten years after the creation of the CAP in chocolate, few apprenticeship centers had actually formed training sections.

I had interviewed Monsieur Daumoinx in Paris just a month before his trip, and he was confident that he could persuade local *chocolatiers* to create a CAP training section. After all, the national initiatives seemed to converge well with those taken on the local level. Both groups astutely manipulated a preindustrial corporate idiom and celebrated their specialized skill as *chocolatiers*. Parisian leaders and local craftsmen alike espoused an esoteric French standard of taste in confectionery consumption. Both groups selectively appropriated and reworked multiple histories in the cultivation of a craftsman ideal designed to enhance the luxury cachet of, and consumer demand for, their artisanally made goods. Moreover, the new attention given to training and the professionalization of the craft seemed to serve well the interests of both Parisian leaders and local craftsmen. Yet instead of welcoming this opportunity, family owners strongly opposed it.

Just before Jacques Daumoinx's meeting with craft producers, confectionery wives from the southwest attended a sales training seminar offered by the local Centre féminin d'études de la pâtisserie, which played a crucial role in training women in confectionery marketing and sales. In addition to one-day seminars, the center organized a popular and well-attended yearly national convention that different regions took turns hosting. Participants at the November seminar enthusiastically discussed the upcoming convention program planned in Beaune, Burgundy. I traveled there to attend the training workshops offered by Parisian business consultants. One seminar, "Performing for Excellence," drew over one-third of the convention participants but provoked intense debate and a near revolt by the women who attended it.

Both reactions to national training initiatives illuminate the tensions and disagreements that arise between business consultants, culture brokers, craft leaders, and family owners. This chapter explores the dialectical interaction of national and global processes with local practices of selfhood and work identity. It traces the management of change in the construction of gendered work identities and the enactment of practices based on family entrepreneurship.

## *Chocolatier* Activists

To gain support for their initiatives, the leadership solicited national-level figures—high civil servants, private consultants, and prominent intellectuals—but simultaneously worked through activists on the local level. They relied primarily on Monsieur Mourier to persuade local independents to endorse their professionalization of the *chocolatiers'* craft. Indeed, when I left Paris to move to Bayonne, Guy Urbain suggested that I contact Monsieur Mourier first. Local craftsmen and state officials at the Bayonne and Pau Chambers of Trade all acknowledged him to be the unofficial head of the *chocolatier* craft community. This was a status Mourier affirmed through his widely disseminated discursive narratives on craft and his energetic organization of public rituals celebrating mastership.

By his own reckoning, Mourier had fifty years' experience as a craftsman. After training for a year as a restaurant chef's apprentice, Mourier switched to pastry making, completed a two-year apprenticeship, and then worked in several pastry businesses in Pau and Bordeaux before the outbreak of World War II. After spending most of the war as a cook in a German detention facility, Mourier returned to France, married, and created a sugar candy business in Pau in 1945 at twenty-five years of age.

In the 1970s he got specialized training in chocolate production, and he and his wife expanded their productive capacity. In 1990, at age seventy, Mourier felt he had succeeded in two fundamental ways. He had created a viable economic patrimony and kept both the ownership and the control of business operations within his family (three generations then worked full time in the business, including his wife, only son, daughter-in-law, and youngest grandson). Mourier insisted that his professional life has always been informed by a love of the craft (*l'amour du métier*) and a fierce dedication to preserving French artisanship. Yet his rise to prominence as a craft activist was a very recent development.

Until the mid-1980s, Monsieur Mourier did not assume a leadership role in defending or promoting the craft of chocolate, although he did enjoy renown as a skilled practitioner and enthusiastic mentor to newly self-employed artisans. Two events precipitated a change. First, the incursion of Belgian franchises to Pau had a dramatic immediate impact. Most Palois *chocolatiers,* including Mourier and the Joliots, experienced a steep short-term drop in sales.

Second, he learned that the confederation (Confédération Nationale des Détaillants et Artisans-détaillants de la Chocolaterie, Confiserie et Biscuiterie) was directly addressing this problem. Mourier began to attend the yearly trade conventions as well as the congress held every four years. He was both surprised and impressed by the "positive energy" and by attempts to institutionalize an autonomous craft identity.

Mourier attracted considerable local attention through his promotional efforts. In the autumn of 1987 he announced the creation of the Club of Palois Chocolatiers by calling a press conference that assembled not only local journalists and the seventeen members of the new club (clad in white vests and chef hats) but also well-known local politicians such as the mayor of Pau. The club received significant coverage in the local press, making the front page of the local daily, *La République des Pyrénées,* where club members were dubbed "the apostles of discriminating taste." Mourier remembered:

We said to ourselves, we have to defend ourselves, we cannot allow ourselves to be inundated by Belgian franchises selling an inexpensive chocolate candy. What kind of chocolate is it? It is large *[gros],* full of fat *[gras],* and very sweet. It is not the same quality. . . . We needed a mechanism that would allow us to talk about our craft, about the nature of French artisanship, about the fact that our prices are higher because our products are better.

Since 1987, members of the Club of Palois Chocolatiers have organized numerous promotional activities. These included the creation of a Palois chocolate specialty, the production and display of the "world's largest chocolate" (registered with the Guinness Book of World records) weighing 200 kilos and filled with 15,000 chocolate candies, the hosting of two induction ceremonies (in 1988 and 1991) for the national Confrérie des Chocolatiers de France (Brotherhood of French Chocolate Makers), and the organization of the 1991 conference on chocolate.

His efforts attracted the notice of the confederation leadership. They asked him to assume the presidency of the newly created Advanced Center for Confectionery Studies (Université de la Confiserie), which operates under the aegis of the confederation and provides advanced training seminars to the owners and employees of confectionery businesses in all parts of France.

In his role as a confederation spokesman, Mourier was called upon to represent both himself and the craft to many outsiders—state representatives, politicians, a local and tourist clientele, journalists, members of the general public, artisans in other crafts, and foreign confectioners. This public advocacy role required Mourier to recount his own personal and craft histories, to articulate a standard of excellence, and to recruit promising apprentices. Over the course of my fieldwork I had many opportunities to observe him. The histories he told selectively emphasize certain episodes while suppressing others. Mourier crafted a mythic narrative account of a master craftsman whose life experiences logically and inexorably led to his position as patriarch of a successful confectionery house and as leader in the regional craft community.

This public version of his life history suppressed his training as a chef and emphasized his spectacular (and very unusual) rise from an apprentice at age seventeen to a position as head of production in a workshop employing twelve skilled craftsmen at the age of nineteen. Mourier attributed this precocious advancement to talent, hard work, and dedication. In fact, larger historical circumstances suggest a more plausible explanation. Mourier was nineteen in 1939, a period when French men were rapidly inducted into the army in anticipation of impending war. This left workshops and factories severely short of help and gave younger workers and apprentices the opportunity to circumvent or advance rapidly within a hierarchy based on skill and experience (compare Clavel 1962).

Mourier always emphasized the aesthetic dimension to his work and the time he devoted to the fashioning of chocolate confectionery art. He underscored the talent he exhibited for drawing and music and the recognition he has earned in craft contests as a confectionery artist. He celebrated his membership in the Confrérie and boasted that he was the proud brotherhood sponsor *(le parrain)* of one of the 1990 Best Craftsman Contest winners.

Like many artisans, Mourier was extremely sensitive about the timing of his departure from school and the amount of his formal education. In public interviews, he stressed his ambition to stay in school and to pursue a career in the fine arts. He insisted that in spite of "excellent grades," which had earned him the right to continue on in the full cycle of secondary education, his father required him to leave school and admonished him "to become a chef like your father." He had bad memories of his first year of apprenticeship because of an abusive master chef. Mourier explained that after his father's sudden death when he was just sixteen years old, he was free to leave the kitchen.

Mourier projected an image of effortless familial accord and continuity by repeatedly describing the Mourier house "as the family firm par excellence." Privately he acknowledged having his share of family difficulties, which included his wife's persistent health problems and inability to assume the role of *patronne*. Although he greatly admired his daughter-in-law's gift for commercial relations and her skillful management of the boutique, he was deeply ambivalent about his son's ability to run the business successfully after his death.

Mourier projected a similarly idealized image of the local craft community in Pau when he justified his activism as a desire "to expand and develop the magnificent solidarity which reigns among us [Palois *chocolatiers*] and which profits us all." I had the opportunity to witness personally the conflicts and tensions dividing this group when I attended their strategy sessions over the course of my fieldwork.

## A CAP in Chocolate for the Southwest?

Just one week after the Bordeaux meeting, Mourier met with the president of the Atlantic Pyrenees Chamber of Trades in Bayonne, the principal of the apprentice training center, and the supervisor of apprenticeship contracts.[1] They were amenable to creating a special CAP on the condition that at least ten apprentices could be found and that the new CAP would be a complement to the existing CAP in pastry production. The staff recommended that apprentices first complete the two-year CAP in pastry production and then prepare the CAP in chocolate in one additional year. Current French law allows an abbreviated training period for a second CAP in a companion craft. Soon after my arrival in Bayonne, a tentative agreement was reached to offer one training section in the Atlantic Pyrenees department.

However, the decision as to which Chamber of Trades would host the new section (Mourier favored Pau and Bergeron wanted Bayonne) emerged as both a difficult and a political one. Although the Bayonne staff acknowledged Mourier as the regional craft leader, they also held Bergeron in high regard. Bergeron was an active member of the pastry makers' organization and also belonged to the confederation. He attended the yearly trade shows and meetings of both organizations and had close ties to the most celebrated Parisian *pâtissiers* and *chocolatiers*, including Robert Linxe. Despite Bergeron's frequent public criticism of the state-run apprenticeship programs, he strongly supported them in a number of ways. Bergeron trained apprentices in his business every year (in 1990–91 he had three), and he regularly conducted practicum classes for apprentices and skilled craftsmen at the Bayonne Chamber of Trades school. He also served on judging panels for the examinations required for the CAP and the master artisan diploma.

In spite of these potential disagreements, Mourier immediately began to spread the news of the new training section. He appeared as a guest on a local radio program and used that public forum to "celebrate the new attention paid to the training and credentialing of young *chocolatiers*, which signals a craft on the move." Mourier also mentioned the new CAP "soon to be available to young people in the region" at the 1991 chocolate conference. He invited Jacques Daumoinx, who attended the 1991 conference, to appeal directly to the "local and regional state representatives present in the audience to support the new training initiatives as a means of ensuring the continuity of a venerable French tradition of artisanship."

Soon after this, the negotiations for opening the new training section became mired in the question of its location. As the news spread, it became apparent that there was little support for the new section. Even the positions of Mourier and Bergeron—both officially proponents of the new section and specialty *chocolatiers*—were riven with contradictions. First, the strategies they pursued with regard to their own children's education belied their public discourse celebrating manual training and its links to revitalized artisanal crafts. Second, while advocating the necessity to provide specialized credentials, they denounced the policing power of the state in the definition of apprenticeship regulations and the arbitration of disputes. They wanted state certification but not the control that accompanied it. Mourier and Bergeron decried the competing authority of public school teachers and administrators in the direct transmission and evaluation of craft skill.

Trained exclusively on the job, Mourier was scornful of the low quality of state centers. Mourier justified his attitude by referring to a personal investigation he had conducted of the facilities, equipment, and teachers in centers in several southwest departments. He judged them all to be deficient. In Mourier's view the time spent there was wasted: "Who are the people teaching these sections? Bah, civil servants [*fonctionnaires*]. They're not *true professionals* in the craft. They don't have any say in what apprentices need to learn or how they should learn it. They just do what they are told by state administrators. They could care less if the training is incorrect. They know they'll be paid regardless of the result" (emphasis added).[2]

Within his own family, Mourier played an important role in advising his two grandsons on their career plans; he insisted that they both stay in school. In 1990 his elder grandson was successfully pursuing a career in the French diplomatic corps. His younger grandson had just entered the business, but not before completing a baccalaureate degree. Only when it was clear that he had no specific goals did Mourier enroll him at the Paris School for the Food Trades, where he earned a CAP in chocolate. Mourier also arranged for his grandson to gain experience in the workshops of colleagues in Belgium, Austria, and Biarritz (with Bergeron).

Bergeron shared Mourier's reservations concerning apprenticeship. One Monday afternoon I was observing the apprentices' practicum class at the Bayonne Chamber of Trades school when Monsieur Bergeron appeared. He had attended a meeting on the future of Basque coast artisanship and stopped to talk with Monsieur Motte, one of two instructors for first- and second-year apprentices in pastry production. Monsieur Bergeron had seen me several times at the Monday evening master artisan classes. Although he knew I was also observing the daytime practicums, he feigned surprise when he caught sight of me. He greeted me warmly and then announced in a loud voice, "Madame, you find yourself at the heart of the problem we in the food crafts now face in France."

When I saw him shortly after in his workshop he waxed philosophical on the shortcomings of the system:

Out of the three apprentices I have right now only one is worth his salt. The problem is the system. There is a critical shortage of manpower in artisanal crafts like pastry, chocolate, and sugar candy making, and yet the schools still advise the brightest kids to prepare an academic degree. There are no jobs for kids with those degrees. But in the manual trades we get the weakest kids. It is really a problem because in chocolate and sugar you have to have general knowledge (*culture générale*) in addition to hands-on training. . . . The problem really began the day [the Ministry of] National Education stuck its nose in the process. Now artisanal apprentices fail in two ways. The state says they have to go to school while they work, but going one week out of four doesn't do a thing [mandated by the Bayonne Chamber of Trades]. The state also says they have to learn a manual craft in two years—it's impossible. Plus, they can't work late at night or too early in the morning [after midnight or before 5 AM]. I knew more at the end of my first year [out of three] as an apprentice than these kids know when they take the CAP [examination]. Yes there were abuses in the past. There were incredibly hard obstacles to overcome, you had to be able to hold out for fourteen to fifteen hours straight, you had to learn the rhythm. Now it's nothing. Apprentices get paid and have regular hours. If they don't master the craft, too bad, the public education system has to produce a certain number of CAPs in a year. At the end of their training they'll get their diploma no matter what they know.

Like Mourier, Bergeron very much regretted not having stayed in school and was a tireless autodidact, reading voraciously on art and design to improve both his technique and general knowledge. He was immensely proud that his only daughter had earned a baccalaureate degree and married well—that is, out of the craft, to a local architect.

I first learned of the new CAP from Monsieur Motte, on the first day I attended his practicum classes. It is significant that, in spite of the generally negative view that local craftsmen held of the teaching staff at apprentice training centers, both instructors in Bayonne had considerable work experience as well as impressive professional credentials. Both possessed the master artisan diploma in pastry production, which, unlike the CAP, was widely acknowledged to require a period of rigorous training and to guarantee mastery. However, their decision to teach rather than practice the craft effectively disqualified them from membership within a community of practice inextricably tied to confectionery houses. For local craftsmen, all public school apprenticeship instructors were civil servants who lacked initiative and independence, otherwise why would they work for the state rather than for themselves? Why would they prefer a salaried status to ownership of their own businesses? All such instructors were judged to be incapable of instilling a craft ethos and work ethic in young apprentices. Even those possessing credible experience and credentials did not enjoy the authority or status they could reasonably have expected as confectionery house owners or heirs. Indeed, I heard persistent rumors that one of the instructors had not really earned his master artisan diploma; instead, it was said, state representatives bent the rules and "gave" him the master artisan diploma because it was the state-mandated credential for the teaching position they needed to fill.

The question of the instructors' competence was intimately linked to the issue of control over the definition and transmission of skill. An experiential, personalized model of transmitting craft skill and norms within a family workshop was challenged by state disciplinary practices. Apprentices in state schools attend structured, often crowded, classes, follow an arbitrary, standardized curriculum mandating theoretical knowledge in technical and general areas, and pass state examinations with a substantial written component.

Moreover, there was often little coordination between the seasonal production demands of confectionery sales and the design of practicum curricula in apprenticeship centers. For example, a lesson in hand-dipping chocolates was given in early November in the Bayonne center, a period before house production began for the delicate centers that could not be coated by machine. In the section I observed, one short hour was devoted to a brief explanation on the tempering of chocolate and on the demonstration of this technique. Each apprentice in the class had only two turns to try his hand at a technique that appeared deceptively simple but, in fact, required considerable practice to master.

In addition, the sequencing and teaching of specific skills in the apprenticeship center differed radically from the hierarchy of tasks through which apprentices ideally progress in the confectionery workshop. In the workshop they began by performing the unskilled tasks of preparing raw materials and advanced slowly over time to master the multiple transformations of the basic raw materials. The aesthetics of confectionery practice—decorative pieces in pulled, blown, or spun sugar and chocolate art—came later. However, apprentices were often taught skills that conformed to a logic of pragmatics—the availability of raw materials, specialized tools, and machinery; important events at the Chamber of Trades for which the apprentices were systematically enlisted to prepare hors d'oeuvres and sweets; or the scheduling of craft contests in which apprentices were expected to participate. For example, in the spring of 1991, Monsieur Motte's practicum class for second-year apprentices spent considerable class time over a two-month period on the execution of an artistic piece in chocolate for an apprentice craft contest. Although the piece was supposed to be the work of the apprentices, Monsieur Motte had in fact both designed and executed much of the piece himself, assigning only ancillary tasks to the apprentices.

During my attendance of Monsieur Motte's Monday classes I heard no more mention of the new section in chocolate. I questioned owners, skilled workers, and apprentices about the proposed new training section. Workers and apprentices were largely unaware of the new diploma; family owners, on the other hand, uniformly opposed its opening.

I initially interpreted this attitude in terms of the rivalries opposing pastry makers and *chocolatiers* I had observed in Paris. The most vocal opponents were the owners of the Mathieu, Carrère, and Harcaut businesses—all of whom had originally trained as pastry makers. Indeed, on the first day I met Michel Harcaut, he complained vociferously about the state's regulatory role: "Do you know that apprentices can't do dishes or work overtime? In this country you are considered an adult at eighteen . . . that means you can get a driver's license, you can do your military service, but you can't work before 5 AM and that continues to the age of twenty-five!"

Yet as time went on it was apparent that the owners of the specialty *chocolateries*—Aguirre, Dalbaitz, and Salinas—also opposed the opening of the new section. The owners of these three houses had all been informally trained in the family workshops. As the newest independents in chocolate production, the De Closets were largely unknown among their confectionery colleagues. Although they were very anxious to claim membership in the local craft community, they were reluctant to express their views on this important issue. Monsieur Bergeron publicly supported this initiative, but his opposition to locating the new training section in Pau provoked an ongoing stalemate that prevented the new section from opening. The initiative was dealt a mortal blow in 1994, when the president of the Bayonne Chamber of Trades, who had strongly supported the new CAP, was forced to resign in the wake of allegations that he had diverted public monies for his private use. His successor had no interest in the new section.

Part of the solution to the riddle of the training section lies in looking at the different craft identities held over the course of the work cycle. Craft identities rely on culturally constructed and historically conditioned meanings; they concern strategic claims based on constantly evolving interests. Historically in the southwest, confectionery house owners were usually practitioners of several companion crafts, such as chocolate and sugar candy, or pastry and chocolate, or even bread, pastry, and chocolate. They affirmed craft identities that encapsulated skills of a number of companion crafts learned on the job or in professional training courses offered at nationally recognized private cooking schools and deemed closest to on-the-job training.

Through a discourse of craft mastership they constructed a community of artisans practicing companion crafts either simultaneously or consecutively. The construction of multiple, overlapping identities is a strategy that has proven to be a highly adaptive response to the effects of a shifting political economy. For example, during the interwar period, a large community of elite consumers on the Basque coast sustained a vibrant gift market for luxury candies, and producers of chocolate thrived. In response to the disappearance of this clientele, the restructuring within chocolate manufacture, and high postwar consumer demand for fresh pastries, the number of specialty *chocolatiers* declined, whereas the numbers of *pâtissiers* soared. In the late 1970s, dark chocolate—the local tradition of confectionery consumption—came to define and dominate a new Parisian, even transnational, taste protocol. Like the raw materials extracted from peripheral regions and refined for consumption in sophisticated metropolises elsewhere, dark chocolates were reconceived as prestige goods and imbued with an aesthetic discourse by Parisian *chocolatiers*, craft leaders, and cultural tastemakers (compare Kearney 1995a, 554). This newly reclassified object was recycled back to the southwest and to other regions as a symbol of national culture and superior taste (compare Savigliano 1995). In response to sharply increased demand for dark, vintage chocolates among a larger middle-class tourist clientele, many specialty *pâtissiers*, including Messieurs Carrère, Mathieu, and Bergeron, had their successors learn or themselves learned chocolate making and promoted their status as master *chocolatiers*. Even those known primarily as bakers or baker-pastry makers hired *chocolatiers* or *pâtissiers* trained in chocolate and promoted their status as producers of "traditional" Bayonnais chocolates.

Thus, house owners opposed the training section because it did not fit the way they constructed and reproduced an identity based on craft. They favored a guild model grounded in self-regulation and local control. This model privileged personal relations between masters and apprentices as well as tests of skill organized by craftsmen themselves. House owners already had experience with existing state-run programs in pastry making and were unanimously negative in their appraisal of the training provided there. They refused to surrender additional control over the training and credentialing of future *chocolatiers* to instructors in public apprenticeship centers versus craftsmen in the workshop. Advising young people to prepare narrowly specialized vocational diplomas in one craft was equally untenable. Creating multiple, labile identities proved to be a better strategy when shifting markets demanded the augmentation of existing skills or the mastery of new skills and the diversification of product lines. The only truly legitimate authenticators of skill were the craft contests, window displays, mentoring relationships between masters and journeymen or apprentices, sponsored memberships within exclusive producer organizations such as the Confrérie des Chocolatiers de France, and training courses by well-known artisans at private cooking schools—all organized by craftsmen themselves.[3] Although house owners actively promoted their skill as master *chocolatiers* and the southwest as the authentic cradle of French chocolate production, they strongly resisted the professionalization of the craft sought by the national leadership.

## Centre féminin d'études de la pâtisserie

Until the early 1960s, little attention was paid to sales and marketing training for women in the boutique. The dearth of training for artisanal wives was not conceived as a problem until the dissemination of a postwar business model predicated on scientific management and marketing procedures. It is significant that the first initiative to address this problem was organized by artisanal wives themselves. In 1960 the Centre féminin d'études de la pâtisserie (Women's Center for Pastry Studies) was created under the aegis of the National Confederation of Pastry Makers and patterned on its administrative organization. Five artisanal wives (including Madame Bassignana from Oloron near Pau) provided the catalyst for creating a national training organization run by and for women in confectionery sales.

In 1991 the center's national board included a president, vice-president, treasurer, and secretary and representatives from twelve regions in France. Each region had its own elected board charged with organizing training workshops for its membership. In addition, the national board sponsored a yearly convention that was attended by artisanal wives and salaried saleswomen from all over France.[4]

As a result of 1982 legislation extending professional training benefits to employees in artisanal businesses (with ten or fewer workers), the cost of training seminars was largely subsidized by artisanal employers and the state. Training seminars in confectionery production and retail sales flourished as a result. In 1990–91 training for saleswomen was available in three private venues: national producer organizations such as the confederation; private culinary schools including the Parisian school started by the *pâtissier* Gaston Lenôtre and the National Confederation of Pastry Makers' school in Yssingeaux near Lyon; and the Women's Center for Pastry Studies. Training largely took the form of half- to two-day seminars and workshops and involved either hands-on workshops in packaging and window dressing or how-to seminars in American-style marketing—how to create demand, how to position and promote products, how to increase sales.

The center played an important role in training local saleswomen. Its regionally elected leaders organized well-attended one-day seminars twice a year, and women from the southwest frequently participated in the annual convention. In February 1991 women from the Burgundy region hosted the convention, and I traveled there to interview members of the center's national board, workshop leaders, and convention participants as well as to attend the training workshops. One hundred sixty women (the majority of whom were married to self-employed artisans), twenty of their artisan husbands, a handful of sales representatives from major French suppliers of packaging, wrapping, and perishable raw materials, and the president of the National Confederation of Pastry Makers, Jean Millet, attended the convention.[5]

The convention program offered five workshops, two centering on sales, one on obtaining bank credit, and two on the aesthetic presentation of confectionery gifts. I focus here on the most well-attended workshop—"Performing for Excellence." Both its content and reception illuminate the tensions and conflicts produced by the complex dialogue among business consultants, craft leaders, and family business owners centering on training for retail sales managers and the need for modern marketing in confectionery boutiques. It also reflects an enduring hegemonic discourse on artisanship as inevitably antimodern and on artisans defined not by what they have—often abundant economic capital—but by what they lack—social and cultural capital.

The seminar began when two representatives from a Parisian consulting firm introduced themselves—Monsieur Toulier and his assistant Mademoiselle Taillevent. Monsieur Toulier conducted the entire seminar while his assistant observed impassively. He presented a survey they had conducted on confectionery consumption and sales. Their data consisted of "a nonrepresentative, qualitative questionnaire given to seventy-five people leaving confectionery houses with a purchase" and also "observation of sales over two four-day periods." Monsieur Toulier explained that participants would determine the workshop themes most relevant to their own needs, divide into small groups, and discuss them at length. He presented the educational credentials of the firm's fifteen consultants: "We have graduates of practically all the Grandes Ecoles, from Polytechnique, Hautes Etudes Commerciales, Arts et Métiers, and from all the excellent professional schools." He emphasized their diversified experience among large and small business in the private and public sector and their reliance on methods borrowed from psychology and sociology.

Beginning at 9:30 AM, he took two hours to outline the four main components of quality and performance: customers, products, market, and teamwork. He repeatedly asked for audience input but rarely stopped long enough to allow for the formulation of responses. Forty-five minutes later, his discussion of "the product" provoked the first unsolicited audience reactions:

Now, let us consider products. I am convinced that you know them very well, their impact on the clientele, the ingredients of new products, ways of presenting them, naming, however you don't consider a number of important factors related to them. For example, the differentiation of the fragile, personalized product from the mass-produced version. Products must be adjusted to market demand, you must know the market. There is a whole logic to master—the choice of name, color, form, ingredients. If the product is merely for [individual] pleasure, different criteria apply. What is your product? What do you sell? There is the whole strategy of product positioning. We're going to help you to ask yourselves certain questions. For example, about [product] diversification. Do you really need such a large assortment of products? Many are alike. How do you differentiate one from another? In your dispensaries *[officines]* there are piles of products stacked side by side, not sold in the same way even on the same day. In fact it [product sales] seems to be a function of the number of people standing in line. . . . Pay attention to attitude, there is a shocking lack of attention to customer reception in your dispensaries *[officines]*. Now, I'm not attempting to impose a set of criteria for good performance, just to develop the capacity for reflection. What are your strengths and weaknesses? We need to work together, to learn a common vocabulary: consumers, market, product positioning—by the end you will be experts. There are things you do very well and things you do less well and we can easily identify the difference, not the techniques of pastry and chocolate [production] but in the improvement of the overall quality of your businesses' functioning. How do you differentiate the service you provide in your dispensaries *[officines]* from huge hypermarkets?

Monsieur Toulier's first use of the term *officine* for the boutique provoked incredulous laughter; the second, a significant exchange of looks among the women at my table; and the third, verbal protests from around the room. *Officine* is a term that suggests not only pharmacists' work but can also mean a center for shady transactions or illicit traffic. One woman spoke out: "Monsieur, you need a better word, one that is more appropriate to describe our products. *Officine* suggests illness and healing to me. Our candies and cakes are all goods for the soul [as much as for the body]." To which Monsieur Toulier responded in a teasing tone: "But you yourselves suggest that your main competitors are pharmacists in the neighborhood!" Many participants laughed but another called out: "I really love my products and what I do. That name *[officine]* says absolutely nothing to me."

As the morning wore on, Monsieur Toulier interspersed comments designed to reinforce positively the work performed in boutiques— "you've worked very, very well"—with criticisms of the very principles that define confectionery sales. He also continued to use the term *officine*. "I'm horrified by the individual names you give your goods—the names have no relation to the product." Referring to boutique hours and customer service, he remarked, "Based on my actual experience it would be better to make one's purchase before 7 PM, in fact not to frequent you[r boutiques] at all between 6 and 7 PM [because of the lukewarm reception]. Have you considered that consumers work longer hours and that the busiest retail hour of the day is the one when you are preparing to close? He noted the critical importance of advertising in the current market and its neglect by small business owners. He suggested that they develop a spirit of teamwork and bridge the divide between the workshop and the boutique. "Let's look at Japanese management styles and American decision making: division of tasks, collective decisions, and cooperation of all." He admonished them to move away from seasonal sales and the cultivation of a loyal, regular clientele. "You need to develop a new kind of customer, you have to learn the laws of the market. You need to create first the need and then the desire for a product." Finally, using the metaphor of a high fidelity system, he announced the fundamental problem. "You have quality individual components but too often you change them without thinking about the overall quality of the sound, the system. Attention to overall quality is what works the least and so our task here today is to isolate the necessary criteria to study in order to gain an understanding of consumer relations."

Since Toulier had not allowed a morning break, there was a collective sigh of relief when participants were finally dismissed for a two-hour lunch. I was invited to eat with a board member and then took advantage of the long break to interview Madame Bourguignon, the center's president from 1981 to 1990. She was pleased that I chose the workshop on quality. "We have worked hard to gain the respect of our husbands and [male] craft leaders, to show that the center is about more than just ribbons and bows."

Madame Bourguignon explained that the center's organizers had initially experienced resistance and had enjoyed little support from pastry leaders because "the [male] artisans are very macho, they felt that the women's initiatives undercut their traditional authority. . . . None of them believed that women could be professional, that they could be relied upon to keep their word. It took many years for us to achieve the status of full voting members of the executive board [of the National Confederation of Pastry Makers]." She paused and asked if I knew who Jean Millet was, and when I responded positively, she added, "It has taken me many years to feel accepted by him. In fact, we have only recently begun to use our first names and the *tu* form." When I asked why it was that the women's center had *"féminin"* in its title, she smiled and replied, "We had to be feminine without being too feminine. You see, we couldn't be too assertive, we had to act like professionals, that is, no jewels, heavy makeup, pouts, tears, or flashy clothes." She stopped, laughed, and continued, "We knew we were having an impact when the men started to invite the same speakers [invited first by the center] to their own meetings!"

When the workshop reconvened two hours later, the participants were in high spirits, relaxed from the wine and stimulated by conversation at lunch. Monsieur Toulier announced that the afternoon session would be devoted to the consumer questionnaire. This would help "to identify a number of weaknesses" threatening the competitive future of confectionery businesses.

Toulier began by describing the entirely new habits of confectionery consumption evident from the survey. "Only fourteen out of the seventy-five [respondents] ate cakes at the end of the family meal. . . . It is obvious that consumption now corresponds to modern rhythms. People don't eat sweets in the same way as in the past. A new trend is the purchase of sweets any time, in the morning or mid-afternoon for pleasure, alone, for a break, with friends. What products are called for when the satisfaction of individual pleasures expands at the expense of ones shared with family?" As he exhorted workshop participants to change based on his survey results and observations of sales, individual retorts broke out and, like a Greek chorus, collective protests of *"Non,"* *"Pas du tout* (not at all)," *"Mais vous exagérez!* (you're exaggerating)" rose in unison. When Toulier proclaimed the end of a sharp divide between the consumption habits of men and women, his listeners shouted with laughter. One woman yelled out, "But Monsieur, if you had interviewed only men you would have gotten a completely different result. They love our sweets and they are so much easier to serve than women!" When he announced that the privileged moments of consumption were no longer religious holidays and ceremonial occasions, they adamantly disagreed.

One participant directly challenged him. "At what time of the year was the questionnaire conducted?" His reply indicating early December and January again provoked a huge outburst: "Well, no wonder!" "That's the explanation!" Another participant explained: "Early January is the period of Epiphany cakes, when people go to visit without being invited and eat cakes and also chocolate in the afternoon. The same is true of early December." Another asked, "What do you know about the people who completed your questionnaire? Do their answers reflect their actual behavior? Don't they just show individual habits? Couldn't it give a misleading image?" Undaunted, Toulier replied, "Since you mention chocolate, have you considered the rising consumer demand for chocolate? People want it in any form, at any time." One woman at my table responded sarcastically, "Oh really, Monsieur? You are telling us things we don't know." Her voice was scarcely audible above the general commotion.

Toulier forged on but the women paid less and less attention and the din from their private conversations swelled in magnitude. He had to call for order repeatedly. Halfway into the afternoon session, Jean Millet entered the conference room. I later learned that one of the convention organizers had in a panic persuaded him to come in an effort to restore order. Millet soon moved from the back of the room to one of the central front tables but the women paid no heed.

Finally Toulier announced that the moment for small group work had arrived. The assignment was to formulate ten questions in an effort to better categorize different types of consumers. Moulier repeated the instructions three times but few women listened. Instead the women at my table shared stories of horrific customers and their own sales secrets. The climax to the drama occurred near the end of the afternoon after Toulier announced that the small group work had ended and he was attempting with little success to elicit questions from each table. By this point he was reduced to pleading for both input and quiet. "Please Mesdames, have pity on the organizer and respect for what little remains of his voice." In response one woman raised her voice and asserted, "I really want to say, Monsieur, that one of the things I hate most is to see some woman (*une bonne femme*) come through the boutique door right at 7 PM. There is nothing worse." This apparent non sequitor provoked uproarious laughter interspersed with loud agreement and effectively silenced Toulier. He attempted to continue the discussion while the participants chatted on blithely ignoring him.

The workshop was the subject of much debate among convention organizers and sales representatives. I took the train back to Paris with Toulier's assistant, who expressed her outrage at the women's rudeness and their backward outlook. When I asked why she thought the seminar had been unsuccessful, she bridled and retorted, "What more can you expect from women with so little cultural background?" However, my conversations with many of the participants revealed that the negative reactions to the seminar were entirely understandable. Toulier got off to a bad start by insisting on educational credentials. The topic of education is culturally loaded because of the link between class status and educational attainment (Bourdieu 1984). It is a particularly sensitive subject for craftspeople given the devalued vocational certificates they hold. Rather than being impressed and reassured, women were put on the defensive by this tactic. This initial impression was reinforced by Toulier's handling of the entire workshop. He asserted his authority as much on the basis of his superior education and class position as on his knowledge of marketing and sociology. His verbal attempts to validate women's work and to elicit their responses were systematically undercut by his condescending tone and arrogant refusal to yield the floor to them. His insistence on using the term *officine* for the boutique was all the more offensive because he knew and correctly used the craft term *laboratoire* for the workshop. The word *officine* disparaged the work controlled by women as it simultaneously evoked negative stereotypes associated with petty bourgeois entrepreneurs who supposedly cheat customers by altering merchandise and overcharging them.

The women who attended the convention were not at all resistant to change. Rather, they were very interested in using more up-to-date approaches, and with their own customers they promoted their center training. Participants in the other sales seminar I attended responded enthusiastically to a different team of Parisian consultants who demonstrated how to expand sales of corporate confectionery gifts through role plays featuring telemarketing techniques. What upset the women in Toulier's workshop was his interrogation and indictment of the very organizing principles of confectionery houses: personalized service, product diversification, seasonal and ceremonial merchandising, a gendered division of family labor, individualized creations, evocative naming of candies, as well as advertising through window displays, craft contests, word of mouth, tourist and culinary guides, and feature stories in local papers rather then expensive advertising. During the dinner following the Toulier seminar, one woman expressed a view shared by many: "My business is a success. I don't need some guy from Paris telling me that everything I've done for the past fifteen years is wrong." That Toulier should have predicated the need for dramatic change on the basis of a survey questionnaire and a mere four days of observation was particularly galling. It was a research methodology they astutely criticized and rightly rejected as invalid.

Finally, through their disruptive behavior women undermined a knowledge broker they judged to be ineffective and reaffirmed their general reputation as unruly. The allusion to the arrival of a dreaded female (bourgeoise) customer at closing time was no accident. Based on his social class, Toulier was being implicitly compared to bourgeoises who feign expert knowledge of confectionery goods, make unreasonable demands on female sales help, and flout their superior class position, social connections, and educational capital. On the other hand, based on his gender, Toulier was put in the category of male customers who are easy to manipulate and control compared to women, whose tenacity earned them a reputation for being difficult but discriminating customers. Another implied message was that if women customers were demanding, women owners were even more formidable. When Toulier's costly expertise proved useless they simply ignored him and used the workshop to educate and entertain themselves.

The debate provoked by the failure of the workshop suggests lingering tensions and ambiguities at the core of women's work. The lack of both adequate sales training and a recognized professional identity for retail sales help continued to pose problems for artisans seeking to recruit women as marriage partners or as salaried help. The increasing popularity of management science and marketing theory as legitimate professional pursuits and the creation of prestigious business schools have made the possession of formal state credentials more important and desirable. In contrast to the state training for perspective producers, in 1990–91 there were no specialized educational programs or certification procedures for women in retail confectionery sales. We have already met two artisans at the Mathieu house who were not self-employed largely because their wives, both schoolteachers, refused to

give up established careers and accept the constraints of house ownership. Another woman I interviewed in Beaune was a nurse before her
marriage and bitterly regretted her decision to renounce what she
described as a recognized career for an ill-defined status and ambiguous
professional identity in confectionery sales. For the same reasons, it was
becoming increasingly difficult to recruit responsible, permanent salaried help in the boutique. Fewer employees were willing to invest emotional labor and to work long hours over weekends, evenings, and holidays in return for the minimum wage. The construction of identities
based on management of the family boutique was fragile at best in a context marked by increased emphasis on professionalization in retail sales.
Many people—state representatives, craft leaders, and center officers—
voiced the need to create formalized training and to validate it with a
recognized credential.

## Conclusion

These chapters demonstrate that the politics of authenticity is enormously complicated. The institutionalization of a national
professional identity for French *chocolatiers* in post-Maastricht Europe
and its rejection by local craftspeople illustrate the power of localist
claims and the capacity of a tiny group often depicted as marginal to assert its counter-hegemonic narratives of skill and models of authenticity. On the one hand, a guild model of authenticity fits well with the reassertion of local, culturally constituted identities, work practices, and
commodities as a source of distinction in the context of global markets
and ubiquitous transnationalism (Harvey 1989). On the other hand, it
collides with a professional model articulated and disseminated through
myriad channels from public schools and mass media to state ministers
and parents. The successful opposition to a CAP training section in the
name of craft ironically mirrors a more prevalent cultural resistance to
vocational training in the name of academics.

The next and final chapter centers on chocolate as a cultural commodity whose semiotic power and consistent use in diverse media
through time make it a resonant metaphor for the French Self and exotic Others in situations of great change.

# CHAPTER 10

# Chocolate as Self and Other

The choice, consumption, display, and representation of foods are necessarily tied to the formation and reformation of identities—cultural, class, ethnic, racial, and national. Whether over the *longue durée* or in the short term, foods play a dynamic role in the construction of identity among different people. They mark the boundary between the Self and Other as a way of defining who we are in opposition to our Others. It is in this sense that we can interpret Annales historian Fernand Braudel's use of Brillat-Savarin's famous aphorism to describe European culture: "Tell me what you eat and I will tell you who you are." In this process of dialectic differentiation, different peoples use certain foods as metaphors of the Self and stereotypes of the Other. The foods in question can be staple items such as rice for the Japanese (Ohnuki Tierney 1993, 3–11) or ceremonial foods such as luxury chocolate for the French.

Since its integration into European foodways, chocolate has been a symbolically powerful foodstuff in the French culinary imaginary. The evolving uses of chocolate parallel changing social relations from the Old Regime to the present. As a sweetened drink linked to kingly rituals and elite etiquette in the seventeenth century, it stood for monarchical rule, divine right, sumptuary consumption, and courtly intrigue. To be invited "to go to the king's morning chocolate" *(aller au chocolat)* was to enjoy royal favor and social status; to be like chocolat *(être chocolat)* was to be deceived or to play the fool. As a substance surrounded with ambiguous moral and medical notions, chocolate evoked persistent anxieties in its early consumers. This may have had to do with reports of its constant adulteration with unhealthy fillers as well as its convenient use to disguise poison or cantharides.[1] To act like chocolat *(faire le chocolat)* meant to be naive or gullible and to court numerous social risks, from deception to death. Until the Second Republic (1848), when slavery was formally abolished in French overseas possessions, chocolate also stood for the importation of goods produced on Caribbean plantations by African slave labor. The noun *chocolat* has long signaled not only a tropical foodstuff but also men of African descent (Trésor de la langue française 1977).

The incorporation of chocolate into the culture of the eighteenth-century salon and the café, social institutions of the aristocracy and rising bourgeoisie, heralded the twilight of feudal Christendom and the rise of a capitalist order espousing political enfranchisement and democratic principles. In the nineteenth century increased consumption of chocolate in new inexpensive forms—such as solid bars and powdered drink mixes—by members of the emerging urban working class was made possible by expanding industrialization, the acquisition of empire primarily in western Africa, and the seeding of cacao plantations there. Various fictional accounts reveal the enduring ambiguity surrounding chocolate as a foodstuff as well as its semiotic virtuosity. For the left-wing novelist Louis Aragon, the powerful organoleptic properties of chocolate and its expanding production in industrial factories made it a resonant metaphor for elite privilege, worker exploitation, and class conflict, all the invidious effects of expanding capitalism. During torrid summer afternoons in the provincial French city that was the site of his famous novel, *Les beaux quartiers,* the odor of chocolate from the factory in which Italian immigrant labor toiled was sickening, "sweet and penetrating like gangrene on the battlefield" (1936, 9). These negative associations may partly explain why in popular nineteenth-century parlance a chocolate box *(boîte à chocolat)* referred not only to a container for candies but to a coffin in which the cadaver was covered with a brown cloth (Goncourt 1860, 856, quoted in Trésor de la langue française 1977).

In the postwar era, the transformation from a rural, imperial, semi-industrialized nation to an urban, postcolonial, and postindustrial one has been marked by greater consumption of chocolate as both a cheap popular snack and an expensive honorific food. The uproar created by the sudden incursion of mass-produced foreign candies into France, the furor generated by proposed European Community (EC) directives threatening to redefine chocolate itself, and the recent attempt to create greater social demand for French *grand cru* chocolates suggest that chocolate, to paraphrase, Lévi-Strauss, is good to think with *(bon à penser)* in France. Although an overwhelming majority of French people claim to like chocolate, their consumption of it remains low compared to that of other Westerners and is strongly circumscribed in France by prescriptive rules and contradictory associations. On the one hand, it encompasses meanings of pleasure, strength, and celebration, as well as social bonds. Chocolate is a source of vitamins, energy, and happiness. Consumed in moderation it is a sign for passion, love, even playful eroticism, and a constituent element of the social order. On the other hand, chocolate also connotes overindulgence, contamination, even illness, and is a symbol of sexual perversion, deceit, and class conflict. Consumed in excess, it is fattening, difficult to digest, even addictive, and a potential threat of social disruption.

Here I examine the images and representations of chocolate in a variety of French media—gastronomic literature, advertising, art, and promotional events—as a means of illuminating contemporary constructions of a French Self. These depictions of chocolate rely strongly on orientalist representations of exoticized Others as a device to sell more chocolate in France (Said 1978). At the same time, the location and imag(in)ing of a contrasting Other is inseparable from the construction and projection of similarly essentialized, occidentalist notions of a civilized French Self (Carrier 1995b, 1–32). These representations of chocolate create and sell Otherness as they highlight the distinguishing characteristics believed to define the Self (compare Creighton 1995). As a metaphor for the Self and a stereotype of the Other, chocolate serves as a window onto the continuities and tensions in French culture and thought concerning alterity, primitivism/exoticism, racism, gender, class, and gifting relations within families and among friends.

As a cultural commodity whose meanings and associations are produced and reproduced as it is exchanged and consumed, chocolate illuminates shifting cultural ideologies and changing social relations. Here I examine the logics of exchange and the production of meaning on two levels. First, I look at the macro level, where constructions of Self and Other are refracted through the prism of modernization, urbanization, and decolonization. Second, I assess positionings of Self and Other at the micro level of social relations within families, among friends, and between social milieux.

## Primitivism / Exoticism

In the 1980s, in ads, promotional events, boutique window displays, and particularly the new chocolate literature, French *chocolatiers* and tastemakers reworked the past, playing on an enduring French fascination with the primitive exoticism of the inhabitants, customs, and cuisines of New World Others. This past formed part of an elaborately constructed mythology surrounding chocolate. The construction of mythologies concerning the origins, names, and properties of particular foods is characteristic of a long French gastronomic literary tradition (Mennell 1996). Moreover, culturally constructed mythologies about commodity flows acquire particular intensity as the spatial, cognitive, and institutional distances between production and consumption increase (Appadurai 1986, 48). Given its complex trajectory from cultivation and harvest in the third world to processing and consumption in the first world, chocolate is particularly suited to the creation of such mythologies. In tandem with efforts to reeducate French palates, this mythology aimed to alter the symbolic associations and culturally constituted uses of chocolate as a device to stimulate consumption. At the end of the 1980s, as we have seen, after rising steadily, French annual per capita consumption of chocolate began to stagnate. Thus, *chocolatiers* renewed efforts to stimulate daily chocolate consumption through the use of chocolate narratives.

Narratives that tell a specifically French history of the discovery of chocolate in the New World reveal the persistent exoticism evident in French and Western thought since the age of European exploration (Todorov 1994, 264–352). Exoticism is deeply embedded in all Western accounts of the historical encounter with the non-West that began in the sixteenth century. That encounter engendered a sustained effort by the West to consolidate its hegemony over lesser "primitive" societies while simultaneously scrutinizing them for clues to its own humanity (Asad 1973, 104). However, the constitutive paradox of exoticism is that the appeal of Others as exotics is based on an ignorance of them as peoples. Thus, the early modern descriptions of "simple," "natural" societies inhabited by "noble savages," while appearing to have real geographical referents in the descriptions of famous philosophers, for example, the cannibals of Montaigne (1969 [1580–1588] I, 251–63); the Tahitians of Diderot (1966 [1772], 411–478); the Caribs of Rousseau (1986 [1754]), and the Natchez of Chateaubriand (1826), are only meaningful in the context of French and, thus, Western ideas of civilization, custom, law, and property. Exoticism, then, is the manifestation of a process whereby the French intensify their own sense of Self by exaggerating the distances and differences separating them from their Others. An exoticized history of chocolate thus relies on the juxtaposition of twinned, essentialized visions of both the indigenous people who first produced chocolate and the French who produce it currently.

This chocolate exotic draws selectively on historical accounts left by European explorers, philosophers, missionaries, scientists, and literati.[2] This constructed history both celebrates and replicates a number of orientalist tropes. It involves a timeless story set in a wild, dangerous land dominated by primal impulses, bizarre customs, and ludic excess (Said 1978). It centers on the "primitive" preparation methods, "strange" flavorings, and "curious" uses of chocolate in the New World.

## Primitive Production and Taste

This chocolate mythology is based on consistently recurrent elements. One such theme highlights the primitive methods used to produce chocolate by Aztec peoples in the New World. Virtually all of the texts published in the 1980s featured the same image of an American primitive with chocolate tools that appeared in a seventeenth-century scholarly work centering on the three substances new to Europe: coffee, tea, and chocolate (Dufour 1685) (see fig. 12). These texts all privilege chocolate use among the Aztecs, and most ignore both its uses and symbolic meanings about the Olmecs and Mayas, who first domesticated chocolate (Coe and Coe 1996, 35–66). It is significant that even the French Annales historian Fernand Braudel featured this image in his magisterial history of the evolution of Western civilization and capitalism to evoke the exotic origins of the New World stimulant (1967, 187).

These representations emphasize that "the drink prepared and consumed by the Aztecs is very different from the product we enjoy today in France" (Constant 1988, 28). Selective portions of early texts provide authentic testimony to the contrast between a crude, imperfectly processed, spicy American drink and the sweet, refined product later perfected by Europeans. Many authors cite Dufour, who explained to his European readers that the Aztecs preferred a cold chocolate drink spiced with chili peppers, warning them that this beverage "would be

Figure 12. American with chocolate pot and stir, 1685. Photo courtesy of the Rare Book and Special Collections Division, Library of Congress.

unbearable to our taste because it would sting excessively our [European] palates . . . it is difficult to digest and causes stomache pains" (1685, 297). A number of guides quoted the French Dominican missionary, Jean-Baptiste Labat, who described chocolate production in the French Antilles in the following way: "The Indians of New Spain are merely content to burn the cacao bean a little, to hull and grind it. . . . They put it in an earthen pot in which they boil it with a bit of pepper, powdered pimento, or pulverized ginger root" (quoted in Constant 1988, 28–29).[3]

Images of Aztec Indians or dark-skinned laborers, men, women, and often children, on tropical plantations are shown harvesting cacao bean pods with hand tools (Constant 1988, 29, 55, 60, 64–65). These images are juxtaposed to occidentalist renderings of European know-how depicting the sophisticated technological advances in machinery and processing that have produced a smoother, more flavorful product in many new forms (Constant 1988, 31, 37, 39, 74, 75, 83). Pictures of loosely organized, preindustrial native family groups laboring on the plantation alternate with engravings of the eighteenth-century artisanal workshop (Rachline 1997, 36–37. 21; Schiaffino and Cluizel 1988, 33, 25, 36) or the nineteenth-century factory shop floor (Constant 1988, 74). The linear arrangement of machines and the structured ordering of white French labor reveal a rationalized, industrial, and gendered division of work. Here male workers monopolize production, performing specialized tasks; women, when they are present, package finished goods in segregated work spaces (Constant 1988, 75).

This new history is a story of sweetness and power, that is, the power to define what constitutes refined taste (Mintz 1985). All these accounts relate how Spanish nuns or monks were the first to domesticate a bitter, cold drink judged to be "more fit for pigs than for human consumption" (compare Constant 1988, 29; Robert 1990, 20). Chocolate was supposedly tamed by adding heat, sugar, and more refined flavorings such as vanilla, cinnamon, amber, and musk. This triumphant transformation heralded the introduction of chocolate to European nobles at court. "Hot, flavored, sweet; virtually nothing recalled its savage origins and, throughout the seventeenth century, the brown ambrosia would attract new followers" (Schiaffino and Cluizel 1988, 18). This account of refined European taste versus barbarous New World use is used to highlight the enduring differences said to characterize contemporary European and American confectionery preferences. One guide explains: "The European [chocolate] tradition . . . is generally characterized by an elegant sobriety and a certain moderation. . . . American sweets, although delicious, often have an air of the newly rich (parvenue): chocolate bundt cakes, devil's foods, angel's [food] cakes with three, four, five layers, overflowing on all sides with fattening creams, disappear under deluges of heavy chocolate icing"(Schiaffino and Cluizel 1988, 60–61).

## Ludic Legends and Mythic Origins

Another recurring theme in these representations centers on indigenous rituals and legends surrounding chocolate use both during the Aztec period and in present-day cocoa-producing countries. These accounts emphasize that in Aztec culture, chocolate was both a food and a medium of exchange used for the payment of tribute as well as the purchase of slaves. One of the legends cited repeatedly recounts the divine provenance of cacao trees in the garden of Eden and their transportation to mortal men by the Indians' plumed serpent god Quetzalcoatl. In all accounts, the myth of Quetzalcoatl—his defeat, exile, and promised second coming—is linked to the 1519 landing of Cortez and recounted as a narrative of loss. They mourn the loss of a great Aztec civilization at the hands of brutish Spanish conquistadors whose lust for gold and vision of conquest blinded them to the value of its resplendent monuments, gardens, and material culture. The following excerpt is representative:

He [Cortez] arrived from the east by sea where Quetzalcoatl had disappeared, under the same calendrical sign as the defeated god, his skin was also white and he brandished the cross, symbol of the four winds, that Quetzalcoatl wore. The monarch [Montezuma the Younger] was convinced that the plumed serpent had returned and Cortez was careful not to enlighten the king. . . . He managed to impose Spanish sovereignty and offered to his mother country a magnificent empire. But the destruction of a refined and brilliant civilization, as well as the pitiless cruelty he displayed, soiled forever its glory. (Robert 1990, 19–20; compare Constant 1988, 24–29; Schiaffino and Cluizel 1988, 16)

What is striking is that the reworking of Aztec origin myths (compare Coe and Coe 1996, 68–77) and the vociferous critique of Spanish colonialism in the New World deflect attention from both the empire building of the Aztecs themselves and the seventeenth-century French colonization of the Antilles organized around the cultivation and harvest of indigo, tobacco, and cacao by African slaves on plantations (Delawarde 1935). What is equally significant in this mythologized history is the total omission of Africa in the story of French chocolate—the French participation in the African slave trade beginning in the seventeenth century, the colonization of Africa throughout the nineteenth century, the seeding of cacao plantations there, and the widespread use of African forastero beans versus Central or South American criollo beans by French industrial manufacturers. This omission effectively elides a problematic colonial past (as well as a troublesome postcolonial present), thereby reenacting the very dynamics of colonialism.

Aztec imagery figures prominently not only in the gastronomic literature centering on chocolate but also in the associational rituals and symbols adopted by a number of contemporary *chocolatier* organizations. In their public induction ceremonies, elders of the Confrérie des Chocolatiers de France don flamboyant robes including a headdress with the effigy of Quetzalcoatl, whom they describe as the Aztec God of Chocolate. Similarly, founding members of the Académie du Chocolat de Bayonne (1994) created a commemorative medal for new members that featured a cacao bean pod flanked on one side by a Basque folk dancer clad in white and, on the other, a brown-skinned, spear-toting Aztec Indian wearing a headdress and striped red and green loin cloth representing the Basque national colors! These examples reveal the basic workings of exoticism. These images reinforced the power of a chocolate mythology because they celebrated an orientalist rendering of Aztec civilization coupled with an occidentalist depiction of local Basque folklore.

## Ritualized Excess and Conspicuous Consumption

French representations of chocolate consumption at Montezuma's court recall visions of ritualistic excess and the agonistic expenditure associated with the potlatch (Bataille 1985; Baudrillard 1981). In these treatments, chocolate is a food of erotic temptation, both irresistible and dangerous—irresistible because of its divine taste and the aphrodisiac properties attributed to it by both Aztec and European aristocrats.[4] Virtually all the accounts relate selected portions of the eyewitness account of Montezuma II's court provided by a member of Cortez's entourage (Diaz del Castillo 1803 [1572]). In a similar rendition offered at the Pau conference, Monsieur Toubon, a retired physician and chocophile, gave his version of conspicuous chocolate consumption at the Aztec court: "I must tell you that Montezuma had a prodigious appetite and capacity for chocolate. It is said that he was served about fifty cups of frothy chocolate in golden cups that were used once and then thrown away." In the question-and-answer period that followed he was asked whether chocolate really is an aphrodisiac. His reply: "Well, I'll respond indirectly to that question by telling the audience that Montezuma is reputed to have had 100 wives and he was served chocolate before each visit to the harem in order to be in good form." French chocolate texts and stories told in confectionery boutiques also cite the prodigious amounts of chocolate consumed by the famous mistresses of French kings. They gleefully quote ecclesiastical denunciations of "chocolate as a food which leads directly to carnal sin" (see Robert 1990, 200).

Chocolate is also considered dangerous because of its addictive properties. These representations glorify the breakdown of willpower and playfully hint at the bizarre excesses to which an acquired habit for fine chocolate can lead, particularly if it is thwarted. Most relate the unsuccessful attempt of a Catholic bishop in colonial Mexico to stop Spanish Creoles from having their chocolate served to them during mass:

The bishop can no longer captivate his listeners by threatening them with hell: they are too preoccupied with giving themselves a foretaste of paradise by drinking chocolate in church. The bishop is reduced to an extreme measure: excommunicate those who in mass dare to imbibe this wicked beverage. Immediate reaction: a boycott of mass is begun . . . the bishop is furious and vituperates but in vain. Some time later they find him ill; he dies and they accuse some satanic parishioner of having sent him poisoned chocolate.[5] (Constant 1988, 30)

Chocolate is dangerous because it is imbued with the alluring but threatening exoticism of this primitive land. Constant's account highlights the dangers associated with travel in the South American tropics, where cacao trees thrive. It is a land of climatic extremes, bizarre flora and fauna, primitive habitations, erotic customs, and sensuous Others. Constant suggests a parallel between Aztec fertility rites marked by "violent orgies" and a pagan custom he personally observed in contemporary Venezuela "where devils in strange masks succumb to curious dances in front of the Catholic church" (1988, 23, 24, 27).

The consuming passions of famous chocolate aficionados in the past such as the gastronome Brillat-Savarin (1755–1826) and nobles such as

Maria-Teresa of Austria (1638–1683), wife of Louis XIV, are interspersed with those of contemporary social elites. The fashion designer Sonya Rykiel has frequently spoken of her chocoholism in published interviews and the preface she authored for Christian Constant's *Le chocolat*. In an 1989 interview I conducted with her in Paris, she explained in a resigned, almost laconic way:

I am pursued by chocolate. . . . I can't remember having ever lived without it . . . it's part of me. When I read a book I eat chocolate, when I go to the movies, I eat chocolate, when I travel I eat chocolate. I keep chocolate hidden in a special place at home and it happens that sometimes I share it, but only with my sisters. Chocolate is a drug and a mystery you shouldn't try too hard to solve.

Social tastemakers express a new individualistic ethos that stands in marked contrast to the collective rituals of gift giving and social commensality that currently mark chocolate consumption. Here, the repeated use of the first person, the listing of everyday consumption contexts, and the reluctance to share all suggest that chocolate is a food being removed from the constraints of sociability. Moreover, this emphasis on individual choice and daily indulgence flouts a bourgeois food aesthetic grounded in restraint, moderation, and strict observance of culinary protocols (Bourdieu 1984; compare Marcel 1984.) Here the use of bourgeois tastemakers to violate class-based food norms in the promotion of a new chocolate aesthetic is strategic. Historically the consuming habits of nobles at the French court provided the accepted standard of refinement and taste, which was imitated by the lower social orders (Elias 1994). This court model still enjoys a powerful resonance in France, where tastemakers, not court nobles, shape taste and drive demand for ever-shifting rules of fashion (Mennell 1996). Tastemakers' preferences for dark, evocatively named chocolates such as "Montezuma," "Caracas," and "Aztec" evoke and invite new consuming passions. They suggest self-pleasuring, playful indulgence, and conspicuous leisure.

This exoticized history of French chocolate highlights the process whereby an unruly substance that served as a bitter, spicy drink to Aztec nobles at Montezuma II's court was "tamed" and made appetizing to the delicate, "civilized" palates of European aristocrats. *Chocolatiers* celebrate the transformation from raw to cooked and also promote chocolate as a substance that fuses nature and culture. Superior chocolate is bittersweet, both exotic and refined. Although linked to a new standard of refinement, French chocolate leads true aficionados to abandon cultural convention in favor of hedonistic indulgence. In these representations chocolate is sweetened but retains the power of its wild, natural origins. It is domesticated yet remains inextricably linked to the consuming habits of elites redefined as both cultured and hedonistic. French consumers are invited to join in the play and follow the lead of master *chocolatiers* and tastemakers, who disdain sweet milk chocolates mass-produced outside of France—both European and American—while indulging their taste for French *grand cru* chocolates.

## Race, Gender, and Chocolate

A few months after I defended my doctoral dissertation, Colette Pétonnet sent me a postcard expressing her congratulations. Captioned *"Chocolat Dansant"* (Chocolate Dancing), it featured a reproduction of a lithograph made by the famous nineteenth-century artist Henri de Toulouse-Lautrec in which a well-known black clown from the Nouveau Cirque, Chocolat, entertains the clientele in a Parisian bar. Sporting skintight pants and a Sherlock Holmes cap pulled low over his eyes, Chocolat strikes an exaggerated pose as he dances. The intensity and affectation of his dance contrast sharply with the indifference of the diners and the blank face of the barman. The recourse to both caricature and stereotype in the rendering of a black man identified as "Chocolate" is not accidental. In nineteenth-century argot, the word *chocolat* signified a black man (Harwich 1992, 178), and even today it is still a euphemism for people of color, as I learned when an apprentice in the Mathieu house, a light-skinned young man of Antillean ancestry, was referred to as "Chocolat."

The consolidation of democratic institutions in the last third of the nineteenth century coincided with a significant expansion of French empire building in western Africa, the increased cultivation of chocolate on plantations there, a concomitant rise in its exportation to and consumption in metropolitan France, and the spread of advertising as an important new medium for the creation of demand for brand-name products. During this period the use of black men, women, and children to sell chocolate was ubiquitous. The depictions of black people in French posters and packages advertising chocolate were shaped by the racist stereotypes of African peoples widely disseminated in three new communication media targeting mass audiences: newspapers, illustrated gazettes, and ethnographic exhibitions in museums and world fairs (Rydell 1993; Schneider 1982). However, a comparison of nineteenth- and twentieth-century chocolate advertising reveals that stereotypical representations of black people have both evolved and remained disconcertingly similar. Whether stereotypes appear in literature, art, advertising, or cinema, whether they are written, spoken, or evoked through imagery, they always imply a politics of identity, of inclusion and exclusion (Rosello 1998, 15). What makes them both pernicious and effective as devices to maintain boundaries between groups, is their capacity to invoke consensus (Dyer 1993, 14–16) even as they are applied to new groups.

In chocolate advertisements from the nineteenth century to the present, chocolate is used as a metonym for black Others.[6] Both the product and the race are marked primarily by their spatial, temporal, and cultural distance from Europe. The cultivation of this distance has always been a strategic component in the creation of demand for chocolate, but it has been managed in the pursuit of different ends at different historical moments. The eighteenth-century fascination with and admiration of "noble savages" and "natural man" gave way to representations of blacks in the nineteenth century as primitive savages bereft of civilization in its many guises from technology, literacy, the arts, and complex institutions to democratic ideals. This shift was accomplished thanks to the rise of racist anthropological typologies positing the existence of inferior races, which engendered both a fervent enthusiasm to civilize them and the attendant imperative to colonize their lands, thus building an empire as a necessary market for French manufactured goods and a source of raw materials to fuel French industrialization (Girardet 1972; Marseille 1984).

Nineteenth-century French chocolate manufacturers sold their products using images of blacks often depicted as naive and childlike inferiors. For example, Menier chocolates used the image of a smiling black man dressed as a domestic on one of their turn-of-the-century labels, and a 1910 poster made for the Félix Potin grocery chain featured an African man looking into a mirror, delightedly comparing the hue of his dark skin to a tablet of chocolate (see Garrigues 1991, 27).

However, the fifty-year-old advertising campaign for the chocolate- and banana-flavored breakfast powder, Banania, is emblematic in its use of racial stereotype. In 1915, the image of a black Antillean woman first used to promote the product was displaced by a smiling Senegalese sharpshooter. Here was the archetypical symbol of the "good savage," the colonial soldier who distinguished himself in the service of French causes, from colonial pacification of indigenous rebel forces in Africa to fighting European foes in two world wars. The advertising slogan, "*Y'a bon*" ("That good"), was borrowed from the uniformly obsequious answers Senegalese soldiers were said to give when questioned about living conditions in the French army: "*Y'a bon cuisine,*" "*Y'a bon capitaine,*" "*Y'a bon pinard* [wine]." Banania's French founder saw the Senegalese sharpshooter as the perfect emblem for a product marketed primarily as a tonic for children, which, as an exotic colonial product, would provide them with the "black strength of cocoa" and the "energy and sunshine of bananas" (Garrigues 1991, 38).

The evolution of the images used to package the Banania box reflects the shift from colonial to postcolonial order. The advent of the interwar Négritude movement, with its reappropriation of colonial stereotypes by black intellectuals, the rise of black nationalist movements in the 1940s, and the reaffirmation of French dominion over its colonial empire in the 1946 Brazzaville conference problematized the imagined relationship between the authoritative white colonizer and his faithful black subject. Following the independence of African nations in the 1950s and early 1960s and the migratory flows that brought large numbers of African men from former French colonies to work in French factories, this relationship was radically reconceived. The exoticism of the harmless, smiling African man was an effective device to sell chocolate when he was back there or in the metropole as a disciplined and contained member of the French military. Once he became the symbol of an immigrant population resident on French soil, this image no longer worked so well. The presence of large numbers of Africans tended to blur the line between the metropolis and the colonies, the dominant and the dominated, creating profound anxiety and fueling new racist stereotypes based on cultural, not biological, differences (Balibar 1988; Taguieff 1990). Following the close of the thirty-year period of rapid expansion and modernization in 1975, the official end of immigration (1974), and the state-initiated family unification of immigrant families, African Others—both men and women—were reconceived as a social and economic problem. African immigrants—both blacks and Arabs—were often depicted in mass media through the racialized and stereotypical images of backward cultural practices and the discourse of the ethnic ghetto. The ghetto was reported as a locus of social disorder and a signifier of the danger posed by unacceptably high concentrations of immigrant (non-European) groups (Grillo 1985; Silverman 1992) for the social body.

In the postwar period, the image of the Senegalese sharpshooter on Banania packaging became progressively stylized, abstract, and incidental to the marketing of the product. It was definitively removed in 1977 and replaced with the symbol of postwar prosperity, population growth, and national regeneration—the face of a rosy-cheeked, smiling child—one of the babies De Gaulle had urged French people to begin making immediately after the war in a campaign to reverse the low birthrates of the interwar period. The African man had become a problematic Other whose geographical proximity only heightened the fears concerning his cultural distance. The figure of the black Other has persisted in contemporary representations of chocolate, but only in a domesticated form distant in time as the enslaved domestic in noble eighteenth-century households (Schiaffino and Cluizel 1988, 29) or the nineteenth-century servant employed by the ascendant bourgeoisie depicted by the wooden model bearing free chocolate samples at the 1991 Intersuc show in Paris (see fig. 13). The exoticism no longer embodied by black African men, but so useful in selling chocolate, was displaced onto and conflated with long-standing racist stereotypes of women of color, both African and South American, the latter presenting the added benefit of being distant in space.

French chocolate advertisements have long used images of black women that reflected widely coded white perceptions of black bodies as rhythmic, magical, and erotically powerful (Clifford 1988, 197–198). A chapter in Christian Constant's *Le chocolat*, entitled "Voyage to Cacao-producing Countries" recounted his personal journey into the "heart of darkness" in search of the best cacao plantations. His encounters recall the late nineteenth-century travel novels of Pierre Loti, which explore the author's erotic relations with women from exoticized lands in Turkey, Tahiti, and Japan (1879; 1880; 1887). Loti's travels and amorous relations mirror the relations of domination between the West and the non-West. "Both the women, because they are foreign, and the countries, because they are feminized, are desired, controlled, and deserted" (Todorov 1994, 314).

In Constant's account, chocolate is used as a metaphor for an eroticized Other. What begins as his education in the latest scientific advances in cacao research during a tour of the University of the West Indies in Trinidad becomes a sensuous gustatory exploration initiated by a local scientist. She engineers his total surrender to the carnal power of chocolate:

After a talk in which only questions relating to hybridization and cloning were addressed, she took me aside and pulled me into a small, dark room. After making sure that we were totally alone, she furtively removed a key from her pocket and carefully unlocked an old wooden cabinet at the back

Figure 13. Black servant bearing chocolate samples, Intersuc, 1991.

of the room. The perfumed air of exotic fragrance was palpable. I held my breath. . . . The double doors [of the cabinet] opened revealing . . . rows of shelves on which were arranged a series of carefully labeled vials full of well-fermented cacao beans. We methodically smelled and tasted each and every one of them. . . . That is how, almost covertly, she honored me with the fruits of her secret garden. (1988, 68–69)

Like Eve in the Garden, the agronomist invites Constant to taste the ripe, natural fruit of the tree of knowledge, the forbidden research samples of cacao beans. Together they violate scientific convention by tasting the contents of each vial. Female nature overwhelms male science; objective, methodical inquiry is subverted by a hedonistic orgy of tasting. Like Adam, Constant has neither the will nor the desire to resist. Yet in a reversal of the biblical story, his surrender allows him to enter, not lose, paradise. It is a fall to celebrate because he discovers the true nature of chocolate taste but also because both the journey to cacao plantations and the knowledge gleaned there when properly marketed in his book and numerous published interviews will not only enhance his reputation and cultural capital but also augment the annual sales of his Parisian boutiques and other marketing schemes.

Since the advent of chocolate advertisements in the nineteenth century, women, both white and black, lower and upper-class, have been widely used to promote the product. Indeed, chocolate ads associate chocolate, like sugar, with luxury, women, and issues of morality (Mintz 1996b, 75). They celebrate female nurturing and domesticity, women's roles as discriminating consumers, as well as female weakness and surrender to temptation. At the same time, in contemporary ads there are significant differences in the representations of black and white women. These advertisements are consistent with the nineteenth-century treatment of black women's bodies as objects of display and symbols of sexual promiscuity (Gilman 1985). In 1997, the Salon du Chocolat included a fashion show of the colors of the Ivory Coast featuring scantily and flamboyantly clad black models with elaborate headdresses that evoked the titillating rhythms and erotic costumes of Josephine Baker's 1920s *Revue nègre*.

Black women and people of color are often used to stand in for chocolate as a natural, raw material rather than to speak for it as a refined consumer good. The 1998 Salon du Chocolat showcased a Miss Cocoa Beauty Contest in which all the contestants were variously shaded women of color. The cover of the April 1997 issue of *La confiserie* featured a smiling black nude against a riotous backdrop of brilliantly colored tropical plants, fruits, beaches, and thatched huts, with the caption "How to sell chocolate, coffee and tea" (see fig. 14). The feature article admonished artisans "to recount the legend" and "to sell the history of chocolate," "just like the fairy tales that French grandmothers tell their grandchildren." It provided both a long and abbreviated version of the exoticized chocolate mythology examined here (1997, 11–15). In the

Figure 14. Front cover, *La confiserie*, "How to sell tropical products," 1997.

postwar issues of *La confiserie,* the few images of female nudity were depicted in chocolate art or window displays, but all centered on people
of color such as Gauguin's Tahitian villagers.

In contrast, white women and white men are used to evoke luxury,
languor, romantic love, and subtly suggestive eroticism. They are also

depicted as knowledgeable consumers of the taste aesthetics associated with vintage chocolate. In a 1997 Nestlé French market commercial for an up-scale *grand chocolat,* the screen is divided into nine squares, each occupied by a chocolate aficionado. All are soberly dressed, white, and solidly middle-class; five are women, the remaining four men. As we view the nine people thoughtfully munching on chocolate, the voice-over explains: "We have chosen nine authorities on chocolate. Only one received a Nestlé grand chocolat. Guess who." The center square, featuring the only smiling person, a woman, is quickly enlarged to occupy the entire screen and the voice assures us: "Objectively Nestlé chocolate has more chocolate and more pleasure."[7]

These ads reinforce the fact that white people are the privileged consumers of exotic products like chocolate that are cultivated and harvested by people of color in the third world but processed and sold in the first world. A 1990 television commercial for a Poulain chocolate bar began with a French consumer opening the wrapper to reveal a live South American jungle scene where Indian men and women dressed in brightly colored ponchos and hats were cultivating cacao bean pods and hand-carrying them across mountainous terrain to the seacoast, presumably for shipment to Europe. These scenes alternated with a close-up of a French father and his daughter in an elegant urban apartment taking turns tasting the fruits of the Indians' labor—dark Poulain chocolate, which the commercial refrain incessantly repeated, as having a flavor, color, and pleasure *"très cacao"* (very cacao). On a similar note, one house owner in Bayonne explained to me the taste differences between subtle, refined South American criollo beans and the stronger, cruder African forastero beans by alluding first to soil conditions and the more robust flavors exhibited by the African beans. Then with a laugh and a look at his head of production, he added, "Plus forasteros have the taste of all those Negroes thrown in." Notions of race and taste are thus linked in overarching structures of political power, economic exploitation, and cultural authority.

Although there is generally much more female nudity in the promotion of consumer products in French print ads and television commercials than in their American counterparts, completely or partially nude black women are featured more often in chocolate promotions than exposed white women. Another example is illustrative. When the multinational Suchard introduced its 1996 French advertising campaign, one poster unleashed a controversy and was promptly withdrawn along with a public apology by the French creator, Patrick Lecercle. The poster featured a nude black woman whose body was decorated with golden tiger strips. Facing front, bent forward and turned slightly to the left with breasts exposed but private parts blocked from view by her right arm, she stared directly into the camera. The caption read, "Even though you said no, we hear yes." French feminists lodged strong protests with both Suchard, a subsidiary of Philip Morris, and the ad agency, Young and Rubicam, which produced the commercial. For them, the salient issue was rape, not race (*Nouvel observateur,* 17–23 October 1996).

The chocolate mythology widely promoted in the 1980s and 1990s relies on the stereotypical portrayal of exoticized and eroticized others. The appeal of an essentialized, unchanging Other in the distant third world may be that it deflects attention away from what is perceived to be a problematic Other at home, within the suburban communities of non-European immigrants in France. At a time when the boundaries defining Europe are contested and blurred, the representations of race and gender in the promotion of chocolate are an attempt to re-establish cultural distance. These images also serve to reinforce the myth of French cultural and national homogeneity through time (compare Creighton 1995). French and European identities are constructed along the divide between nature and culture. Nature is the preserve of the Other: natural, untamed, and female; Culture is the prerogative of the French and Europeans: civilized, controlled, and male. The transformation of chocolate, in its journey back from the New World and its promotion as a *grand cru* product preferred by French elites, illustrate this opposition.

## Rituals of Confectionery Gift Exchange

Rituals of confectionery exchange embody the contradictory positionings of Self and Other within myriad social contexts as well as the ambiguity of gifting relationships. Although they appear disinterested and voluntary, they are given, accepted, and repaid under obligation (Mauss 1990 [1925]). These gifts often imply an act of patronage, although they do not flow exclusively or even primarily from the more powerful to the less powerful. Corporate and bureaucratic managers, business owners, politicians, professionals, and parents give gifts, but so do employees, voters, clients, students, and children. However, the flow of gifts necessarily constrains and obligates both the giver and the recipient, and these obligations are exploited by both groups. For example, both my landlady and her husband held secure if modestly remunerated positions as civil servants. They have a son whose exemplary music talent had earned him entrance to the elite Paris Conservatory of Music. Their extreme daily frugality contrasted with the lavish confectionery gifts they made to their son's local music mentor and his Parisian professors. These gifts coincided with the period during which their son was preparing a competitive examination for the placement of musicians as paid members of state orchestras.

As a graduate student doing fieldwork among *chocolatiers,* I was only too aware of the obligations inherent in patronage. I sent chocolates to all the members of my dissertation committee, recycling in turn some of the confectionery gifts I had received from the family owners in my study—anxious to have their goods tasted by New York elites. Owners of confectionery houses regularly made gifts of their goods to powerful potential patrons. They courted both local notables and national politicians. For example, the De Closets arranged through a friend with connections in the Socialist Party to have their house specialty delivered directly to then president François Mitterrand. Although they never heard what Mitterrand's reaction might have been, it was a story they astutely exploited among their clientele.

The exchange of confectionery gifts is a matter of managing the obligations and risks of social interaction and class status. Confectionery gifts can express, strengthen, challenge, or undermine social relations because they represent an important medium through which to communicate social messages. The content of these messages is enhanced by the symbolically resonant ceremonial occasions on which chocolates are typically exchanged. For instance, Madame Bonnet has had recurrent problems with her mother-in-law and disliked the closeness between her husband and his mother. After one particularly unpleasant confrontation, Madame Bonnet registered her frustration and anger by not offering the confectionery gift her mother-in-law had come to expect on Mother's Day. Mademoiselle Ribout, too, used chocolate to send a strong message to a relative whom she felt had consistently neglected her. She is an unmarried saleslady who has spent her entire career in the same confectionery boutique. She had ongoing arguments with her niece, the mother of her godson, concerning the frequency of their contact. Easter of 1989 arrived several weeks after one particularly acrimonious argument, and Mademoiselle expressed her resentment by not purchasing the large chocolate egg her godson anxiously awaited each year.

Confectionery gifts not only challenge but also affirm existing social relations in the face of personal and familial ordeals. Chocolate serves as a source of comfort, reassurance, and pleasing aesthetic distraction. One Bayonnais gentleman sent an exquisite package of assorted chocolates, champagne, and sugared fruits valued at $200 to a favorite niece whose baby was hospitalized with meningitis. Elaborate gifts coaxed from the most perishable and delicate of media, such as chocolate, are a resonant medium through which to celebrate the triumph over adversity and the fragility of human life. For example, every year at Christmas time, Monsieur Laborde sent a lavish chocolate gift box valued at $100 to a close friend to commemorate her recovery from an illness that nearly claimed her life. "I honor her life and our friendship," he explained.

The circulation and display of the honorific gifts mentioned above render class position visible and confer social prestige. Confectionery gifting rituals have increasingly lent themselves to extravagance and ostentation. They are a strategic component in the symbolic struggle for social distinction waged among members of a larger, affluent, middle-class clientele. Through their gifts, consumers conspicuously display professional, friendship, and kin ties but also social networks, career success, and expansive life styles. At various times throughout the seasonal round, middle-class consumers placed special orders for custom-designed pieces in chocolate or purchased the confectionery art pieces featured in the boutique window. Some of these pieces marked rites of passage such as weddings and engagements but many were deritualized, linked instead to individual circumstances, corporate relations, or local and regional politics. For example, a grateful patient commissioned a costly set of chocolate dentures and dental tools from Michel Chaudun to thank his dentist. One customer of Francis Boucher ordered a life-sized chocolate terrier as a peace offering for his wife when he refused to allow real dogs in their home. Another of his male customers ordered a meter-high chocolate rabbit extending flowers with one arm as a gift to his girlfriend. On a whim, one of Boucher's female customers ordered pale pink marzipan and asked his advice on the best way to shape it into human ears—thirty to be precise—to be presented to her dinner guests. When I returned to Paris in 1998, I found a large plaster bust of Marianne, the symbol of the French Republic, in Francis Boucher's office. It was brought by the organizers of a political dinner who wanted a chocolate replica of Marianne to honor the women who had been elected to their regional council in 1998.

If the *chocolatier's* art exemplifies the principles of Veblenian consumption, it also reveals the ritualistic extravagance and agonistic display associated with the potlatch (compare Tobin 1992). In 1993 Monsieur

Bergeron, a *chocolatier* noted for his artistry and technical prowess, planned a promotional event in Biarritz that was reported in regional publications throughout France. He and two assistants made a giant chocolate Easter bell weighing 1400 kilos and measuring a story in height. It was officially weighed and measured in the presence of a Bayonnais sheriff, lifted by a crane onto a flatbed truck, and promenaded ceremoniously through the streets of the city to the town hall, where the mayor, Didier Borotra, awarded Bergeron the municipal seal for his mastery of his craft. The bell was displayed in the central hall before being shattered and the pieces scattered in the city garden for an Easter morning chocolate hunt for local youngsters (*La confiserie* 1993, 89).

On a return trip to the Basque coast in the summer of 1995, I paid a visit to Monsieur Bergeron and found him in his workshop in the late afternoon, roughing out the contours of a black panther from a meter-long block of dark chocolate. He had been commissioned to provide a demonstration of his art for a group of women accompanying their husbands on a business trip to Biarritz. He explained that he would put the finishing touches on the panther during the demonstration, then display and photograph it. It would subsequently be ceremoniously shattered, distributed to, and he added with a chuckle, "eaten by the group of surprised and delighted ladies."

## Conclusion

The postwar period in France has been marked by increased consumption of chocolate as both a cheap popular snack, the quintessential postmodern commodity, and as an expensive honorific food, a highly desirable postmodern gift. In this chapter I emphasize mass media images of chocolate that are designed to promote its exchange and consumption. My emphasis here has been to highlight the complex processes whereby chocolate as a cultural commodity acquires and sheds culturally specific meanings, properties, and values as it is circulated and consumed at a particular point in time and across different historical periods.

I have highlighted rituals of confectionery gift exchange because accounts of advanced capitalist economies usually privilege only mass-produced commodities. Moreover, commodities and exchange are still too often defined in ways that reify the contrasts between gifts and commodities, associating the gift with societies governed by personalized reciprocal exchanges and the commodity with societies dominated by alienated market transactions. Chocolate provides an ideal medium with which to examine the cultural and ritual dimensions of a society that represents itself and is widely represented as one of the privileged Civilizations of reason and disciplined economic interest.

At the same time, my close reading of recent attempts by social elites and Parisian *chocolatiers* to alter the symbolic associations and to reconfigure gifting rituals arose out of Bourdieu's critique of gift exchange theory. The examples I chose reveal the strategic parallels between confectionery gift exchange and the calculating spirit of more ostensibly "economic practices" even when gifting gives the appearance of complete disinterestedness (Bourdieu 1977, 177). Thus, at the micro level the offering and withdrawal of chocolate gifts is intimately linked to strategies aimed at altering power differentials, family dynamics, class status, and social distinction.

At the macro level, chocolate is an effective medium through which to examine the continuities and tensions in French culture, thought, and history concerning alterity, primitivism/exoticism, racism, gender, and national identity. The creation and worldwide promotion of a new chocolate taste standard cannot be divorced from France's colonial past. This past deeply informs the construction of the exoticized discourse of consumption and the eroticized images of peoples of color who stand in for chocolate as a substance that retains the seductive power of its "wild," "natural" origins outside France and Europe. As the 1998 Salon du Chocolat revealed, these images are still quite useful in selling chocolate.

The new taste standard cannot be separated from the postcolonial present, in which French spheres of influence under the banner of *francophonie* are perceived to be under siege and where foodstuffs have become the privileged arena for affirmation of French exceptionalism in the face of the latest manifestations of a menacing globalization, namely, imports of beef with added hormones and genetically altered plants. Moreover, the pure dark chocolate standard so unambiguously endorsed by French crafts leaders and social elites was promoted at a time when cacao prices were very low. Within the European Commission, the temporary reprieve won by purist nations with regard to the use of cocoa butter replacers may not last, given the opposition voiced by huge multinationals and other member nations of the European Community and the heightened role of deterritorialized transnational capital in the making of chocolate empires and the elaboration of production priorities.

# Epilogue

Eight years after the intensive period of my field research ended, my relations with the French *chocolatier* community continue. Unfolding events in Paris, Brussels, and Strasbourg repeatedly engage *chocolatiers* directly with representatives and structures of power. The politics of identity and representation chronicled in this book are still aimed, with even renewed urgency, not only at French and European technocrats but also at powerful culture brokers, a constantly expanding international clientele for vintage chocolate, and the anthropologist.

*Chocolatiers'* identity struggles have been and continue to be waged in and through written, visual, and performative texts. From my earliest contact with them in 1989, these artisans welcomed my interest in their craft by opening their businesses and by supplying me with a plethora of scholarly, popular, and administrative texts. In fact, I still receive a complimentary subscription to their craft journal. And *chocolatiers* continue to solicit and appropriate portions of my published research as a device to validate their particular goals. Texts, then, have been central to our relations, not as theoretical models, but as critical sources of data and strategic sites of negotiation. I focus now on a series of return visits to France and exchanges with *chocolatiers* in Bayonne and Paris because of the issues they raise for Western anthropologists who do field research in Euro-American cores and study up or across rather than down. As anthropology's focus has become increasingly urban, cosmopolitan, and Western, our conventional understandings of ethnographic authority, access, and power relations have been contested and problematized in new, more complex ways. This contestation has been and remains intimately linked to issues of power.

In the spring of 1996 I received a package from Jean Mourier. He enclosed a videotape made in his workshop as well as a copy of the March issue of *La confiserie*. He drew my attention to a feature article on his business of which he was justifiably proud and then added, rather mysteriously, that there was another article sure to interest me. As I studied the table of contents and found the article entitled, "*Chocolatiers* Seen through American Eyes," I began to feel quite uneasy. Between 1991 when I left France and 1993 when I defended my dissertation, I had received periodic inquiries about the status of my writing from both craft leaders in Paris and local *chocolatiers* in Bayonne. Had I finished the thesis? When would it be published? Could they have a copy of it?

I had written to Guy Urbain in 1993, explaining the problems posed by the translation of a 400-page document and offered instead to provide a copy in English. A year later, in 1994, both he and Alain Grangé separately sent urgent requests for my thesis—in English. They were very anxious to present it at their craft congress, to which several well-placed French and European technocrats had been invited. Although I duly sent the thesis priority mail along with a request for a copy of the French translation along with the translator's name and credentials, I had heard nothing from them until the package with the journal article arrived in May 1996. When I read the article I was shocked to discover that craft leaders had published a French synopsis of my dissertation without bothering to provide the information I had requested or to obtain my permission. I noted immediately that the article was presented as if I had authored it. My shock gave way to disbelief and then to anger when I discovered that the synopsis actually bore very little resemblance to my thesis.

Just two months later, in the summer of 1996, I received a phone call from Patrick Sarlate in Bayonne, inviting me, on behalf of Mayor Jean Grenet, to participate in the Year of Chocolate festivities then being planned for October. Would I give a public lecture on my field research among the local craft community? As an enticement, he added that not only would the city provide me with a round-trip ticket but the mayor would publish all the lectures in a special volume by a respected French press. Although I was deeply shaken by the misrepresentation and publication of my material, I also felt a profound obligation to accept the invitation. I very much wanted to present a portion of my research to the craft families who had so generously shared their work and lives with me, some of whom had become friends. Also, during my return visit to Bayonne in 1995, Patrick Sarlate and Madame Rénaud had arranged for my induction into the Académie du Chocolat de Bayonne and for a series of interviews with local journalists that were published in the local newspaper. I therefore accepted his invitation without hesitation but with considerable apprehension.

The source of my anxiety was directly connected to the politicized nature of ethnographic encounters with educated consultants engaged in an ongoing politics of identity. It also reveals the potentially conflicting imperatives of postmodern, reflexive theory and the professional ethics that inform fieldwork practices. These ethical rules require the protection of our consultants by assuring that their participation is informed, voluntary, and anonymous. So what do ethnographers do when consultants reject anonymity and insist on being identified? How do anthropologists manage situations when consultants are as interested in appropriating and publishing the research findings as "their" ethnographers? Ethical rules also demand that when potential conflicts arise between the interests of ethnographers and their consultants, those of the consultants should prevail. But what happens when there are conflicting interests among consultants that have serious political and professional implications for the entire group? Is it possible, or even desirable, to negotiate a balanced rapport with consultants who are themselves actively involved in the solicitation and production of texts that both affirm their collective identity and advance their vested interests?

My attempts to protect *chocolatiers'* anonymity both puzzled and annoyed them because most wanted me to use their real names and to promote both the craft and their individual houses. It should, therefore, have come as no surprise when I read the synopsis of my thesis to see that the real names and identities of the craft families in the southwest had been substituted for the pseudonyms I used. I initially experienced this substitution as a blatant attempt on the part of the Parisian leaders to further their identity politics through the guise of an apparently objective scholarly text. I was worried about reaction to the article in the southwest because I had spent a great deal of time explaining why anonymity was necessary. Would local craft families see it as a betrayal of the confidence they had placed in me? Would they blame me or the Parisians?

I was also concerned that a confrontation on this issue might endanger the relationships I had sought to nurture and maintain among both craft leaders and local families. I was upset, and also offended, because I saw the substitution of the pseudonyms as a betrayal of the trust I thought I had established with Guy Urbain, who edited the craft journal. I therefore purposely squeezed an extra day onto my weekend trip to Bayonne in October 1996. I felt certain he would give me a full accounting of how and why this had happened.

When I look back now, Guy Urbain's reaction should have been entirely predictable. When we met at the confederation headquarters in Paris, he was genuinely mystified over my upset about the question of anonymity and replied, "But it was obvious to all of us who you were talking about so why not put in the real names? In fact the membership would have wondered what we were up to if we hadn't!" I reminded him of my concern about the quality of the translation given the urgency of the request and asked somewhat testily who had been authorized to translate the thesis. "But I did," he had replied in a wounded tone. When I asked as tactfully as I could how he felt confident translating a doctoral thesis given his limited command of English and lack of background in anthropology, he shrugged and assured me that his frequent trips to the United States had improved his English. "Besides," he added, "I know my craft, don't I?"

The title of the journal article had seemed supremely ironic to me in its use of the metaphor of the eye. The irony was, of course, that the "hegemonic ethnographic gaze" of the anthropologist had been met and transformed by the so-called objects of that gaze. When I wrote the thesis I was very conscious of the problematic use of a unitary narrative voice and a seamless holistic perspective in the rendering of culture, craft, or any other. I tried to present a less tidy, more nuanced picture of the craft, one that privileged the competing voices surrounding it. However, the journal article was notable for its suppression of these multiple voices and presented, instead, both a single narrative of *chocolatier* tradition and an aestheticized image of a craft community united in the pursuit of common goals.

It elided my discussion of the complex evolution and myriad uses of the words *tradition, community,* and *authenticity.* The notion of craft tradition—one I was said to admire with "passion"—was presented as an unchanging set of practices and associational rituals effortlessly reproduced through time.

As I flew to Bayonne that weekend I was nervous about facing local *chocolatiers* who might have read the article and interpreted my thesis as a confirmation of the continuing hegemony of sophisticated metropoles like Paris in contrast to provincial centers like Bayonne. I was also afraid that they might see my analysis as a validation of the power and authority of powerful Parisians to define the craft and to control its representation. Therefore, when Patrick met me at the airport, one of the first things I asked about was the journal article. Although he had not read it himself, he said he had heard good things about it from Monsieur Mourier. No one else had apparently mentioned it. They had been too busy preparing for the Year of Chocolate activities.

Until the publication of that article and my 1996 return visit to France I did not fully grasp the tremendous stakes my research represented for my "subject" community or the constantly evolving relationship between hierarchies of power and ethnographic authority. Of course, from the beginning I understood that *chocolatiers'* attempts to write craft culture and to make their own history were totally logical in a society that views its literary productions as a constituent element of national culture and identity (Clark 1987). Similarly, *chocolatiers'* attempts to control the representation of their craft were totally understandable given artisans' own ambiguous position in French history. Artisans have at various periods of history found themselves under the intense scrutiny of an array of intellectuals and state officials. Indeed, the production of texts by working people, many skilled artisans, has a long history in France (Perrot 1992). In the industrializing context of the nineteenth and twentieth centuries, the deskilling of artisans and the collapse of their crafts generated intense debates on the nature and pace of large-scale change. Texts written by or in collaboration with intellectuals were often controlled or heavily influenced by the political agendas of those intellectuals.

The early 1990s was just such a moment for French *chocolatiers.* In their ongoing negotiations, they wanted the authority a scholarly text would provide them. However, the Parisian leaders who read my thesis were distinctly uncomfortable with my attempts to render craft culture in all its disorderly complexity. Their negotiations in the areas of training, certification, and, most recently, production norms relied on sending a clear message in the name of craft. Their presentation of *chocolatier* tradition as unchanging corresponded well to the French state's recognition and recent support of genuine crafts and regional products, *de terroir,* of the soil. It also related well to the 1992 European legislation enacted to authenticate distinctive foods tied to a particular place or production tradition (Bérard and Marcheney 1995). My analysis of craft tradition as continuous adaptation, while consistent with much anthropological theory on culture, was hardly one that *chocolatiers* wanted to disseminate in 1996. This was a point on which both Parisian leaders and local *chocolatiers* agreed.

At the same time, both craft leaders and local activists such as Jean Mourier and Patrick Sarlate were acutely aware of my new status as a professor at Georgetown—an American university they were all familiar with because a Spanish prince had recently graduated from the School of Foreign Service. When I was a graduate student, my status as an anthropologist merely perplexed some of the people I knew. For instance, my landlady misunderstood the word *ethnologue* (anthropologist) for *oenologue* (wine connoisseur) and wondered why I was studying *chocolatiers*.

When I began my field research I already had command of French, knowledge of high culture, and experience as a college professor. But this status as an intellectual rarely gave me the authority I might have expected. I was still a student and an American. Members of the craft community and local people solicited advice I felt inadequate to give on marketing and sales—America being the land of commercialism and big business—and were surprised, sometimes even incredulous, when I demonstrated knowledge of their history—Americans being the people without history, and therefore, civilization.

However, my return as a professor of French civilization and anthropology was a bit more disturbing. Like many local folk, one of the journalists who interviewed me in 1995 understood my investigation of the craft community as folklore, a subject of largely historical interest. It was only when I described my position in a French department and my study as an anthropological one that his attention sharpened. "So what do you tell your students about us?" he asked in a suspicious tone. I managed to ease his fears, but this concern was echoed at a dinner party given several days later for the new inductees into the Académie du Chocolat de Bayonne. Académie president Madame Rénaud asked me a question that provoked gales of laughter among the ten guests seated at my table. "So what do you tell your students about us? Do you describe us like the Zulus in Africa?"

The subtext of Madame Rénaud's question highlights some of the problems that arise when the ethnographic gaze focuses on aspects of Western civilization itself. This issue is particularly salient in France, a society whose eighteenth-century thinkers coined the term *civilization* and theorized human history as a unitary scale of progress culminating in the superior accomplishments of the West (Bénéton 1975). In the nineteenth century, French philosophers, writers, and historians further refined a universalist notion of civilization, making it equivalent to French republican values and to French high culture itself.

Madame Rénaud's question also speaks to the status of competing civilizations within a shifting hierarchy of nation-states. If France's loss of empire reflected and signaled her diminished political, economic, and military power in the postwar period, many French people believe the nation's cultural hegemony is perfectly intact. In this view the submission of elements of French culture and civilization to anthropological analysis can be seen as controversial, even subversive. This view privileges France and assumes that the ethnographic gaze should more properly be trained on African peoples—a view that is apparent in the representations of chocolate as Self and Other.

At the same time, it suggests that the use of anthropologists by subject communities with an agenda may be an ever increasing feature of ethnography in the West as anthropology of the West gains a more authoritative presence in the construction of knowledge about "Us." French intellectual elites play a crucial role in molding and diffusing knowledge about France. While philosophers and historians have traditionally dominated French intellectual culture, anthropologists enjoy more legitimacy now than in the past. This fact was clearly not lost on the organizers of the Year of Chocolate when they asked me to give a public lecture along with two historians, an agro-engineer, and a representative from Valrhona.

All these questions weighed heavily on my mind as I prepared for my lecture. How could I present an ethnography of craft that did not simply reproduce the ideology of craft celebrated in *chocolatiers'* numerous collective initiatives? I wanted to project the richly nuanced picture I had observed throughout my field research of a group of social actors astutely asserting their place within both the past and the present—with all the attendant contradictions and tensions that process implies. Of course, I wanted my lecture to be well received by the other scholars, but more importantly I wanted it to be *heard,* not just by the bourgeois organizers of the event, but by the craft families whose work and lives form the core of this book. I well remember how disappointed I was in 1995 when only bourgeois professional and business people signed up for the dinner held after my induction into the Académie du Chocolat de Bayonne. Michèle Harcaut tactfully explained that she and her husband would have gone "if other members of the craft community had been there." Serge Mathieu stated bluntly what she merely suggested when he exclaimed, "That was a bourgeois affair. You've seen how they are. They wouldn't have wanted us there."

It was a painful reminder that my liminal status as an American and an outsider gave me the freedom to move between class milieux, one that local people—both craft families and bourgeois elites—simply did not have.

In the end I centered on *chocolatiers'* strategic initiatives and allowed them to speak through the theoretical frames of two French sociologists. I used Emile Durkheim's writings on social ritual and Maurice

Halbwachs's work on collective memory to analyze their recent elaboration of craft rituals and commemorative texts. Famous French scholars then did the labor of connecting their work and products to the craft and culinary patrimony they were intent on authenticating and preserving. Although no craft families, except the Sarlates, attended the dinner following the lecture, I noted with pleasure that many of them were present at the lecture. During that dinner, Madame Rénaud again performed the ritual of induction, this time for Nikita Harwich, one of the historians who lectured on the history of chocolate production and consumption in the New World. She was seated at my table, and after it was completed, she turned to me saying with a smile, "If it's true that rituals bind us as a group and shape our understanding of the past, then we are making our own history tonight, don't you think?"

I end by suggesting that field research in urban environments with educated consultants necessarily involves new methodological concerns, ethical dilemmas, and representational issues, which are not easily accommodated by either realist or postmodern ethnographies. At issue here are the differing claims to authority and control over texts as well as the ethics that underlie those claims. In writing this book, I have obviously chosen to reintroduce the messy inconsistencies of craft culture and the contested histories of *chocolatier* tradition. I did so because they give a truer picture of French artisans as a people *with* and *in* history. They have not disappeared, but the history they make is not always one of their choosing. Drawing this picture is crucial because it reveals the complex and contingent nature of the processes of domination and makes visible the dialectical interaction of competing interests. I am only too aware that it may collide with *chocolatiers'* ongoing efforts to solicit and use powerful centers in Paris, Brussels, Strasbourg, and New York for validation of their own strategic ends.

I offer no facile solutions to the dilemmas I have raised in this epilogue. I do suggest that one way to achieve a more nuanced understanding of the complex realities informing contemporary ethnography is to maintain an ongoing dialogue and exchange of texts with our consultants. While such exchanges will problematize ethnographic authority and no doubt transform our understandings of field research, they also offer the opportunity to create new conversations about the process of domination and the hierarchies of power in contemporary Europe. As Madame Rénaud rightly suggested, these conversations will open a space within which we can discuss how we make and understand our own particular histories.

# Fieldwork Sample

I conducted ethnographic research in eight craft businesses located in three Basque coast towns—Bayonne, Biarritz, and
Saint-Jean-de-Luz. I collected data on the everyday organization and
performance of work including seasonal production cycles, hierarchies
of skill, the division of labor by function, age, and skill, training methods, and the merchandising and sale of goods. My principal focus was
the owners and heirs of craft businesses and how they perceived and
managed a series of tensions and contradictions related to the short-
term maintenance and long-term reproduction of their work.

I also investigated the complexities of salaried work. Once a week,
on Mondays, the day when local *chocolateries* were closed, I attended
the practicum classes of the confectionery apprenticeship program at
the public vocational school housed within the Bayonne Chamber of
Trades. Since French law mandates that apprentices divide their time
between school and work, I was able to compare the real and perceived
differences between the training conducted in both locales. I observed
first- and second-year apprentices as well as the master artisan classes for
salaried workers hoping to become self-employed.

Throughout the seasonal round I observed *chocolatiers* at work and
occasionally participated in their work during peak production periods.
I wrapped candies, displayed goods, or ran errands, tasks reserved for unskilled, temporary female employees. On trips to Paris I systematically
investigated the culture of the *chocolatiers'* professional organization as
well as the image of the craft presented to the membership and the public. I interviewed the current and past presidents, vice-presidents, and

treasurers as well as members of the executive board. I collected data from their archives on membership statistics, training, trade shows, and organizational structure. I have been able to study the craft journal, *La confiserie,* from its beginnings in the 1920s to the present thanks to the generosity of its editor, Guy Urbain.

In 1990 there were a total of fifty-eight *pâtisseries, confiseries,* and *chocolateries* operating in the three coastal towns. I chose eight to investigate in detail basing that choice on the following criteria. First, I selected only those combining production and sales because there remains a strong consensus among artisans and the general public that family artisanship necessarily includes both activities. However, the distinction between small merchant retailers and artisans who sell what they produce is sometimes blurred. This is particularly true in food crafts, where both French and foreign franchise outlets merely resell candies produced elsewhere. Some producers make frequent use of the label *"fabrication artisanale"* to differentiate themselves from both the franchise outlets and the small shopkeepers who resell industrially produced goods. Indeed, the appropriation and deformation of what artisans see as the true French craft model has been the catalyst for much *chocolatier* activism.

Second, since my primary focus is on chocolate I selected businesses that either specialized exclusively in it or produced an important supplementary line of chocolates. The eight businesses forming the core of this book are representative in this regard. All produce chocolate candies but only three do so exclusively. Five of the eight businesses considered here in detail produce mainly candy specialties: Dalbaitz, Bourriet, De Closet, Salinas, and Aguirre. The remaining three, Mathieu, Carrère, and Harcaut, produce primarily pastries but also a seasonal line of chocolates.

The third criterion involved a representative mix of older, established houses and newly created ones. I wanted to compare first-generation owners with second-, third- or fourth-generation entrepreneurs in terms of practices designed to ensure the short-term viability and long-term reproduction. Of the eight families considered, one has continually produced for four generations, three others for three generations, one for two, and three are in their first generation of business ownership.

The fourth criterion centered on craft activism. I was particularly interested in owners who had been actively involved in the organization of collective initiatives. They were engaged in constructing and projecting a distinct notion of craft community. They perceived themselves and were perceived by others to be activists who promoted change within their houses and the craft as a whole. Five of the eight owners were recognized in this role. Although they were not representative of the whole, they reflected many ideas held by others concerning the need for continuity in what they saw as the traditional organization and performance of craft work as well as the need for innovative change. However, both their views and initiatives have generated sometimes intense disagreement. The Aguirre business is a case in point. The current owners refused to participate in the recent creation of the *chocolat de Bayonne*. Bayonnais craftspeople considered this a reprehensible decision given what they saw as the importance of collectively promoting regional chocolate production. Their refusal elucidates an ongoing internal dialectic among local artisans.

Finally, I wanted a representative sampling of houses from the resort towns of Biarritz and Saint-Jean-de-Luz as they constitute part of a regional economy heavily dependent on tourism. Thus, I included five Bayonnais businesses and three outside of Bayonne—two in Biarritz and one in Saint-Jean-de-Luz.

My fieldwork among French *chocolatiers* was conducted at a time when they were engaged in difficult, ongoing negotiations with technocrats in Paris and Brussels. From our first contact in 1989, most not only welcomed my interest in their craft by opening their businesses and archives to me but frequently attempted to control my representation of their work. They also solicited and selectively published portions of my doctoral dissertation, significantly misrepresenting my analysis. Needless to say, they eagerly await the publication of a book on French chocolate. As I argue in the epilogue, these actions were totally understandable given the stakes and the history of their relations with French intellectuals (see Terrio 1998).

Nonetheless, this posed a significant dilemma for me. Throughout my fieldwork, *chocolatiers* and I wrestled for control of each other's knowledge. They were sometimes careful to distinguish between data I could and could not use—sensitive personal and, particularly, financial data—precisely because most wanted me to use their real names and to promote both the craft and their businesses. My attempts to protect their anonymity both annoyed and puzzled them. In the end, I changed the names of the Basque coast craftspeople and did not divulge information on the economics of the craft or on sensitive personal matters. The names of craft leaders, who play a very public role in Paris and the southwest as well as public figures such as elected officials have not been changed.

# Notes

## Chapter 1. Introduction

1. After initially accepting the Confrérie's invitation, Alain Juppé sent a local politician to be inducted in his place.

2. I interviewed Ms. Douce in Paris on 14 May 1998, and studied press coverage of all three salons as well as a video Event International commissioned of the 1997 edition of the Salon du Chocolat. I visited the New York Chocolate Show on 25 November 1998 (see *New York Times,* 16 December 1998).

3. Here I use the term *tastemaker* to include food critics, restaurateurs, journalists, fashion designers, advertising professionals, and intellectuals (compare Appadurai 1986, 32; Harvey 1989, 290).

4. See Appadurai (1986), Baudrillard (1981), Bourdieu (1984), Carrier (1995a), Douglas and Isherwood (1979), Harvey (1989), Jameson (1991), Miller (1995, 1997), Mintz (1996a, 1996b), Sahlins (1976), Tobin (1992), and Zukin (1991). Recent work on craft remains largely focused on crafts in nonindustrial societies (Helms 1993) and on the differential impact of world demand on local craft in the developing world or in first world peripheries (Bradburd 1995; Buechler 1989; Cooper 1980; Ennew 1982; Helfgott 1996; Nash 1993; Spooner 1986). Some notable exceptions include Bertaux and Bertaux-Wiame (1978), Hareven (1992), Herzfeld (1995, 1997), Kondo (1990), Moeran (1984), and Ulin (1996).

5. Scholars who favor the theory of chocolate's arrival at the French court include Harwich (1992) and Peeters (1989). Partisans of the ecclesiastical diffusion theory include Argonne (1713), Barbaret (1887), Braudel (1967), Coe and Coe (1996), and Franklin (1893). Those mentioning Bayonne as the French cradle of chocolate include local historians Constantin (1933), Hourmat (1990), and Léon (1893).

6. Postwar studies of the petite bourgeoisie either examined postwar patterns of political mobilization among the traditional petite bourgeoisie (artisans and shopkeepers) in order to assess its potential as a breeding ground for right-wing extremism (Borne 1977; Hoffmann 1956; Mayer 1986) or studied the

capacity of petty bourgeois to reproduce themselves within an expanding capitalist order (Baudelot and Establet 1974; Bertaux and Bertaux-Wiame 1978; Bourdieu 1984; Jaeger 1982; Zarca 1979a, 1979b, 1986, 1987). Many concluded that small independent producers could not reproduce themselves in a society dominated by capitalist relations. Bourdieu's (1984, 345–354) depiction of the declining petite bourgeoisie is emblematic in this regard. He argues that traditional craftsmen have an inherent disadvantage in the symbolic struggles for status that differentiate and advance social classes in France. Their intermediate status drives petit bourgeois to an arduous, unceasing struggle for admittance into the dominant bourgeois class. The very aesthetic that defines traditional artisans—an "ethos of conscientiousness," appreciation of "order, rigour and care," hostility to "all inclinations of modernity," "religious and political conservatism," resentment against the "new morality," and a consumerist ethos—dooms their social ambitions to failure. Their "Malthusian" strategies as well as their "regressive" attachment to "old" France reveal and perpetuate a crippling lack of the "capital"—economic assets, social contacts, and cultural authority based on educational attainment—needed to effect social mobility. They are thus examples of both cultural anachronism and social immobility.

7. See Michael Herzfeld's (1995, 1997) fascinating analysis of the contradictory images embodied by Greek artisans.

8. Numerous scholarly and popular works examine or depict the negative images associated with shopkeepers and artisans in their roles as petty bourgeois entrepreneurs. A partial list includes Clavel (1962), Darnton (1985), Dutourd (1952), Ernaux (1974, 1983), Rousseau (1762), and Zola (1883). There is a huge literature on the mobilization of artisans and their attraction to nineteenth-century left-wing movements. Some notable examples include Aminzade (1981), Hanagan (1980), Johnson (1975), Merriman (1979), Perrot (1974), Reddy (1984), Scott (1974), and Sewell (1980). On artisans and shopkeepers in right-wing political movements, see Borne (1977), Hoffmann (1956), Mayer (1986), Nord (1986), and Poujade (1955).

9. If earlier analyses of modernity excluded craft, so do postmodern theories. For example, Jameson's analysis is framed in a unilinear evolutionary mode. According to him, in postmodernism "the survival, the residue, the holdover, the archaic, has finally been swept away without a trace. In the postmodern, then the past itself has disappeared . . . nature has been triumphantly blotted out, along with peasants, petit-bourgeois commerce, handicraft" (1991, 309–310). This account, like those that focus exclusively on the alienation of modern labor (Braverman 1974; Buroway 1985), ignores the economic, political, and sociocultural conditions that might account for craft as a thriving, nonanachronistic, activity. It also neglects the complex, mediating role played by centralized institutions as well as the ongoing expansion of late capitalism itself.

10. Two scholarly works, one by two anthropologists and one by two historians, deconstructed "tradition" as both a commonsense and a social scientific category inherited from nineteenth-century thought (Hobsbaum and Ranger 1983; Handler and Linnekin 1984). Both rejected the received notion of tradition as an unchanging body of customs and ideas handed down across generations, treating it instead as a social construction. Hobsbaum and Ranger's analysis nonetheless implies that there is an objectivist history to uncover be-

hind the invention. In contrast, Handler and Linnekin argue that tradition, like culture, is ceaselessly reinvented. They reject all objectivist views of history that distinguish an authentic from an invented past. Ulin has recently criticized their view because it overemphasizes the ability of social actors to act apart from their pasts and their culture even as it relativizes and equates all discourses concerning the past. However, in his own study of southwest French wine cooperatives, Ulin sometimes underestimates the agency of local actors to understand and act on their pasts, just as he overemphasizes both the hegemonic effects of global economic processes and the authority and invulnerability of estate wine growers in Bordeaux. The 1998 Bordeaux wine scandal is a case in point.

11. Several works have contributed in significant ways to my thinking on rituals as political acts embedded within complex histories (Aretxaga 1997, 80–104; Kertzer 1988) and on the politics of authenticity (Bendix 1997).

12. See the appendix for a description of the research sample.

## Chapter 2.    Bread and Chocolate

1. I would like to thank Sidney Mintz for suggesting that I tell the story of French chocolate by beginning with French bread.

2. See chapter 10 for an analysis of the different social and symbolic meanings attached to chocolate.

3. State intervention in defense of the neighborhood *boulanger* was reported regularly in the autumn of 1996 on French national television. It continued in 1997 with the 2 January 1997 Antenne 2 broadcast describing a new law restricting the use of the label *boulangerie* to those bakers who made bread from scratch on the premises. See also *New York Times,* 5 January 1997, and *Washington Post,* 15 January 1997. Early the following year, on 6 February 1998, the French Council of State abrogated the 1997 law restricting use of the label *boulangerie.*

4. Compare the displacement of rice as a staple to a side dish in contemporary Japan (Ohnuki-Tierney 1993).

5. Readers should remember that the haute cuisine for which France was and is justly famous was largely reserved for privileged milieux.

6. In 1960 there were seven supermarkets in France. By 1989 there were 6,493 supermarkets and 747 hypermarkets (with 2,500 square meters of floor space) (INSEE 1990).

7. See Herpin (1988). One anthropologist who specializes in food systems contrasted the village France of the 1950s, where cuisine was *"gastro-nomique"* meaning tightly ordered by a culinary grammar encompassing strict rules, to the urban (and suburban) France of 1990, where culinary structures were beginning to disintegrate and becoming *"gastro-anomique"* (Fischler 1990, 205).

8. The number of fast food establishments grew from 109 in 1980 to 2,036 in 1991 (Fantasia 1995, 203).

9. Louis le Duff, CEO of the Brioche Dorée chain, noted the failure of the first fast food restaurants in France (the first French McDonald's opened in 1972), and in 1977 he targeted a new market niche for the between-meal snack. The lighter noontime meal and the eight o'clock dinner hour created the need for an obligatory afternoon stop at the neighborhood *boulangerie-pâtisserie* for a

quiche, pastry, or sweet roll. His stores consciously imitated traditional bakery décors but made production appear to be an integral part of consumption. Workers prepared croissants and brioches from industrial mixes in the workshop but baked them in full view of consumers (Pynson 1987, 23). McDonald's, meanwhile, concluded that there would be too much resistance to their fast food formula in France and leased exclusive use of its franchise to Raymond Dayan in 1977. When the fast food formula was a success, in spite of the violent diatribes launched against it by the French culinary establishment and prominent intellectuals, the company successfully sued to get it back. When the McDonald's corporation regained control of its French franchises in 1982, it planned a decade of rapid expansion, which engendered a series of acquisitions and mergers of French fast food chains with the larger industrial food groups in processing, commercial catering, or hotel chains (Fantasia 1995, 207).

10. Until recently, the most popular type of chocolate candy center was the *praliné*. *Praliné* centers consist of a mixture of roasted, finely ground caramelized almonds and/or filberts, sugar, and ground chocolate couverture. *Chocolatiers* also made *ganache* centers from ground chocolate, milk or cream, butter, sugar, and various flavors: whisky, liqueur, candied or alcohol-macerated fruit, reduced fruit purées, or fruit essences. Other specialties one could expect to find included sugared orange peels, chocolate-coated nuts, marzipan centers, hard sugar candies, nougat centers, sugared fruits *(fruits confits)*, nuts and chestnuts, as well as a fruit confection made from fruit pulp combined with sugar, cooked slowly, and allowed to set *(pâte de fruits)*.

11. The Best Craftsman of France contest was created in 1923 during a period marked by upheaval in many crafts. It remains the most prestigious and highly coveted state award. The contests are organized by the National Work Exhibits (Exposition Nationale du Travail), a state-sponsored exhibition of outstanding craft works. The Ministry of Education grants representatives of crafts the right to organize and stage the contest. In 1990, eighteen such exhibits had been held in crafts as diverse as food, hair dressing, decorative arts, metalworking, ceramics, glassmaking, cutlery, and gunsmithing.

12. In 1990 and 1991, craft leaders at the Paris headquarters of the Confédération Nationale des Détaillants et Artisans-détaillants de la Chocolaterie, Confiserie et Biscuiterie (hereafter, the confederation) elaborated policy and took collective initiatives on behalf of a nationwide membership. Their attempt to professionalize a craft identity was strongly contested by the local *chocolatiers* and members of companion crafts. See chapter 8.

13. Jacobs Suchard was acquired by the American multinational, Philip Morris, in 1990.

14. In 1995 the confederation, under the leadership of Alain Grangé, directly petitioned the foreign affairs minister to oppose the proposed directive on chocolate manufacture. The French minister supported the confederation position by expressing his opposition to the proposed directive in a 1995 letter to the president of the European Commission, Jacques Santer. Guy Urbain, the editor of the *chocolatiers'* journal, *La confiserie,* collected almost 30,000 signatures from concerned French consumers and in January 1996 personally presented them to the European Commission representative on consumption pol-

icy in Brussels (Urbain 1996b, 8–15). Despite these efforts, on 17 April 1996, the European Commission, with seven out of fifteen members present, voted five to two in favor of the proposal to allow up to 5 percent MGV in chocolate and to permit manufacturers to use the official designation of "chocolate" (*Nouvel observateur*, 16–22 May 1996; *Libération*, 19 April 1996).

This decision generated heated debate and renewed lobbying efforts by opponents. For their part, cocoa-producing nations estimated that the new directive would sharply reduce exports of cacao beans to Europe, the biggest importer of African beans, and would create a 20 percent drop in cocoa prices on the global cocoa exchange, generating losses as high as $780 million a year for producer nations (*Revue de presse*, 6 November 1997).

After months of intense negotiations, on 23 October 1997, the European Parliament voted overwhelmingly in favor of the purist position. Although members upheld the 1996 Commission ruling permitting the addition of MGV, they delayed its application until a reliable testing method could be found to determine its exact proportion in chocolate. The Parliament mandated that the designation "quality chocolate" was exclusively reserved for products made with cocoa butter. An important amendment stipulated that manufacturers who use MGV would be required to put a consumer label on the front of the wrapper indicating the addition of a "noncocoa substitute." The Parliament also directly targeted English and Irish milk chocolates by forcing them to rename their products because, according to European standards, they contained too much milk and not enough cocoa solids (interview with Alain Grangé, 15 May 1998; *Libération*, 24 October 1997; *New York Times*, 24 October 1997; *Revue de presse*, 6 November 1997).

The French press, cultural tastemakers, and government representatives opposed the 1996 Commission ruling on the basis of preserving quality and purity. One French journalist exclaimed, "It's a crime of no taste, of the least discriminating palate, of the smothered taste bud. . . . Think of it—soy in hot chocolate, palm oil in the *ganache*, colza oil in chocolate mousse, and who knows what in the *truffle*, the *éclair* or the candy center" (*Nouvel observateur*, 16–22 May 1996). In contrast, the British framed the debate in terms of the free market and common sense. Caroline Jackson, a British member of the European Parliament, fumed: "Debates over food should be about safety, not about what makes a chocolate bar really chocolate . . . this isn't radioactive" (*New York Times*, 24 October 1997). Compare the defense of the use of cocoa butter equivalents by manufacturers in the United Kingdom, Denmark, and the Republic of Ireland (Talbot 1994, 247).

The campaign waged against MGV continues unabated. On 18 January 1999 Guy Urbain led a delegation to the European parliament in Strasbourg, armed with more than 4,000 petitions from irate Basque coast consumers collected by Patrick Sarlate, President of the Guild of Chocolatiers in Bayonne. The Vice-President of the Académie du Chocolat de Bayonne, Jean Labadie, expressed his anger at the economic folly of the European Commission directive: "We are going to buy vegetable additives from countries like Malaysia and create havoc in African cocoa producing nations. And then to ease our conscience we will rebate to the Africans 20% of what we spent on the additives. It will cost therefore as much [as making chocolate with cocoa butter] but instead of eating real chocolate we will be eating shit." Sarlate and Bayonnais municipal leaders have organized a local debate on the question on 22 March 2000.

## Chapter 3.    Reeducating French Palates

1. See the interview with Lenôtre recorded for Champs-Elysées 1988, series 6, number 9.

2. I interviewed Alexandre Sacerdoti, the president of Valrhona, in his office at company headquarters in Tain-l'Hermitage on Monday, 11 May 1998.

3. The craft of *chocolatier* was progressively mechanized over the nineteenth and twentieth centuries, provoking a two-stage restructuring. First, small and medium-sized family *chocolatiers* who mechanized their workshops displaced craftsmen manually producing chocolate from beans (an arduous process involving ground beans on heated stones virtually unchanged since pre-Columbian days). These small-scale family producers were in turn definitively displaced by large-scale industrial manufacturers. The first machines for grinding cacao beans were invented in the late eighteenth century and adopted slowly and sporadically by French firms. It was during the nineteenth century that the production of chocolate from fermented cacao beans was rationalized and broken down into separate processing phases for which specialized machines were developed (Barbaret 1887; Harwich 1992). By the 1950s, the fabrication of chocolate and cocoa had shifted entirely to industrialized mass production. See chapter 4 for more detail.

4. Cacao beans are removed from ripe pods and allowed to ferment naturally in the sun or artificially in ovens. This is critical because the complex chemical changes that occur during this process give chocolate its distinctive taste and aroma. The fermented beans are dried, bagged, and shipped to processing plants in Europe or North America. Upon their arrival they are cleaned, hulled, and roasted. Next, they are shattered into large fragments called nibs, then mixed with pulverized sugar, heated, and, finally, ground under intense pressure. This produces a thick, dark mass called chocolate liquor, which serves as the basis for chocolate and cocoa. The liquor is subjected to high pressure to extract the fat or cocoa butter. The residual cake-like mass (chocolate press cake) is ground to produce cocoa powder. In an additional processing phase, cocoa butter (or vegetable fat equivalents or replacers, since cocoa butter can be sold to the pharmaceutical industry at a handsome profit) is added and the combined mass refined by multiple rollers, in a process known as conching for fifty to ninety-six hours to ensure smoothness and impart flavor (Minifie 1989).

5. A series of record harvests, the cultivation of robust cocoa trees on Ivory Coast plantations, and the emergence of Malaysian and Indonesian cacao growths produced a glut of beans on the world market and lowered prices (Harwich 1992, 226–227).

6. The Day of Taste has become the Week of Tastes held every October in France. During this week, food professionals provide demonstrations in schools and their own businesses to educate children as well as adults in the subtleties of taste differentiation.

7. See Coady 1995; Constant 1988; Girard 1984; Jolly 1983; *Le guide des croqueurs du chocolat* 1988; Linxe 1992; Robert 1990; and Schiaffino and Cluizel 1988.

8. On 1 May 1998, I conducted a telephone interview with Bernard Duclos, Valrhona executive vice president for sales and marketing in North America. He explained that the Valrhona marketing strategy was premised on the creation of a brand name based on the highest quality, pure (no cocoa butter equivalents or replacers) dark chocolate made from 98 percent criollo beans, grown to order on plantations in Venezuela and Indonesia. He speculated that the idea for adopting a wine connoisseur taste standard arose naturally from the location of company headquarters in Tain-l'Hermitage, amid numerous Rhône valley vineyards. Mr. Duclos refused to discuss Valrhona's total production volume, market share, or marketing budget.

9. Incomplete knowledge about *couverture* among artisanal *chocolatiers* produces curious results in texts published as authoritative taste guides. For example, a recent chocolate connoisseur guide rates chocolates organized by small, medium, and large commercial producers and lists the raw materials or *couverture* used in their production (Coady 1995). When asked about the source of their *couverture,* some producers refused to divulge house secrets. Those who did described *couverture* in terms of some combination of four different factors: mere verification that the manufacturer was French; the propriety brand name of the industrial manufacturers who share the French market, such as Valrhona, Cacao Barry, Callebaut, Weiss; the variety of cacao bean, such as criollos; and the geographical region where the cacao was or is cultivated, such as Guanaja.

10. In 1923, the Gold Coast exported 197,000 tons of cacao, more than the entire combined cacao production of the Americas (Harwich 1992, 190).

11. The discovery and incorporation of chocolate into European foodways generated a plethora of conflicting moral and medical attributes relating to it. A series of historical texts published in the seventeenth and eighteenth centuries detailed differing medical opinions. The debate in humoral medicine centered on whether chocolate was a hot or cold substance and what humors it was likely to provoke given the temperaments of the people who drank it. Spanish authorities considered chocolate to be a dry, cold food and judged the addition of hot substances such as cinnamon, cloves, anise, amber, and musk necessary to temper and balance its cold properties (Colmenero de Ledesma 1644). One writer even declared chocolate to be a "cold poison"; no additives could make it safe to drink (Maradon 1618, quoted in Peeters 1989). These same scholars also warned that excessive, or even regular, consumption of chocolate could cause weight loss and other weaknesses.

French scholars writing in the eighteenth century, a period of French ascendancy and power in Europe, refuted the prevalent Spanish views. In his comprehensive *Encyclopédie, ou dictionnaire raisonné des arts et des métiers, par une société des gens de lettres,* Diderot argued strongly for a pure chocolate drink free from the spices that overheated the body and posed health hazards (1751–1772, iii, 360). The widely read French cleric Jean-Baptiste Labat also insisted that chocolate was, by virtue of its oily and bitter properties, a hot food (Labat 1742, iii, 368).

12. Physician Hervé Robert's text (1990), enthusiastically greeted by *choco-*

*latiers,* attempted to disprove by scientific means all of the myths concerning chocolate's deleterious effects.

13. Chocolate contains more than 300 identified substances, including theobromine and methylxanthine—two mildly addictive, caffeine-like substances—and phenylethylamine, a stimulant chemically similar to the human body's own dopamine and adrenaline (Young 1994, 13).

## Chapter 4.   Unsettling Memories

1. Local historians and educated Bayonnais whom I knew chronicled the city's history by referring to the passage of important persons: from the armies of the French monarch Charles VII, who besieged and reconquered Bayonne in 1451, ending three centuries of English rule, to the forces of General Charles de Gaulle, whose 1944 arrival in Bayonne marked liberation from the German occupation of the Atlantic coast. This chronicle may have as much to do with a persistent French preoccupation with elite culture and history as it does with the desire to refute received notions of Bayonne as a provincial backwater. It also speaks to the way the French are still taught history. They memorize events that emphasize the centripetal forces of national centralization as well as the centrifugal forces that threaten it.

2. With the exception of a brief interlude of a leftist municipal council headed by a Socialist mayor from 1945 to 1947, postwar councils have been dominated by centrist politicians from business and professional backgrounds.

3. Since the 1970s, tourism in the Atlantic Pyrenees department has developed in two different directions: upscale and popular. On the one hand, the number of two-, three-, and four-star hotels increased, as did the occupancy rate for these hotels between 1975 and 1990. The number of vacation residences on the Basque coast multiplied from 7,954 in 1968 to 19,485 in 1990. On the other hand, Basque coast campgrounds increased their capacity from 29,800 campers to 34,038 between 1977 and 1990 (Pyrénées Atlantiques 1994).

4. The southwest boasts myriad recreational and sports activities in the Pyrenees mountains to the south, in picturesque Basque villages inland to the east, and on miles of rocky coastline and beaches. These include water and snow skiing, surfing, wind surfing, cycling, hiking, golf, tennis, jai alai, and bullfights in the arena in Bayonne and nearby Dax as well as the summer heritage festivals held in the coastal towns.

5. Historically, there has been relatively little industrial development either on the coast or inland. Since 1963, DATAR, the state government agency created to stimulate industrial growth in rural, underdeveloped regions in the west and southwest of France, has been only moderately successful in attracting high technology industries to the region.

6. One much-quoted local historian disputed Bayonne as the genesis of French chocolate production and was equally skeptical about the role presumably played by Portuguese Jews in introducing it to the southwest. However, he did not dispute the fact that Jews practiced the craft there (Cuzacq 1949). In contrast, other prominent Bayonnais historians (Constantin 1933; Hourmat 1990; Léon 1893) argued that Jews introduced chocolate making to Bayonne.

7. French monarchs intervened repeatedly to reaffirm the original rights accorded Portuguese Jews in the southwest. These rights were officially registered with the Parliament of Paris in 1550 and reconfirmed by Henry III in 1574, Louis XIV in 1656, who specifically addressed the Jews in Bayonne, and Louis XV in 1723 and 1754 (Nahon 1981). This intervention did not, however, end ongoing religious anti-Judaism or prevent the emergence of racist anti-Semitism in the nineteenth century.

8. The 1822 Commercial Register of Bayonne listed fifteen *chocolatiers* in the Petit and Grand Bayonne neighborhoods. The register did not include the neighborhood of Saint Esprit because it was a part of the contiguous Landes department from 1789 to 1857. By 1856, the Bayonne commercial almanac listed thirty-one *chocolatiers* in Bayonne. This number shrank to seven in the 1936 register of commerce and trades located in the archives of the Bayonne Chamber of Commerce and Industry. Of these seven, only five made chocolate from cacao beans and the remaining two purchased semi-finished chocolate *couverture*.

9. The history of the Dalbaitz house necessarily involves the trajectories of two craft families, the Dalbaitz who founded it and the Joliots, a craft family from Pau who purchased it and currently operate it. The history of this house is also linked with that of the Etchegaray house because the founder of the Dalbaitz house apprenticed there. The trajectories of these two houses remain intertwined. Madame Rénaud-Etchegaray, a direct descendant of the founder, is currently the president of the newly created Académie du Chocolat de Bayonne (1994) and works closely with the head of the Guild of Chocolatiers (1994) and Bayonnais *chocolatier* Patrick Sarlate, the husband of Hélène Joliot Sarlate. I collected a history of the Joliot house in Pau from Maurice Joliot, who apprenticed in the Pau family workshop between 1938 and 1939 and worked as head of production from 1945 until his retirement in 1978. Joliot declined to discuss World War II and divided his story into a pre- and postwar narrative. In a separate interview, I collected a similar history from his wife Odette, who in 1991 was still working part time, forty-four years after her entry into the business. I also interviewed Odette's daughter, Sylvie Joliot, who operated the business with her husband, Bernard. Maurice Joliot's first cousin Paul began work in the Bayonne workshop in 1939, but he had passed away in 1986. Therefore, my chronicle of that workshop had to begin in the immediate postwar period and it was made possible by study of family archives, commercial archives, and Chamber of Trade archives, as well as detailed recollections of Paul Joliot's wife, his daughter, Hélène, son-in-law, Patrick Sarlate, the granddaughter of the founder of the Dalbaitz house, Brigitte Ustaritz, and one retired artisan, Dora Hublon, who spent her entire working life there. I tape-recorded a two-hour interview with Dora Hublon in her home on 14 March 1991. In order to reconstruct the history of the Etchegaray house, I conducted two formal interviews, a one-hour interview with Madame Rénaud-Etchegaray and a separate three-hour interview with Madame Rénaud-Etchegaray (1925– ), her husband, Dr. Charles Rénaud, and a retired Etchegaray worker, Michel Carré (1925– ). Michel Carré entered the business six months after France declared war on Germany in 1939 and worked there until it closed in 1953. I also conducted two follow-up telephone interviews with Madame Rénaud. All of the names of consultants and the confectionery houses on the Basque coast have been changed to protect their anonymity.

10. Of the chocolate *couverture* made at the Etchegaray house, 90 percent was dark, and the remaining 10 percent was milk chocolate. Madame Rénaud, Auguste Etchegaray's granddaughter, never heard the word *ganache* used to describe the few creamy centers made in her family's workshop. She reminded me that the label *ganache* was commonly used for a stupid or inept person.

11. The intense concentration of chocolate manufacture over the past twenty-five years is evident in the evolution of the Tobler company. Founded in 1867, it merged with the Swiss multinational Suchard in 1974 to form Interfood. Its subsequent purchase by the Jacobs-Suchard group in 1982 was a mere prelude to a relentless series of acquisitions including the Dutch firm Van Houten in 1986 and the Belgian company Côte d'Or in 1987. In June 1990 the whole Jacobs-Suchard group itself was acquired by an American tobacco consortium, Phillip Morris (Harwich 1992, 234).

12. In Bayonne, it seems that some *chocolatiers* refused to work exclusively for the French population. La Maison des Rois, located on the Port Neuf, closed immediately after the war. Although I could find no official explanation for its closure in the Chamber of Commerce archives, three elderly Bayonnais independently confirmed that the business was closed because its owner had openly collaborated with the Nazi occupiers. As one gentleman put it, "La Maison des Rois, was also *la maison des Allemands* [the house of the Germans], and its pretty owner had her head shaved in public as a result. She left Bayonne immediately after that." This incident was confirmed by two other Bayonnais. Monsieur Carrère was a teenager during the war and went to school with the owner's son. "Well, I can't say if his mother collaborated or not. All I know is that he was the only kid I knew who had his pockets stuffed with chocolate all the time." Another couple confirmed this but expressed their strong displeasure that I raised the issue. I was at their house for a late afternoon tea and was discussing the sudden closure of the Maison des Rois as a punishment for collaboration. The husband was a retired engineer who had taken a great interest in my research. His wife glared at me over her cup and said sarcastically, "Thank you, Madame, for reminding us of our history."

13. It is important to issue a caveat regarding the reliability of commercial records in France. A number of factors make them problematic as a source of reliable information. First, owners of craft businesses combining production and sales activities must register with both the Chamber of Commerce and Industry and the Chamber of Trades. In reality, most businesses register only with one, not both. In gathering historical data from the early 1920s on (when the Chambers of Trades were created), it is necessary to check records from both the Chamber of Trades and the Chamber of Commerce. However, the Bayonne Chamber of Trades had no prewar archives and those of the Chamber of Commerce were incomplete and improperly catalogued for the interwar period. Second, commercial records are supposed to be updated when an existing business is sold, fails, or changes its productive capacity. Since business failures are high in some crafts, some go unreported. A far greater problem involves the nature of production because changes are rarely reported. Some of these problems became apparent as I compared my knowledge of existing businesses in 1991 based on family archives with the "official" archive. An example from the Bourriet business will illustrate. Records from 1991 showed 1978 as the date when the business

opened. This was inaccurate. The business was created in 1946 by the Bourriets, who sold it in 1978 to the current owners. The dominant productive activity was listed as pastry making in 1978. This too was wrong. By 1991 the owners had earned a national reputation as *chocolatiers*. Although they still maintained the same confectionery boutique in downtown Biarritz, they also served as wholesalers of a line of house specialties to a national network of pastry makers.

14. Patrick Sarlate purchased his chocolate, as did his wife's cousins in Pau, from the two major French suppliers of industrial *couverture* to small producers: Valrhona and Cacao Barry.

## Chapter 5.   What's in a Name?

1. This was a state requirement that, in the southwest at least, was not enforced. Nonetheless, employers and workers alike considered the master artisan diploma a rigorous credential guaranteeing an advanced level of empirical skill as well as a theoretical understanding of craft materials and management principles.

2. See Rogers (1991, 77–78) for a discussion of the Aveyronnais *ostal,* where both the patronym and the place name were constituent elements in the identity of persons and family farms.

3. A cardinal rule among craft families was never to divulge their own particular political views. Craft families also agreed on the necessity to avoid potentially divisive topics such as politics and religion in the boutique and to choose politically neutral themes for their seasonal window displays. In 1989 the intersection of political history and confectionery traditions produced an interesting polemic. Early in that year many owners of *chocolateries* were preparing to commemorate the bicentennial of the French Revolution through their annual Easter window displays. The owners of a confectionery house in the sixteenth administrative district in Paris (a high-status, conservative area) had her fears about the divisiveness of this theme. Therefore, in the Epiphany cakes *(galettes des rois)* sold in early January, they placed gold-plated busts of revolutionary figures in lieu of the traditional ceramic beans said to bring good luck in the New Year. One customer who found the bust of Robespierre, architect of the Revolutionary Reign of Terror, returned to the boutique in a rage and threw it on the counter exclaiming that she would never keep the bust of a "filthy regicide" in her house. Their fears confirmed, the owners avoided the display of chocolate guillotines and *sans-culottes* in red freedom caps for Easter. Commemoration of the bicentennial in *chocolateries* was also avoided in western France, where local *chouans* were persecuted for their fierce opposition to the 1789 Revolution and to the imposition of Republican rule following the overthrow of the monarchy.

4. My conclusions concerning consumers' confectionery knowledge were confirmed by all of the saleswomen in my research sample and also by a 1990 state study of the craft commissioned by the Office of Artisanship within the Ministry of Commerce and Artisanship at the request of the professional organization of *chocolatiers*.

5. The relations among women and the rules governing linguistic forms of address were different from those obtaining between craftsmen in the work-

shop. Women who were structural equals sometimes used one another's first name but avoided the familiar form of address prevalent in French work settings among those in the same profession or job. This may have had at least something to do with the projection of a bourgeois image in the boutique. In a bourgeois social milieu, the familiar *tu* is used relatively less than the formal *vous*. Some wives emphasized their superordinate position with sales help by opting for this familiar form of address with them. Others used the *tu* form only with sales help whom they had known over a long period of time and with whom they maintained warm personal relations. Still others avoided the familial idiom informing the traditional encompassing role of the *patronne* in the boutique and consciously used the polite *vous* form even if they had very cordial, personalized relations.

## Chapter 6.    "Our craft is beautiful . . ."

1. Confectionery house owners justified the high prices they charge—compared to supermarkets and franchises—based on their small-scale, skilled-based mode of production and sales. Many used the following formula for establishing prices for goods produced on the premises: the price of raw materials multiplied by 6. They explained that this coefficient was necessary in order to amortize the costs of the commercial property, lease, labor, machinery, taxes, and so forth.

2. When it was first created in 1947, the Bonbonnière was not a confectionery house in the strict sense of the term because it did not combine production and sales activities. A family name was not given to this business because it was created by an unmarried woman who merely resold candies made elsewhere. Although a line of candies was produced on the premises first by Monsieur LeBlanc and later by his son, the irregular living situation of the first artisanal couple explains why the house name was never formally changed.

3. Madame Carrère was referring to (1) the 1956 prenuptial agreement, (2) the formal partnership of her husband and her mother-in-law established in 1966 following Louis Carrère's death, (3) the substitution of Simon Carrère as partner in the place of his grandmother, Gracie Carrère, after her death in 1983, and (4) the formal transfer of control to Simon Carrère in 1991.

4. The De Closets were so attractive as successors because they were looking for an inexpensive piece of commercial property, were cash buyers, and Monsieur De Closet had both training and experience working in chocolate, albeit an industrial chocolate factory.

5. Prices of *pâtisseries* and *chocolateries* were based on a number of factors, the most important being yearly sales turnover. Commercial real estate agents determined the market value of the house by taking 75–100 percent of the average sales turnover of the three years preceding the sale. Although they also looked at net profit, they normally gave more weight to annual sales, adjusting the market value upward or downward based on the business location (proximity to public transportation and other retail outlets), the amount of the monthly lease, the length of time remaining on the lease (in cases where craft families did not own the "walls" or building in which the house is located), the age and con-

dition of equipment included, and the physical plant (the amount of floor space and condition of the building) (Bonnard 1991).

6. Despite its prime location, local craft families considered the asking price very high because most estimated that an equivalent sum would be needed to expand and modernize both the workshop and the boutique.

7. Sarlate was reelected in 1983, 1989, and 1995 and in 1995 was appointed assistant mayor for cultural affairs.

8. The three Joliot daughters were married with prenuptial contracts excluding their spouses from accumulated family assets including legal title to the business. In 1991 Hélène Sarlate and her mother held title to the business and split the profits equally.

## Chapter 7.   Craft as Community, Chocolate as Spectacle

1. The brotherhood emphasis on Aztec origin myths and ceremonial rituals associated with chocolate ignores the history of the origin of domesticated chocolate among the Olmecs (1500–400 B.C.), the Mixe-Zoqueans, the ancestors of the Olmec-derived culture called Izapan, and the Classic Maya (A.D. 250–900) of the lowlands of the Yucatán peninsula and northern Guatemala. Elegantly painted or carved vessels found in the tombs of Maya elites revealed that chocolate was consumed in a complex variety of forms—in Maya drinks, gruels, porridge, powders, and probably solid substances to which numerous flavorings were added (Coe and Coe 1996, 36–66).

2. A *chocolatier* from Bordeaux, one from Lyon, and thirteen of their *confrères* joined forces to create the first chapter. They wrote the brotherhood's charter and commissioned a Parisian couturier to design the processional robe and headdress. In January 1997, there were twenty-nine Confrérie chapters in France.

Brotherhood elders pay for their own transportation and lodging, but local organizers finance their meals and entertainment in the host city.

3. In Dorinne Kondo's excellent study of confectionery craft work in contemporary Tokyo (1990), she usefully challenges teleologies of manual work as alienation in advanced capitalism and connects the construction of artisanal identities to salient Japanese notions of work, social personhood, family household *(ie)*, and a larger political economy in flux. However, her account gives very little sense of how workers construct and affirm their identities as confectioners, not simply artisans. We have no idea how individual confectioners assert and maintain membership within a larger craft community beyond the workplace. Kondo reveals the tension between a traditional work ethos embodied by older artisans and the increasingly rationalized managerial and entrepreneurial practices favored by the family owners of the workplace that was the focus of her ethnographic research. However, we do not know whether this tension is pervasive, concealing divergent ways of conceiving and performing craft work, or masks the existence of competing interests among owners of confectioneries in Tokyo and outlying areas.

4. Apprentices were paid a percentage of the minimum wage based on their age and experience on the job. Their salaries increased incrementally up to a maximum of 75 percent of the minimum wage (Bayonne Chamber of Trades 1991).

5. Craft families were extremely reluctant to disclose financial information of any kind, and when they did it was offered with the proviso that I not publish it. However, one evening in the master artisan class, Monsieur Bergeron was the guest artisan and he talked about trade economics, specifically, the formula used to calculate retail prices. He instructed them to multiply the price of the raw materials by a factor of six. In the year 1990–91, Bourriet chocolates retailed for 280F, or $60 a kilo.

6. The *brevet de technologie supérieure* (BTS) is a two-year business studies diploma, following completion of the baccalaureate degree, where instruction was provided within the vocational secondary school *(lycée d'enseignement professionnel)*.

7. Artistic pieces could not be more than 50 centimeters long, 40–50 centimeters wide, and 65 centimeters high (Concours de Chocolatiers 1991, 2).

## Chapter 8.    From Craft to Profession?

1. The choice of Madame Lombard as president of the judging panel was a strategic one. See below.

2. The full name of the confederation is La Confédération Nationale des Détaillants et Artisans-Détaillants de la Confiserie, Chocolaterie, et Biscuiterie.

3. See Agulhon 1994; CEREQ 1994; Bachelard 1994; Baudelot and Mauger 1994; Cambon 1993; Gehin 1993.

4. This avant-garde included statesman Jean Monnet, Socialist politician Pierre Mendès-France, the Servan Schreiber family, and journalist Françoise Giroud. They wanted to create a new class of university-educated middle managers to challenge and reform the pre–World War II hierarchical structure of industry in which small entrepreneurs were pitted against workers. They helped to shape a view of postwar society further refined by French sociologists in terms of its rising and declining sectors. *Cadres,* the salaried bourgeoisie, represented the new middle class and were defined as progressive in contrast to older middle classes, particularly the petite bourgeoisie, destined to disappear altogether.

5. For example, vocational diplomas earned after the completion of the secondary cycle lead to special university programs that prepare students for technical supervisory positions in industry. They do not lead to higher public university degrees and, even less, to the most prestigious institutions that train the nation's elite, the Grandes Ecoles.

6. I have reconstructed a history of the confederation from consultation of the journal it publishes, *La confiserie,* from 1920 to the present and from dozens of hours of formal and informal interviews with activists and board members Francis Boucher, Françoise Boucher (no relation to Francis Boucher), René Chaleix and his wife, Christian Chambeau, Jacques Daumoinx, Benoît Digeon, Alain Grangé, Suzanne Lioret, Madeleine Lombard, and Guy Urbain and son, Alain Urbain. I also interviewed the principal, Mademoiselle Sauvage, teachers, and staff at the Paris School for the Food Trades.

7. The CAP in pastry making (also encompassing sugar candy, ice cream, and chocolate) was established in 1955.

8. These contracts date to 1936, when a series of paralyzing labor strikes prompted the Popular Front government of Socialist Prime Minister Léon Blum to institute the first mandatory collective bargaining agreements for all trades and industries. These state-mandated agreements bring together representatives of employers' and workers' associations in order to determine shop floor regulations, wages, and labor benefits. These agreements are renegotiated annually.

## Chapter 9.    Defending the Local

1. Unlike most French departments, which have one Chamber of Trades, the department of the Atlantic Pyrenees has two, one in the west in Bayonne and the other in the east in Pau. Here I center on the Bayonne Chamber of Trades.

2. All French public school teachers are employees of the highly centralized Ministry of National Education. They are certified by state examination, hired, assigned to specific teaching posts, and paid by the state.

3. Two of the most reputable private schools providing training in both production and sales in the food crafts are the Lenôtre school outside Paris (founded by the renowned pastry chef and *chocolatier* Gaston Lenôtre) and the Ecole Nationale Supérieure at Yssingeaux near Lyon, created and administered by the National Confederation of Pastry Makers. The name of the latter evokes the most selective public universities in France, the Grandes Ecoles, which provide advanced graduate education in the humanities (Ecole Normale Supérieure), public administration (Ecole Nationale d'Administration), social science (Ecole des Hautes Etudes en Sciences Sociales), mathematics and science (Ecole Polytechnique), and business (Hautes Etudes Commerciales).

4. From five founding members in 1960, the center's membership grew to a high of 600 in 1985 before dropping slightly to 550 in February 1991. The center president, Madame Bourguignon, noted that the membership statistics did not accurately reflect the numbers of women who received training in the center's seminars. She estimated that number to be five times the total membership.

5. The organizers estimated attendance to be 30–40 percent lower than usual due to the depressed business climate created by the 1991 Gulf War.

## Chapter 10.    Chocolate as Self and Other

1. See Coe and Coe (1996) for a description of the adulteration and misuse of chocolate.

2. The *chocolatiers* and tastemakers who promote chocolate through their texts, lectures, and tastings purport to present objective and authoritative histories of its discovery and early use. Unlike professional historians, they repeat identical incidents liberally adapted from historical accounts, often cite quotations without giving bibliographic references, and do not provide complete and accurate lists of works cited. On the other hand, these strategies are very effective in the construction of mythologies; strict empirical accuracy cannot serve their particular ends.

3. This essentialized rendering ignores the complex realities of class-based uses and social rituals surrounding chocolate in Mayan and Aztec culture as well as the tremendous variety of foods in which chocolate was an ingredient. Mayans added chile as well as many local flavorings such as vanilla and "ear flower" to their chocolates (Coe and Coe 1996, 64), just as the Aztecs used numerous flavorings from local flowers and plants to produce many varieties of spicy and sweetened chocolate (Coe and Coe 1996, 88–93).

4. This is significant because there is no evidence to support the claim that Aztecs viewed chocolate as an aphrodisiac; in fact, it was viewed as a culturally appropriate and pleasingly exotic replacement for *octli*, a mildly alcoholic native drink surrounded with ambivalence in Aztec society, where the usual penalty for drunkenness was death (Coe and Coe 1996, 77–78).

5. This incident is taken from Thomas Gage, English chronicler of Mesoamerican Indian life in the colonial period (1958 [1648], 143–145).

6. I include the images and texts found in the new chocolate literature and promotional venues such as commercial chocolate shows as a form of advertising along with billboards, product packaging, TV commercials, and window displays. All had aimed to represent French chocolate in ways that would increase consumer demand for it.

7. I would like to thank Michelle Williams formerly of J. Walter Thompson agency in New York for sharing this clip of the Nestlé television advertisement.

# References

Agulhon, Catherine. 1994. *L'enseignement professionnel: quel avenir pour les jeunes?* Paris: Éditions de l'Atelier / Éditions Ouvrières.

*Almanach commercial de Bayonne.* Bayonne, 1856.

Aminzade, Ronald. 1981. *Class, politics, and early industrial capitalism.* Albany: State University of New York Press.

Appadurai, Arjun, ed. 1986. *The social life of things.* Cambridge: Cambridge University Press.

Appadurai, Arjun. 1988. "How to make a national cuisine: cook books in contemporary India." *Comparative studies in society and history* 30 (1): 3–24.

Aragon, Louis. 1936. *Les beaux quartiers.* Paris: Denoël and Steele.

Aranzadi, Thomas de. 1920. "La pierre à chocolat en Espagne." *Revue d'ethnographie et des traditions populaires* 1: 169–173.

Aretxaga, Begoña. 1997. *Shattering silence: women, nationalism, and political subjectivity in Northern Ireland.* Princeton: Princeton University Press.

Argonne, Bonaventure d'. 1713. *Mélanges d'histoire et de littérature.* Paris: Claude Prudhomme.

Asad, Talal, ed. 1973. *Anthropology and the colonial encounter.* New York: Humanities Press.

Assier-Andrieu, Louis. 1981. *Coutume et rapports sociaux: étude anthropologique des communautés paysannes du Capcir.* Paris: Centre National de la Recherche Scientifique.

Augé, Marc. 1994. *Pour une anthropologie des mondes contemporains.* Paris: Aubier.

Auslander, Leora. 1996. *Taste and power: furnishing modern France.* Studies on the History of Society and Culture, vol. 24. Chicago: University of Chicago Press.

Auvolat, Michel. 1985. *L'artisanat en France.* Paris: La Documentation Française.

Azéma, Jean-Pierre. 1979. *De Munich à la libération.* Paris: Seuil.

Babcock, Barbara. 1995. "Marketing Maria: the tribal artist in the age of mechanical reproduction." In Brenda Jo Bright and Lisa Bakewell, eds., *Looking high and low: art and cultural identity*, 124–150. Tucson: University of
Arizona Press.

Bachelard, Paul. 1982. *L'artisanat dans l'espace français*. Paris: Masson.

———. 1994. *Apprentissage et pratiques d'alternance*. Paris: L'Harmattan.

Badone, Ellen. 1991. "Ethnography, fiction, and the meanings of the past in
Brittany." *American ethnologist* 18 (3): 518–545.

Bakewell, Lisa. 1995. "Belles artes and artes populaires: the implications of difference in the Mexico City art world." In Brenda Jo Bright and Lisa Bakewell, eds., *Looking high and low: art and cultural identity*, 19–54. Tucson:
University of Arizona Press.

Balibar, Etienne. 1988. *Race, nation, classe: les identités ambiguës*. Paris:
La Découverte.

Barbaret, Joseph. 1887. *Monographies professionnelles, IV*. Paris: Berger-Levrault.

Bataille, Georges. 1985. *Visions of excess: selected writings, 1927–1939*. Translated
and edited by Allan Stoekl. Theory and History of Literature, no.14. Minneapolis, MN: University of Minneapolis Press.

Baudelot, Christian, and Roger Establet. 1974. *La petite bourgeoisie*. Paris:
Minuit.

Baudelot, Christian, and Roger Mauger. 1994. *Jeunesses populaires: les généra-
tions de la crise*. Paris: L'Harmattan.

Baudrillard, Jean. 1981. *For a critique of the political economy of the sign*. Translated by Charles Levin. St. Louis: Telos Press.

Bayonne Archives Municipales. N.d. HH 189: 435–446.

Bayonne Chamber of Trades Archives. 1991.

Beckett, S. T., ed. 1994. *Industrial chocolate manufacture and use*, 2d ed.,
8–24. London: Blackie Academic and Professional.

Bédier, J. 1991. "Réflexions sur la profession." *La confiserie* 296: 41–47.

Bendix, Regina. 1997. *In search of authenticity: the formation of folklore*. Madi-
son: University of Wisconsin Press.

Bénéton, Pierre. 1975. *Histoire de mots: culture et civilisation*. Paris: Fondation
Nationale de Sciences Politiques.

Benjamin, Walter. 1969 [1936]. "The work of art in the age of mechanical
production." In Hannah Arendt, ed., *Illuminations: essays and reflections*,
219–223. Translated by Harry Zohn. New York: Harcourt, Brace.

Bérard, Laurence, and Philippe Marcheney. 1995. "Lieux, temps et preuves:
la construction sociale des produits de terroir." *Terrain* 24: 153–164.

Bernachon, Maurice, and Jean-Jacques Bernachon. 1985. *La passion du chocolat*.
Paris: Flammarion.

Bertaux, Daniel, and Isabelle Bertaux-Wiame. 1978. *Transformations et per-
manence de l'artisanat boulanger en France*. Paris: Maison des Sciences
de l'Homme.

Bertaux, Daniel, Jacqueline Dufrene, and Françoise Kersebet. 1983. *Evolution, technologie, investissements, et conditions de travail dans la boulangerie artisanale*. Paris: Action Thématique Programmée/Travail-Emploi-
Conditions de Travail, Centre National de Recherche Scientifique.

Bestor, Theodore. 1992. "The raw, the cooked, and the industrial: commoditization and food culture in a Japanese commodities market." Paper delivered at Department of Anthropology, New York University.

Betbeder, Marie. 1991. "Etre apprenti aujourd'hui." *Le monde de l'éducation* 185: 44–46.

*Biarritz: au vent du large et de l'histoire.* 1988. Biarritz: Maury.

Blanchard, Richard. 1909. "Survivances ethnographiques au Mexique." *Journal de la Société des Américanistes,* n.s., 6.

Blasquez, Adélaïde. 1976. *Gaston Lucas, serrurier.* Paris: Plon.

Bloch, Ernst. 1977. "Nonsynchronism and the obligation to its dialectics." *New German critique* 11: 22–38.

Boltanski, Luc. 1988. *The making of a class: cadres in French society.* Translated by Arthur Goldhammer. Cambridge: Cambridge University Press.

Bonnard, F. 1991. *Petite entreprise: un expert comptable vous conseille.* Paris: Les Editions d'Organisation.

Borne, Dominique. 1977. *Petits bourgeois en révolte? Le mouvement poujade.* Paris: Flammarion.

Bourdieu, Pierre. 1977. *Outline of a theory of practice.* Translated by Richard Nice. Cambridge: Cambridge University Press.

———. 1984. *Distinction: a social critique of the judgement of taste.* Translated by Richard Nice. Cambridge: Harvard University Press.

Bradburd, Daniel. 1995. "Marketing backwardness: Sardinian cheese, authenticity, and the production of a commodity." Paper delivered at the annual meeting of the American Anthropological Association.

Braudel, Fernand. 1967. *Civilisation matérielle et capitalisme (xve–xviiie siècles).* Paris: Armand Colin.

Braverman, Harry. 1974. *Labor and monopoly capital.* New York: Monthly Review Press.

Brettell, Caroline. 1995. *We have already cried many tears: the stories of three Portuguese migrant women.* Prospect Heights, IL: Waveland Press.

Bright, Brenda Jo. 1995. "Introduction." In Brenda Jo Bright and Lisa Bakewell, eds., *Looking high and low: art and cultural identity,* 1–18. Tucson: University of Arizona Press.

Brillat-Savarin, Jean Anthelme. 1839 [1826]. *Physiologie du goût ou méditations de gastronomie transcendente ouvrage théorique, historique, et à l'ordre du jour.* Paris: Charpentier.

Bringa, Tone. 1995. *Being Muslim the Bosnian way.* Princeton: Princeton University Press.

Bruner, Edward, M. 1994. "Abraham Lincoln as authentic reproduction: a critique of postmodernism." *American anthropologist* 16 (2): 397–415.

Buechler, Hans. 1989. "Apprenticeship and transmission of knowledge in La Paz, Bolivia." In Michael Coy, ed., *Apprenticeship: from theory to method and back again,* 31–50. Albany: State University of New York Press.

Buroway, Michael. 1985. *The politics of production: factory regimes under capitalism.* London: Verso.

*Calendrier commercial de Bayonne.* 1822.

Cambon, Christian, with Patrick Butor. 1993. *La bataille de l'apprentissage: une réponse au chômage des jeunes.* Paris: Descartes.

Capdevielle, Jacques, Hélène Meynard, and René Mouriaux. 1990. *Petits bou-*

*lots et grand marché.* Paris: Presses de la Fondation Nationale des Sciences Politiques.

Carrier, James. 1995a. *Gifts and commodities.* London: Routledge.

Carrier, James, ed. 1995b. *Occidentalism. images of the West.* Oxford: Clarendon Press.

Casella, Philippe. 1989. *La profession de chocolatier.* Paris: Agence Nationale pour le Développement de l'Education Permanente.

Céreq. 1994. Apprenticeship: which way forward? Organisation for Economic Co-operation and Development. Paris: Organisation for Economic Co-operation and Development; Washington, DC: OECD Publications and Information Center.

Chakrabarty, Dipesh. 1992. "The death of history? Historical consciousness and the culture of late capitalism." *Public culture* 4 (2): 47–66.

Chalvon-Demersay, Sabine. 1984. *Le triangle du XIVe.* Paris: Maison des Sciences de l'Homme.

Chambre de Commerce et d'Industrie de Bayonne. 1981. *L'activité économique dans l'arrondissement de Bayonne et le canton de Martin-de-Seignanx.*

Chambre des Métiers, Lot-et-Garonne. 1961. Contrat d'apprentissage.

*Champs-Elysées.* 1988. Series 6, number 9.

*Champs-Elysées.* 1989. Series 8, number 5.

Chateaubriand, François René de. 1827 [1826]. *The Natchez: an Indian tale.* London: H. Colburn.

Chiva, Matty. 1985. *Le doux et l'amer.* Paris: Presses Universitaires de France.

*Chocolat, Bayonne.* 1997. Conférences de Bayonne. Biarritz: J & D Editions.

Clark, Priscilla Parkhurst. 1987. *Literary France: the making of a culture.* Berkeley: University of California Press.

Clavel, Bernard. 1962. *La maison des autres: la grande patience.* Paris: Lafont.

Clifford, James. 1988. *The predicament of culture: twentieth century ethnography, literature and art.* Cambridge: Harvard University Press.

Coady, Chantal. 1995. *The chocolate companion: a connoisseur's guide to the world's finest chocolate.* New York: Simon and Schuster.

Cobban, Alfred. 1985. *A history of modern France: old regime and revolution, 1715–1799.* New York: Penguin.

Coe, Sophie D. 1994. *America's first cuisines.* Austin: University of Texas Press.

Coe, Sophie, and Michael Coe. 1996. *The true history of chocolate.* London: Thames and Hudson.

Colmenero de Ledesma, Antonio. 1644. *Chocolata inda opusculum.* Nuremberg: Wolfgang Enderi.

Comaroff, Jean L., and John Comaroff. 1997. *Of revelation and revolution: the dialectics of modernity in a South African frontier.* Vol. 2. Chicago: University of Chicago Press.

Conan, Eric, and Henry Rousso. 1998. *Vichy: an ever present past.* Translated by Nathan Bracher. Hanover, NH: University of New England Press.

"Concours de Chocolatiers." 1991. Anglet: Les BTS Action Commerciale.

"Concours Meilleur Ouvrier de France, Chocolatier-Confiseur." 1990. Paris: Confédération Nationale des Détaillants et Détaillants-Fabricants de la Confiserie, Chocolaterie et Biscuiterie.

Constant, Christian. 1988. *Le chocolat: le goût de la vie.* Paris: Nathan.

Constantin, André. 1933. "A propos du chocolat de Bayonne." *Cahiers du Centre Basque et Gascon d'Etudes Régionales,* vol. 4, pp. 1–20. Bayonne: Editions du Musée Basque.

Cooper, Eugene. 1980. *The wood-carvers of Hong Kong.* Cambridge: Cambridge University Press.

Coornaert, Emile. 1966. *Les compagnonnages en France: du moyen age à nos jours.* Paris: Ouvrières.

———. 1968. *Les corporations en France avant 1789.* Paris: Ouvrières.

Coy, Michael, ed. 1989. *Apprenticeship: from theory to method and back again.* Albany: State University of New York Press.

Creighton, Millie R. 1995. "Imaging the other in Japanese advertising campaigns." In James Carrier, ed., *Occidentalism: images of the West,* 135–160. Oxford: Clarendon Press.

Cuzacq, René. 1949. *Tryptyque bayonnais: jambon, baïonnette, chocolat de Bayonne.* Mont-de-Mersan: J. Glize.

Darnton, Robert. 1985. *The great cat massacre and other episodes in French cultural history.* New York: Basic Books.

Daumoinx, Jacques. 1991. "Les certifications de qualité." *La confiserie* 296: 26.

Delawarde, Jean-Baptiste. 1935. *Les défricheurs et les petits colons de la Martinique au XVIIe siècle.* Paris: Buffault.

Descolonges, Pierre-Marie. 1987. *Faut-il un CAP ou une formation complémentaire pour former un jeune au métier de chocolatier-confiseur?* Paris: Centres d'Etudes et de Recherches sur les Qualifications, Ministère de l'Education Nationale–Ministère des Affaires Sociales et de l'Emploi.

Desrosières, Alain, and Laurent Thévenot. 1988. *Les catégories socio-professionnelles.* Paris: La Découverte.

Diaz des Castillo, Bernal. 1803 [1572]. *The true history of the conquest of Mexico.* Salem, MA: Cushing and Appleton.

Diderot, Denis, ed. 1751–1772. *Encyclopédie, ou dictionnaire raisonné des arts et des métiers, par une société des gens de lettres.* Paris: Briasson.

———. 1966. *Supplément au voyage de Bougainville.* Paris: Gallimard.

Douglas, Mary, and B. Isherwood. 1979. *The world of goods.* London: Allen Lane.

Douglass, William. 1988. "The Basque stem family household: myth or reality?" *Journal of family history* 13: 75–89.

Douyrou, Marcel. 1991. "Le chocolat et les chocolatiers." *Bulletin du Cercle Généalogique du Pays Basque et Bas-Adour* 91: 5–15.

Dufour, Philippe Sylvestre. 1685. *Traitez nouveaux et curieux du café, du thé et du chocolate.* The Hague: Adrian Moetjens.

Durand, Marc, and Jean-Paul Frémont. 1979. *L'artisanat en France.* Paris: Presses Universitaires de France.

Dutourd, Jean. 1952. *Au bon beurre: ou Dix ans de la vie d'un crémier.* Paris: Plon.

Dyer, Richard. 1993. *The matter of images: essays of representation.* New York: Routledge.

Elias, Norbert. 1994 [1939]. *The civilizing process.* Translated by E. Jephcott. Cambridge, MA: Blackwell.

Ennew, Judith. 1982. "Harris tweed: construction, retention and representation of a cottage industry." In Esther Goody, ed., *From craft to industry: ethnography of proto-industrial cloth production,* 166–199. Cambridge: Cambridge University Press.

Ernaux, Annie. 1974. *Les armoires vides.* Paris: Gallimard.

———. 1983. *La place.* Paris: Gallimard.

Fabian, Johannes. 1983. *Time and the other: how anthropology makes its object.* New York: Columbia University Press.

Fantasia, Rick. 1995. "Fast food in France." *Theory and society* 24 (2): 210–243.

Fassin, Eric. 1991. "Entretien avec Olivier Mongin." *Revue* 1: 82–95.

Faure, Alain. 1979. "L'épicerie parisienne au XIXe siècle ou la corporation éclatée." *Mouvement social* 108: 113–130.

Faure, Christian. 1989. *Le projet culturel de Vichy.* Lyon: Presses Universitaires de Lyon.

Ferguson, Priscilla Parkhurst (Clark). 1998. "A cultural field in the making: gastronomy in 19th century France." *American journal of sociology* 104 (3): 597–641.

Fernandez, James W. 1986. *Persuasions and performances: the play of tropes in culture.* Bloomington: Indiana University Press.

Fischler, Claude. 1990. *L'homnivore.* Paris: Odile Jacob.

Flandrin, Jean-Louis. 1979. *Families in former times: kinship, household, and sexuality.* Translated by Richard Southern. Cambridge: Cambridge University Press.

Foucault, Michel. 1979. *Discipline and punish: the birth of a prison.* Translated by Allan Sheridan. New York: Pantheon.

Fourastié, Jean. 1979. *Les trente glorieuses ou la révolution invisible de 1946 à 1975.* Paris: Fayard.

Franklin, Alfred Louis. 1893. *La vie privée d'autrefois, 12e à 18e siècles.* Paris: Plon-Nourrit.

Friedman, Jonathan. 1994. *Cultural identity and global process.* London: Thousand Oaks.

Furlough, Ellen. 1993. "Packaging pleasures: Club Méditerranée and French consumer culture, 1950–1968." *French historical studies* 18 (1): 65–82.

Gage, Thomas. 1958 [1648]. *Thomas Gage's travels in the new world.* Edited by J. Eric S. Thompson. Norman: University of Oklahoma Press.

Garrigues, Jean. 1991. *Banania, histoire d'une passion française.* Paris: May.

Gault, Henri, and Millau, Christian. 1976. *Gault et Millau se mettent à table.* Paris: Stock.

Gehin, Jean-Paul. 1993. *Apprentissage ou formation continue? Stratégies éducatives des entreprises en Allemagne et en France.* Paris: L'Harmattan.

Gilman, Sander. 1985. *Difference and pathology: stereotypes of sexuality, race and madness.* Ithaca, NY: Cornell University Press.

Gimlin, Deborah. 1996. "Pamela's place: power and negotiation in the hair salon." *Gender and society* 10 (5): 505–526.

Girard, Sylvie. 1984. *Le guide du chocolat et de ses à-côtés.* Paris: Messidor-Temps.

Girardet, Raoul. 1972. *L'idée coloniale en France de 1871 à 1962.* Paris: Gallimard.

*Glossaire du métier de confiseur-chocolatier.* 1991. Paris: Confédération Nationale des Détaillants et Détaillants-Fabricants de la Confiserie, Chocolaterie, et Biscuiterie.

Grenadou, Ephraïm, and Alain Prévost. 1966. *Grenadou, paysan français*. Paris: Seuil.

Grillo, Ralph. 1985. *Ideologies and institutions in urban France: the representation of immigrants*. Cambridge: Cambridge University Press.

Grimod de la Reynière, A.-B. L. 1984 [1803–1812]. *Almanach des gourmands servant de guide dans les moyens de faire excellente chère par un vieil amateur*. 8 vols. Paris: Valmer.

Guide Michelin. 1989. *Guide de tourisme, Pays Basque*. Paris.

Gupta, Akhil, and James Ferguson, eds. 1997. *Anthropological locations: boundaries and grounds of a field science*. Berkeley: University of California Press.

Hanagan, Michael. 1980. *The logic of solidarity: artisans and industrial workers in three French towns, 1871–1914*. Urbana: University of Illinois Press.

Hanley, D. L., A. P. Kerr, and N. H. Waites. 1984. *Contemporary France: politics and society since 1945*. London: Routledge.

Handler, Richard, and Eric Gable. 1997. *The new history in an old museum*. Durham, NC: Duke University Press.

Handler, Richard, and Jocelyn Linnekin. 1984. "Tradition, genuine or spurious." *Journal of American folklore* 97 (385): 273–290.

Hareven, Tamara K. 1992. "The festival's work as leisure: the traditional craftsmen of Gion festival." In John Calagione, Doris Francis, and Daniel Nugent, eds., *Worker's expressions: beyond accommodation and resistance*, 98–128. Albany: State University of New York Press.

Harvey, David. 1989. *The condition of postmodernity*. Cambridge: Blackwell.

Harwich, Nikita. 1992. *Histoire du chocolat*. Paris: Desjonquères.

Hauser, Henri. 1927. *Ouvriers des temps passés*. Paris: Félix Alcan.

Helfgott, Leonard M. 1996. *Ties that bind: a social history of the Iranian carpet*. Washington, DC: Smithsonian Institution Press.

Helms, Mary W. 1993. *Craft and the kingly ideal*. Austin: University of Texas Press.

Herpin, Nicholas. 1988. "Le repas comme institution." *Revue française de sociologie* 39 (3): 503–521.

Herzfeld, Michael. 1985. *The poetics of manhood: contest and identity in a Cretan mountain village*. Princeton: Princeton University Press.

———. 1987. *Anthropology through the looking glass: critical ethnography in the margins of Europe*. Cambridge: Cambridge University Press.

———. 1995. "Hellenism and occidentalism: the permutations of performance in Greek bourgeois identity." In James Carrier, ed., *Occidentalism. images of the West*, 218–233. Oxford: Clarendon Press.

———. 1997. "The aesthetics of individualism: artisanship, business, and the state in Greece." Paper delivered at the annual meetings of the American Anthropological Association.

Héviat, Isabel. 1990. *Corpus de référence, chocolatier (document de travail)*. Paris: Agence Nationale pour le Développement de l'Education Permanente.

Hobsbaum, Eric, and Terence Ranger, eds. 1983. *The invention of tradition*. Cambridge: Cambridge University Press.

Hochschild, Arlie Russell. 1983. *The managed heart: commercialization of human feeling.* Berkeley: University of California Press.

Hoffmann, Stanley. 1956. *Le mouvement poujade.* Paris: Armand Colin.

Hourmat, Pierre. 1990. *Bayonne.* Bayonne: Ouest-France.

————. 1997. "Contribution à l'histoire du chocolat de Bayonne." In *Chocolat, Bayonne,* 29–35. Biarritz: Conférences de Bayonne, J&D Editions.

INSEE. 1985, 1990. *Données sociales.* Paris: Documentation Française.

Jaeger, Christine. 1982. *Artisanat et capitalisme: l'envers de la roue de l'histoire.* Paris: Payot.

Jameson, Fredric. 1991. *The politics of post-modernity; or the cultural logic of late capitalism.* Durham, NC: Duke University Press.

Johnson, Christopher H. 1975. "Economic change and artisan discontent: the tailors' history, 1800–1848." In Roger Price, ed., *Revolution and reaction: 1848 and the Second French Republic,* 87–114. London: Croom Helm.

Jolly, Martine. 1983. *Le chocolat, une passion dévorante.* Paris: Olivier Orban.

Kaplan, Steven L. 1996. *The bakers of Paris and the bread question, 1700–1775.* Durham, NC: Duke University Press.

Kaplan, Steven L., and Cynthia Koepp, eds. 1986. *Work in France: representation, meaning, organization, practice.* Ithaca, NY: Cornell University Press.

Karp, Ivan, Christine Mullen Kreamer, and Steven D. Levine. 1992. *Museums and communities: the politics of public cultures.* Washington, DC: Smithsonian Institution Press.

Karp, Ivan, and Steven D. Levine. 1991. *Exhibiting culture: the poetics and politics of museum display.* Washington, DC: Smithsonian Institution Press.

Kearney, Michael. 1995a. "The local and the global: the anthropology of globalization and transnationalism." *Annual review of anthropology* 24: 547–565.

————. 1995b. *Reconceptualizing the peasantry: anthropology in global perspective.* Boulder, CO: Westview Press.

Kertzer, David. 1988. *Ritual, politics, and power.* New Haven: Yale University Press.

Kondo, Dorinne. 1990. *Crafting selves: power, gender, and discourses of identity in a Japanese workplace.* Chicago: University of Chicago Press.

————. 1992. "Aesthetics and politics in fashion." In Joseph Tobin, ed., *Remade in Japan: everyday life and consumer taste in a changing society,* 176–203. New Haven: Yale University Press.

Kopytoff, Igor. 1986. "The cultural biography of things: commoditization as process." In Arjan Appadurai, ed., *The social life of things,* 64–91. Cambridge: Cambridge University Press.

Kuisel, Richard F. 1993. *Seducing the French: the dilemma of Americanization.* Berkeley: University of California Press.

Labat, Jean-Baptiste. 1979 [1742]. *Voyage aux îles de l'Amérique.* Paris: Seghers.

Lamphere, Louise. 1997. "Work and the production of silence." In Gerald Sider and Gavin Smith, eds., *Between history and histories: the making of silences and commemorations,* 263–283. Toronto: University of Toronto Press.

Lang, Jennifer Harvey, ed. 1988. *Larousse gastronomique.* New York: Crown.

Lave, Jean, and Etienne Wenger. 1991. *Situated learning.* Cambridge: Cambridge University Press.

Lebaube, Alain. 1990. "L'apprentissage: la loi de 1987 n'a pas modifié la tendence." *Le monde,* 24 October.

Lefebvre, Henry. 1991. *The production of space.* Oxford: Basil Blackwell.

Le Gendre, Gilles. 1986. "La grande saga du chocolat." *Le nouvel économiste* 522: 38–42.

*Le guide des croqueurs du chocolat.* 1988. Paris: Olivier Orban.

Léon, Henry. 1893. *Histoire des juifs de Bayonne.* Paris: Armand Durlacher.

Lequin, Yves. 1977. *Les ouvriers de la région lyonnaise, 1848–1914.* Lyon: Presses Universitaires de Lyon.

————. 1986. "Apprenticeship in nineteenth century France: a continuing tradition or a break with the past?." In Steven L. Kaplan and Cynthia Koepp, eds., *Work in France: representation, meaning, organization, practice,* 457–474. Ithaca, NY: Cornell University Press.

Lévi-Strauss, Claude. 1962. *La pensée sauvage.* Paris: Plon.

Le Wita, Béatrix. 1994. *French bourgeois culture.* Translated by J. A. Underwood. Paris: Maison des Sciences de l'Homme.

Lioret, Suzanne. 1979. *La dragée haute.* Clermont-Ferrand: Guy de Bussac.

Linxe, Robert. 1992. *La maison du chocolat.* Paris: Robert Laffont.

Loti, Pierre (pseud. Julien Viaud). 1989 [1879]. *Aziyadé.* Translated by Marjorie Laurie. London: Kegan Paul International.

————. 1976 [1880]. *The marriage of Loti.* Translated by Wright and Eleanor Frierson. Honolulu: University of Hawaii Press.

————. 1897 [1887]. *Madame Chrysanthème.* Translated by Laura Ensor. London: George Routledge.

Marceau, Jane. 1977. *Class and status in France: economic change and social immobility, 1945–75.* Oxford: Clarendon Press.

Marcel, Odile. 1984. *Une éducation française.* Paris: Presses Universitaires de France.

Marseille, Jacques. 1984. *Empire colonial et capitalisme français: histoire d'un divorce.* Paris: Albin Michel.

Martin Saint-Léon, Etienne. 1901. *Le compagnonnage, son histoire, ses coutumes, ses règlements et ses rites.* Paris: Colin.

Mathieu, Johann. 1990. *La confiserie de chocolat: diagnostic de l'univers et recherche d'axes de développement.* Paris: l'Institut d'Observation et de Décision, la Direction de l'Artisanat du Ministère de l'Artisanat et du Commerce.

Mauss, Marcel. 1990 [1925]. *The gift.* Translated by W. D. Halls. New York: Norton.

Mayer, Nonna. 1986. *La boutique contre la gauche.* Paris: Fondation Nationale des Sciences Politiques.

McDonald, Maryon. 1989. *We are not French! Language, culture and identity in Brittany.* London: Routledge.

Mendras, Henry. 1970. *The vanishing peasant: innovation and change in French agriculture.* Translated by Jean Lerner. Cambridge: MIT Press.

Mennell, Stephen. 1996. *All manners of food: eating and taste in England and France.* Urbana: University of Illinois Press.

Mercier, Jacques. 1989. *Le chocolat belge.* Brussels: Glénat.

Merriman, John, ed. 1979. *Consciousness and class experience in nineteenth century Europe.* New York: Meier.

Miller, Daniel, ed. 1995. *Acknowledging consumption*. London: Routledge.

Miller, Daniel. 1997. *Capitalism: an ethnographic approach*. London: Berg.

Minifie, Bernard W. 1989. *Chocolate, cocoa, and confectionery science and technology*. 3d ed. New York: Van Nostrand Reinhold.

Mintz, Sidney W. 1985. *Sweetness and power: the place of sugar in modern history*. New York: Penguin.

———. 1996a. "Chocs, Coke and cacao." *Times literary supplement*, 9 August 1996.

———. 1996b. *Tasting food, tasting freedom: excursions into eating, culture, and the past*. Boston: Beacon Press.

Moeran, Brian. 1984. *Lost innocence: folk craft potters of Onta, Japan*. Berkeley: University of California Press.

Monnassier, Bernard. 1991. "Comment évaluer la valeur de votre affaire." Lecture delivered at the Atelier de Réflexion, Intersuc, Paris.

Montaigne, Michel de. 1969. *Essais*. Paris: Garnier-Flammarion.

Myerhoff, Barbara. 1992. *Remembered lives: the work of ritual, storytelling and growing older*. Ann Arbor: University of Michigan Press.

Nadel-Klein, Jane. 1991. "Reweaving the fringe: localism, tradition, and representation in British ethnography." *American ethnologist* 18 (3): 500–517.

———. 1995. "Occidentalism as a cottage industry: representing the autochthonous 'other' in British and Irish rural studies." In James Carrier, ed., *Occidentalism: images of the West*, 109–134. Oxford: Clarendon Press.

Nahon, Gérard. 1981. *Les nations juives portugaises du sud-ouest de la France (1684–1791)*. Paris: Fundaco Calouste Guilbenkian, Centro Cultural Portugais.

Nash, June, ed. 1993. *Crafts in the world market*. Albany: State University of New York Press.

Noiriel, Gérard. 1990. *Le creuset français: histoire de l'immigration, xixe–xxe siècles*. Paris: Seuil.

Nora, Pierre, ed. 1984–1992. *Les lieux de mémoire*. Paris: Gallimard.

Nora, Pierre. 1992. "L'ère de la commémoration." In Pierre Nora, ed., *Les lieux de mémoire-les France*, 977–1012. Paris: Gallimard.

Nord, Phillip. 1986. *Paris shopkeepers and the politics of resentment*. Princeton: Princeton University Press.

*Nouvel observateur*, no. 1667, 17–23 October 1996.

Ohnuki-Tierney, Emiko. 1993. *Rice as self: Japanese identities through time*. Princeton: Princeton University Press.

Okely, Judith. 1996. *Own or other culture*. London: Routledge.

Ortner, Sherri. 1984. "Theory in anthropology since the sixties." *Comparative studies in society and history* 26: 126–166.

Parman, Susan. 1990. *Scottish crofters: a historical ethnography of a Celtic village*. Fort Worth, TX: Holt, Rinehart and Winston.

Parodi, Maurice. 1981. *L'économie de la société française depuis 1945*. Paris: Armand Colin.

Paxton, Robert O. 1972. *Vichy France*. New York: Columbia University Press.

Peeters, Alice. 1989. "Boire le chocolat." *Terrain* 13: 98–104.

Perdiguier, Agricol. 1977. *Mémoires d'un compagnon*. Paris: Maspéro.

Perrot, Michelle. 1974. *Les ouvriers en grève*. Paris: Mouton.

———. 1992. "Les vies ouvrières." In Pierre Nora, ed., *Les lieux de mémoire-Les France,* 87–129. Paris: Gallimard.

Pontet-Fourmigué, Josette. 1990. *Bayonne: un destin de ville moyenne à l'époque moderne.* Biarritz: J & D.

Poujade, Pierre. 1955. *J'ai choisi le combat.* Saint-Céré: Société Générale des Editions et des Publications.

Programme savoir-faire et techniques, dossier 1. 1988. Paris: Mission du Patrimoine ethnologique. Ministère de la Culture et de la Communication des Grands Travaux et du Bicentennaire.

Prost, Antoine. 1968. *Histoire de l'enseignement en France.* Paris: Colin.

———. 1990. "Où va l'enseignement en France?" Lecture delivered at Maison Française, New York University.

———. 1997. *Education, société et politiques: une histoire de l'enseignement en France, de 1945 à nos jours.* Paris: Seuil.

Prost, Antoine, and Gérard Vincent, eds. 1991. *A history of private life,* vol. 5: *Riddles of identity in modern times.* Translated by Arthur Goldhammer. Cambridge: Harvard University Press.

Pudlowski, Gilles. 1991. "Ces chocolatiers sont les meilleurs de France." *Cuisine et vins de France* 468: 24–30.

Pynson, Pascale. 1987. *La France à table.* Paris: Découverte.

Pyrénées Atlantiques. 1994. *Structure du tourisme: l'observation économique du tourisme.* Mission Touristique Départementale.

Rachline, Michel. 1997. *Les secrets d'un grand chocolat.* Collection Encyclopédie 3000, série gastronomie. Paris: Atlas.

Raissiguier, Catherine. 1994. *Becoming women, becoming workers: identity formation in a French vocational school.* Albany: State University of New York Press.

Rambali, Paul. 1994. *Boulangerie: the craft and culture of baking in France.* New York: Macmillan.

Rancière, Jacques. 1986. "The myth of the artisan: critical reflections on a category of social history." In Steven L. Kaplan and Cynthia Koepp, eds., *Work in France: representation, meaning, organization, practice,* 317–334. Ithaca, NY: Cornell University Press.

Rappaport, Joanne. 1998. *The politics of memory: native historical interpretation in the Colombian Andes.* Durham, NC: Duke University Press.

Reddy, William. 1984. *The Rise of Market Culture.* Cambridge: Cambridge University Press.

Reed-Danahay, Deborah. 1996a. "Champagne and chocolate: "taste" and inversion in a French wedding ritual." *American anthropologist* 98 (4): 750–761.

———. 1996b. *Education and identity in rural France: the politics of schooling.* Cambridge: Cambridge University Press.

Richards, Audrey. 1938. *Hunger and work in a savage tribe.* London: George Routledge.

Rigby, Brian. 1991. *Popular culture in modern France: a study of cultural discourse.* London: Routledge.

Robert, Jean. 1984. *Des travaux et des jours en piémont pyrénéen.* Bidache: Jean-Pierre Gyss.

Robert, Hervé. 1990. *Les vertus thérapeutiques du chocolat.* Paris: Artulen.

Rogers, Susan C. 1991. *Shaping modern times in rural France: the transformation and reproduction of an Aveyronnais community.* Princeton: Princeton University Press.

Rosello, Mireille. 1998. *Declining the stereotype: ethnicity and representation in French cultures.* Hanover, NH: University of New England Press.

Rosenberg, Harriet O. 1988. *Negotiated world: three centuries of change in a French Alpine community.* Toronto: University of Toronto Press.

Ross, Kristin. 1995. *Fast cars, clean bodies: the decolonization and the reordering of French culture.* Cambridge: MIT Press.

Rousseau, Jean-Jacques. 1966 [1762]. *Emile ou de l'éducation.* Paris: Garnier-Flammarion.

———. 1986 [1749,1754]. *The first and second discourses.* Translated by Victor Gourevitch. New York: Harper and Row.

Rousso, Henry. 1990. *Le syndrome de Vichy de 1944 à nos jours.* Paris: Seuil.

Rydell, Robert W. 1993. *World of fairs: the Century-of-Progress expositions.* Chicago: University of Chicago Press.

Sahlins, Marshall. 1976. *Culture and practical reason.* Chicago: University of Chicago Press.

Sahlins, Peter. 1989. *Boundaries: the making of France and Spain in the Pyrenees.* Berkeley: University of California Press.

Said, Edward. 1978. *Orientalism.* New York: Vintage.

Savigliano, Michael. 1995. *Tango and the political economy of passion.* Boulder, CO: Westview Press.

Schiaffino, Mariarosa, and Cluizel, Michel. 1988. *La route du chocolat.* Paris: Gentleman.

Schivelbusch, Wolfgang. 1992. *Tastes of paradise: a social history of spices, stimulants, and intoxicants.* Translated by David Jacobson. New York: Pantheon Books.

Schneider, William H. 1982. *An empire for the masses. the French popular image of Africa, 1870–1900.* Westport, CT: Greenwood Press.

Scott, Joan W. 1974. *The glassblowers of Carmaux.* Cambridge: Harvard University Press.

———. 1988. *Gender and the politics of history.* New York: Columbia University Press.

Sébillot, Paul. 1980 [1895]. *Légendes et curiosités des métiers.* New York: Arno Press.

Sewell, William H., Jr. 1980. *Work and revolution in France: the language of labor from the Old Regime to 1848.* Cambridge: Cambridge University Press.

———. 1986. "Artisans, factory workers and the formation of the French working class, 1789–1848." In Ira Katznelson and Aristide Zolberg, eds., *Working class formation: nineteenth century patterns in Western Europe and the United States,* 45–62. Princeton: Princeton University Press.

Shore, Cris. 1993. "Ethnicity as revolutionary strategy: communist identity construction in Italy." In Sharon Macdonald, ed., *Inside European identities,* 27–53. Oxford: Berg.

Sider, Gerald, and Gavin Smith, eds. 1997. *Between history and histories: the making of silences and commemorations.* Toronto: University of Toronto Press.

Silverman, Maxim. 1992. *Deconstructing the nation: immigration, racism and citizenship in modern France.* London: Routledge.

Singleton, John, ed. 1998. *Learning in likely places: varieties of apprenticeship in Japan.* Cambridge: Cambridge University Press.

Singly, François de, and Clothilde Lemarchant. 1991. "Belle-mère et belle-fille: la bonne distance." In Martine Segalen, ed., *Jeux de familles,* 119–136. Paris: Presses du Centre National de la Recherche Scientifique.

Sonenscher, Michael. 1987. "Mythical work: workshop production and the *compagnonnages* of the eighteenth century." In Patrick Joyce, ed., *The historical meanings of work,* pp. 31–63. Cambridge: Cambridge University Press.

Spooner, Brian. 1986. "Weavers and dealers: the authenticity of an oriental carpet." In Arjun Appadurai, ed., *The social life of things,* 195–235. Cambridge: Cambridge University Press.

Stewart, Susan. 1984. *On longing: narratives of the miniature, the gigantic, the souvenir, the collection.* Baltimore: Johns Hopkins University Press.

Taguieff, Pierre-André. 1990. *La force du préjugé: essai sur le racisme et ses doubles.* Paris: Gallimard.

Talbot, G. 1994. "Vegetable Fats." In S. T. Beckett, ed., *Industrial chocolate manufacture and use,* 242–257. London: Blackie Academic and Professional.

Terrio, Susan J. 1996. "Crafting *grand cru* chocolates in contemporary France." *American anthropologist* 98 (1): 67–79.

———. 1997. "Les chocolatiers de la Côte Basque: le renouvellement d'une tradition professionnelle." In *Chocolat, Bayonne,* 43–55. Biarritz: Conférences de Bayonne, J&D Editions.

———. 1998. "Deconstructing fieldwork in contemporary urban France." *Anthropological quarterly* 71 (1): 18–31.

Tobin, Joseph J., ed. 1992. *Remade in Japan: everyday life and consumer taste in a changing society.* New Haven: Yale University Press.

Todorov, Tzvetan. 1994. *On human diversity: nationalism, racism and exoticism in French thought.* Translated by Catherine Porter. Cambridge: Harvard University Press.

*Trésor de la langue française, dictionnaire de la langue du XIXe siècle et du XXe siècle (1789–1960).* 1977. Edited by Paul Imbs. Paris: Editions du Centre National de la Recherche Scientifique.

Trouillot, Michel-Rolph. 1997. "Silencing the past: layers of meaning in the Haitian revolution." In Gerald Sider and Gavin Smith, eds., *Between history and histories: the making of silences and commemorations,* 31–61. Toronto: University of Toronto Press.

Truant, Cynthia. 1979. "Solidarity and symbolism among journeymen artisans: the case of *compagnonnage.*" *Comparative studies in society and history* 21: 214–226.

Turner, Victor. 1969. *The ritual process: structure and anti-structure.* Chicago: Aldine.

Ulin, Robert C. 1996. *Vintages and traditions: an ethnohistory of southwest French wine cooperatives.* Washington, DC: Smithsonian Institution Press.

Union of Industrial Chocolate Makers. 1990. *Etude sur le chocolat.* Paris.

Urbain, Guy. 1966. "Enquête." *La confiserie* 103: 29–31.

———. 1967. "Les perspectives d'avenir du métier de confiseur spécialiste de France." *La confiserie* III: 53–61.

———. 1985. "Histoire de la confiserie." *La confiserie* 251: 31–45.

———. 1986. "Pourquoi?" *La confiserie* 259: 17–19.

———. 1988. "Histoire des confiseurs." *La confiserie* 272: 36.

———. 1991a. "La genèse d'une décision." *La confiserie* 296: 59–61.

———. 1991b. "Les artisans chocolatiers à la reconquête des palais." *La confiserie* 296: 66.

———. 1991c. "Organiser une séance d'initiation." *La confiserie* 296: 29–32.

———. 1993. *La confiserie* 315: 89.

———. 1996a. "Fait main en France: les artisans chocolatiers-confiseurs vus avec les yeux de l'Amérique." *La confiserie* 336: 66–71.

———. 1996b. "La bataille pour le vrai chocolat." *La confiserie* 336: 8–15.

———. 1997a. "Expert en cacao." *La confiserie* 345: 11–25.

———. 1997b. "Radioscope." *La confiserie* 346: 17.

———. 1998. "Le Festival d'Art Gourmand à Intersuc." *La confiserie* 353: 13–28.

Van Gennep, Arnold. 1946. *Manuel de folklore français contemporain*. Paris: A. et J. Picard.

———. 1960. *The rites of passage*. Chicago: University of Chicago Press.

Vialles, Noélie. 1994. *Animal to edible*. Translated by J. A. Underwood. Cambridge: Cambridge University Press.

White, Hayden. 1978. *Tropics of discourse*. Baltimore: Johns Hopkins University Press.

Wilson, Thomas, and M. Estellie Smith, eds. 1993. *Cultural change and the new European Community*. Boulder, CO: Westview Press.

Wolf, Eric. 1982. *Europe and the people without history*. Berkeley: University of California Press.

Young, Allen M. 1994. *The chocolate tree: a natural history of cacao*. Washington, DC: Smithsonian Institution Press.

Zarca, Bernard. 1979a. "Artisanat et trajectoires sociales." *Actes de la recherche en sciences sociales* 29: 3–26.

———. 1979b. "L'ami du trait: l'itinéraire d'un compagnon-charpentier." *Actes de la recherche en sciences sociales* 29: 27–44.

———. 1986. *L'artisanat français*. Paris: Economica.

———. 1987. *Les artisans: gens de métier, gens de parole*. Paris: L'Harmattan.

Zdanty, Steven M. 1990. *The politics of survival: artisans in twentieth century France*. Oxford: Oxford University Press.

Zola, Emile. 1984 [1883]. *Au bonheur des dames*. Paris: Fasquelle.

Zukin, Sharon. 1991. *Landscapes of power: from Detroit to Disney World*. Berkeley: University of California Press.

# Index

Page numbers in *italics* denote illustrations. Owners and workers referred to by pseudonym have not been indexed.

Text: 10/13 Galliard
Display: Galliard
Composition: G&S Typesetters, Inc.
Printing and binding: Malloy Lithographing, Inc.
Maps: Bill Nelson Cartography
Index: Victoria Baker